WOMEN MAKING MUSIC

WOMEN MAKING MUSIC

The
Western Art Tradition,
1150–1950

Edited by
JANE BOWERS
and
JUDITH TICK

UNIVERSITY OF ILLINOIS PRESS

Urbana and Chicago

This publication has been supported by a subvention
from the American Musicological Society.

———————————

Illini Books edition, 1987

This book is printed on acid-free paper.

Library of Congress Cataloging in Publication Data
Main entry under title:

Women making music.

  Includes bibliographical references and index.
    1. Women musicians.   2. Music—History and criticism.
I. Bowers, Jane M.   II. Tick, Judith.
ML82.W67   1986   780'.88042   85-8642
ISBN 0-252-01470-7

To my daughter Erica
and in memory of my dear friend, Walter Gerboth

JUDITH TICK

To my mother, Jess Bowers,
who generously gave me moral and financial support for my work,
and in memory of Virginia Woolf,
whose *A Room of One's Own* inspired my first investigations into
women in music

JANE BOWERS

Contents

Contents

Illustrations

Illustrations

Acknowledgments

This book has taken a long time to come into being. Many people have helped it and us along the arduous journey into print, either through their intuitive faith in the rightness of this project or through their objective criticisms. The following have read portions of the manuscript: Julia Allen, Adrienne Fried Block, Renata Bridenthal, Janet E. Dunleavy, Sarah Fuller, Virginia Hancock, Amy Kesselman, Carol Oja, Janet Regnell, Ellen Rosand, Judith Rosen, Howard Smither, and Elizabeth Wood. Brian Aaron, Ellen Lerner, and Joanne Meyers have contributed their research skills. And Adrienne Fried Block, Lucille Goodman, Doris Kretschmer, Stephen Oleskey, Judith Rosen, and Elizabeth Wood have helped with their constant encouragement, enthusiasm, and discerning guidance. To all of them we offer our thanks and sincere appreciation.

Especially heartfelt thanks also go to the American Association of University Women, which provided fellowship funds to Jane Bowers during two different years in support of her work on this book.

WOMEN
MAKING MUSIC

1

Introduction

JANE BOWERS and JUDITH TICK

"Do look after my music!" These words, uttered by the composer
Irene Wienawska Poldowski shortly before she died in 1932, capture
the spirit and intent of this book. We are "looking after" women's
music—and women musicians themselves—by remembering them
through the methods historians apply in their attempts to objectify
the past.

What is history if not the special caretaking of what has gone
before? For women in music this past has been untended, uncared
for, certainly absent from the conventional mainstream music history books from which most of us acquired our knowledge of Western music. If this past is to be turned into history, it needs a particular kind of looking backward that is the scholarly counterpart of
Poldowski's exhortation to "look after."

The absence of women in the standard music histories is not
due to their absence in the musical past. Rather, the questions so far
asked by historians have tended to exclude them. One reason for
such neglect has to do with the nature of musicology as it has developed in this century. Musicologists have paid little attention to the
sociology of music, whether this be concerned with the social class
and economic status of musicians, stratification in the professions,
or access to educational opportunities. They have focused instead
on documents (manuscripts, prints, and treatises), relatively few of
which exist for women's music in the periods that have been most
thoroughly investigated. In addition, musicologists have emphasized the development of musical style through the most progressive
works and genres of a period, whereas most women composers were
not leaders in style change, in part, at least, because they were excluded from the professional positions that engendered new developments. They came late to new forms and genres; their ability to compose in the "higher forms" (orchestral music and opera), for example,

was questioned throughout the nineteenth and early twentieth centuries, not taken as a matter of course. Finally, the institutional musical structures most studied by musicologists are those that either excluded women altogether or included them only in small numbers.

We offer the present volume, therefore, to expand the scope and purview of music history. This collection of historical studies of women in Western art music, the first written by musicologists from different specializations within the discipline, seeks to emphasize the process through which women's contributions to Western music history have been shaped. In chronological order, it documents achievements of outstanding individual artists and also explores the history of women as a distinct sociological group within the musical professions and musical life as a whole. It is inspired by the awareness that women have been, and to some extent still are, a minority subgroup within music, with all that implies about ambivalence, achievement, and the slow evolution of opportunity for women to realize and fulfill their musicality within Western culture. A brief overview of women's past as musicians may help elucidate that evolution and provide a backdrop against which the achievements described in the individual studies can be more clearly viewed.

In the early centuries of the Christian church there is little doubt that women took part in singing at divine worship. But as the church grew, so did the opposition to women's participation in liturgical rites. As sacred singing schools were established, the performance of church music increasingly became the province of trained male singers and of the priesthood. In convents, however, from their foundation in the fourth century on, women continued to sing, and during the late Middle Ages the activities of nuns as composers and performers are well documented. The first substantial group of extant compositions by a woman composer are those of the twelfth-century abbess Hildegard of Bingen.

During this era, female troubadours and trouvères also set courtly poems to music. Aristocratic women frequently sang and played for their own pleasure, and women of other classes occasionally made their living as itinerant performers and household musicians. When professional minstrels were incorporated in Paris in 1321, eight women signed the statutes of the confraternity. For the late Middle Ages as a whole, nevertheless, it is fair to state that women were excluded from musical positions of high status and lacked direct access to most professional opportunities, rewards, and authority. This state of affairs was to continue for some time.

During most of the fifteenth and early sixteenth centuries,

women had virtually no access to the two kinds of training that constituted the principal means of acquiring a thorough music education—study at a cathedral school or apprenticeship to a master player. The principal music professions were also closed to them. Nevertheless, a few women musicians, primarily singers, made their living in low-status jobs—as members of traveling companies of minstrels, household musicians, and the like. It is not surprising that we know of very few women who composed music during this period, since only those persons who had the opportunity for extensive theoretical training had much hope of mastering the complicated polyphonic style that then prevailed.

All this does not mean that women were not musically active, however. Daughters born into noble or rich merchant and banking families were frequently provided with private music teachers, and as adults they continued to perform within their private social circles. Some noblewomen, moreover, became important patrons of music. This point underlines the relevance of class in determining women's access to musical instruction and performing opportunities. Neither women nor men of the upper classes became professional musicians, as a rule. But women who came from the classes from which most male musicians emerged had virtually no chance for musical training unless they were born into musical families.

Shortly after the mid-sixteenth century, important changes in the activities and status of women musicians began to take place. The most sweeping and radical of these changes was the increased participation of women in professional singing, first as members of predominantly female ensembles at Ferrara and at other northern Italian courts. Because they became highly prized as singers, for the first time young women were sought out and brought to courts specifically to be trained as musicians. The rapid growth of opera and of musical establishments in upper-class households during the seventeenth century provided work for a substantial number of women singers, some at the very apex of the profession. By 1700, women were securely established in all branches of singing in Italy, except for religious music.

During the same period women composers began to emerge from virtual obscurity. The first compositions by a woman to be published appeared in Venice in 1566. Throughout the rest of that century and the next, numerous other works by Italian women followed. While many of the composers were upper-class amateur musicians or nuns who faded into obscurity after a youthful publication or two, others—including Francesca Caccini, Barbara Strozzi, and

Isabella Leonarda—composed seriously over a long period. Still, women did not embrace the entire range of musical genres. They wrote little instrumental music, no full-length operas, and few oratorios and sacred pieces for large forces, mainly because they could not enter professional careers that would have allowed or encouraged them to do so.

In France, professional female singers first became prominent around the middle of the seventeenth century, in opera productions and court ballets. Somewhat later, aristocratic circles began to provide opportunities for women to perform as singers and instrumentalists, particularly on the harpsichord. At first, daughters and wives of professional male musicians were most numerous among the women who performed in Parisian musical circles. Later, ordinary women from other ranks joined them. Ultimately, however, the establishment of public concerts provided women with their greatest opportunities, for here they were free to promote their own careers as soloists. At the *Concert Spirituel*, established in 1725, women sang and performed on the harpsichord, organ, fortepiano, flute, violin, harp, and horn, sometimes playing their own compositions. But public concerts did not provide women with any of the more routine employment opportunities from which men benefited; none of the extant lists of personnel indicates that women were hired to play in the orchestras that accompanied at nearly all the concerts.

Another musical profession into which French women moved, as early as the late 1600s but primarily during the late 1700s, was music teaching. As increasing numbers of aristocrats and bourgeois took up singing and playing, opportunities to offer private lessons expanded accordingly. Institutional teaching posts were rarely awarded to women, however. The two-year tenure of Hélène de Montgeroult as professor of piano at the newly established Paris Conservatory seems to have been a rare exception.

In other countries during the eighteenth century, as in France, developments in opera, concert life, and amateur music making led to new opportunities for women musicians. Some joined the burgeoning ranks of touring virtuosos. Others, very late in the century, were occasionally appointed church organists, although none is known to have been hired as a chapel master. In Rome in 1774 a young Italian woman, Maria Rosa Coccia, did take and pass an examination qualifying her as *maestra di cappella*. Both she and the judges of her examination came under heavy attack, however, and her consequent notoriety seems to have curbed her musical ambitions considerably.[1]

6

As women entered the music professions in increasing numbers and as the new concert life and a vastly expanded music-publishing industry offered artists greater freedom and flexibility, women began to emerge as composers in France, Germany, Austria, and England. In France this was under way by 1700; in other countries, primarily after 1750. Although the late start women had had in composing instrumental music was made up for at this time, it was principally the smaller instrumental genres—sonatas for keyboard, pieces for harp, and chamber works—and solo songs that they cultivated. These were intended for domestic consumption by amateur musicians, many of whom were also women. Few symphonies came from women's pens; even concertos, which some composer-performers wrote as solo vehicles, were exceptions. Unusual women, however, such as Elisabeth Jacquet de la Guerre, composed over a wide range of genres and styles. John Hawkins, the noted eighteenth-century historian, described her as "an excellent composer, . . . [who] possessed such a degree of skill, as well in the science as [in] the practice of music, that but few of her sex have equalled her."[2]

As patronage shifted from a feudal to a market economy, women benefited from the new developments even in aspects of the trade. In France, for example, they became music engravers and publishers. Overall, though, their status as outsiders remained unquestioned, exemplified by their acceptance as soloists with orchestras and their virtual exclusion as orchestra members. As composers, teachers, and instrumentalists, most women continued to inhabit the fringes of the profession. Only in singing were they in the musical mainstream.

During the nineteenth century, women's career expectations and achievements increased with widening educational opportunities, an enhanced consciousness of women's abilities based on their prior achievements, and, late in the century, contact with feminist currents. Perhaps the most crucial change was the establishment of public secular conservatories, a number of which were open to women. In England, the Royal Academy of Music, chartered in 1839, became a haven for women musicians, who were admitted to certain classes, if not to all. In Leipzig, although Clara Rogers, the English singer and composer, was refused permission to study composition at the conservatory in the 1860s, by 1877 Ethel Smyth was able to enroll. As women increasingly gained advanced instruction in music, women composers set their sights higher than domestic music. In France, for example, Louise Bertin, Louise Farrenc, and Augusta Holmès tackled some of the largest genres of their day—grand opera, symphonies, symphonic poems, and dramatic odes. Amy Beach in the United States and Ethel Smyth in England astonished audiences and critics alike with their powerful symphonic works, which in no sense exhibited the limitations normally associated with women's work.

Women made greater strides as performers as well. Although singing, both in opera and on the concert stage, remained their major outlet, more women became prominent instrumental virtuosos, first as pianists, and later as performers on other instruments, such as the violin. Some reached the peak of their profession—among them, Clara Schumann, indisputably one of the greatest pianists of the century. Women also excelled on the organ, some achieving solo careers. The growing acceptance of women as church organists coincided, however, with the decreasing status of church musicians in general.

Although opportunities for employment increased in the nineteenth century, they did not keep pace with the new kinds of training women were receiving as musicians. Women were needed to support the new conservatories as students, but they remained less employable than men. The sense of frustration women felt under these circumstances led them to organize. One response was to form women's orchestras and chamber-music groups. What most members of "lady orchestras" wanted, however, was to join already established groups of male musicians. In the United States, only when the musicians' union became affiliated with the American Federation of Labor in 1904 was it forced to admit women. At the same time, women in France organized to press for admission to theater orchestras.[3] When cultural feminism surfaced around the turn of the century, we find women organizing concerts of women's music, compiling handbooks and dictionaries about women musicians, and writing articles about the "woman question" in music, much as we do today.

As women assumed larger roles in musical life, the ideology of opposition also became stronger. When confronted with the plea by late nineteenth-century German women for professional musical training, traditionalists responded that sex-integrated education would dilute the seriousness of professional study. Ideas about musical creativity solidified into a rock of masculine prerogative. "All creative work is well-known as being the exclusive work of men," wrote the German author of a popular two-volume history of music translated into English and widely distributed in both England and the United States.[4]

In 1894 the psychologist Havelock Ellis wrote that "there is certainly no art in which [women] have shown themselves more helpless." Their lack of achievement, he asserted, was proof of their biological inferiority. Other writers concurred; music was a "masculine idea." Goethe's image of the eternal feminine and Victorian notions about women's proper sphere and calling fueled hot debates over the innate natures of man and woman. We have yet to recover from the ensuing onslaught of graphic imagery in which this piece was labeled masculine, that one feminine; this aspect of theory declared appropriate for men, that for women; this instrument deemed suitable for the lady, that for the gentleman. Many women fell into line. By turning out parlor songs and other kinds of sentimental music, they fulfilled social expectations about their proper role as composers.

During the twentieth century, massive social changes—particularly the entrance of women into the paid labor force at progressively higher professional levels—have overcome some of the ideologies about women's artistic place. Women's activities in music have finally shifted from the primarily domestic or private sphere to the primarily public sphere. Although the concept of music as an "accomplishment" for young girls lingers on—even today more families provide music lessons for their daughters than for their sons—generally speaking, great importance is no longer placed upon it. Women have increasingly sought out music education at the higher levels and have attempted to compete with men as equals in professional activities. On the whole, women musicians in this century have behaved less self-consciously than their predecessors. As composers, they have worked within a larger variety of genres and have moved to the forefront of new musical experiments at one time or another; Ruth Crawford Seeger in the United States and Elisabeth Lutyens in Britain are just two cases in point. The kind of self-disparagement in which even Clara Schumann indulged is far less common today.

As performers, women have taken up a much wider variety of instruments than in the past century. For the most part lacking entrée into "mixed" orchestras in the early 1900s, women established their own. Although it was not until substantial numbers of male musicians were away during World War II that women were welcomed into mixed orchestras in significant numbers and positions, they had been preparing themselves both musically and politically for such work for some time. In the field of conducting, to which women were largely new in the late nineteenth century, they have also pressed for the right to work with mixed ensembles, although for long most opportunities remained limited to women's orchestras and choruses. In teaching, women have attained positions in public schools, conservatories, and universities, although they remain clustered in the lower grades or ranks, and many women still function primarily as low-status private teachers.

It is a positive sign that twentieth-century women have found it less necessary to be virtuosos to support themselves as musicians. More women who are merely talented have been able to enter and succeed in the musical professions than earlier. Nevertheless, pressure from the disparity between the numbers trained and the numbers recognized, hired, or advanced equally has led to another wave of cultural feminism. Within the last decade or so there has been a resurgence of women's performing groups, concerts and festivals of women's music, and feminist organizations formed to promote professional advancement. Although musicians and musicologists such as Ethel Smyth, Yvonne Rokseth, Marie Bobillier (Michel Brenet, pseud.), Kathi Meyer, and Sophie Drinker—pioneers to whom the present generation is in debt—gave the study of women in music its essential impulse, the current activity is part of the new feminism and the larger field of women's studies that began to emerge in the 1960s and 1970s.

As one noted women's historian has asserted, the first questions to be asked of all subjects that have suffered historical neglect are compensatory. They require fundamental fact-finding to establish what women have actually done, experienced, and achieved.[5] Who were the women musicians? What was their historical tradition? What has been their special contribution to music making?

In one way or another all the chapters in this book address themselves to these questions. Some are motivated by what Elizabeth Wood has described as "replicating the 'who' and 'what' of conventional historical narrative in order to rewrite women into it."[6] Matilda Gaume's essay on Ruth Crawford Seeger, for example, is the first published scholarly investigation of the life and works of an important American composer who is not mentioned in such a comprehensive history as William Austin's *Music in the Twentieth Century*. Ellen Rosand's study of Barbara Strozzi (who is omitted from Manfred Bukofzer's *Music in the Baroque Era*) is the first scholarly treatment of an outstanding composer of baroque cantatas. Jane Bernstein discusses Ethel Smyth, a prominent figure in British opera history, while Judith Olson recounts the life of Luise Adolpha Le Beau, a celebrated composer of instrumental music in late nineteenth-century Germany. Nancy Reich's study of Clara Schumann is hardly the first investigation of this famous pianist. Most of the literature, however, treats Schumann as a devoted wife and mother, a "consecrated, loyal priestess," a figure in a great romance, or a party to a "passionate friendship." Reich extricates her from such stereotypes to acknowledge her as first and foremost a great artist.

Other chapters examine a host of frequently less distinguished, often obscure women musicians who worked within predominantly male institutions. Among these are Maria Coldwell's chapter on women as secular musicians in fourteenth-century France and Howard Brown's similarly focused work for fifteenth-century Italy. Chapters that treat women collectively also sometimes chronicle important turning points for women in Western musical life that had great resonance in the culture at large. Anthony Newcomb recounts the beginnings of a professional class of female singers in late sixteenth-century Italy and its significance for the stylistic development of vocal music. Jane Bowers explains the emergence of the first significant group of European women composers in late sixteenth- and seventeenth-century Italy. Julie Anne Sadie chronicles the entrance of French women into a wide variety of musical professions under the ancien régime. In a study of cultural sex-role definitions that affected both men and women of the late nineteenth century, Judith Tick describes the coming-of-age of American women as both composers and performers.

Answering compensatory questions about women musicians, however, is only one goal of this book. Another is to consider the effects of women's minority status within music upon their activities and achievements. We think it symbolic that the author of the earliest printed history of Western music allotted women musicians (*Frauen Musicantinnen*) a special subcategory in his index.[7] Themes associated with minority status run through many of the chapters in varying degrees. How has sex as a historical variable affected the opportunities women as a class have had to realize their musical creativity? What is the connection between socialization and creative achievements? How have prejudice and discrimination—roughly parallel to belief and behavior—shaped the history of women in music?

Brown, for example, speculates on why fifteenth-century women did not compose music or at least did not admit to doing so. Bowers investigates the deterrents to composing that Italian women faced during the next two centuries. Marcia Citron explores the conflicts women felt between their obligations to professional and private spheres of activity as well as the attitudes that constrained their publication of music and public appearances as performers in late eighteenth- and early nineteenth-century Germany. Olson illuminates the resistance with which the professional ambitions of the pioneering Le Beau were met. Tick examines the social grammar of prejudice that produced a double standard for American women composers, who were accused of triviality if they wrote domestic music or of inappropriate virility if they wrote symphonic works. Nearly all touch upon the consequences of women's unequal access to music education. Many also consider the extent to which socialization for marriage and motherhood or the responsibilities of those roles affected musical careers. Reich's account of Clara Schumann's struggle to maintain her sense of priority as a performer and Gaume's description of the long hiatuses in Ruth Crawford Seeger's composing career are but two cases in point.

Examples of the problems and conflicts that invariably accompany minority status could be multiplied many times. The cumulative testimony of primary sources from the lives of individuals presented in this book—autobiographies, diaries, letters, dedications to musical works, and interviews—demonstrates women's crippling internalization of their culturally determined marginality. Anne Yardley cites examples of intense psychological barriers to creativity among medieval nuns. Rosand quotes the self-deprecating tone adopted by Strozzi in the dedications to her early prints, and Bernstein reports on how the young Smyth was so grateful to have some songs accepted for publication (after having been told that "no composeress had ever succeeded") that she forgot to ask for a fee. In chapter after chapter, evidence accumulates to suggest that even those women who pursued atypical musical careers were affected by the status of women in general. Sadie quotes the courageous letter Julie Candeille published in her own defense against the "treacherous insinuations" of detractors. Carol Neuls-Bates cites conductor Ethel Leginska's exhortation of women to "rebel, . . . break loose from traditions and go [your] own way!"

Another effect of women's minority status within the musical professions was their establishment of alternative musical institutions. According to Yardley and Bowers, some nuns developed remarkable musical ensembles in convents, which in turn encouraged them to compose. In the all-female orchestras studied by both Neuls-Bates and Tick, women became conductors and performers on such "masculine" (or male-identified) instruments as the French horn and timpani.

While some women forged alternative musical institutions, others responded to the role restrictions society assigned them by cultivating music within the private sphere, as a feminine "accomplishment." Coldwell, Brown, Newcomb, Sadie, Citron, and Bernstein all demonstrate the enormous length and breadth of this tradition, which exhorted aristocratic and later bourgeois women to learn to sing and play musical instruments to entertain their families and social circles. By accepting and fulfilling these special gender-identified roles, women contributed significantly to musical culture. Awareness of music as a feminine accomplishment functions didactically to remind us that women's history often lies outside men's typical domains. We need not accept the private sphere as the only proper one for women's musicality in order to acknowledge the considerable skill and dedication many women over centuries have devoted to making music within it. Rather than being dismissed as frivolous conventions, these activities need to be investigated further to ascertain their importance to the cultures of specific historical eras.

To the extent that these chapters focus on groups more than on individuals, they belong, in spirit if not in methodology, to what has been called the "new history"—the revolution in historical method and subject matter in the last two decades.[8] They deal with concerns—socialization, institutional patterns of music education, and access to professional outlets—that have not been traditional for conventional historical musicology. Their consideration forces us to realize the bond between society and creativity.

In his book *How Musical Is Man?*, ethnomusicologist John Blacking suggests that the presence of so much music in the world makes it reasonable to suppose that music, like language and possibly religion, is a species-specific human trait, perhaps genetically inherited as well as socially acquired.[9] In this volume we ask the question How musical is woman? We ask this, not only because of the intense interest it generates about the nature of musical creativity, but also because we wish to attend to the works of beauty and expressiveness that women—individually and as a class—have created over the centuries.

NOTES

1. On Coccia, see esp. C. Lozzi, "Una giovinetta romana: Maestra di Musica ammirata dal Martini e dal Metastasio," *Gazzetta musicale di Milano*, Anno 55 (1900), pp. 297–98; Alberto Cametti, "Altre notizie su Maria Rosa Coccia," ibid., pp. 342–44.

2. John Hawkins, *A General History of the Science and Practice of Music*, new ed. (1853; reprint, New York: Dover Publications, 1963), p. 779.

3. For the situation in France, see Mathilde Daubresse, "La Femme musicienne d'orchestre: Enquête," *Le Guide musical* (Paris) 50 (1904): 571–77; Arthur Pougin, "Le Violon, les femmes et le Conservatoire," *Le Ménéstrel* 90, no. 14 (1904): 108–9.

4. Emil Naumann, *The History of Music*, 2 vols., trans. F. Praeger (1882–86), 2:1267.

5. Gerda Lerner, *The Majority Finds Its Past: Placing Women in History* (New York: Oxford University Press, 1979), p. 166.

6. Elizabeth Wood, "Review Essay: Women in Music," *Signs* 6 (1980): 284.

7. Wolfgang Caspar Printz, *Historische Beschreibung der Edelen Sing- und Kling-kunst* (Dresden: J. C. Mieth, 1690).

8. Gertrude Himmelfarb, "A History of the New History," *New York Times Book Review*, 10 January 1982, p. 9.

9. John Blacking, *How Musical Is Man?* (Seattle: University of Washington Press, 1973), p. 7.

2

"Ful weel she soong the service dyvyne": The Cloistered Musician in the Middle Ages

ANNE BAGNALL YARDLEY

From repetitions of St. Paul's admonition that women should keep silent in the churches to Donald Jay Grout's statement that "Gregorian Chant consists of a single-line melody sung to Latin words by unaccompanied men's voices,"[1] women's role in the performance of sacred music in the Middle Ages has been denied implicitly or explicitly by most scholars.[2] Few people are aware that *she* as well as *he* "soong the service dyvyne"[3] not occasionally but daily, following the full complexity of the liturgical year. Throughout the Middle Ages, the nunnery offered women an opportunity to sing, arrange, and compose music for the worship of God. Indeed, in most convents, the performance of liturgical music was the central communal activity.

The religious vocation was considered a high calling in the Middle Ages, and the number of religious houses was therefore large. While the majority of these institutions were monasteries,[4] there nevertheless existed a sizable number of nunneries.[5] Among the many medieval nunneries, there were great variations in the size and economic status of individual houses. They ranged from large well-endowed establishments that drew members primarily from the royalty, to small, poverty-stricken establishments that had considerable difficulty supporting their religious communities.[6] Musical practices in these institutions of course differed considerably.

Fortunately, a variety of such primary source materials as conventual rules and customaries, musical manuscripts, bishops' visitation records, and other documents provide a concrete basis for an examination of musical practices in medieval nunneries. Four key areas will be emphasized here: the education of nuns as it related to

Plate 1
Master of St. Jerome, Nuns in choir

Source: London, British Library, Cotton Domitian A XVII,
folio 177v. By permission of the British Library

their musical activities, the liturgical practices and organizational structure of nunneries as compared with those of monasteries, the performance of plainsong and polyphony by religious women, and the composition of liturgical music by nuns.

The education of nuns in the Middle Ages was as varied as were the establishments to which they belonged. Some houses supported nuns of great intellectual distinction,[7] while others struggled to find nuns competent enough to perform the Divine Office. The dichotomy that existed between these two extremes should not obscure the fact that almost all nuns learned the basic skills of reading and singing as novices[8] and that many continued to study theological and devotional works after taking their vows.

To participate fully in the performance of the liturgy, nuns had to acquire the literary and musical skills necessary for this activity, and such training was the basis of the education offered novices in most medieval nunneries. Many contemporary comments concerning the admission of novices attest to the importance of reading and singing in the education of a nun. Bishop Gray's injunctions in 1432 to the nuns of the Benedictine Abbey at Elstow, England, for instance, set forth the requirements for an entering nun: "We enjoin and command that from now on you admit no one as a nun of the said monastery unless . . . taught in singing and reading and the other necessary things in this part, or it is probable that in the near future she may easily be instructed and will be able to manage such things as the burdens of the choir and the other things connected with religion."[9]

In spite of such high ideals, many nuns appear to have received a meagre education that barely equipped them to perform the liturgy and left them unable to understand Latin, the language in which they sang and were supposed to converse. Although nuns on the continent may have had a better grasp of Latin than English nuns, even there documents addressed to nuns were often in the vernacular, a rarity for monastic documents. For instance, the important early fourteenth-century manuscript from the French abbey of Origny-Sainte-Benoîte is written in Old French;[10] and the medieval customary from Las Huelgas de Burgos in northern Spain is written in medieval Spanish.[11] Bishops and priests often communicated with nuns in the vernacular rather than attempting to teach them Latin, a fact that is documented by translations of the Benedictine Rule into Middle English, injunctions issued in both French and Middle English, and many other sources.[12]

Nevertheless, many nuns read and studied devotional writings throughout their lives as a way of fostering their spiritual development. St. Benedict had envisioned such study as part of the monastic life, and his rule calls for the distribution of one book to each member of the house every year at the beginning of Lent.[13] The early fifteenth-century customary from Barking Abbey, a large Benedictine nunnery near London, confirms that this practice was still followed in the late Middle Ages.[14] The remains of various medieval libraries offer further evidence that nuns read major theological and devotional books, often in the vernacular.[15]

At Syon Abbey, near London, the only English house of the Bridgettine order, the priests and monks associated with the house provided spiritual guidance for the nuns. These men were known for the quality of their scholarship and the excellence of their preaching.[16] They translated many Latin writings into Middle English specifically for the nuns. Among these works is *The Mirror of Our Lady*, written by an anonymous author in the mid-fifteenth century and published in 1530. It contains a treatise on the divine service and an explication and translation of the text of the unique Bridgettine liturgy in honor of the Blessed Virgin Mary. In the introduction, the author states, "For since many of you, though you can sing and read [Latin], cannot understand its meaning, therefore . . . I have translated your reading and your entire service into English, that through understanding them . . . you may more devoutly and intelligently worship her [Mary] by singing, reading, and saying them."[17] From this book, as well as many other documents, it is clear that nuns were exposed to theological interpretations of the Scriptures and liturgy as part of their education.

A few religious women, however, were not content with the range of subjects heretofore described and were interested in both expanding their own knowledge and communicating that knowledge to others.[18] Hroswitha, a tenth-century canoness[19] at the convent of Gandersheim, one of the earliest and most important German convents, wrote many plays that occupy an important position in the history of dramatic literature. In her play *Paphnutius*, the opening dialogue between the master, Paphnutius, and his disciples about the nature of music reveals Hroswitha's familiarity with Boethian music theory (*musica speculativa*).[20]

Yet Hroswitha was somewhat troubled, not only by her knowledge and talents, but also by the recognition she achieved. In a preface to her plays addressed to "certain learned patrons of this book," she wrote, "You have, however, not praised me but the Giver of the grace which works in me, by sending me your paternal congratulations and admitting that I possess some little knowledge of those arts the subtleties of which exceed the grasp of my woman's mind."[21] She continued by crediting God for her gifts and describing the conflict she felt between humility and an awareness of her gifts. Such remarks provide some insight into the barriers a religious woman faced in expressing her creative impulses: as a woman she was assumed to have limited intellectual ability, and as a member of a religious community she was expected to show humility. Hroswitha resolved this dilemma in typically medieval fashion by explaining that she was merely a vessel through which God revealed himself.

The most impressive educational tour de force produced by a medieval nun was undoubtedly Herrad of Landsberg's encyclopedic "Hortus deliciarum" ("Garden of Delights"), a compendium of contemporary knowledge. Herrad was the abbess of Hohenburg, a prestigious nunnery in Alsace, which drew its members from the surrounding landed gentry. During the time when she ruled the house (1167–95), there were about sixty nuns in the convent. In the "Hortus deliciarum," Herrad attempted to gather together all the knowledge of her day into one volume as an instructional aid for her nuns.[22] This beautifully and copiously illustrated manuscript, destroyed by a fire in 1870, contained carefully documented selections from a variety of authors on many topics. Interspersed with these writings were Herrad's poems addressed to the nuns. Almost all of her poems, including the opening exhortation, were set to music. Of the two pieces for which the music is extant, one is a monophonic song, *Primus parens hominum*, and the other is a two-part piece for Christmas, *Sol oritur occasus*.[23] The "Hortus deliciarum" is an indication of the exceptional educational level at Hohenburg. The wide variety of sources cited in the manuscript, the high artistic quality of the illuminations, and the creativity of the overall conception of the work all demonstrate that the abbey of Hohenburg was an important cultural center where nuns received an excellent education.

The education of nuns, whether at Hohenburg or at the smallest nunnery in Europe, was structured primarily to enable nuns to participate fully in the communal worship of the nunnery. The Benedictine Rule which, from the sixth century onward, established the character and outline of religious life,[24] emphasized the centrality of the liturgy within the religious community. Since this rule applied equally to nuns and to monks, most aspects of the liturgical-musical tradition were virtually identical in monasteries and nunneries. The same concepts of worship applied, the same organizational structure existed, and the same basic repertoire was performed.[25] Only in the service for the consecration of virgins and in the performance of liturgical drama did the liturgical-musical practices of nunneries and monasteries differ significantly.

The concepts of worship that were at the foundation of medieval monastic life were also expressed in the Benedictine Rule.[26] This rule, as well as other medieval sources, emphasized the importance of the mental attitude of the individual nun or monk toward musical performance rather than her or his vocal abilities. Pride in vocal abilities was seen as an impediment to true worship. Devotion to God and concentration on the text of the liturgy were emphasized.

The organizational structures for monasteries and nunneries were very similar. The officials or functionaries who had responsibility for the operation of the house shared similar titles and functions (e.g., in an abbey, the abbess and abbot). In convents three types of officials—abbess, prioress, and cantrix—were actively involved in the musical leadership of the establishment; and the responsibilities of each paralleled those of her male counterpart (i.e., abbot, prior, and cantor).[27]

The roles of abbess and prioress in the musical life of the convent were primarily ceremonial, as befitted their status as leaders. They intoned certain chants on feast days and, in general, fulfilled a leadership role in the service, singing versicles and reading lessons.[28] At Barking Abbey they were both members of a group of six soloists who played a special role on feast days, singing the soloistic portions of the liturgy and leading the choir in processions.[29]

The cantrix was the official most responsible for the musical life of the nunnery. Her duties included organizing the choir, designating soloists, choosing the correct chants for the liturgical occasion, taking care of the liturgical books, making the table or weekly rotational chart, and assembling the music for such occasions as local saints' days.[30] Various extant sources refer to the necessity of filling this office with an intelligent and able nun.[31]

Another important similarity in the musical practices of monasteries and nunneries was the repertoire itself, which varied not according to the gender of the inhabitants but according to the location and order of a particular house.[32] Nuns followed the same liturgical day as monks, singing the same daily offices and mass, and observed the same major church feasts with variations for saints of local importance. Extant source material points universally to the regularity of liturgical worship in nunneries.[33]

The major liturgical occasions on which the musical practices in both English and continental nunneries differed from those in

monasteries were the service of consecrating virgins and the performance of liturgical dramas at Easter. The service of consecration of a
virgin differed markedly from its monastic counterpart, unlike such
services as the consecration of an abbess, which merely made appropriate pronoun changes.[34] The service was rooted in the image of the
nun as the bride of Christ and was influenced during its development
by the contemporary marriage ritual, the ordination ceremony, and
the liturgical drama. The service for monks invoked instead the image of "putting on the new man in Christ."

In its original form in the fourth and fifth centuries the service
for the consecration of a virgin included a simple public recognition
of the virgin's vow and the blessing of her veil and any other dis-
tinctive clothing.[35] These elements remained central to the service
throughout its expansion; but by the fifteenth century, eight distinct
events had become an integral part of the service: (1) blessing of the
habit, (2) entrance of the virgin wearing the habit, (3) signing of the
vow of obedience, (4) blessing and presentation of the veil, (5) blessing and presentation of the ring, (6) presentation by the virgin of
bread and wine to be blessed for communion, (7) fastening of the
veil, and (8) departure of the virgin. Most of these actions were accompanied by chants from a variety of sources (e.g., the liturgy for
Saint Agnes and Saint Agatha), sometimes sung by all the virgins together and sometimes by each individually.

The same dramatic impulse that led to the development of the
liturgical drama also influenced the consecration service. René Metz
has pointed out that the major tenth-century expansion of the consecration service took place at the same time as the early development of medieval drama. In particular, the consecration service became, during the tenth century, a dramatic rendition of parts of the
liturgy of St. Agnes, from which it took many of its chants.[36] St.
Agnes, a fourth-century virgin martyr, refused earthly marriage to
become the bride of Christ. She was seen as an important example
for nuns.

The dramatic nature of the consecration service can easily be
seen in an early sixteenth-century manuscript from the English
nunnery of St. Mary's in Winchester.[37] The detailed Middle English
rubrics in the source give minute instructions for the liturgical actions, providing evidence of the visual and dramatic effects of the
service. During the delivery of the rings, for example, the bishop
blessed the rings, sprinkled them with holy water, and placed them
on the fourth fingers of the novices, who responded by singing an
antiphon from the service of St. Agnes, "By His ring my Lord Jesus

Christ has wed me and like a wife he has adorned me with a crown." During the singing of this antiphon, the virgins were instructed to hold their hands high enough that the people might see the rings, a dramatic gesture that clearly demonstrated the liturgist's awareness of audience.

The performance of liturgical drama in nunneries and monasteries differed not in intention, as did the consecration services, but in resources. In nunneries, unlike monasteries, mixed casts were available, since each convent retained at least one priest for the celebration of the Mass. Sources from the Abbey of Origny-Sainte-Benoîte in France and from Barking Abbey and Wilton Abbey in England give instructions for the performance of the Easter drama with three nuns playing the roles of the Marys and priests playing the roles of the angel and other male characters, such as Christ and his disciples.[38] Since all three of these abbeys were large establishments, they had several chaplains who could participate in the drama. In the version of Origny-Sainte-Benoîte, the exchange between the Marys and a merchant is also included. The text of this portion, as well as that of many other sections and the rubrics throughout, are in French.[39] It is significant that the Easter drama, which includes important female characters in the cast, seems to be the only drama that was incorporated into the liturgical practices of these nunneries.

Evidence for the use of a mixed cast in liturgical drama is of interest to those who study the performance practice of medieval music. Sources relating to other aspects of the performance of liturgical music in medieval nunneries—the role of the cantrix in regulating chant performance, rehearsal techniques, problems that arose in the performance of chant, and, most important, the rendition of polyphony—shed light on the same subject.

The cantrix, whose role has been briefly described above, exercised considerable musical leadership within the nunnery. In addition to her organizational duties, she had responsibility for choosing pitch and tempo for the chants and for creating a balanced sound between the two halves of the choir which were usually seated opposite each other. The cantrix at Syon Abbey was specifically told "to set the song evenly and moderately, neither too high nor too low, nor too fast nor too slow, but seriously and devoutly according to the solemnity of the feast or day."[40] It is interesting to note that the importance of the liturgical occasion was expected to influence the cantrix's choice of tempo.

This glimpse into the practical side of conventual musical life leads us to wonder about rehearsal techniques. Unfortunately little information concerning rehearsals is extant, and we are forced to speculate about most aspects of this subject. We may surmise that the nuns spent some time rehearsing, especially in preparation for such services as the consecration of nuns, which occurred only rarely. One intriguing piece of evidence from a fourteenth-century English manuscript suggests that the nuns practiced vocal exercises similar to those used in the twentieth century. These exercises appear in a Psalter from the Benedictine nunnery at Wherwell and, although based on the hexachord, demonstrate a use of scalar passages, skips, and movement by thirds that is familiar to modern singers (figure 1).[41]

Bishops' records of their visitations of nunneries also yield realistic information about the performance of chant. From these sources we learn of the problems that frequently arose in nunneries: lateness to service, drowsiness at matins, an excess of talking, and a tendency toward haste and sloppiness in performance. While the problems were all understandable, even predictable, they needed to be rectified if discipline of the type required for communal living was to be maintained. The bishops constantly exhorted the nuns to approach their task reverently and with real devotion, as is demonstrated in the following injunction from John Longland, bishop of Lincoln, to the Benedictine nuns at Nun Cottam:

First, inasmuch as all religion is grounded in and ordained principally to honor and serve God both by night and day, and especially that the divine

Figure 1

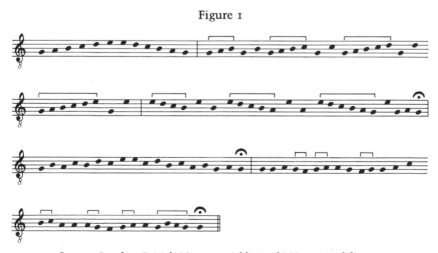

Source: London, British Museum, Additional MS. 27866, folio 147

23

service in the choir should be sung and said reverently and distinctly, . . . and since I have detected in my regular visitation that you have not done it this way but quickly, hastily, and without devotion, . . . I charge you . . . that from henceforth you make sure that the divine office is sung distinctly, in a serious and devout manner, with good pauses and punctuation and without any undue haste or speed; and that you keep the due hours and times of the divine services.[42]

This passage is typical of instructions given to both nuns and monks in the Middle Ages.

Although serious scholars generally concede that nuns in medieval convents performed plainsong, they often ignore any role nuns may have played in the performance of polyphony. Nevertheless, both medieval comments about polyphony and manuscripts containing polyphonic pieces make it clear that women did participate in the adornment of chant through polyphony. For example, in 1261 Odon Rigaud, archbishop of Rouen, specifically forbade the nuns of Montivilliers to continue to perform conductus, motets, and farces.[43]

Further evidence that nuns participated in the performance of polyphony comes from an examination of manuscripts that contain some polyphonic pieces whose provenance can be traced to medieval nunneries. Table 1 gives a number of extant sources that have a definite or probable connection with a nunnery.[44] Although most of these manuscripts contain no more than a few polyphonic pieces, each suggests that the nuns at the convents to which the manuscripts were connected were involved to some degree in the performance of polyphony.

By far the most extensive source of polyphonic music in table 1 is the manuscript from the Monasterio de Las Huelgas near Burgos in northern Spain. This abbey was a wealthy and important religious center in the Middle Ages.[45] Founded in 1180 by Alfonso VIII of Castile, the abbey drew its members primarily from women of royal lineage and was often the site of consecrations, royal burials, and other such activities. The abbess was given considerable authority, both spiritual and temporal, and was exempted from episcopal authority.[46] The number of noblewomen, many of whom brought servants with them, was restricted to one hundred in 1257. Both the use of the nunnery for royal ceremonies and its location near Burgos, which was a major stop on the pilgrimage route to Santiago de Compostela, insured a constant stream of visitors and an influx of ideas from other areas of the world.

The early fourteenth-century polyphonic codex, discovered at

Las Huelgas in 1904 by two monks from Silos, is recognized as one of the major medieval sources of polyphony.[47] It contains an international repertoire that draws heavily on French sources but includes some local compositions. The Las Huelgas Codex contains 136 polyphonic pieces, of which the majority (87) are for two voices, while 48 are for three voices, and one is for four voices. The repertoire includes motets, *Benedicamus* settings, sequences, settings of the Mass ordinary, and organa.[48]

A two-voice vocal exercise found on folio 154v of the codex clearly indicates that the Las Huelgas nuns were instructed in singing polyphony. The text of the lower voice begins with solmization syllables and continues: "And you Carthusian virgins and nuns adorned with gold because you are suitably talented for all this, take care to produce polyphony, with the other voice sounding along in this way."[49] The solmization syllables of the lower voice also indicate the manner in which the singers should change from one hexachord to another; for example, the syllable *sol* is replaced by *ut* on a single note.[50] Both the text of the piece and the use of solmization syllables demonstrate that the piece had a pedagogical rather than a liturgical function, a clear suggestion that the nuns at Burgos were trained in the art of polyphony. A passage from a late thirteenth-century customary instructing the nuns to sing "in three voices" on the first Sunday in Advent confirms the practice of female polyphonic performance at Las Huelgas.[51]

Since medieval nuns were continuously involved in the performance of a large corpus of liturgical music representing several centuries of growth, they had many opportunities to absorb the musical idioms of the liturgical tradition. It is not surprising, therefore, that some nuns, like Herrad, also composed music in traditional idioms. It is difficult, nevertheless, to determine how active religious women were as composers, since the identities of most medieval composers remain unknown. Some nuns (e.g., St. Mechtilde of Magdebourg and Adelheid of Landau) were credited by their contemporaries with the composition of sacred music, but no direct evidence of their music is extant.[52]

Fortunately, no problem surrounds the identity of one nun composer, Hildegard of Bingen, who left behind her a fairly substantial body of plainchant. Born in 1098, Hildegard was placed in a convent at Disibodenberg on the river Nahe at the age of eight and was taught psalm singing and needlework there. The house at Disibodenberg was under the rule of an abbot, and the convent of nuns had been added only shortly before Hildegard's time. Hildegard became head

Table 1
Polyphony in Manuscripts from Medieval Nunneries

Manuscript	Date	Source	Polyphonic Contents
Strasbourg, Bibliothèque nationale et universitaire, "Hortus deliciarum" (destroyed)	12th century	Augustinian nunnery of St. Odilien of Hohenburg, Alsace	1 Two-voice conductus (preserved in Engelhardt's copy)
Wilhering, Stiftsbibliothek, MS. IX.40	12th century	Cistercian nunnery of Wilhering, Austria	1 Two-voice motet of the late 13th century on flyleaf
Donaueschingen, Fürstlich Fürstenbergische Bibliothek, MS. 882	13th century	Dominican nunnery of Brunnenhof near Mohringen, Germany	3 Two-voice pieces
Geneva, Bibliothèque universitaire, MS. Lat. 155 (olim. lat. 30a)	13th century	Probably Dominican nunnery on German-Swiss border	Same pieces as Donaueschingen MS above
Karlsruhe, Badische Landesbibliothek, MS St. Georgen 31	13th century	Nunnery in south Germany or Switzerland	1 Two-voice piece (also in Donaueschingen and Geneva MSS)
Bologna, Biblioteca G. B. Martini, MS Q11	14th century	Nunnery in central Italy	7 Two-voice pieces, including settings of Mass ordinary, two motets
Burgos, Monasterio de Las Huelgas, Codex	14th century	Nunnery of Las Huelgas near Burgos, Spain	136 Pieces, including motets, conductus, Benedicamus settings, sequences, organa for Mass
Limoges, Bibliothèque municipale, MS. 2	14th century	Abbey of Fontevrault in France	3 Two-voice pieces, one a Credo (MS prepared for the abbey's sixteenth abbess, Alienor Dreux-Bretagne)

Table I (continued)

Manuscript	Date	Source	Polyphonic Contents
Fribourg, Bibliothèque de la Maigrauge, MS. 4	14th century	Possibly Franciscan nunnery of Maigrauge, Switzerland	1 Three-voice troped *Agnus*, 1 two-voice *Kyrie*
Karlsruhe, Badische Landesbibliothek, MS St. Peter Perg. 16	14th century	Perhaps Augustinian nunnery in the Neuwerkloster, Erfurt, Germany	1 Organum
Lüneburg, Kloster Lüne	14th– 15th century	Benedictine nunnery in Lüneburg, Germany	1 Two-voice *Benedicamus* setting
Mainz, Stadtbibliothek, MS. II. 138	14th– 15th century	"White" nun cloister in Germany	1 Two-voice piece: *Vernans virtus sacramenti*
Berlin-Tübingen, Staatsbibliothek, Stiftung Preussischer Kulturbesitz (olim. Preuss. Staatsbibl.), MS germ. 8° 190	15th century	Possibly Franciscan nunnery near Utrecht, Netherlands	47 Pieces: sequences, antiphons, hymns, Dutch lieder
Oxford, Bodleian Library, MS Can. lit. 291	15th century	Dominican nunnery in Italy	2 Two-voice *Benedicamus* settings
Rome, Biblioteca Apostolica Vaticana, MS Lat. 4749	15th century	Benedictine nunnery	1 Three-voice *Benedicamus* setting
Vienna, Österreichische Nationalbibliothek, Codex (series nova) 12875	15th century	Franciscan nunnery of St. Margareta, Amsterdam, Netherlands	1 Two-voice Dutch lied, *Mit desen nywen iare*

of the convent in 1136; in 1147 she moved it to Rupertsberg near Bingen, where it was no longer under the direct control of the abbot. There she adopted the Benedictine Rule for the eighteen nuns who followed her. She continued as abbess until her death in 1179.[53]

Hildegard has long been recognized as a major twelfth-century mystic and author. Besides producing several theological works, she wrote medical and scientific treatises, corresponded with many important contemporary figures, and composed the text and music of both sacred and dramatic works. By all accounts she was a woman of strength, intelligence, and religious fervor. Although past scholars tended to ignore her musical works, such scholars as Joseph Schmidt-Görg, M. Immaculata Ritscher, and Peter Dronke have recently begun to study her lyric works in detail.[54]

Around 1150−60 Hildegard collected her sacred music into a work entitled "Symphonia harmoniae caelestium revelationum" ("Symphony of the Harmony of Heavenly Revelations"). This collection, containing seventy-seven pieces, includes forty-three antiphons, eighteen responsories, and seven sequences, all with complete musical notation. The music was intended for feast days of both well-known saints like Mary and saints of primarily local importance like Rupert. Hildegard's corpus of musical works has been compared by Dronke in size and scope to Notker's "Liber hymnorum," written three hundred years earlier.[55]

In one manuscript the liturgical works were followed by a dramatic work, *Ordo virtutum*, which was also set to music.[56] This play (c. 1141−51), which is credited with being the earliest extant liturgical morality play, predates by about two centuries any other works in this genre.[57] It is clearly a landmark in the history of liturgical drama.

Schmidt-Görg, Ritscher, and Dronke all stress the great individuality of Hildegard's work in both its poetic and its musical aspects. Dronke's entire study deals with writers whose work seems not to follow traditional paths but rather to exhibit a degree of originality that is difficult to explain with reference to an inherited tradition. Dronke points to Hildegard's "wholly individual use of imagery," that is, the way in which she was able to incorporate well-known images into her own vocabulary so as to give them new meanings.

Dronke's emphasis on Hildegard's unusual and individual use of poetic images is mirrored by Ritscher and Schmidt-Görg's views of her uncommon and idiosyncratic use of contemporary musical idioms. Both of the latter writers stress her ability to create endlessly varied transmutations of the standard melodic formulae that form the basis of her compositions. Her remarkable flexibility in the use of melodic forms can perhaps be seen most clearly in her sequences, which never exhibit exact melodic and metric repetition of paired versicles and which, on occasion, move back to the rare, early form of the repetitionless sequence.[58] Dronke feels that Hildegard's sequence form establishes a close tie between the poetry and music, and that in her versicle pairs "the images and meaning of the second both mirror and carry forward those of the first."[59]

Some of Hildegard's works were written to honor saints who had local or regional significance for the house at Rupertsberg, notably St. Rupert and St. Ursula. Most religious houses, in fact, had a body of music written especially to celebrate the saint or saints in whose honor the house was constructed. Even when the saint had churchwide recognition, a local house would generally require a larger number of chants and lessons for its own celebrations.

A careful study of the repertoire of individual nunneries brings to light several instances of such compositions. For example, a fifteenth-century hymnal from Barking Abbey contains both the text and music of three hymns in honor of St. Ethelburga, first abbess of Barking in the seventh century, and one hymn text in honor of St. Erkenwald, Ethelburga's brother and founder of the abbey.[60] Both the texts and the musical settings are unique to this manuscript.[61] I include here the first verse of the hymn *Assit nobis* used at vespers throughout the octave of St. Ethelburga (figure 2). Since these unica, which offer no indication as to their creator, exist in a manuscript that originated at a nunnery, one can assume female authorship just as one would assume male authorship had Barking Abbey been a monastery.[62]

Further studies of the repertoire from nunneries both in England and on the continent would undoubtedly point to many other such compositions.[63] Since plainsong formed such an integral part of a

Figure 2

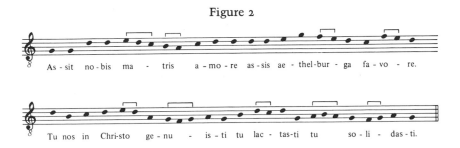

As - sit no - bis ma - tris a - mo - re as - sis ae - thel-bur - ga fa - vo - re.

Tu nos in Chri-sto ge - nu - is - ti tu lac - tas-ti tu so - li - das - ti.

Source: Cambridge, Trinity College Library, MS. 1226, folio 41

nun's daily life, it would not be surprising to find that many nuns wrote chant melodies for the hymns, antiphons, and responsories necessary to honor saints of local importance. Although these women, like many of their male counterparts, might not have reached the creative heights of Hildegard of Bingen, they would nevertheless have been active contributors to medieval musical repertoire.

Viewed from several perspectives, medieval nuns seem to have had far more opportunity to develop their musical talents than did most of their contemporaries who did not choose the religious life. Not only did they obtain at least a minimal education in reading and singing and spend several hours each day performing the liturgy, but they could also—if they had sufficient ability and experience—attain the position of cantrix, with its responsibilities for organizing the musical life of the convent, and find outlets for their creative compositional endeavors within the nunnery. Counterbalancing these advantages were the emphasis on humility and abnegation characteristic of the religious life, the restrictiveness of the daily routine, and the widely held social attitudes that downgraded women's abilities.

Even Hildegard apparently deemed it necessary to justify her work through references to external forces. Like Hroswitha, Hildegard declared that she was merely a vessel for divine revelations.[64] While it was not uncommon for men to justify their work similarly, women also disclaimed their ability to compete with men (see, for example, Hroswitha's remark about the subtleties that "exceed the grasp of my woman's mind"). Such protestations suggest that it required a certain amount of courage for nuns to demonstrate their creativity openly.[65]

None of the information presented here concerning musical life in medieval nunneries is cause for a major revision in the common understanding of sacred music in the Middle Ages. Nevertheless, an increased sensitivity on the part of scholars to the musical activities of nuns should bring about a better integration of the achievements of nuns with those of monks.[66] Discussions of "the monastic tradition" should mention the roles of both nuns and monks. The almost exclusive association of Gregorian chant with "unaccompanied men's voices" should be revised. Such standard reference books as the *New Grove Dictionary* should include articles on Benedictines and Franciscans rather than on "Benedictine Monks" and "Franciscan Friars." While these changes would be small individually, their cumulative effect would be significant. It has been an all too well kept secret that the nunnery in the Middle Ages offered women a chance to sing back to St. Paul.

NOTES

1. Donald Jay Grout, with Claude V. Palisca, *A History of Western Music*, 3d ed. (New York: W. W. Norton & Co., 1980), p. 36.

2. The following studies represent important exceptions to this rule: Michel Brenet [Marie Bobillier], "La Musique dans les couvents de femmes depuis le moyen âge jusqu'à nos jours," *La Tribune de Saint-Gervais*, 4me année (1898), pp. 25–31, 58–61, 73–81; Yvonne Rokseth, "Les Femmes musiciennes du XIIe au XIVe siècle," *Romania* 61 (1935): 464–80; and Kathi Meyer, *Der chorische Gesang der Frauen mit besonderer Bezugnahme seiner Betätigung auf geistlichem Gebeit* (Mittenwald: Arthur Nemayer, 1917).

3. "Ther was also a Nonne, a Prioresse,
   That of hir smylyng was ful symple and coy;
   Hire gretteste ooth was but by Seinte Loy;
   And she was cleped madame Eglentyne.
   Ful weel she soong the service dyvyne,
   Entuned in hir nose ful semely,
   And Frenssh she spak ful faire and fetisly,
   After the scole of Stratford atte Bowe,
   For Frenssh of Parys was to hire unknowe."
   Geoffrey Chaucer, *The Canterbury Tales*, ed. F. N. Robinson, 2d ed. (Boston: Houghton Mifflin Co., 1957), prologue, lines 118–26.

4. Throughout this article I shall use the term *monastery* in the specific rather than the generic sense (i.e., a house of male religious inhabitants) and use the terms *convent* and *nunnery* to refer to female houses.

5 In England in the 1530s, for example, there were approximately 710 monasteries and 140 nunneries. See David Knowles and R. Neville Hadcock, *Medieval Religious Houses: England and Wales* (London: Longman Group, 1971), p. 494. The table on the cited page indicates that there were about 1,900 nuns and canonesses in these houses.

6. Consider the following portion of a letter from the Benedictine nuns at Polsloe, England, written in response to a request that they accept a lay sister: "And if it please your debonair highness to know our simple estate, we are so poor (God knows it and all the country) that what we have suffices not to our small sustenance, who must by day and night do the service of God, were it not for the aid of friends; nor can we be charged with seculars without reducing the number of us religious women, to the diminution of God's service and the perpetual prejudice of our poor house." See Eileen Power, *Medieval English Nunneries, c. 1275 to 1535* (1922; reprint ed., New York: Biblo & Tannen, 1964), p. 193.

7. The German convent at Gandersheim, the home of Hroswitha, for example, had an excellent library and a tradition of well-educated women like the abbess Gerberga.

8. Many houses had provisions for lay sisters or nonchoir sisters, who were not trained to sing the liturgy, however. An alternative form of worship

was usually required. At a Franciscan nunnery near London, for instance, the lay sisters were required to say the Lord's Prayer seventy-two times daily in lieu of singing the Divine Office. See Anne D. Bagnall, *Musical Practices in Medieval English Nunneries* (Ann Arbor, Mich.: University Microfilms, 1975), pp. 38–40.

9. A. Hamilton Thompson, ed., *Visitations of Religious Houses in the Diocese of Lincoln*, 3 vols., Lincoln Record Society, vols. 7, 14, 21 (Horncastle: W. K. Morton & Sons, 1914), 7:53.

10. Saint-Quentin, Bibliothèque municipale, MS. 86 75. See the description of certain rituals by Telchilde de Montessus in "Note sur le rituel de 1315 de l'abbaye d'Origny-Sainte-Benoîte," *Revue Bénédictine* 82 (1972): 243–62.

11. Burgos, Abbey de las Huelgas, unnumbered MS.

12. See Power, *English Nunneries*, pp. 246–55. For a discussion of the educational level in nunneries in the early Middle Ages, see Suzanne Fonay Wemple, *Women in Frankish Society: Marriage and the Cloister 500–900* (Philadelphia: University of Pennsylvania Press, 1981), pp. 175–188.

13. Benedictine Rule, ch. 48.

14. The procedure for the distribution of books is set forth in J. B. L. Tolhurst, ed., *The Ordinale and Customary of the Benedictine Nuns of Barking Abbey*, 2 vols., Henry Bradshaw Society, vols. 65 and 66 (London: Harrison & Sons, 1927), 1:70.

15. N. R. Ker's invaluable book, *Medieval Libraries of Great Britain: A List of Surviving Books*, 2d ed. (London: Offices of the Royal Historical Society, 1964), provides this information for English houses. See also A. I. Doyle, "Books Connected with the Vere Family and Barking Abbey," *Essex Archaeological Society Transactions*, n.s. 25 (1958): 239–43; and Diane Dolan, *Le Drame liturgique de Pâques en Normandie et en Angleterre au moyen âge*, Publications de l'Université de Poitiers, Lettres et Sciences Humaines, vol. 16 (Paris: Presses Universitaires de France, 1975), p. 123.

16. See the discussion in David Knowles, *The Religious Orders in England*, vol. 3, *The Tudor Age* (Cambridge: Cambridge University Press, 1959), p. 213.

17. The translation is my own. The original appears in J. H. Blount, ed., *The Myroure of Oure Ladye*, Early English Text Society, e.s. 19 (London: N. Trübner & Co., 1873), pp. 2–3. See pp. vii–viii for a discussion of the date of the original manuscript.

18. For an introductory study of two such religious women, Hroswitha of Gandersheim and Herrad of Landsberg, the reader is referred to Lina Eckenstein, *Woman under Monasticism: Chapters on Saint-Lore and Convent Life between A.D. 500 and A.D. 1500* (Cambridge: Cambridge University Press, 1896), pp. 160–83, 238–55. See also the *New Catholic Encyclopedia*, s.v. "Herrad of Landsberg" and "Roswitha."

19. Canonesses usually lived together in small groups and recited the Divine Office together. They did not take a vow of poverty and were free to leave at any time. See the *New Catholic Encyclopedia*, s.v. "canoness."

20. For an English translation of *Paphnutius*, see Christopher St. John, trans., *The Plays of Roswitha* (New York: Benjamin Blom, 1923), pp. 93–129. See Anne Lyon Haight, ed., *Hroswitha of Gandersheim: Her Life, Times, and Works, and a Comprehensive Bibliography* (New York: Hroswitha Club, 1965), pp. 3–15, for general background on Hroswitha and the convent at Gandersheim. Both Benedictine nuns and canonesses lived there.

21. Haight, *Hroswitha of Gandersheim*, p. 22.

22. The major source of information about the manuscript is Christian M. Engelhardt, *Herrad von Landsperg und ihr Werk: Hortus Deliciarum* (Stuttgart: J. G. Cotta, 1818). Volume 1 contains a commentary on the work; volume 2 contains several plates that reproduce illustrations from the manuscript.

23. These two pieces are found in Engelhardt, *Herrad von Landsperg*, vol. 2, table 10. Although Engelhardt mentions that most of the other poems were set to music, he does not differentiate between polyphonic and monophonic settings.

24. See the *New Catholic Encyclopedia*, s.v. "Benedictine Rule," for a discussion of the origins and dissemination of this rule.

25. The one major difference in structure lay in the presence of a priest who acted as the chaplain in a nunnery. He was primarily involved in the Mass and not in the offices, and his participation did not substantially affect the musical experience of the nuns.

26. See Bagnall, *Musical Practices*, pp. 2–30, for a discussion of extant copies of the Benedictine Rule from medieval English nunneries. Chapters 5–7 of the rule deal with basic concepts of monastic life; chapters 8–19 deal with the Divine Office.

27. In ascertaining the musical functions of these officials, the Ordinal from Barking Abbey was particularly helpful and provided much of the information used here.

28. On ferial (i.e., non–feast day) occasions, the leadership role in the service was rotated among the members of the community. The person who led the service was called the *ebdomaria* and held the position for a week at a time.

29. The rubrics for Christmas vespers instruct the nuns: "Incipient abbatissa, priorissa, presentrix [sic], et succentrix et due ex senioribus. Similiter in omnibus principalibus festis ad primas vesperas reponsorium a sex." See Tolhurst, *Ordinale*, 1:24. From the Barking Ordinal and from the lists of nuns found in visitation records, it would appear that the terms *precentrix* and *succentrix* were sometimes used to refer to the cantrix and her assistant. Usually the term *cantrix* was used when a single person was referred to, and *precentrix* and *succentrix* when two nuns were specified. The Middle English terms *chantress* and *subchantress*, and the Old French terms *grant chantre* and *sous chantre*, were also used to refer to the cantrix and her assistant.

30. Hilpisch, in *Benedictine Nuns*, p. 35, states that "the chantress was important; generally only one who had been especially trained would be

chosen. She was not only, as today, a director of the choir but, since there was much room for development in the liturgical life, she was expected to compose hymns and set them to music. Thus she had to be both poet and musician at the same time. Since the library consisted principally of liturgical hymns, she was ordinarily librarian also. Under her direction the copying and illustrating of manuscripts was carried on in the scriptorium." Unfortunately Hilpisch does not give the sources of his information.

31. See, for example, the fifteenth-century *Additions to the Rule* of Syon Abbey in George J. Aungier, *The History and Antiquities of Syon Monastery, the Parish of Isleworth, and the Chapelry of Hounslow Compiled from Public Records, Ancient Manuscripts, Ecclesiastical and Other Documents* (London: J. B. Nichols & Sons, 1840), pp. 359–60. This source gives detailed information for the only Bridgettine house in England.

32. Benedictine houses, for example, usually adopted the missal of the diocese in which they were located. A specific statement to this effect is found in the Barking Ordinal (fol. 219). See Tolhurst, *Ordinale*, 1 : ix, for a discussion of the practices at Barking Abbey.

33. For a discussion of the liturgical-musical practices in a German Dominican nunnery, see Hildegard Wachtel's dissertation, *Die liturgische Musikpflege im Kloster Adelhausen seit Grundung des Klosters 1234 bis um 1500*, Freiburg Diözesan-Archiv, n.f. vol. 39 (vol. 66 of the entire series) (Freiburg im Breslau: H. Rombach & Co., 1938). See especially pp. 57–64 for a discussion of the responsibilities of specific individuals within the nunnery.

34. René Metz's work, *La Consécration des vierges dans l'église romaine: Étude d'histoire de la liturgie* (Paris: Presses Universitaires de France, 1954), is a thorough study of the version of this service found in the Roman pontifical and used widely on the continent. For a more detailed discussion of the extant source material in England, see Bagnall, *Musical Practices*, pp. 130–56. The service was basically the same in England as it was on the continent.

35. Walter Howard Frere discusses this phase of the development of the liturgy in *Pontifical Services Illustrated from Miniatures of the XVth and XVIth Centuries*, Alcuin Club Collections, vol. 3 (London: Longmans, Green, & Co., 1901), pp. 57–58. Since communities of religious women focused primarily on their virginity and secondarily on their religious functions while those of religious men reversed these priorities, it is not surprising that the different emphases were reflected by markedly different consecration services.

36. Metz, *La Consécration des vierges*, pp. 221–22.

37. Cambridge, University Library, MS. Mm iii. 3. The text of the manuscript has been edited by W. Maskell in *Monumenta Ritualia Ecclesia Anglicana*, 2d ed., 3 vols. (1882; reprint, Westmead, Eng.: Gregg International Publishers, 1970), 2 : 308–31.

38. See Edouard de Coussemaker, *Les Drames liturgiques du moyen âge* (1860; facsimile ed., New York: Broude Bros., 1964), for a discussion of the Origny-Saint-Benoîte manuscript (pp. 337–44) and for a reproduction of

the manuscript itself (pp. 256–79). The version of the drama at Barking Abbey is described in Tolhurst, *Ordinale*, 1:106–10, and discussed in Diane Dolan, *Drame liturgique*, pp. 121–40. Though the manuscript from Wilton Abbey is now lost, a copy was made by Dom Jausions of the Abbey of Solesmes in 1862, and that version is thoroughly discussed in Georges Benoît-Castelli, "Un Processional anglais du XIVème siècle: Le Processional dit 'de Rollington'," *Ephemerides liturgicae* 75 (1961): 281–326.

39. See W. L. Smoldon, "Liturgical Drama," *New Oxford History of Music*, vol. 2, *Early Medieval Music up to 1300*, ed. Don Anselm Hughes (London: Oxford University Press, 1955), p. 188.

40. *Additions to the Rule* in Aungier, *History and Antiquities*, p. 360. The translation is my own.

41. London, British Library, Add. MS. 27866, fol. 147. This Psalter contains music for both the ferial antiphons and the Office of the Dead.

42. Edward Peacock, "Injunctions of John Longland, Bishop of Lincoln, to Certain Monasteries in his Diocese," *Archaeologia* 47 (1882): 55–56.

43. "Nimia iocositate et scurrilibus cantibus utebantur ut pote farsis, conductis, motulis." See Pierre Aubry, ed., *Cent motets du XIII*e *siècle*, 3 vols. (1908; reprint, New York: Broude Bros., 1964), 3:17n. For information on other such injunctions, see the discussion in Rokseth, "Les Femmes musiciennes," pp. 477–78.

44. This list has been compiled on the basis of listings in *Répertoire international des sources musicales*, 4 vols. (München-Duisberg: G. Henle, 1966–72): vols. B IV 1, *Manuscripts of Polyphonic Music: 11th–Early 14th Century* (1966), and B IV 2, *Manuscripts of Polyphonic Music: c. 1320–1400* (1969), ed. Gilbert Reaney, and vols. B IV 3 and 4, *Handschriften mit mehrstimmiger Musik des 14., 15., und 16. Jahrhunderts* (1972), ed. Max Lütolf; as well as the listing in Arnold Geering, *Die Organa und mehrstimmigen Conductus in den Handschriften des deutschen Sprachgebietes vom 13. bis 16. Jahrhundert* (Bern: Paul Haupt, 1952).

45. For a brief history of the abbey, see the *New Catholic Encyclopedia*, s.v. "Huelgas de Burgos, Abbey of." An extensive history of the abbey is Don Amancio Rodriguez Lopez, *El real monasterio de las Huelgas de Burgos y el hospital del rey: Apuntes para su historia y colección diplomática con ellos relacionada*, 2 vols. (Burgos: Lain Calvo, 1907).

46. See Joan Morris, *The Lady Was a Bishop* (New York: Macmillan, 1973), for a discussion of nunneries in which the abbess had quasi-episcopal authority, and especially pp. 83–99 on Las Huelgas.

47. This manuscript has been edited, published in facsimile, and transcribed by Higinio Anglès in *El codex musical de las Huelgas*, 3 vols. (Barcelona: Institut d'estudis Catalans, Biblioteca de Catalunya, 1931). Volume 1, a commentary on the manuscript, includes a history of the abbey on pp. v–xxii.

48. See Robert Stevenson, *Spanish Music in the Age of Columbus* (The Hague: Martinus Nijhoff, 1960), pp. 35–36, for the number of each type of composition. For a study and transcription of the polyphonic settings of the

Mass ordinary, see Max Lütolf, *Die mehrstimmigen Ordinarium Missae-Sätze vom ausgehenden 11. bis zur Wende des 13. zum 14. Jahrhundert*, 2 vols. (Bern: Paul Haupt, 1970), 1:262–83 and vol. 2 passim.

49. I am greatly indebted to Professor Ernest Sanders of Columbia University for his translation of this passage. A transcription is found in Anglès, *Codex*, 2:405.

50. See measure 5 of the Anglès transcription.

51. Anglès, *Codex*, 1:110–11. Despite the evidence of female performance, Anglès asserts that much of the repertoire would have been sung by the twenty chaplains associated with the abbey. He bases this assertion on the range of a few pieces, which are notated a fourth or fifth lower than in concordant sources (1:xi, 231–32). Two important points argue against his thesis that such transposition implies performance by male voices: (1) the notation of pitch in the Middle Ages was relative, not absolute; and (2) there is no indication in manuscripts intended for nunneries that women would sing the music at a higher pitch level than men, although they obviously must have done so. If, as Anglès argues, the transpositions were made to change the range of the pieces from that suitable for men and boys to one suitable for men only, the changes would in fact make the pieces performable by either an all-male or an all-female choir. Stevenson, in *Spanish Music*, p. 38, is particularly misleading on this point: he makes no mention of nuns in his commentary on the Las Huelgas choir. Indeed, he seems to think that the only choice of choirs in medieval Spain was between boys and men or men alone.

52. See Meyer, *Der chorische Gesang der Frauen*, pp. 40–44, for information on such nuns.

53. For biographical information about Hildegard, see *The New Grove Dictionary of Music and Musicians* (1980), s.v. "Hildegard of Bingen," 8:553–56; Joseph Schmidt-Görg, "Hildegard von Bingen," in *Die Musik in Geschichte und Gegenwart*, ed. Friedrich Blume, vol. 6 (1957), cols. 389–91; *New Catholic Encyclopedia*, s.v. "Hildegarde, St."; Eckenstein, *Woman under Monasticism*, pp. 262–63; and Frances and Joseph Gies, *Women in the Middle Ages* (New York: Thomas Y. Crowell Co., 1978), pp. 63–96.

54. Prudentia Barth, M. Immaculata Ritscher, and Joseph Schmidt-Görg, eds., *Hildegard von Bingen: Lieder* (Salzburg: Otto Müller, 1969), a complete edition of Hildegard's songs in diplomatic facsimile, contains an introductory stylistic discussion by Schmidt-Görg. See also M. Immaculata Ritscher, "Zur Musik der heiligen Hildegard," in *Colloquium amicorum Joseph Schmidt-Görg zum 70. Geburtstag*, ed. Siegfried Kross and Hans Schmidt (Bonn: Beethovenhaus, 1967), pp. 309–26; and Peter Dronke, *Poetic Individuality in the Middle Ages: New Departures in Poetry 1000–1150* (Oxford: Oxford University Press, 1970), pp. 150–92, 209–31. The absence of any mention of her work in standard writings on medieval music is startling.

55. Dronke, *Poetic Individuality*, p. 152.

56. Ibid., pp. 152–53. Schmidt-Görg states, in his article in *Die Musik*

in *Geschichte und Gegenwart*, that Hildegard's pieces are not, strictly speaking, liturgical, since they were intended for use primarily in her own convent. Since their function, however, was liturgical, I believe they may properly be described as such.

57. See Bruce W. Hozeski, *"Ordo Virtutum*: Hildegard of Bingen's Liturgical Morality Play," *Annuale Mediaevale* 13 (1972): 45–69, for a translation of *Ordo virtutum* into English, along with a brief introduction.

58. Most scholars discuss the twelfth-century sequence by referring only to Adam of St. Victor's sequences, in which the rhyme and rhythm of paired versicles are regular; see, for instance, Richard H. Hoppin, *Medieval Music* (New York: W. W. Norton & Co., 1978), p. 166. Hildegard's works do not exhibit this regularity.

59. Dronke, *Poetic Individuality*, p. 158. The reader who does not have access to Hildegard's complete works (in Barth et al., *Hildegard von Bingen*) will find transcriptions of two sequences in the appendix to Dronke, *Poetic Individuality*, and of a third sequence in Peter Dronke, *The Medieval Lyric* (New York: Harper & Row, 1969), pp. 233–35.

60. Cambridge, Trinity College Library, MS. 1226. The three hymns for St. Ethelburga are found on fols. 41–42. The hymn to St. Erkenwald includes blank staves without music.

61. Often new texts were set to preexisting melodies. This practice of adaptation was in itself a valid area of musical-liturgical work and probably one in which many nuns were involved. Hymn tunes in particular were commonly supplied with new sets of words. Although I do not have any firm evidence of a nun undertaking such a process, it was a standard medieval procedure, and a study of manuscripts would probably confirm that some nunneries adopted preexistent tunes for setting local texts.

62. The fifteenth-century processional from the English nunnery of Chester includes five antiphons and a responsory that are unique to that manuscript. For a description and transcription of the unica, see Bagnall, *Musical Practices*, pp. 119–21, 208–9. The manuscript itself (EL 34 B.7) is at the Huntington Library in San Marino, California.

63. Sarah Fuller has suggested to me that a study of the troper-prosers from nunneries might be fruitful in finding such compositions. It is certainly an area that needs further study. See Hildegard Wachtel's study of the music at Adelhausen (n. 33 above) for a description of the sequence manuscript from that nunnery.

64. Hildegard stated, in the introduction to one of her works (*Scivias*) that a "voice from heaven" told her: "Thou art timid, timid in speech, artless in explaining, unlearned in writing, but express and write not according to art but according to natural ability, not under the guidance of human composition but under the guidance of that which thou seest and hearest in God's heaven above." See Eckenstein, *Woman under Monasticism*, p. 264.

65. Barbara L. Grant, "An Interview with the Sybil of the Rhine: Hildegard von Bingen (1098–1179)," in *Women and Music, Heresies*, no. 10 (1980), p. 7, suggests that a terrible illness Hildegard suffered was due to her

refusal to write down her visions because of her "fear of what certain men might say about [her] authority to speak, the authenticity of [her] visions." In "Five Liturgical Songs by Hildegard von Bingen (1098–1179)," *Signs* 5 (1980): 557–58, Grant further discusses Hildegard's struggle to find her own voice.

66. An example of the positive effects of such scholarship is found in David Fallows's review of Christopher Page's recording of "Hildegard of Bingen: Eight Sequences and Hymns" (*Early Music* 11 [1983]: 263–65). Fallows suggests that Hildegard's achievements show many things of importance to the proper understanding of twelfth-century music.

3

Jougleresses and *Trobairitz*: Secular Musicians in Medieval France

MARIA V. COLDWELL

The early medieval period was a time of relative power and freedom for women. Especially in northern Europe, women had many of the same legal and economic privileges as men. Women could inherit property and manage estates; they could belong to most guilds and take over their husbands' businesses as widows; peasant women worked equally with their male counterparts.[1] In France Charlemagne's wife and her aristocratic female contemporaries were expected to administer the financial and domestic affairs of their husbands' estates. Charlemagne's daughters were substantially endowed upon his death and were able to lead independent lives away from the court of their brother.[2] From the tenth century, many fiefs throughout France were held by women, from Boulogne and Calais in the north to Toulouse, Carcassonne, Nîmes, and Montpellier in the south.[3]

The twelfth century saw the spectacular rise to power of Eleanor of Aquitaine, who in 1132 inherited an enormous duchy, larger than the kingdom of France. Her inheritance made her the most politically desirable woman in Europe; but despite her successive marriages to two kings, Louis VII of France and Henry II of England, she managed to maintain control over her ancestral lands until her death.[4] At the age of eighty she was responsible for bringing her granddaughter, Blanche of Castile, from Spain to marry the heir to the French throne, the future Louis VIII. In her turn Blanche became the most powerful woman in France, acting as regent for her son, Louis IX, who was only twelve when his father died. Even after Louis IX came of age, Blanche remained a powerful force, regularly advising and accompanying her son. When he departed for a Crusade in 1248, it was

39

his sixty-year-old mother whom he designated as regent; she remained in that position until her death in 1252.[5]

From the thirteenth century onward, however, women's power and autonomy began to decline in France and elsewhere in Europe. After the death of Philip the Fair in 1314, in a desperate move to prevent the French throne from passing to the son of the late king's sister—Edward III of England—the French barons declared that ancient Frankish Salic law prohibited any inheritance of the kingdom through females, a proclamation that quickly became convention.[6] By the late fourteenth century, the beginning of the Renaissance, women's economic and political power had deteriorated significantly, and it continued at a low ebb throughout this period of expanding freedom and enlightenment for men.[7]

Many commentators have noted that the general image of woman in the Middle Ages was two-faced, the faces belonging to Mary, the saint, and Eve, the evil temptress.[8] The Church, with its view of women as ideally chaste and pure but in practice weak and sexually dangerous, was primarily responsible for this dichotomy. The growth of Marian cults and devotional societies in the twelfth and thirteenth centuries was paralleled by the development of the notion of courtly love in the secular sphere. Courtly love elevated the idealized aristocratic woman to a pedestal of power, in affairs of the heart if not in those of state. However, it seems clear that courtly love was essentially a literary phenomenon and did little to improve the actual status of women.[9] The world of courtly love can perhaps be seen as a fantasy created to compensate women for their declining influence in the real world. It is somewhat ironic that women were active participants in the construction of the "code" of courtly love. Marie, countess of Champagne and daughter of Eleanor of Aquitaine, was both patron and advisor to Andreas Capellanus, whose *Treatise on Love* (sometimes called *The Art of Courtly Love*), written about 1200, is the bible for students of courtly love.[10] Marie was also an important figure in the spread of troubadour poetry and music to northern France as a patron of trouvères and literary figures including Conon de Béthune, Gace Brulé, and Chrétien de Troyes. Eleanor of Aquitaine herself was the patron (and lover?) of the troubadour Bernart de Ventadorn. Marie de France, author of the earliest French Arthurian lais (narrative poems not intended to be sung), was a member of Eleanor's court. Thibaut, the count of Champagne and a famous trouvère, wrote many of his chansons for Blanche of Castile, his queen and the object of his admiration and love.

The noblewoman of medieval France was frequently highly cultured but generally not formally educated. Her training was probably an apprenticeship in the home of another lady, perhaps her own mother or her future mother-in-law.[11] The skills of managing a large household were the most important for her to acquire. Several late medieval didactic treatises addressed to middle- and upper-class women concerning their education consider the proper accomplishments a young woman should have: excellent manners, the ability to play chess and other courtly games, a knowledge of falconry, some skill in reading and writing, and sometimes skill in singing and playing musical instruments.[12] Garin lo Brun's *Ensenhamens* from about 1200 advises women to sing and recite poetry for their guests, and to welcome troubadours and jongleurs with gifts so their praises will be spread abroad by the musicians.[13] *La Clef d'Amors*, an early fourteenth-century French imitation of Ovid's *Ars amatoria*, states that singing is a beautiful and noble thing for a young woman and that playing the psaltery, the *timbre*, the *guiterne*, and the *citole* are highly desirable skills.[14] Chrétien de Troyes's imaginary heroine Philomena knew how to read and write, how to compose poetry, and how to play the psaltery, the *lire*, the *gigue*, the *rote*, and the vielle.[15] Frêne, the heroine of the early thirteenth-century romance *Galeran de Bretagne*, was educated in an abbey, where she was also trained well in music. She knew Saracen tunes, Gascon and French songs, songs from Lorraine, and Breton lais; and she was an excellent harpist.[16]

The musical education of ladies in France seems quite typical of Europe in general; compare the early fourteenth-century Italian treatise *Del reggimento e costumi di donna* of Francesco da Barberino, which suggests that a young woman sing for her own amusement (but not in public) and that she learn to play the vielle or some other good and upright instrument, particularly the harp.[17] The immodesty of singing in public is not generally mentioned in French sources, although Robert de Blois does suggest that a woman should sing publicly only if she is asked to, and then she should do so without making a fuss.[18]

The musical education of aristocratic women was not very different from that of their male counterparts.[19] In fact, as amateur musicians, aristocratic women seem to have been the equal of men in medieval France. In the context of medieval French romances, women certainly perform just as frequently as men, and there are some genres in which they clearly predominate. The carol or dance song is one such genre. In a scene from *Le Roman de la Violette* (early thirteenth century), the carol singers include "my lady Nicole," the countess of Besançon, the duchess of Burgundy, "a very educated girl who was the sister of the count of Blois," the sister of the count of St. Paul, the lady of Couci, the châtelaine of Niort, and a lady from Normandy.[20] Johannes de Grocheo, one of the few medieval musical theorists who write about secular music, mentions female singers in defining certain kinds of dance songs. According to Grocheo, the *rotundellus*, *stantipes*, and *ductia* are all sung "by girls and youths."[21]

Women were not limited in performance to simple dance songs, however; they also sang the more elevated troubadour and trouvère chansons. Euriaus sings songs by the troubadour Bernart de Ventadorn and the trouvère Moniot d'Arras in *Le Roman de la Violette*. Pyrabiaus sings motets in *Méliacin*, even though she knows very well she is a bad singer.[22] Many women in the romances sing lais to the accompaniment of their instruments. In *The Romance of Horn*, Lenburc sings lais to the harp. She first tunes her harp, raising its pitch, and then begins her song.[23] The various versions of the anonymous "Tristan" in prose (mid–thirteenth century) contain several long descriptions of women singing lais to the accompaniment of their harps. In one passage Tristan is traveling incognito and meets a very talented young woman. She brings her beautiful golden harp before him and prepares to play, tuning the harp so that "the higher strings accord with the lower." She asks what he would like to hear, suggesting that the lais of "my lord Tristan" are the best. She decides to play his *"Lay de victoire,"* and he affirms that it is certainly one of Tristan's best. She makes a prelude and begins to sing. She sings and plays so sweetly that Tristan tells her afterward that she is the best young female harpist and singer he has heard for some time.[24] In one manuscript version of the "Tristan" in prose, musical notation is given for sixteen songs, three of which are sung by Isolde.[25]

The instruments women play in the romances and those suggested as appropriate in the didactic treatises are the harp, the vielle, the psaltery, the rote, the lire, the gigue, the guiterne, the citole, and the timbre, all but the last stringed instruments. In a recent survey of thirteenth-century French manuscript illuminations depicting music, this list of instruments is confirmed. Of the pictures including female instrumentalists, three show vielle players, four show harpists, two depict rebec players, and one a gittern player.[26]

Not only did women sing and play monophonic music, they also performed polyphonic secular music when it became popular in the fourteenth century.[27] In the autobiographical narrative, *Le Livre du Voir-Dit*, Machaut describes Péronne d'Armentières, "Toute Belle," as "the best singer born in a hundred years." Péronne may have composed many of the lyric poems included in the *Voir-Dit*, but she apparently did not compose music. She constantly badgered Machaut in her letters (included in the *Voir-Dit*) to set both her poems and his to music, for she didn't want to sing anything else. Even when she broke off the romantic relationship, she suggested that he might occasionally want to send her some more songs.[28]

Péronne's inability to compose polyphony is not surprising. While there were some female composers of troubadour and trouvère songs, no female composers of secular polyphony are known. Relatively little skill was required to compose monophonic tunes, and aristocratic men and women were on equal ground in the composition of troubadour and trouvère chansons. But with the development of polyphony, only those men with access to musical training in cathedral schools or universities could develop the requisite skills for composing.[29] The aristocracy, both male and female, were unable to keep up with the technical requirements of composition, and it became increasingly the art of clerics in the fourteenth and fifteenth centuries.

Aristocratic women were not the only female musicians in medieval France; women from lower social classes were also musically active. Those who made their living from music fall into two general categories: (1) traveling *jougleresses* and (2) more stationary servants and courtesans. The latter seem to have been much more a fixture in Moorish Spain than in France. The tradition of singing and dancing slave girls and harem members extends back into Near Eastern Islamic history.[30] As early as the eighth century, Arabian conquests had brought captive women of various races and classes into slavery. Many of them were trained as singers and instrumentalists at the music schools of the Hijāz and ʿIrāq to supply harems of the nobility, not only with beauty, but also with musical talent.[31]

Some of these women were sold to Arabian nobility in Spain. An early eleventh-century account describes a performance by one of these women in Malaga. Ahmed bin Muhammed Al-Yemeni, a visitor in Spain, was troubled by insomnia one night. The street noises keeping him awake suddenly calmed, however, when he heard some beautiful instrumental music being played and soon afterward a clear and beautiful woman's voice. He found a window overlooking the neighbor's courtyard and saw there some twenty people sitting with desserts and drinks listening to a female musician who was keeping her audience spellbound. The next day Al-Yemeni made inquiries and learned that the slave girl was from Baghdad, and one of the best singers of Al-Mansur bin Abi Amir.[32] Moorish customs had a great influence on native Christian Spaniards: wealthy Christians, too, began to keep "singing-girls" as entertainers. As late as the fourteenth century, Juan Ruiz refers to the Spanish *cantaders* (singing girls) singing, dancing, and playing the tambourine.[33]

Documentary and iconographic evidence suggests that women in Spain played a wide variety of musical instruments. Moorish women routinely learned to play the lute, the *rabel* (rebec), the *manucordio* (monochord), and the organ so as to be a "solace for their husbands."[34] The two women musicians pictured in the illuminations of the *Cantigas de Santa Maria* of King Alfonso the Wise (late thirteenth century)[35] are both playing percussion instruments— wooden clappers (apparently played like castanets) and an Arabic drum. Plate 2 shows the woman playing an Arabic drum (which is held over her shoulder) while a man plays a long horn (perhaps a type of shawm). Plate 3, an illustration from Alfonso's *Book of Chess, Dice, and Backgammon*,[36] shows a woman playing the lute or *oud* while two other women play chess. The two chess players are wearing jewelry and rather elegant head dresses, but the lute player is not; she appears to be a servant or professional entertainer to the (Christian) ladies.

Moorish musicians from Spain must have occasionally traveled through France; at least that is the implication of certain episodes in romances where French noblewomen disguise themselves as minstrels by darkening their faces with herbs, putting on traveling cloaks, and carrying instruments. In *Aucassin et Nicolette*, for example, Nicolette acquires a vielle, learns to play it, and then disguises herself as a *jogleor*[37] (apparently a common sort of passenger on Mediterranean boats) to escape her captors in Carthage. When she arrives in Provence, she travels from castle to castle singing the story of Aucassin and Nicolette until she ends up at Beaucaire, where Aucassin is staying, and they are reunited.[38]

Another tale using the motif of disguise as a jougleresse, again with reference to darkening the color of the skin, appears in *Bueve de Hantone*, where the heroine Josiane stains her skin with an herb, dyes her blonde hair, and dresses as a jougleresse, taking up her vielle. Her repertory consists of "notes, lais, and songs" about Tristan and Isolde, Menelaus, Paris, and Troy. An old man, Soybaus, who travels with her, plays the harp and makes his instrument accord with her vielle in playing together.[39]

In the medieval romances, traveling French jougleresses are relatively common characters. Perhaps 5 to 10 percent of the traveling

Plate 2
Woman playing an Arabic drum

Source: "Las Cantigas de Santa Maria,"
El Escorial, MS j.b. 2, old MS page 330, new foliation f. 295v.
Reproduced in Julian Ribera, *La Musica de las Cantigas* (Madrid:
Tip. de la Revista de archivos, 1922)

Plate 3
Woman playing a lute

Source: "Libro de Ajedrez"
(Book of Chess, Dice, and Backgammon of Alfonso the Wise), El Escorial, MS j.T. 6.
Reproduced in Julian Ribera, *La Musica de las
Cantigas* (Madrid: Tip. de la Revista de archivos, 1922)

minstrels mentioned in the romances are female. Frêne, in *Galeran de Bretagne*, is forced to leave the abbey where she was educated as a child and to set out alone on a mule with only a few personal belongings, including her harp. While traveling she pays her way at inns by playing the harp and singing. She eventually performs as a minstrel at the castle of her long lost beloved and is recognized for the noblewoman she really is.[40] In *Guillaume de Dole*, when minstrels come from "all the earth" to entertain the emperor Conrad, a female minstrel from Troies, "la bele Doete," sings a pastourelle for him.[41]

The evidence of the romances is supported by actual documents from the period. Professional musicians' guilds allowed women members.[42] The statutes of the guild of minstrels in Paris, dating from 1321, have eight women among the thirty-seven signers: Isabelet la Rousselle; Marie la Chartaine; Liégart, the wife of Bienviegnant; Marguerite, the wife of the "monk" (?); Jehane la Ferpiere; Alipson, the wife of Guillot Guerin; Adeline, the wife of G. Langlois; and Isabiau la Lorraine. Each of the individual articles in the document specifies that it includes both "menestreus et menestrelles" or "jougleurs et jougleresses." Although later documents of the guild do not mention women specifically, their right to be part of the community had already been established in 1321. The number of women members may have diminished gradually throughout the fourteenth century, however, due to the increasingly onerous conditions required for admission to the guild as master players.[43]

The tax records of the city of Paris provide some references to female musicians living in that city. In a tax book of 1297, Bietriz d'Arraz, the "jugleresse," is listed as residing in the Rue aux Jugleurs, and Eudeline the "salterionnesse" (psaltery player) lived by St. Germain d'Auxerres. A tax book of 1313 states that there lived by the church of Ste. Geneviève one Marie, "citolerresse, regratière" (citole player and peddler).[44]

Certain household accounts also record payments to women performers. In 1239 Louis IX gave one hundred sous to "Mélanz, cantatrix." In 1276 sixteen sous were paid to Alison, the "vieleresse," by the count of Flanders, Guy de Dampiene. In 1320 the accounts of the hôtel d'Artois list a payment to Jehanne, who played the organ.[45] In the accounts of the Burgundian court in the late fourteenth century are several records of payments to women singers: four livres de Tours to Jeanne de la Page and three other "chanteresses" who entertained the duke of Burgundy in 1372; and various sums to Berthelomette "la menestriere," Aiglautine de Tournay "la chanteresse," and Robinette and Jehanette, two "chanteuresses de Paris" in the 1370s.[46]

The records of the duke of Berry show payments to female musicians from Lyons in 1372, to others from Paris and Puy in 1374, and to a singer named Catherine, who sang with her husband for the court in 1377.[47]

Women in medieval France were more than performers of music, however; they were also creators of music. Women are considered to be the earliest poets to use the vernacular in the Middle Ages. The earliest known romance lyrics are the *kharjas*, verses in a Mozarabic dialect appended, presumably by the woman who sang them, to long strophic Arabic poems called *muwashshahs*.[48] "Woman's songs," poems in which the speaker is a woman, regardless of the actual sex of the author, occur in all the medieval love-lyric vernacular traditions: as *cantigas de amigo* in Portugal, as *Frauenlieder* in Germany, as *chansons de femme* in France.[49] The woman's song is a "popularizing" (as opposed to an "aristocratizing") genre, that is, one that imitates folk styles and has a less elevated tone than the standard courtly love lyric.[50] In the French tradition, woman's songs include the *chanson d'ami* (a love song from the woman's point of view), the *chanson de malmariée* (song of an unhappily wedded woman), the *chanson de toile* (needlework song relating a romantic tale), and the *aube* (*alba* or parting song of lovers at dawn).[51] Most of these texts have been transmitted anonymously, so the proportion actually written by women is unknown. When chansons de toile[52] are mentioned in the context of romances, however, they are always sung by women: Léonor and her mother sing them to Guillaume and Nicole in *Guillaume de Dole*, and Marote sings one while doing embroidery in *Le Roman de la Violette*.[53]

Woman's songs as a literary genre must be distinguished from the songs in various genres actually written by women. The female authors whose names have survived in the manuscripts of troubadour and trouvère song include twenty women troubadours and a smaller number of female trouvères.[54] These women generally wrote within the tradition of the aristocratic courtly love lyric and yet necessarily had to transform that tradition to stay within its limits. In their poems the women troubadours did not simply switch roles with the men and elevate their male lovers to pedestals; rather, they remained the objects of desire and expressed a wish to be worshiped properly.[55] Most of their poems avoid outright praise of their lovers, and many are written in an adversarial style: half of the surviving texts are *tensos* or debate songs, which frequently have men as opponents. The true *cansos* or love songs are generally complaints against unfaithful lovers or evil gossipers.

Plate 4
Portrait of Comtessa de Dia

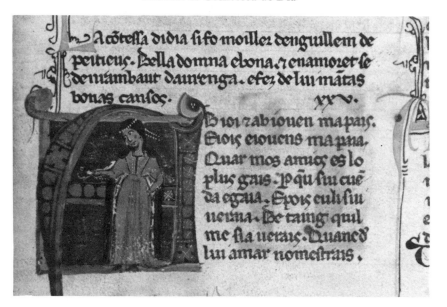

Source: Paris, Bibliothèque nationale,
fonds français 854, folio 141

The female troubadours whose poems survive include Castelloza from Auvergne, the wife of a nobleman who fought in the fourth crusade; Azalais de Porcairagues; Marie de Ventadorn; and Tibors, sister of the troubadour Raimbaut d'Orange and wife of Bertrand de Baux, a patron of Raimbaut.[56] Only one of the trobairitz's songs survives with music, A chantar m'er de so que no volria by the Comtessa de Dia[57] (see plate 4). The comtessa's vida says that she was the wife of Guillem de Poitiers and the lover of Raimbaut d'Orange, but finding a historical personage who corresponds to these scant facts is problematic.[58] In A chantar the comtessa berates her unfaithful lover and reminds him of her virtues. The poem is cast in five strophes with a tornada or concluding half-strophe. The music, which is identical for each of the five strophes, is in a typical form for such a canso: AAB (see figure 3). The last line of the A section is musically identical to the last line of the B section. Although the poem exists in several manuscripts, the melody is contained only in Le Manuscrit du Roi.[59] There it is written in the typical

48

Figure 3
A chantar m'er de so
Comtessa de Dia

A chan – tar m'er de so qu'eu no vol – ri – a

Tant me ran – cur de lui cui sui a – mi – a

Car eu l'am mais que nul – ha ren que si – a

Vas lui no•m val mer – ces ni cor – te – zi – a

Ni ma bel – tatz ni mos pretz ni mos sens

Qu'a – tres – si•m sui en – ga – nad' e tra – hi – a

Com de – gr'es – ser s'eu fos de – sa – vi – nens.

I must sing of that which I would rather not:
I am so aggrieved by him of whom I am the friend.
For I love him more than anything that be,
But pity and courtliness do not avail me with him,
Nor my beauty, nor my worth, nor my wits:
For I am thus tricked and betrayed
As I should be if I were ugly.

Source: Paris, Bibliothèque nationale, fonds français 844, folio 204. Recorded by Studio der Frühen Musik on *Chansons der Troubadours*, Telefunken SAWT 9567-B; by Hesperion XX on *Cansos de Trobairitz*, Odeon/Reflexe 1C 065-30941Q; and by Clemencic Consort on *Troubadours*, volume 2, Harmonia Mundi 397

tenor-range C clef; in no way is it distinguished from the melodies of male troubadours. If a woman sang the piece, she would certainly have sung it in a more comfortable range for her, and she could similarly have sung any of the male troubadours' pieces at a higher pitch level.[60]

Only a few songs by female trouvères have been uncovered. In *Le Manuscrit du Roi*, one trouvère chanson with music is attributed to a woman, Maroie de Dregnau of Lille, an otherwise unknown poet. *Mout m'abelist quant je voi revenir* has just one seven-line strophe of text preserved, and like the piece by the Comtessa de Dia, its musical form is AAB.[61] The poem speaks of the ennobling power of love, even during the worst season of the year (see figure 4 and plate 5). *Amours, u trop tart me sui pris*, attributed to Blanche of Castile, queen of France, is found in a fragmentary manuscript[62] (see figure 5). It is a prayer to the Virgin in four strophes; the last two lines of each strophe constitute a musical/textual refrain. Friedrich Gennrich has printed the piece in one of his collections, using modal rhythm in his transcription.[63] The original notation of troubadour and trouvère chansons generally indicates no specific durational values; most of the transcriptions here (see figures 3, 4, and 6) are done in a free style that would allow a performer to follow the shifting accents of the texts in giving the pieces some rhythmic shape. Some musicologists, including Gennrich, however, apply repetitive rhythmic patterns to the chansons to produce a consistent musical meter. The transcription in figure 5 is taken directly from Gennrich's publication.

Two trouvère chansons without music in a manuscript at Bern are attributed to the Duchesse de Lorraine.[64] In the same manuscript the very famous crusade song, *Chanterai por mon corage*, is attributed to the Dame de Fayel (the lover of the famous trouvère, the Châtelain de Couci). The piece is found in several other manuscripts with music and is attributed in *Le Manuscrit du Roi* and elsewhere to Guiot de Dijon. The text is certainly written from a woman's point of view, but that is no reason for preferring the attribution to a female author. Since the Dame de Fayel has no other songs extant, the Bern manuscript's attribution is probably fanciful.

Several Old French *jeu-partis* (debate songs) have women as authors or coauthors. Ten (or 5½ percent) of the 182 pieces edited by Långfors in his collection of jeu-partis have women participants.[65] Only three of these ten poems survive with music, however: *Je vous pri Dame Maroie*, by Dame Margot and Dame Maroie; *Douce dame ce soit sans nul nomer*, by Perrot de Beaumarchais and a nameless

Plate 5
Mout m'abelist quant je voi revenir, Maroie de
Dregnau de Lille

Source: Paris, Bibliothèque nationale,
fonds français 844, folio 181

lady; and *Amis, quelx est li mieuz vaillanz*, by an anonymous lady
and her lover or friend.[66] The last is written to the tune of Bernart de
Ventadorn's canso, *Can vei la lauzeta moder*, but the other two have
melodies presumably written by one of the participants. Figure 6
gives the two surviving melodies for the debate between Margot and
Maroie. Both of the sources are thought to come from the Arras region, and it is a bit surprising to find in them two completely different melodies for this text.[67] The subject of the debate is a question of
courtly behavior: if a woman's lover is simply too shy to speak up,
should she be able to take the initiative? Dame Maroie answers in

Figure 4
Mout m'abelist quant je voi revenir
Maroie de Dregnau de Lille

Mout m'a - be - list quant je voi re - ve - nir

Y - ver gre - sill et ge - le - e à - pa - roir

Car en toz tans se doit bien res - jo - ir

Be - le pu - ce - le et jo - li cuer a - voir

Si chan - te - rai d'a - mors por mieuz va - loir

Car mes fins cuers plains d'a - mo - rous de - sir

Ne mi fait pas ma grant joi - e fail - lir.

It pleases me much when I see
Winter's hail return and frost appear,
For in all times, a beautiful maid
Should certainly rejoice and be of light heart.
So I shall sing of love, that I may grow in worth,
For my fine heart full of amorous desire
Does not allow my great joy to fail.

Source: Paris, Bibliothèque nationale, fonds français 844, folio 181

Figure 5
Amours, u trop tart me sui pris
Roïne Blance

Love, with whom too late I am allied,
Has instructed me through its lordship,
Sweet lady of Paradise,
That I should want to sing a song of you:
For the joy which can endure,
One should serve and love you.

Source: Paris, Bibliothèque nationale, fonds français, nouvelles acquisitions 21677

the affirmative, so Dame Margot must defend the negative. The poem has six strophes altogether, three sung by each of the participants.

The subjects of the women's compositions presented here are similar to men's. The poems show a woman who has been rejected by her lover, a woman who is happy in love, a woman who sings in adoration of the Virgin, and two women debating a point of courtly love. All of these themes and forms can be found in the male poetry of the time; the women's poems differ only in their shift of perspective on the subjects. These songs are not "woman's songs" in the literary

Figure 6
Je vous pri dame Maroie
Dame Margot and Dame Maroie

I beg you, lady Maroie, to respond to me.
An elegant lady is well and truly loved,
And she loves also, this you surely know;
But he who loves her is so shy
That he dares not avow his love, and he cannot bring himself
To make himself known. So tell me truly what you think,
Should she declare herself or keep still?

Sources: Arras, Bibliothèque municipale, MS. 657, folio 141v; Rome, Biblioteca
Apostolica Vaticana, Reg. MS. 1490, folio 140r

sense, but "songs by women"; they represent a broad spectrum of courtly love poetry. Just as men could write woman's songs, women could write in the elevated aristocratic style generally associated with men.

Although the references to female musicians in archival records, romances, and pictures are relatively few, it seems possible to conclude cautiously that there were no outstanding prejudices against women performing and composing in medieval France. If the evidence of the romances is to be believed, noblewomen sang and played just as frequently as men did; indeed, proficiency as a musician was a highly desirable quality for a woman, according to educational manuals of the time. Women professional musicians, especially the lower-class jougleresses who traveled in France and elsewhere in Europe, are mentioned with some regularity in romances and archival records. The important statutes of the Parisian guild of minstrels indicate that women were allowed as members and given the same privileges as their male counterparts.

Woman's songs—texts written from a woman's point of view—form an important subgroup of troubadour and trouvère poetry. Songs actually composed by women are few in number, but they cover the whole spectrum of courtly love poetry. The female troubadours whose lives can be documented were generally noblewomen, recipients of troubadour verse as well as authors of it; the class status of the largely undocumented female trouvères is not clear. Although there were few female composers, they apparently had reasonable opportunity to write and circulate secular pieces. Only in the fourteenth century, when secular music became generally polyphonic, did women's opportunity to compose fall far behind men's, because women lacked access to musical training in ecclesiastical schools and universities.

Women's status as musicians in medieval France seems to have paralleled their political status: when Eleanor of Aquitaine ruled southern France, women composed and performed on a relatively equal basis with men; but when Salic law prohibited the passage of the French crown through women, women were no longer able to compete as composers with men. This parallel is probably coincidental, since the advent of secular polyphony can hardly be seen as a conscious attempt to discriminate against women composers. The fourteenth century did see increased specialization and professionalization in music, however, and women were excluded from the new group of professional composers that emerged at this time. During

55

the same period when women's legal freedom and economic power were declining, their musical status was also being limited.

NOTES

1. This is the view of most recent historians. See Kathleen Casey, "The Cheshire Cat: Reconstructing the Experience of Medieval Woman," in *Liberating Women's History*, ed. Berenice A. Carroll (Urbana: University of Illinois Press, 1977), pp. 224–49; Jo Ann McNamara and Suzanne F. Wemple, "Sanctity and Power: The Dual Pursuit of Medieval Women," in *Becoming Visible: Women in European History*, ed. Renate Bridenthal and Claudia Koonz (Boston: Houghton Mifflin, 1977), pp. 90–118.

2. McNamara and Wemple, "Sanctity and Power," p. 103.

3. Gaston Richard, *La Femme dans l'histoire* (Paris: Octave Doin et Fils, 1909), p. 78.

4. See especially Amy Kelly, *Eleanor of Aquitaine and the Four Kings* (Cambridge, Mass.: Harvard University Press, 1950).

5. A short biography of Blanche of Castile is contained in Frances and Joseph Gies, *Women in the Middle Ages* (New York: Thomas Y. Crowell Co., 1978), pp. 97–119.

6. McNamara and Wemple, "Sanctity and Power," pp. 112–13.

7. Casey, "Cheshire Cat," p. 226; Joan Kelly-Gadol, "Did Women Have a Renaissance?" in *Becoming Visible*, ed. Bridenthal and Koonz, pp. 137–64. See also Howard Brown's essay, ch. 4 of this vol., for information about the position of women during the Renaissance.

8. See Eileen Power, "The Position of Women," in *The Legacy of the Middle Ages*, ed. Charles G. Crump and Ernest F. Jacob (Oxford: Oxford University Press, 1926), pp. 401–33; E. William Monter, "The Pedestal and the Stake: Courtly Love and Witchcraft," in *Becoming Visible*, ed. Bridenthal and Koonz, pp. 119–36; Gies, *Women in the Middle Ages*, pp. 37–59.

9. John F. Benton says (in "Clio and Venus: An Historical View of Medieval Love," in *The Meaning of Courtly Love*, ed. Francis X. Newman [Albany: State University of New York Press, 1968], p. 35): "Courtesy was created by men for their own satisfaction, and it emphasized a woman's role as object, sexual or otherwise. Since they did not encourage a genuine respect for women as individuals, the conventions of medieval chivalry, like the conventions of chivalry in the southern United States, did not advance women toward legal or social emancipation. When men ignored chivalry, women were better off."

10. Andreas Capellanus, *The Art of Courtly Love*, trans. John J. Parry (New York: Columbia University Press, 1941). It has also been suggested, as in Joan M. Ferrante and George D. Economou, eds., *In Pursuit of Perfection: Courtly Love in Medieval Literature* (Port Washington, N.Y.: Kennikat Press, 1975), p. 3, that Andreas's book is a satire mocking courtly love rather than a

bible for it. Whether or not such a thing as courtly love even existed is a matter of debate. For an extensive bibliography of the literature on courtly love, see Roger Boase, *The Origin and Meaning of Courtly Love* (Manchester: Manchester University Press, 1977).

11. Eileen Power, *Medieval Women*, ed. M. M. Postan (Cambridge: Cambridge University Press, 1975), is a particularly good source on women's education. See esp. pp. 76–88.

12. A rather extensive study of these treatises may be found in Alice A. Hentsch, *De la littérature didactique du moyen âge s'adressant spéciale-ment aux femmes* (Halle, 1903). Eileen Power has edited and translated one of the most practically oriented of these in *The Goodman of Paris (Le Mé-nagier de Paris): A Treatise on Moral and Domestic Economy by a Citizen of Paris (ca. 1393)* (London: George Routledge & Sons, 1928).

13. Hentsch, *De la littérature didactique du moyen âge*, p. 47.

14. *La Clef d'Amors*, ed. Auguste Doutrepont (1890; reprint, Geneva: Slatkine Reprints, 1975), lines 2589–607. Guiterne and citole are both plucked string instruments; see Laurence Wright, "The Medieval Gittern and Citole: A Case of Mistaken Identity," *Galpin Society Journal* 30 (1977): 8–42; *timbre* most probably means *tambourine*, but it might also mean *bell*.

15. Chrétien de Troyes, *Philomena*, ed. C. de Boer (Paris: P. Geuthner, 1909), lines 196–204. Lire may be a bowed or plucked lyre; gigue is apparently a type of fiddle; rote is a small harp or psaltery; *vielle* is the standard French term for *fiddle*.

16. Jean Renart, *Galeran de Bretagne*, ed. Lucíen Foulet (Paris: Champion, 1925), lines 1167–72. Frêne is just one example of a woman educated in a convent. Convents were an alternative to castles for the education of aristocratic children, both male and female; but there is little direct evidence of their curricula. By the late Middle Ages, education for the nuns themselves was frequently at a rather low level. See Power, *Medieval Women*, pp. 81–82. See also Anne Yardley's essay, ch. 2 above.

17. Hentsch, *De la littérature didactique du moyen âge*, p. 107.

18. Robert de Blois, *Le Chastoiement des dames* (13th cent.), cited ibid., p. 78.

19. One description of a young nobleman's education may be found in Donna R. Barnes, ed., *For Court, Manor, and Church: Education in Medieval Europe* (Minneapolis: Burgess Publishing Co., 1971), p. 29, in an abridged version of an essay by William Stearnes Davis, "Aimery Learns to Become a Knight," from *Life on a Medieval Barony* (New York: Harper & Row, 1923). The account dates from about 1220: "Before he was fifteen, Aimery had thus learned to read and write, to ride and hawk, to play chess, checkers, and backgammon, to thrum a harp and sing with clear voice, to shoot with the arbalist, and to fence with considerable skill."

20. Gerbert de Montreuil, *Le Roman de la Violette ou de Gerart de Nevers*, ed. Douglas L. Buffum (Paris: Société des Anciens Textes Français, 1928), lines 92–151. Yvonne Rokseth, in "Les Femmes musiciennes du XIIe au XIVe siècle," *Romania* 61 (1935): 465–68, gives several other short refer-

ences to women dancing and singing in medieval French romances; as does Helene Jacobius in "Erziehung des Edelfräuleins im alten Frankreich nach Dichtungen des XII. XIII. und XIV. Jahrhunderts," *Zeitschrift für romanische Philologie,* supp. 16 (Halle: Max Niemeyer, 1908), p. 69n.

21. Ernst Rohloff, ed., *Der Musiktraktat des Johannes de Grocheo* (Leipzig: Deutscher Verlag, 1943), p. 51.

22. No complete edition of *Méliacin* exists, although an abridged version has been made: Girard d'Amiens, *Le Roman du cheval de fust; ou, De Méliacin,* ed. Paul Aebischer (Geneva: Droz, 1974). All of the lyric pieces in the text can be found in Edmund Stengel, "Die altfranzösischen Liedercitate aus Gerardin's d'Amiens Conte du cheval de fust," *Zeitschrift für romanische Philologie* 10 (1886): 460–72.

23. Thomas, *The Romance of Horn,* ed. Mildred K. Pope (Oxford: B. Blackwell for the Anglo-Norman Text Society, 1955), lines 2810–14. Jacobius, "Erziehung des Edelfräuleins," pp. 68–69, also cites passages from *Durmart le Gallois* (lines 3225ff.) and *Sone de Nansay* (lines 12569ff.) where women sing lais and accompany themselves on the harp.

24. Jean Maillard, "Coutumes musicales au moyen âge d'après le Tristan en prose," *Cahiers de civilisation mediévale* 2 (1959): 345–47.

25. Tatiana Fotitch and Ruth Steiner, *Les Lais du roman de Tristan en prose* (Munich: Wilhelm Fink, 1974), nos. 2, 4, and 14.

26. Genette Foster, *The Symbolism of Music and Musical Instruments in Thirteenth-Century French Manuscript Illuminations* (Ann Arbor, Mich.: University Microfilms, 1977). The following list from Foster's catalog does not include any angels, sirens, depictions of Musica, animal hybrids, or Old Testament characters; it contains only realistically portrayed women: Paris, Bibliothèque de l'Arsenal 2510, fol. 10, portrait of a woman playing a vielle; Paris, Bibliothèque nationale, fonds français 350, fol. 88v, woman tuning harp with left hand, playing with right; ibid., fol. 345, woman plucking harp with both hands; ibid., fonds français 1463, fol. 91, woman plucking large triangular harp with right hand; ibid., fol. 99, same harpist; ibid., fonds latins 796, fol. 212v, girl with rebec and bow; London, British Museum, Egerton 274, fol. 7v, woman plucking gittern with plectrum; ibid., Stowe 17, fol. 112, woman playing vielle; ibid., fol. 129v, woman playing rebec; Oxford, Bodleian Library, Douce 118, fol. 160v, woman wearing long blue gown and golden crown playing vielle. Numerous other illustrations depict women dancing to the accompaniment of male musicians. A volume of illustrations of medieval women (Sibylle Harksen, *Women in the Middle Ages* [New York: Abner Schram, 1975]) shows in plate 61 a female "flute" player (with an instrument that looks more like a shawm). This crowned figure from a late fourteenth-century English choir stall, if indeed a female, may, however, be intended as an absurdity rather than as a realistic portrayal.

27. Rokseth, "Les Femmes musiciennes," p. 469, cites a passage from Gautier de Coinci, *Les Miracles de Nostre Dame,* in which angels are described as a three-part female choir, the archangels "singing," the maidens

and angels adding the "discant," and the holy virgins and saints adding the "treble." She also cites a passage (p. 478) from the romance *Escoufle* in which a choir of nuns sings motets, conductus, and *farcies.* The Las Huelgas Codex offers concrete evidence of women's involvement in polyphonic singing; see Anne Yardley's essay, ch. 2 above.

28. Guillaume de Machaut, *Le Livre du Voir-Dit,* ed. Paulin Paris (Paris: Société des bibliophiles françois, 1875), pp. 47–49. Sarah Jane Williams, in "The Lady, the Lyrics, and the Letters," *Early Music* 5 (1977): 463–64, makes a case for Péronne's being the poet of many of the lyrics in the *Voir-Dit.*

29. For a discussion of musical training at these schools, see Nan Cooke Carpenter, *Music in the Medieval and Renaissance Universities* (Norman: University of Oklahoma Press, 1958).

30. Henry George Farmer, *A History of Arabian Music* (London: Luzac & Co., 1929), contains brief biographies of several women singers and instrumentalists of the Abbasids (eighth and ninth centuries) in Arabia (pp. 132–36, 162–63). A. R. Nykl, *Hispano-Arabic Poetry and its Relations with the Old Provençal Troubadours* (Baltimore: J. H. Furst Co., 1946), offers poems by several Arabic women in Spain.

31. Nadia Abbott, "Women and the State in Early Islam," *Journal of Near Eastern Studies* 1 (1942): 351.

32. Julian Ribera, *Music in Ancient Arabia and Spain,* trans. and abr. Eleanor Hague and Marion Leffingwell (Stanford: Stanford University Press, 1929), pp. 115–16.

33. Ibid., pp. 113–14.

34. Juan Ruiz, *Libro de Buen Amor,* ed. and trans. Raymond S. Willis (Princeton: Princeton University Press, 1972), pars. 470, 1513.

35. *La Música de las Cantigas de Santa María del Rey Alfonso el Sabio,* 3 vols., ed. Higinio Anglès (Barcelona: Disputación Provincial, Biblioteca Central, 1943–64). Volume 1 is a facsimile (reprint, 1964); volumes 2 (1943) and 3 (1958) contain commentary and transcriptions.

36. See also *Libro de Ajedrez: Das Spanisch Schachzelbuch des Königs Alfons des Weisen von Jahr 1283,* facsimile, prologue by John G. White (Leipzig: Karl W. Hiersemann, 1913).

37. The possibility exists that Nicolette was disguising herself as a male jongleur, but probably her singing would have given her away as a female. I think *jogleor* in this passage is being used in its generic sense and could mean a female as easily as a male. In *Bueve de Hantone* (see n. 39 below), the female form, *jougleresse,* is specifically used.

38. *Aucassin et Nicolette,* ed. Jean Dufournet (Paris: Garnier-Flammarion, 1973), sec. 38.

39. *Der festlandische Bueve de Hantone,* Fassung III, ed. Albert Stimming (Dresden: M. Niemeyer, 1914), lines 11945–2185. The lines describing Josiane and Soybaus playing together are as follows: "Lors commencha Josienne a chanter, / Notes et lais bien a vieler, / Li vius Soybaus commencha a harper, / Bien se commenchent lor son a acorder" (lines 12087–90).

40. See n. 16 above.

41. Jean Renart, *Le Roman de la Rose ou de Guillaume de Dole*, ed. G. Servois (Paris: Société des Anciens Textes Français, 1893), lines 4553–58.

42. Etienne Boileau's *Livre des métiers* of 1270 lists 5 out of 110 guilds that were female monopolies and only a few guilds (including those of scholars, lawyers, notaries, goldsmiths, and portrait painters) that prohibited women. Boileau's list and the Parisian tax rolls of 1292 and 1300 show that 108 out of 321 occupations were open to women, including surgery, butchering, glass-blowing, bit- and bridle-making, and chain-mail forging. See Casey, "The Cheshire Cat," p. 247n.

43. The statutes are presented, along with other documents, in Bernard Bernhard, "Recherches sur l'histoire de la corporation des Ménétriers ou Joueurs d'instruments de la ville de Paris," *Bibliothèque de l'Ecole des Chartes* 3 (1841–42): 377–404; 4 (1842): 525–48; and 5 (1843): 254–84, 339–72.

44. These references were pointed out to me by Lawrence Gushee. The tax records in question have been published by Karl Michaëlsson in *Le Livre de la Taille de Paris (1313)* and *Le Livre de la Taille de Paris (1297)* (Göteborg: Wettergren & Kerber, 1951, 1962).

45. Rokseth, "Les Femmes musiciennes," p. 474.

46. Craig Wright, *Music at the Court of Burgundy, 1364–1419: A Documentary History* (New York: Institute of Medieval Music, 1979), pp. 28–29.

47. André Pirro, *Histoire de la musique de la fin du XIVe à la fin du XVIe* (Paris: Renouard, 1940), p. 25.

48. For more information about kharjas, see Peter Dronke, *The Medieval Lyric* (New York: Harper & Row, 1968), pp. 86–108.

49. See John F. Plummer, ed., *Vox Feminae: Studies in Medieval Woman's Songs*, Studies in Medieval Culture, 15 (Kalamazoo, Mich.: Medieval Institute Publications, 1981).

50. This is the terminology of Pierre Bec in *La Lyrique française au moyen âge (XIIe–XIIIe siècles): Etudes* (Paris: A. & J. Picard, 1977).

51. These thematic types survived into the Renaissance; see Howard Brown's essay, ch. 4 below.

52. The surviving chanson de toile texts have been edited by Michel Zink, *Les Chansons de toile* (Paris: Champion, 1977).

53. *Guillaume de Dole*, lines 1147ff.; *Roman de la Violette*, lines 2299ff.

54. The distinction between *troubadour* and *trouvère* is a linguistic one: troubadours wrote in the langue d'oc or Provençal, trouvères in the langue d'oïl or Old French. Twenty-three surviving poems by the *trobairitz* (female troubadours), including four anonymous poems, have been edited and translated by Meg Bogin in *The Women Troubadours* (New York: Paddington Press, 1976).

55. Two recent articles have brought this out: Marianne Shapiro, "The Provençal Trobairitz and the Limits of Courtly Love," *Signs* 3 (1978): 560–71; Pierre Bec, "'Trobairitz' et chansons de femme: Contribution à la con-

naissance du lyrisme feminin au moyen âge," *Cahiers de civilisation medié-vale* 22 (1979): 235–62.

56. Bogin, *Women Troubadours*, pp. 81, 162–79.

57. To put the number of surviving women's melodies in perspective, about 2,600 poems by more than 450 troubadours have been preserved in anthology manuscripts of the thirteenth and fourteenth centuries, but fewer than 300 melodies by about 40 troubadours have survived. See Richard Hoppin, *Medieval Music* (New York: W. W. Norton, 1978), pp. 270–71, for further discussion.

58. See Bogin, *Women Troubadours*, pp. 163–64.

59. "Le Manuscript du roi," Paris, Bibliothèque nationale, fonds français 844; *Le Manuscript du roi*, ed. Jean and Louise Beck, facsimile (Philadelphia: University of Pennsylvania Press, 1938).

60. A record of songs by women troubadours has been issued by Hesperion XX (an early music ensemble): *Cansos de Trobairitz*, Odeon/Reflexe 1C 065-30941Q. Most of the pieces on the record have texts (or parts of texts) by women, but the texts are set as contrafacta to preexistent melodies composed by men.

61. To my knowledge, the edition of the melody here is the first published modern transcription of the piece.

62. Paris, Bibliothèque nationale, nouvelles acquisitions français 21677.

63. Friedrich Gennrich, *Rondeaux, Virelais und Balladen*, 3 vols. (Dresden and Göttingen: Max Niemeyer, 1921–63), 2 (1927): 125–26. Jean Maillard has also edited the piece, in his *Anthologie de chants de trouvères* (Paris: A. Zurfluh, 1967), pp. 63–64. There is some doubt as to the queen's authorship of this song. It may possibly be by her admirer, Thibaut de Champagne, *le roi de Navarre*. According to Maillard, however, "une certaine faiblesse de style permet de douter d'une telle attribution [to Thibaut]. De toute manière, s'il s'agit d'une galanterie du Roi de Navarre d'avoir abandonné la paternité de cette oeuvre au profit de celle qu'il a pu aimer, nous aurions manqué de courtoisie en annulant de notre propre chef cette rubrique" (p. 10). Maillard's subjective judgment of the piece and patronizing attitude aside, the manuscript attribution to the queen stands.

64. Bern, Stadtsbibliothek, MS. 389.

65. Arthur Långfors, *Recueil général des jeux-partis français* (Paris: Champion, 1926). The pieces with women participants are Långfors 139, 143, 144, 145, 153, 156, 165, 167, 169, and 179.

66. *Je vous pri Dame Maroie*, Långfors 144, Raynaud 1744, is found in Arras, Bibliothèque municipale 657, fol. 141v, and Rome, Biblioteca Apostolica Vaticana, Reg. 1490, fol. 140r; *Douce dame ce soit*, Långfors 145, Raynaud 876, is found in the "Chansonnier de Noailles," Paris, Bibliothèque nationale, fonds français 12615, fol. 511; *Amis, quelx est li mieulz vaillanz*, Långfors 153, Raynaud 365, is found in the "Chansonnier Cangé," ibid., fonds français 845, fol. 13v.

67. In the trouvère repertory as a whole, it is not at all unusual to find two unrelated melodies for a single text.

4

Women Singers and Women's Songs in Fifteenth-Century Italy

HOWARD MAYER BROWN

In opposition to Jacob Burckhardt, who claimed that during the Italian Renaissance upper-class women "stood on a footing of perfect equality with men" at least with respect to social intercourse,[1] recent scholars—notably Joan Kelly-Gadol and Margaret Leah King—have emphasized the inequalities between men and women and the difficulties women encountered in pursuing careers.[2] King has pointed out that women could not easily continue their humanistic studies after girlhood. And Kelly-Gadol has argued persuasively that in the fifteenth and sixteenth centuries Italian noblewomen

were increasingly removed from public concerns—economic, political and cultural—and although they did not disappear into a private realm of family and domestic concerns as fully as their sisters in the patrician bourgeoisie, their loss of public power made itself felt in new constraints placed upon their personal as well as their social lives. . . . All the advances of Renaissance Italy, its protocapitalist economy, its states, and its humanistic culture, worked to mold the noblewoman into an aesthetic object: decorous, chaste, and doubly dependent—on her husband as well as the prince.[3]

She cites Caterina Sforza as an exception, since Caterina derived her political power in ruling Forlì and Imola solely from her own skill and from superior force—from *fortuna* and *virtù*, as it were. Isabella d'Este, on the other hand, for all her great ability as a diplomat, enjoyed what political influence she had only indirectly and provisionally through her husband and his family. But she, too, was exceptional in directing so much of her immense energy and talent into commissioning, encouraging, and influencing composers, artists, and men of letters.[4] It is a commonplace of music history to assert that her patronage of Tromboncino, Cara, and other Italian composers was one of the decisive factors that led to the eventual shift in taste away from the French chanson and toward native Italian forms and styles.

The older view that women were regarded as equal with men in the Renaissance derives from the fact that some humanists had decided a classical education was as important for a girl as for a boy. But one should neither exaggerate the size of this circle of learned women, nor misconstrue the nature of the educational policy of the humanists.[5] It is true that some noblewomen, like Cecilia Gonzaga, were gifted students of the classics—Cecilia had been educated like her brothers by Vittorino da Feltre—and that others, such as Isotta Nogarola, Costanza Varano, and Cassandra Fedele, were themselves humanists whose literary achievements have won for them a small if secure place in the history of Italian letters.[6] Most of these learned women, however, seem to have given up their humanistic studies early in their lives to marry, or else they retired from an active life.

A humanist education would have been available only to a limited number of the leading families in Italy, most of them noble or from the class of rich merchants and bankers, and not all of those would have wished to take advantage of the new educational opportunities for their daughters. Moreover, the humanists were doubtless more concerned to provide intellectually equal companions for their male students than to create a new class of liberated women. Alberti and others make clear that the first duties of most Italian women in the fifteenth century were to maintain the home, regulate the social life of the family, care for and educate the children, do good works, and supervise the religious education of those around them.[7] Vespasiano da Bisticci, the crusty old Florentine bookseller who had amassed the great libraries of many of the famous men whose lives he described, may well have expressed the prejudices of many members of his class when he wrote—in answer to charges of antifeminism—that virtuous women pleased him, so long as they followed St. Paul's two injunctions: "to bring up their children in the fear of God, and . . . [to] keep quiet in church."[8] Similarly, the battle between Clarice Orsini, wife of Lorenzo de' Medici, called the Magnificent, and Angelo Poliziano, tutor to her children, is symptomatic of the tension in fifteenth-century society between traditional values of Christian piety and the new ideals of humanism.[9] Put simply, Poliziano wanted the Medici children to be studying Greek and Latin, when Clarice wished them to be reading Scripture and perhaps singing sacred songs. But although Poliziano lost on that occasion, the cause of classical education—for men and women alike—continued to gain ground during the Renaissance and beyond.

63

The new educational policies of the humanists may have led eventually to a greater acceptance of women who wrote learned works of classical erudition or poetry or both. That, at least, is the conclusion I draw from comparing Poliziano's rather patronizing amazement at the accomplishments of Cassandra Fedele, in a letter to Lorenzo de' Medici, with the generally positive critical response to such important sixteenth-century poets as Veronica Gambara and Vittoria Colonna. There were a number of distinguished women poets in the sixteenth century besides Gambara and Colonna—including Isabella di Morra, Gaspara Stampa, and the courtesans Veronica Franco and Tullia d'Aragona—and the participation of women in composing and performing music increased greatly after mid-century.[10] But no circle of women composers grew up in the fifteenth or early sixteenth centuries, so far as we know. The reasons why are not difficult to understand.

In the first place, if some noble Italian women of the late fifteenth century did write music, modesty and a sense of decorum would most likely have prevented them from admitting it. While the ideal courtier was encouraged to become a skillful singer and performer on several instruments—and apparently was even expected to improvise his part on occasion—he should not seem to take an overweening pride in his accomplishments, lest someone suppose music his principal profession.[11] It is true, of course, that some members of the nobility are identified in musical manuscripts of the time as composers of secular music. I think immediately of Charles the Bold, Henry VIII, and Leo X.[12] Perhaps, though, their names were attached to the music they wrote simply because they were political figures of the highest rank, whereas lesser nobility would have disseminated anonymously whatever works they exceptionally wrote. If that were the case, then a few anonymous compositions might have been composed by noble women as well as by noble men, although in all likelihood we shall never be able to identify them.

The most important reason why women were not likely to compose music in the late fifteenth century stems from their exclusion from participation in church services.[13] Most composers during the period began their musical education as choirboys studying at cathedral schools. After their voices changed, they went on for further study—some to universities—and then they traditionally made their careers as singers, choirmasters, or organists in a church or at court. To be sure, there were a few exceptions to that general practice, even in the fifteenth century. Bartolomeo Tromboncino, for example, seems to have begun his service at the court of Mantua as an instrumentalist.[14] Since Tromboncino was also the son of an instrumentalist, he probably received his education through the alternative system of apprenticeship to a master player. Tomasso Damiano, who is represented in the Montecassino manuscript by two compositions, was a recorder player at the Neapolitan court in 1456.[15] But these two men—and there were others like them—broke with the prevailing conventions. Most of the Franco-Flemish "stars" who dominated Italian choirs in the late fifteenth century, and probably most of the native Italian musicians as well, were educated at cathedral schools and, perhaps, at universities, educational institutions presumably closed to women.[16]

On the other hand, humanists and more traditional commentators alike agreed that ladies and gentlemen could perform music for pleasure, as a social grace. Indeed, skill in singing or playing an instrument was one of the chief attributes in making a lady of the Renaissance "decorous." In a sense, music-making in a courtly context can be considered a woman's activity, or at least something done for women. As Castiglione wrote,

> Do you not see that the cause of all gracious exercises that give us pleasure is to be assigned to women alone? Who learns to dance gracefully for any reason except to please women? Who devotes himself to the sweetness of music for any other reason? Who attempts to compose verses, at least in the vernacular, unless to express sentiments inspired by women?[17]

Certainly music-making was thought to be an appropriate activity for upper-class girls and young women as early as the fourteenth century. Francesco da Barberino's handbook for the conduct of various classes of women included singing, playing appropriate instruments, and dancing among the accomplishments suitable for a well-born girl. Boccaccio, in the *Decameron*, had his women tell stories and take part in entertaining each other equally with men;[18] some of the women even sang songs they themselves had written, although whether they had composed the music as well as the poetry Boccaccio does not make clear.

That music was a desirable field of study for patricians in the fifteenth century as well is evident, for example, from the importance Isabella d'Este attached to her Flemish music master, the composer Johannes Martini, when she moved from Ferrara to Mantua as a young bride.[19] It is evident, also, from the obvious respect and affection Johannes Tinctoris, the Flemish theorist and composer employed as chapelmaster at the court in Naples, showed in dedicating three of his treatises to his erstwhile student, Beatrice of Aragon, the daughter of the Neapolitan king, who eventually became the wife of King Matthias Corvin and reigned in Budapest as queen of Hungary.[20] Parisina, marchesa of Ferrara, Valentina Visconti, wife of Louis duc d'Orléans, and Isabella of Bavaria, wife of Charles VI, all played the harp, and Beatrice di Tenda and Ippolita Sforza the lute.[21] Similar examples of noble Italian women educated in music, many of them by the *oltremontani* who flocked south in the fifteenth century, could be multiplied many times over. And the value of a musical education to members of the patrician bourgeoisie in the fifteenth century is demonstrated by one of the letters the Florentine widow Alessandra Macinghi negli Strozzi wrote to her son in Naples assessing possible candidates for marriage. She asked whether one of these girls, Gostanza di Pandolfo, was uncultivated (*zotico*) and was told that the girl knew how to read fairly well, was agile, and knew how to dance as well as sing.[22]

Not everyone, of course, would have agreed that these were desirable accomplishments. Vespasiano da Bisticci complained about the girls of his old age who had an unseemly regard for weddings, balls, and "other vanities." They "take infinite pains over the choice of their dancing masters," he wrote, "and think more of letting their feet move exactly in time with the music than of aught else."[23] And Pietro Bembo, who may have been an exceptionally stern parent, in 1541 forbade his daughter to learn to play a musical instrument because, as he put it, "il sonare è cosa da donna vana e leggera," and he wished her to be serious and chaste, conditions apparently assured her if she continued her study of sewing and letters—the educational program approved by her father.[24]

Women regularly took part in entertainments at Italian courts in the fifteenth century or at least figured prominently among the allegorical, mythological, and historical characters who appeared in the *tableaux vivants* and other semistaged spectacles that were a standard feature of banquets celebrating special events and *intermedii* between acts of spoken drama.[25] We can seldom be certain whether the women who sang at such festive occasions were court ladies displaying their talents, particularly gifted townspeople called in to help celebrate a notable event, the wives and daughters of the regularly employed chapel and chamber musicians, or, just possibly, women hired by the court for the express purpose of singing secular music. In a few cases, women's roles might even have been taken by men or boys in transvestite disguise.[26] Although most of the notices are worded in a way that suggests women actually sang, normal practice at the court of Ferrara in the late fifteenth century seems to have been to exclude women from spoken drama,[27] even though they took a prominent part in the *intermedii* between acts. There were no professional actors at the Ferrarese court. The duke recruited courtiers, gentlemen, university students, and whoever else could be persuaded to help act in the plays he requested; but all the women's roles were taken by men.

Certainly courtiers, leading citizens, and other well-born dilettantes, women and men alike, performed secular music regularly at court—a point persuasively demonstrated by Heinrich Besseler as a common practice throughout western Europe in the fifteenth century.[28] But it seems likely that courtiers seldom if ever joined professional musicians to sing in costume as mythological, allegorical, or historical characters in an *intermedio*. Such impersonations might have suggested that the performer took too professional an interest in the art of music. On very special occasions, a great lady might deign to entertain the guests without compromising herself. Thus Isabella d'Este sang to the lute after one of the festive meals organized to celebrate the wedding of her brother Alfonso to Lucrezia Borgia in 1502.[29] But she sang in her own persona and not in the guise of a goddess, queen, or personified attribute. She also danced a hat dance (*ballo del cappello*) on that occasion, displaying her choreographic ability in a way apparently acceptable to fifteenth-century sensibilities, for there are numerous records of well-born ladies dancing for the entertainment of spectators. For example, Isabelle of Aragon led the performance in her honor in 1490 by dancing before the assembled guests.[30] Vespasiano da Bisticci described the entertainments given in the Piazza della Signoria in Florence in 1432, when the most beautiful young ladies of the city danced for the ambassadors of the Emperor Sigismund.[31] And a similar citizens' ballet took place in Florence in 1459 for the visit of Pope Pius II and Galeazzo Maria Sforza.[32]

In the late fifteenth century some Italian women seem to have performed secular music as their principal activity. I hesitate to state flatly that a class of professional women musicians existed then, because of the difficulties of defining precisely the term *professional musician* and because there seem to have been not one but several classes of women who were paid for their musical ability. The fugitive character of the careers of lowly traveling minstrels prevents us from ever knowing very much about this class of musician/entertainer. At the other extreme, it is seldom possible to differentiate between women from quite modest families who were hired by courts specifically for their musical talent and women of the lesser nobility who were tolerated at great courts because they sang well.[33]

Certainly women, as well as men, wandered through the land earning what living they could from giving plays, performing music, and entertaining the populace. Occasionally they entertained the nobility as well, so court records note gifts to traveling companies, such as a payment to two *"batteleurs et leurs femmes"* who played farces before the duchess of Savoy in 1474.[34] Among Edmund Bowles's anthology of pictures illustrating the musical life of the fifteenth century—the most extensive such collection published to date—there are a few works of art that show women playing or singing in a context which suggests they were well-born dilettantes, and one that shows a "professional" female instrumentalist, who is an itinerant entertainer, hitting a tambourine while her female companion does acrobatic tricks and her male companion plays pipe and tabor.[35]

A few letters and archival notices suggest that the professional woman singer was also not unknown at Italian courts, although some of these may have been gifted gentlewomen, servants hired for their musical ability, or simply wives of chapel or chamber musicians. Thus, two secular singers, *"menestriers de bouche,"* Paris and his wife Parise, came to Savoy in 1396 to devote themselves to the service of the court.[36] In 1455, when the ten-year-old Galeazzo Maria Sforza visited Venice, the seven Milanese gentlemen accompanying him described, in a letter home, a solemn banquet, following a hunt, at which music was provided by *"alcuni notabilissimi cantatori,"* presumably professionals. Among them was an English lady who sang so sweetly that she seemed to have a divine, not a human, voice.[37] In 1468, the marquis Guglielmo di Monferrato wrote a letter recommending a certain "Anna cantatrice" to the court of Milan.[38] Since she came to offer "belli giochi et solatii" to Galeazzo Maria Sforza on the occasion of his marriage to Bona di Savoia, it may be that she, like so many other minstrels who congregated whenever some festal occasion made it likely that their services would be in demand, should be counted among the peripatetic free-lance minstrels rather than the chamber virtuosos.

But presumably the pregnant hunchback—if that is in fact what "una dona goba denante et de dreto" means—who sang "optimo soprano" during the banquet given in Innsbruck in 1493 by the duke and duchess of Austria in honor of the wedding of Bianca Maria Sforza and the emperor Maximilian I, must certainly have been a commoner and thus probably a professional, for a noble woman

68

would surely not have been described in that way.[39] And there can be little doubt that Giovanna Moreschi, the wife of Marchetto Cara, was a professional singer at the Mantuan court.[40] The Gonzagas employed another woman singer as well during the early sixteenth century: Paula Poccino, who is mentioned by Isabella d'Este, for example, as having brought honor to Mantua by singing with Bartolomeo Tromboncino and several of their Mantuan companions during a performance of Plautus's comedy *Asinaria*, which was given as a part of the festivities celebrating the marriage of Alfonso d'Este and Lucrezia Borgia in Ferrara in 1502.[41] A manuscript anthology of frottola texts now in the Biblioteca Nazionale Centrale in Florence reveals the names of three Florentine women who, if they were not professional musicians, sang well enough to have been associated with a group of pieces: Maria, the wife of Bianchino da Pisa; Masina, who is otherwise unknown; and Lionarda Arrighi, wife of the composer Baccino degli Organi.[42]

There may even have been professional women instrumentalists in the fifteenth century. Women playing harp, tambourine, and possibly other instruments can be seen performing in a gallery overlooking a wedding ceremony in a fresco by Domenico di Bartolo (c. 1400–1477) painted in the reception room of the Spedale della Scala in Siena, a foundling hospital committed to encouraging their girl foundlings to marry when they came of age.[43] The instrumentalists, then, must be professional musicians hired for the occasion, members of the staff, or foundlings themselves.

Other fifteenth-century Italian works of art confirm the active participation of women in the performance of secular music in a courtly context. In almost every case, though, so far as one can tell, they show well-born amateurs rather than professionals singing and playing instruments. In the charming pen drawing depicting Tristan and Lancelot playing chess at the house of the Lady of the Lake (plate 6), for example, the elaborate coiffure and elegant dress identify the lady harpist as a member of the court rather than as a servant.[44] The lady holding a lute who looks down at the viewer from the ceiling of the Sala del Tesoro in the Palazzo di Ludovico il Moro in Ferrara (plate 7) certainly belonged to the upper classes.[45] And, while the picture of Fiammetta playing the fiddle and Pamphilo the lute (plate 8) merely illustrates literally the text of Boccaccio's *Decameron* in a Venetian edition of 1492, it at least demonstrates that the image of well-born youths making music together was still acceptable to late fifteenth-century readers.[46]

Other pictures better known to modern viewers make the same

Plate 6
Scene from the romance "Lancelot," c. 1446

Source: Florence, Biblioteca nazionale centrale,
Pal. Cod. 556, folio 105
Photograph by G. B. Pineider, Florence

point. Francesco Cossa's delightful frescoes in the Palazzo Schifanoia in Ferrara, which elaborate the attributes of each month of the year, include for the month of April crowds of young courtiers surrounding a car on which Venus rides. Some of the courtiers, women and men alike, hold instruments: lutes, recorders, and a rebec.[47] And the "concert" by Ercole de' Roberti or, more likely, Lorenzo Costa, in which a gentleman accompanies a lady and a second gentleman on the lute, must also illustrate a common occurrence of daily life, in which courtiers (or, in this case, possibly professional musicians) of both sexes took equal part in the performance of secular music.[48]

Costa, in fact, allows us to be quite certain about the participants in one session of secular music-making he painted—a group portrait of the children of Giovanni Bentivoglio II of Bologna—since he labels each person (plate 9). In so doing, he explicitly confirms Besseler's hypothesis that amateurs and professionals were apt to perform together, though the active participation of the women is ambiguous, to say the least, since they alone have their mouths closed and seem to be looking on rather than singing. Four of Giovanni's

Plate 7
Benvenuto Tisi, called Garofalo or Ercole Grandi, Women with lute and
viol, fresco detail

Source: Ferrara, Palazzo di Ludovico il Moro, Sala del Tesoro
Photograph courtesy of Musei civici d'arte antica, Comune di Ferrara

Plate 8
Illustration from Giovanni Boccaccio, *Decamerone* (Venice, 1492)

Photograph courtesy of Pierpont Morgan Library, New York

Plate 9
Lorenzo Costa, Concert with the children of Giovanni
Bentivoglio II of Bologna

Source: Lugano, Thyssen-Bornemisza Collection
Photograph courtesy of Thyssen-Bornemisza Collection

73

children—Signora Bianca Rangona, Monsignore [Antongaleazzo] Bentivoglio, Hermes, and Alessandro—are joined around a sheet of music by two professional singers, a priest, "Pistano" (presumably a courtier), Costa himself, and a court lady, Signora Caterina Manfredi, who may have been related to the rulers of Faenza at the time.[49]

What sorts of music did Italian women perform in the fifteenth century? The repertory of lower-class urban dwellers, itinerant professionals, workers, and the like can at best only be partially recovered through indirect evidence, if at all; it is a topic that requires a separate study. The surviving manuscripts of polyphonic secular music presumably enlighten us chiefly about the activities of the upper classes: the nobility, the patrician bourgeoisie, and those members of the middle classes who were better educated than most. To judge from extant fifteenth-century sources, many compositions they knew and enjoyed were originally conceived as settings of French lyric poetry, especially rondeaux and *bergerettes* dealing with romantic love. The overwhelming majority of compositions in Italian fifteenth-century anthologies were supplied with French texts—usually garbled by Italian scribes—or, more commonly, with only the incipits of the French poems to which the chansons were originally intended to be sung. The early sixteenth-century collections, however, are divided between those with a preponderance of French chansons and those that contain a substantial number of songs with Italian texts as well.[50] Upper-class Italians in the fifteenth century doubtless cultivated foreign music for the same reasons they read French romances and imported Flemish pictures and Franco-Flemish artists and musicians.[51] Courtly love songs and stories of heroic knights and their gallant deeds opened up to them an elegant bygone world of high idealism and romantic adventure. Singing chansons and reading about Charlemagne's court, the knights of the Round Table, and famous lovers of past times demonstrated the sophistication of their taste and enhanced their social prestige.

Since French culture played so important a role in the Italian musical life of the fifteenth century, it is helpful to look briefly at the role of women in French literary circles, from which Italian women and men drew so much of their musical repertory. Women are, of course, the principal subject matter of most of the French lyric poems set to music. In fact, a sizable group of poems in the literary and musical anthologies of the time were either written by women or express a woman's point of view. They, too, had their say in establishing the conventions of love and manners in the fifteenth century. One collection of French lyric poems compiled after 1453 quite exceptionally provides the names of almost all the poets represented in it.[52] Most are members of the nobility or court officials; four are women.

Evidently, fashionable ladies could admit to writing poetry, if not music. Kathleen Chesney cites three long sequences of *rondeaux des femmes* in manuscripts of the late fifteenth and early sixteenth centuries.[53] One of the principal collections of lyric poetry printed at the beginning of the sixteenth century, *Le Jardin de Plaisance et fleur de rhétorique*, describes its anthology of rondeaux and ballades as poems written partly by lovers in praise or dispraise of ladies and partly by ladies answering their lovers.[54] A second early sixteenth-century anthology of poetry, *La Chasse et le départ d'amours*, introduces the longest of its several collections of rondeaux and ballades with the fiction that the Perfect Lover ("*L'amant parfaict*"), having been separated from his lady, must needs write poetry to her, to which she replies.[55] The lover's 101 rondeaux and 7 ballades are followed by the lady's 28 rondeaux and a third section in which a poem by one is answered by a "*responce*" from the other. As with so many poetic anthologies of the fifteenth and sixteenth centuries, it is not always possible to tell which of these poems were intended—or, indeed, are appropriate—for music. In any case, some of the lady's rondeaux in *La Chasse et le départ d'amours* were, in fact, set to music by Franco-Flemish composers.[56]

Similar songs expressing a woman's point of view appear as well in the Italian *chansonniers*. Their character and content may be judged by studying more closely those in a typical, if unusually copious, Florentine source of the time, Florence 229.[57] Complete or partial texts can be recovered for about half of the 268 compositions in the manuscript, and most of those are in French. Taking into account pieces with textual incipits only, and those without any textual identification that seem to be rondeau settings because of their phrase structure, there may be as many as 200 compositions in Florence 229 originally conceived with French texts. Of these only a dozen unquestionably express a woman's point of view (see table 2), either because the sense or the syntax makes clear the gender of the speaker or because the poem appears among those said to be written by women in *La Chasse et le départ d'amours*. A few others are ambiguous in their references to gender.

Most of the rondeaux and bergerettes in Florence 229, like those in the French literary anthologies and in other Italian musical manuscripts, deal with romantic love in a courtly context. Save for a few that use legal or alchemical imagery, a few that adopt a more playful

Table 2
Songs with a Woman's Point of View

Number	Title	Composer
4	*Mon pere m'a doné mari*	Heinrich Isaac
29	*Je suis venue vers mon amy*	[Hayne van Ghizeghem or Antoine Busnois]
52	*Ung plus que tous est en mon souvenir*	[Antoine Busnois]
60	*Seule à par moy en chambre bien parée*	Antoine Busnois
64	*C'est mal serché vostre avantage*	Alexander Agricola
66	*Sy j'ayme mon amy (= In mijnen sin)*	Alexander Agricola
85	*La rouset*	Anonymous
86	*Mauldicte soit envie*	[Alexander Agricola]
88	*Ung plus que tous c'est mon confort*	Anonymous
125	*Ha qu'il m'ennuye*	[Alexander Agricola or Jean Fresneau]
129	*Je ne me puis vivre à mon ayse*	Heinrich Isaac
202	*Mes que se fut secretement*	[Loyset Compère or Pietrequin]

SOURCE: Florence, Biblioteca nazionale centrale, MS Banco rari 229. The numbers are those given to the songs in the modern edition. For complete bibliographical information and a transcription into modern notation for each of these songs, see Howard Mayer Brown, *A Florentine Chansonnier from the Time of Lorenzo the Magnificent* (Chicago: University of Chicago Press, 1983).

or more personal tone, and those written in a "popular" mode, the poems are peopled with allegorical personifications—of Hope, Danger, Love, Harm, and Fortune—familiar from the *Roman de la Rose* and the literature it spawned. The poet does not single out for praise those qualities unique to his own lady. Instead he praises her in general terms: she is beautiful, knowledgeable, loyal, or has a good reputation. In short, she is full of virtues, but they are mostly unspecified. Many of the poems could be addressed to any lady of the fifteenth century. It is not a repertory filled with passionate and individual expressions of personal love. In many poems the poet laments the coldness and indifference of his *belle dame sans merci*, and occasionally the poet rebukes his lady in sharper terms. She is devious or deceitful, or she distributes her favors to anyone who asks for them. In some poems the course of true love is stayed by the falsely jealous and the flatterers.

In short, these chansons reflect the long outworn conventions of courtly love.[58] The lover's only goal must be to serve his lady. Love must be kept secret from the world. The enemies of love are enumerated in earlier medieval terms. The only ingredient from the older tradition missing from these archaizing poems is the vision of the ennobling possibility of love. Apparently love had its own rewards in the fifteenth century—presumably physical love and to a lesser degree personal fame—for no others are cited by the poets. At best they can have meant to establish ideal behavior for amorous courtiers and their ladies, but more probably the poems reflect a facet of the play element in a culture that still organized tournaments and jousts to celebrate weddings and provided personified allegorical traits and characters from mythological or ancient times or from exotic lands to entertain guests at banquets. The distance between the grandiose sentiments of courtly service to a lady and social reality can perhaps best be judged by contrasting the high-flown rhetoric of French chansons with the down-to-earth evaluations Alessandra Macinghi negli Strozzi gave of her son's prospective brides.[59]

The songs in Florence 229 expressing a woman's point of view are a microcosm of the anthology as a whole and reflect the fact that women themselves—if they wrote these songs—seem, by and large, to have supported the status quo in the late fifteenth century. Of the dozen songs in Florence 229, four are written in the popular mode, two of them *chansons de mal mariée* expressing the laments of a young girl married to an old man, the third a May song (a narrative that survives only incompletely), and the fourth a curse on envy and jealousy. Seven of the eight courtly poems in the collection offer the same view of romantic love we saw in the men's songs but from the woman's point of view. *Je suis venue vers mon amy* (29) seems to be a simple quatrain expressing the poetess's love, although the text is so corrupt that the precise meaning can no longer be determined. The single bergerette (125) expresses regret that the lover is absent. Two of the five rondeaux, *Ung plus que tous est en mon souvenir* (52) and *Ung plus que tous c'est mon confort* (88), are declarations of love similar to those written by men. In the former, the poetess writes that she will be loyal and grant her friend even more than is due a lady's servant; if he returns her love, he will achieve great fame. The latter, *Ung plus que tous c'est mon confort*, while offering strong assurances of the poetess's affections, expresses the secret nature of true love, a theme commonly found in romantic poetry of the late Middle Ages. "Whatever appearance I may put on," writes the poetess, "I have saved the top place in my heart for him. Even if I give my support to someone else, he is the one, more than all others, who is my true comfort." The death of the poetess's lover in *Seulle à part moy en chambre bien parée* (60) inspires her to thoughts of suicide in one of the most moving poems in the collection; and the poetess of *Je ne me puis vivre à mon ayse* (129) is unhappily involved with the wrong man, since she hates the one she should kiss and loves the one she should displease. In *C'est mal serché vostre avantage* (64), the poetess rejects the advances of a man too old for such nonsense—a reaction somewhat sharp and coarse for so refined a repertory.[60]

Only one of the rondeaux, *Mais que se fut secretement* (202), seems to introduce a wholly new tone into the collection. It reveals an independence and a playfulness on the part of women that may signal the beginning of more nearly equal social relationships, but it probably merely proves the extent to which these poems were divorced from social reality. The poetess's rather coy admission that she would not refuse a man one or two attempts on her virtue, although she would not tolerate more, not only implies an acceptance of sexual license on the part of women quite at odds with the prevailing double standard, but also reflects a light-hearted attitude toward love that is inimical to the serious, constrained, and formal tone of most of the courtly poetry of the period.

Songs written from a woman's point of view are not distinguished from those for men either by range or by musical style. That is, most of the musical settings are for three voices, the *superius* notated in soprano, mezzo-soprano, or occasionally treble clef; the *tenor* in tenor or alto clef; and the *contratenor* in tenor or bass clef. When Italian scribes added complete French poems or, more often, the refrains of rondeaux in garbled form to the manuscripts they copied, they were apt to place the text beneath the superius only, although it is by no means certain whether the composer intended only a single line, two lines, or even three lines to be sung, or whether, indeed, he had a single fixed intention for each composition. In any case, as many chansons written from a man's point of view as from a woman's have top lines that go to the highest *e* of the gamut (a tenth above middle *c*) or even one or two notes higher. If men sang such lines, they would doubtless have needed to sing in falsetto, as we know they did in the fifteenth century.[61] And, given the important role women played in the performance of secular music in fifteenth-century Italy, we are safe, I think, in assuming that women sang more than just those songs written from a woman's point of view.

By and large, fifteenth-century Italians appear to have believed that a woman's place was in the home, although some of the women who enjoyed a humanistic education as good as their husbands' could at least have assumed a more nearly equal role in the give-and-take of social intercourse. Only a few exceptional personalities were allowed to wield political power and most of those only indirectly and provisionally through their husbands. Although women were excluded from cathedral schools and only a very few could have had anything like a career as a professional musician—except, perhaps, by marrying a court singer—the daughters of leading citizens, nobles, and other members of the upper classes received training in music almost, it would seem, as a matter of course.

The chansonniers that reflect the Italian upper-class taste for French culture in the late fifteenth century contain songs that conjure up a largely imaginary world of make-believe and romantic love; they offer, at most, a set of ideals the well-born might have aspired to follow. Most of the chansons in these collections express the male point of view, although some were either written by women or to reveal their side of the established conventions of love and manners. Although women's songs do not make up a numerically significant portion of the repertory, they do enlighten us about the kinds of French music patrician ladies of the Italian Renaissance would have learned to perform for their circle of friends.

While some of the songs written from a woman's point of view might have been reserved for transvestite performance by men or for performance by the few quasi-professional women singers—it is difficult to imagine a Medici wife or Isabella d'Este, for example, singing *Mon père m'a donné mari / A qui la barbe grise point*—others must certainly have been among the compositions the northern music masters taught their rich or noble students. Their presence in collections like Florence 229 confirms and extends Besseler's demonstration that amateurs, including women, took part with professional musicians in the fifteenth century in performing secular music. But perhaps the most significant conclusion to be reached from a study of the songs written from a woman's point of view in Florence 229 is that they seem to support and confirm the prevailing conventions regarding love and manners. There is no evidence to suggest that women resented their special role in society.

NOTES

1. Jacob Burckhardt, *The Civilization of the Renaissance in Italy* (London: Phaidon, 1945), pt. 5, p. 240.

2. Joan Kelly-Gadol, "Did Women Have a Renaissance?" in *Becoming Visible: Women in European History*, ed. Renate Bridenthal and Claudia Koonz (Boston: Houghton Mifflin, 1977), pp. 137–64; Margaret Leah King, "Thwarted Ambitions: Six Learned Women of the Italian Renaissance," *Soundings: An Interdisciplinary Journal* 59 (1976): 280–304; id., "The Religious Retreat of Isotta Nogarola (1418–1466)," *Signs* 3 (1978): 807–22.

3. Kelly-Gadol, "Did Women Have a Renaissance?" pp. 160–61. See p. 149 for an analysis of Caterina Sforza's rule.

4. On Isabella's patronage of music, see William F. Prizer, *Courtly Pastimes: The Frottole of Marchetto Cara* (Ann Arbor: UMI Research Press, 1980), pp. 2–14, where previous studies of Isabella and her relations with musicians are cited. On Isabella's decisive influence on the history of Italian music, see, among other studies, Nanie Bridgman, *La Vie musicale au quattrocento* (Paris: Gallimard, 1964), pp. 109ff.

5. Ruth Kelso, *Doctrine for the Lady of the Renaissance* (Urbana: University of Illinois Press, 1956), in chaps. 3 and 4, pp. 38–77, presents the most detailed study to date of the education of women during the Renaissance and provides a good bibliography of earlier studies. While acknowledging the central place liberal studies had in the education of some women, Kelso dismisses the notion that women were treated as the intellectual equals of men.

6. Cecilia Gonzaga's studies and accomplishments are described briefly in William H. Woodward, *Vittorino da Feltre and other Humanist Educators*, rev. ed. (1897; New York: Columbia University, 1963), pp. 50, 249. Fedele, Nogarola, and Varano are the three women humanists cited in Vittorio Rossi, *Il Quattrocento*, 8th ed. (Milan: F. Vallardi, 1964), pp. 51–52. The best summary of the lives of these and other women humanists is King, "Thwarted Ambitions," which includes references to editions of their works and critical studies. On Nogarola, see also King, "Religious Retreat of Isotta Nogarola."

7. For what Kelly-Gadol calls the "major Renaissance statement of the bourgeois domestication of women," see "I libri della famiglia" (c. 1435), in Leon Battista Alberti, *Opere volgari*, ed. Cecil Grayson (Bari: Laterza, 1960). The treatise has been translated into English by Guido A. Guarino in *The Albertis of Florence: Leon Battista Alberti's Della Famiglia* (Lewisburg: Bucknell University Press, 1971).

8. Vespasiano da Bisticci, *Vite di uomini illustri del Secolo XV*, ed. Paolo d'Ancona and Erhard Aeschlimann (Milan: U. Hoepli, 1951), p. 548. The English translation is from id., *Renaissance Princes, Popes, and Prelates*, trans. William George and Emily Walters (1926; reprint, New York: Harper Torchbooks, 1963), pp. 444–45. Vespasiano also wrote a "Libro delle lodi e commendazioni delle donne illustri."

9. The incident is reported, among other places, in William Roscoe, *The Life of Lorenzo de' Medici called the Magnificent*, 9th ed. (London: Henry G. Bohn, 1847), pp. 273–75, where the relevant exchange of letters between Poliziano and Lorenzo, and Clarice and Lorenzo is published (pp. 458–61). Some of these letters also appear in Angelo Poliziano, *Prose volgari inedite e poesie latine e greche edite e inedite*, ed. Isidoro del Lungo (Florence: G. Barbèra, 1867), pp. 57ff. The whole episode is analyzed at length in Giovanni Battista Picotti, "Tra il poeta ed il lauro," *Giornale storico della letteratura italiana* 65 (1915): 263–303 and 66 (1915): 52–104, reprinted in id., *Ricerche umanistiche* (Florence: Nuova Italia, 1955) (see esp. pp. 39–47), and in Ida Maïer, *Ange Politien: La Formation d'un poète humaniste (1469–1480)* (Geneva: Droz, 1966), p. 353.

10. See Poliziano, *Prose volgari*, pp. 81–82, for the letter. On the participation of women in composing and performing in the late sixteenth century, see the essays by Newcomb and Bowers, chaps. 5 and 6 below.

11. The best-known work setting down ideal behavior for the courtier in the late fifteenth and early sixteenth centuries is, of course, Baldesar Castiglione, *Il libro del Cortegiano*, ed. Bruno Maier, 2d ed. (Turin: Unione tipografico-editrice torinese, 1964). On the courtier's attitude toward music, see Baldesar Castiglione, *The Book of the Courtier*, trans. Charles S. Singleton (Garden City, N.Y.: Doubleday, 1959), p. 104: "Let the Courtier turn to music as to a pastime, and as though forced, and not in the presence of persons of low birth or where there is a crowd . . . let him appear to esteem but little this accomplishment of his, yet by performing it excellently well, make others esteem it highly." I take it that, in recommending "il cantare alla viola" and especially "il cantare alla viola per recitare," Castiglione implies improvisation.

12. On Charles the Bold as a composer, see Howard Mayer Brown, *A Florentine Chansonnier from the Time of Lorenzo the Magnificent* (Chicago: University of Chicago Press, 1983), chap. 9. For examples of Henry VIII's compositions and arrangements, see John Stevens, ed., *Music at the Court of Henry VIII*, Musica Britannica, no. 18 (London: Stainer & Bell, 1962). Leo X's arrangement of Colinet de Lannoy's "Cela sans plus" is discussed, among other places, in Franz X. Haberl, "Eine Komposition des Cardinals Jo. de Medicis (Leo papa X) in einem Manuscript des 16. Jahrhunderts," *Kirchenmusikalisches Jahrbuch* 3 (1888): 39–49.

13. An exception, of course, was made for the liturgical and other sacred music performed in convents and nunneries, a subject that badly needs further study. See the essays by Yardley and Bowers, chaps. 2 and 6 of this vol., and Michel Brenet, *La Musique dans les couvents de femmes depuis le moyen âge jusqu'à nos jours* (Paris: Schola Cantorum, 1898). See also Alessandro Luzio and Rodolfo Renier, "Delle relazioni di Isabella d'Este Gonzaga con Ludovico e Beatrice Sforza," *Archivio storico lombardo* 17 (1890): 372, who report on a visit Isabella d'Este made to Venice in 1493. Among other things, she went "al audir cantare le sore de S.^{to} Zacharia," suggesting that at

least Venetian nuns were notable for their musical abilities as early as the fifteenth century.

14. For a brief summary of Tromboncino's stormy life, see Prizer, *Courtly Pastimes*, pp. 55–61, where previous studies are cited.

15. On Damiano, see Isabel Pope and Masakata Kanazawa, eds., *The Musical Manuscript Montecassino 871* (Oxford: Clarendon Press, 1978), p. 34 and nos. 76 and 137.

16. Paul Oskar Kristeller, "Learned Women of Early Modern Italy: Humanists and University Scholars," in Patricia H. Labalme, *Beyond Their Sex: Learned Women of the European Past* (New York: New York University Press, 1980), pp. 91–116, cites a very few exceptions to the rule that women were by and large excluded from universities during the Renaissance in Italy.

17. Castiglione, *Book of the Courtier*, pp. 257–58. The same sentiment is expressed in a negative way by the misogynist Gasparo Pallavicino, ibid., p. 75: "I think that music, along with many other vanities, is indeed well suited to women, and perhaps also to others who have the appearance of men, but not to real men; for the latter ought not to render their minds effeminate and afraid of death." On music in Castiglione's work, see Walter H. Kemp, "Music in *Il Libro del Cortegiano*," in *Cultural Aspects of the Italian Renaissance: Essays in Honour of Paul Oskar Kristeller*, ed. Cecil H. Clough (New York: A. F. Zambelli, 1976), pp. 354–69, where previous studies are cited. On the "contradiction between the professed parity of noblewomen and men . . . and the merely decorative role Castiglione unwittingly assigned" the ladies in *The Book of the Courtier*, see Kelly-Gadol, "Did Women Have a Renaissance?" pp. 149–52.

18. See Francesco da Barberino, *Del Reggimento e costumi di donna*, ed. Conte Carlo Baudi di Vesme, Collezione di opere inedite o rare dei primi tre secoli della lingua (Bologna: G. Romagnoli, 1875), pp. 30, 53, 75–76; also, Giuseppe Vecchi, "Educazione musicale, scuola e società nell'opera didascalica di Francesco da Barberino," *Quadrivium* 7 (1966): 5–29. On music in the *Decameron*, see Howard Mayer Brown, "Fantasia on a Theme by Boccaccio," *Early Music* 5 (1977): 324–39, where previous studies are cited.

19. See Prizer, *Courtly Pastimes*, pp. 11–12.

20. The dedications of Tinctoris's *Tractatus de regulari valore notarum* and *Complexus effectuum musices* were most recently printed in Johannes Tinctoris, *Opera theoretica*, ed. Albert Seay, 2 vols. in 3 (n.p.: American Institute of Musicology, 1975), 1:125, 2:165–66. The dedication of *Terminorum musicae diffinitorium* is printed in Latin and English in, among other places, id., *Dictionary of Musical Terms*, trans. Carl Parrish (Glencoe: Free Press, 1963; London: Collier-MacMillan, 1963), pp. 2–5.

21. All of these aristocratic ladies are mentioned in Emilio Motta, *Musici alla corte degli Sforza* (1887; reprint, Geneva: Minkoff, 1977), pp. 59–60; some appear in André Pirro, *La musique à Paris sous le règne de Charles*, *1380–1422*, 2d ed. (Strasbourg: Heitz, 1958), pp. 12–13. On medieval women musicians, see the essay by Coldwell, chap. 3 above; as well as Yvonne Rok-

seth, "Les Femmes musiciennes du XIIᵉ au XIVᵉ siècle," *Romania* 61 (1935): 464–80. The essay Rokseth promised there (p. 480) on women musicians in the fifteenth century and later was never published. A number of references to women musicians in the fourteenth century appear, also, in André Pirro, *Histoire de la musique de la fin du XIVᵉ siècle à la fin du XVIᵉ* (Paris: Renouard, 1940), pp. 21–25.

22. See Alessandra Macinghi negli Strozzi, *Lettere di una gentildonna fiorentina del secolo XV al figliuoli esuli*, ed. Cesare Guasti (Florence: G. C. Sansoni, 1877), p. 464: "ella legge così bene. E demandando se l'aveva del zotico, dicemi di no, ch'ell' è desta, e sa ballare e cantare."

23. See Vespasiano, *Vite di uomini illustri*, p. 553. Vespasiano, *Renaissance Princes, Popes, and Prelates*, p. 449, from which the English translation is taken, incorrectly gives "[they] spend the nights in dancing and in other vanities" for the Italian "le menano alle nozze e a' balli e alle vanità."

24. Pietro Bembo, *Opere in volgare*, ed. Mario Marti, I classici italiani (Florence: Sansoni, 1961), pp. 877–78.

25. For some examples of women taking part in fifteenth-century *intermedii* and related theatrical events, see the *farsa* in Jacopo Sannazaro, *Le opere volgari*, ed. Giovanni Antonio and Gaetano Volpi (Padua: Giuseppe Comino, 1723), pp. 422–26; Edmondo Solmi, "La Festa del Paradiso di Leonardo da Vinci e Bernardo Bellincione (13 gennaio 1490)," *Archivio storico lombardo*, 4th ser., 1 (1904): 75–89; Alfredo Saviotti, "Una rappresentazione allegorica in Urbino nel 1474," *Atti e memorie della R. Accademia Petrarca di Scienze, Lettere ed Arti in Arezzo*, n.s., 1 (1920): 180–236; Wolfgang Osthoff, *Theatergesang und darstellende Musik in der italienischen Renaissance*, 2 vols. (Tutzing: Hans Schneider, 1969), 1: 33–38; and Nino Pirrotta, *Li due Orfei da Poliziano a Monteverdi* (Turin: ERI, 1969), pp. 37–59.

26. See, for example, the letter from Filippo Strozzi to his younger brother, Lorenzo, about a *mascherata* given in Florence during the carnival season of 1507, quoted in Frank d'Accone, "Alessandro Coppini and Bartolomeo degli Organi: Two Florentine Composers of the Renaissance," *Analecta Musicologica* 4 (1967): 52, 76. Filippo wrote, "We portrayed la Dovizia (Abundance), who was [impersonated] by Antonfrancesco dressed like a woman with a cornucopia in one hand and a basket full of different kinds of fruit on his head." See also Ferdinand Gregorovius, *Lucrezia Borgia* (New York: Phaidon, 1948), p. 142, for a report of a *rappresentazione* given in Rome in honor of Lucrezia Borgia's wedding to Alfonso d'Este, in which a boy in women's clothes represented Virtue.

27. See Anna Maria Coppo, "Spettacoli alla corte di Ercole I," *Contributi dell'Istituto di Filologia Moderna, Pubblicazioni dell'Università Cattolica del Sacro Cuore* (Milan), 3d ser., Serie storia del teatro, 1 (1968): 31–32. According to Coppo, Anna Sforza once quite exceptionally took the part of Ippolito in a private performance of the *Comedia di Hipolito et Lionora* (p. 32).

28. See Heinrich Besseler, "Umgangsmusik und Darbietungsmusik im

16. Jahrhundert," *Archiv für Musikwissenschaft* 16 (1959): 21–43; also id., "Die Besetzung der Chansons im 15. Jahrhundert," *Kongress-Bericht, Internationale Gesellschaft für Musikwissenschaft, Utrecht 1952* (Amsterdam: Vereniging voor Nederlandse Muziekgeschiedenis, 1953), pp. 65–72. Besseler offers evidence that courtiers performed regularly with professional musicians.

29. See Prizer, *Courtly Pastimes*, p. 3.

30. See Solmi, "La Festa del Paradiso," p. 83.

31. Vespasiano, *Vite di uomini illustri*, pp. 554–56; id., *Renaissance Princes, Popes, and Prelates*, pp. 451–52.

32. The ball, held on 30 April 1459, is described in a long poem in Florence, Biblioteca Nazionale Centrale, MS Magl. VII, 1121, fols. 63–69ᵛ. While much of the ball involved simple social dancing—especially of the saltarello—the anonymous poet also explained that after the first serving of food, the dancing began again, "Et ballato gran pezzo al salterello [*sic*], / ballaron poi a danza variata, / chome desiderava questo et quello." Among the *danze variate*, he named *L'angiola bella, Gli arrosti, Belriguardo, Charbonata, Chirintana, Danza del re, Laura, Lionciel, Mummia,* and *La Speranza,* some of which survive with choreographies in the Italian dance treatises of the fifteenth century. For a list of the treatises and a bibliography of studies of fifteenth-century dance, see Frederick Crane, *Materials for the Study of the Fifteenth-Century Basse Danse* (Brooklyn: Institute of Mediaeval Music, 1968).

On 15 April 1459 Galeazzo Maria Sforza and his entourage stopped for the night between Bologna and Florence, where they were entertained before dinner "per alchuno belle done al modo fiorentino, saltando et fazendo scambieti, di che per tuta la compagnia se prese uno grande piacere" (Galeazzo Maria Sforza to Francesco and Bianca Sforza, Milan, Archivio di Stato, Potenze sovrane, MS. 1461, fols. 86, 88). On 23 April he visited the Medici villa at Careggi and was entertained after dinner by "una festagliola de done," including the first ladies of Florence, who danced "a la fiorentina, con salti et scambieti a la polita" (id. to Francesco Sforza, Paris, Bibliothèque national, MS fonds it. 1588, fol. 226). I am grateful to Rab Hatfield of Florence for telling me of these documents and for furnishing me with a transcription of them.

33. Anthony Newcomb, *The Madrigal at Ferrara, 1579–1597,* 2 vols. (Princeton: Princeton University Press, 1980), 1:7ff., makes the latter point about the famous female singers of Ferrara in the second half of the sixteenth century. For performances of *concerti* in Ferrara in 1529 involving Madonna Dalida Puti, onetime mistress of Cardinal Ippolito I d'Este, see Howard Mayer Brown, "A Cook's Tour of Ferrara in 1529," *Rivista italiana di musicologia* 10 (1975): 223. Einstein, *Italian Madrigal,* 1:93–95, suggests that much of the music composed for women to sing in the early sixteenth century was intended for "women of highly questionable virtue, or by such as were close to them—the *nobili cortigiane* and *dames galantes.*" His statement is surely exaggerated, although sixteenth-century courtesans

were highly adept at music. On the cultural achievements of courtesans, see Georgina Masson's delightful and sympathetic study, *Courtesans of the Italian Renaissance* (New York: St. Martin's Press, 1975).

34. Marie-Thérèse Bouquet, "La Cappella musicale dei duchi di Savoia dal 1450 al 1500," *Rivista italiana di musicologia* 3 (1968): 236.

35. Edmund A. Bowles, *Musikleben im 15. Jahrhundert*, Musikgeschichte in Bildern (Leipzig: VEB Deutscher Verlag für Musik, 1977). The *jongleuresse* appears in plate 158. Plate 159 shows a wandering minstrel playing a folded trumpet with a monkey on his back; the woman next to him seems to be accepting payment from a child.

36. Bouquet, "Cappella musicale dei duchi di Savoia," p. 281.

37. The letter is preserved in Paris, Bibliothèque nationale, MS fonds it. 1587, fol. 90. Of the "damisela anglese" it is said, she "cantava tanto dolcemente, et suavemente, che pareva una voce, non humana, ma divina." I am grateful to Dr. Bonnie J. Blackburn for telling me of the existence of the letter and for providing me with a transcription.

38. The letter is transcribed in Motta, *Musici alla corte degli Sforza*, pp. 299–300. A photographic reproduction of it appears in Guglielmo Barblan, *Storia di Milano*, 17 vols. (Milan: Fondazione Trecanni degli Alfieri, 1953–66), 9 (1961): 821. Edmond vander Straeten, *La Musique aux Pays-Bas avant le XIXᵉ siècle*, 8 vols. in 4 (1867–88; reprint, New York: Dover, 1969), 4:31, lists a "Madama Anna Inglese, musica del S.R.," as having been in the service of the king of Naples in 1480. She is less likely to have been the English woman who sang in Venice in 1455 than to have been the "Anna cantatrice" who came to Milan in 1468; and she may, of course, have been an entirely different person from either.

39. The menu and entertainment are described briefly in A.C., "Il Corredo nuziale di Bianca M. Sforza-Visconti sposa dell'Imperatore Massimiliano I," *Archivio storico lombardo* 2 (1875): 74–75. Music was provided by a trumpet, shawm and bagpipe ("cornamuse con piva"), a combination of lute and fiddle ("liutto cum violla"), and by polyphonic music ("canto figurato") sung by, among others, "una dona goba denante et de dreto, che faceva optimo soprano."

40. On Cara and his wife, see Einstein, *Italian Madrigal*, 1:52; Prizer, *Courtly Pastimes*, pp. 42–43, and docs. 8, 11, 13, 17; id., "Marchetto Cara at Mantua: New Documents on the Life and Duties of a Renaissance Court Musician," *Musica Disciplina* 32 (1978). See also vander Straeten, *La Musique aux Pays-Bas*, 4:31, who lists a "Vannella, moglia del q° Vincinet, cantor fo del S.R.," among the singers of the king of Naples in 1479.

41. The letter is in Mantua, Archivio di Stato, Archivio Gonzaga, busta 2993, vol. 13, fols. 40ᵛ–41ᵛ. See also *I Diarii di Marino Sanuto*, ed. Nicolò Barozzi, vol. 4 (Venice: F. Visentini, 1880), p. 229; Prizer, *Courtly Pastimes*, p. 58. Einstein, *Italian Madrigal*, 1:48, quotes a letter dated 1535, in which Tromboncino, in Vicenza, asks his Venetian correspondent to give his regards to "Madonna Paula," who is perhaps the same Paula Poccino. I am grateful to William F. Prizer for sending me a transcript of the 1502 letter and

for advising me about music in Mantua. Professor Prizer has informed me that a number of letters in the Mantuan archives from 1505 on refer to a musician named Pocino, Poccino, or Pozzino, using the masculine gender, presumably a second musician with the same surname.

42. See Einstein, *Italian Madrigal*, 1:78; D'Accone, "Coppini and Bartolomeo," pp. 48–49.

43. The fresco is reproduced, among other places, in *Guida storico-artistica: Siena, R. R. Spedali Riuniti di S. Maria della Scala* (Milan: L. Alfieri, n.d.); and John Pope-Hennessy, *Sienese Quattrocento Painting* (Oxford: Phaidon, 1947), p. 28, fig. 15.

44. From a manuscript of the romance "Lancelot" prepared in Venice about 1446 (Florence, Biblioteca Nazionale Centrale, Cod. Pal. 556, fol. 105), according to Roger Sherman Loomis, *Arthurian Legends in Medieval Art* (London: Oxford University Press, 1938), where the scene is reproduced on p. 337. Folio 154ᵛ of the same manuscript shows a lady playing a rebec in her castle, while two knights approach.

45. The painting is reproduced and conflicting attributions to Garofalo and Ercole Grandi are briefly discussed in Adolfo Venturi, "Ercole Grandi," *Archivio storico dell'arte* 1 (1888): 196–98; id., *Storia dell'arte italiana*, 11 vols. in 24 (Milan: U. Hoepli, 1901–14), vol. 7, pt. 3 (1914), pp. 1130–41; Giuseppe Agnelli, *Ferrara e Pomposa* (Bergamo: Istituto italiano d'arte grafiche, n.d.), pp. 151–59; Edmund G. Gardner, *The Painters of the School of Ferrara* (London: Duckworth, 1911), pp. 131–32, 177–78; Bernard Berenson, *Italian Pictures of the Renaissance: Central Italian and North Italian Schools*, 3 vols., rev. ed. (London: Phaidon, 1968), 1:155; vol. 3, fig. 1779 (as Garofalo). The fresco needs to be studied more closely by music historians, not only because some of the musicians depicted may be identifiable—Claudio Gallico, *Un libro di poesie per musica dell'epoca d'Isabella d'Este* (Mantua: Bollettino storico mantovano, 1961), who reproduces the fresco opposite p. 120, supposes the two young ladies to be Isabella and Beatrice d'Este—but also because the ceiling includes instruments besides the lute and viol or fiddle shown in plate 7, including an early violin, reproduced in Venturi, *Storia dell'arte italiana*, vol. 7, pl. 855, and more recently in Mary Remnant, *Musical Instruments of the West* (London: B. T. Batsford, 1978), fig. 45 (the lutenist is reproduced there also, as fig. 16). If Remnant's dating of 1505–8 is correct and the fresco has not been heavily restored, this is the earliest known painting of a violin.

46. Reproduced in Max Sander, *Le Livre à figures italiens depuis 1467 jusqu'à 1530*, 6 vols. (Milan: U. Hoepli, 1942), vol. 5, no. 194. Also, a lone elegant lady seated in a tent playing a portative organ is among the anonymous fifteenth-century fresco scenes of courtly life decorating the Castello of Masnago. The scene is reproduced in *Affreschi lombardi del Quattrocento*, ed. G. A. dell'Acqua and F. Mazzini (Milan: Casa di Risparmio, 1965), fig. 55; and Liana Castelfranchi Vegas, *Gli affreschi quattrocenteschi del Castello di Masnago* (Milan: Bramante, 1967), pl. 1.

47. Reproduced, among other places, in Besseler, "Umgangsmusik," pl. 5. See also Giacomo Bargellesi, *Palazzo Schifanoia: Gli affreschi nel "Salone dei mesi" in Ferrara* (Bergamo: Istituto italiano d'arti grafiche, 1945); Paolo D'Ancona, *The Schifanoia Months at Ferrara* (Milan: Edizioni del Milione, 1954). Eberhard Ruhmer, *Francesco del Cossa* (Munich: F. Bruckmann, 1959), figs. 18–44 and pp. 71–75, gives a brief overview of the history and meaning of the paintings and a bibliography of previous studies.

48. Is it possible that the painting depicts professional singers famous enough to be considered an adornment of the court where they sang and thus worthy of a group portrait? The balustrade on which they place their music books and instruments might well be part of a musicians' gallery. The hypothesis needs to be explored further. It would be tempting, for example, to imagine the picture a portrait of Marchetto Cara and his first wife. They were, after all, among the "treasures" of Isabella d'Este's court, and she was understandably proud of them. Costa came to work in Mantua in 1505, although he had painted pictures for Isabella before then. Art historians date the painting about 1490. Unfortunately, no known portraits of Cara exist, and the genesis and early history of the painting are not known. It is reproduced, among other places, in Einstein, *Italian Madrigal*, vol. 1, facing p. 143 (as by Ercole de' Roberti); and in Ranieri Varese, *Lorenzo Costa* (Milan: Silvana, 1967), figs. 26 and 27, with a brief résumé of what is known about the history of the painting and a survey of the attributions made by art historians (see catalog of Costa's work, ibid., pp. 71–72, no. 54).

49. The painting is reproduced and discussed in Detlev Freiherr von Hadeln, "Das Bentivoglio-Konzert von Lorenzo Costa," *Pantheon* 13/14 (1934): 338–40. See also Roberto Longhi, *Officina ferrarese*, new ed. (Florence: Sansoni, 1956), p. 143. The two cantori reveal so little personality that it is doubtful they can ever be identified more closely as individuals working for the Bentivoglio family in the late fifteenth century.

50. For a convenient survey of fifteenth- and early sixteenth-century Italian chansonniers, their provenance and dates, see Allan Atlas, *The Cappella Giulia Chansonnier*, 2 vols. (Brooklyn: Institute of Mediaeval Music, 1975–76), 1:233–58. At least one of the sixteenth-century manuscripts was owned by a woman. Florence, Biblioteca Nazionale Centrale, MS Magl. XIX, 121, carries the ex libris of Marietta, daughter of Francesco Pugi, a Florentine notary; see Bonnie J. Blackburn, "Two 'Carnival Songs' Unmasked: A Commentary on MS Florence Magl. XIX, 121," *Musica Disciplina* 35 (1981): 121–78. For the view that French chansons were almost always performed on instruments in Italy and not sung, see Louise Litterick, "On the Performance of Franco-Netherlandish Secular Music of the Late Fifteenth Century," *Early Music* 8 (1980): 474–87.

51. On French literary culture at the Este court in the fifteenth century, see Giulio Bertoni, *La Biblioteca Estense e la coltura ferrarese ai tempi del duca Ercole I (1471–1505)* (Turin: E. Loescher, 1903), pp. 69–93. On French books in Italian Renaissance libraries, see Dorothy M. Robathan, "Libraries

of the Italian Renaissance," in *The Medieval Library*, ed. James Westfall Thompson (1939; reprint, New York: Hafner, 1967), pp. 529, 532–34, 554, 556–57. On the vogue of importing Flemish pictures, see Erwin Panofsky, *Early Netherlandish Painting*, 2 vols. (Cambridge: Harvard University Press, 1964), 1:1–3.

52. Paris, Bibliothèque nationale, MS fonds fr. 9223. The manuscript was edited in its entirety and further identification for all the poets was supplied by Gaston Raynaud in *Rondeaux et autres poésies du XVe siècle* (Paris: Firmin Didot, 1889).

53. See Kathleen Chesney, "Two Collections of Early Sixteenth-Century French Rondeaux," *Medium Aevum* 40 (1971): 157–71.

54. *Le Jardin de Plaisance et fleur de rhétorique* (Paris: [Antoine Vérard, 1501]), facsimile, with extensive intro. by Eugénie Droz and Arthur Piaget, 2 vols. (Paris: Édouard Champion, 1910–25).

55. *La Chasse et le départ d'amours*, ed. Octovien Saint-Gelais and Blaise d'Auriol (Paris: widow of Jean Trepperel and Jehan Jehannot, 1509), is described in Frédéric Lachèvre, *Bibliographie des recueils collectifs de poésies du XVIe siècle* (Paris: Édouard Champion, 1922), pp. 12–15. I consulted the undated edition, S 218, Douce Collection, Bodleian Library, Oxford. For a discussion of some details with special reference to the poetry written from a woman's point of view, see Mary Beth Winn, "The Apology of Women in *La Chasse et le départ d'Amours* (1509): Another Voice in the 'Querelle de la femme,'" *The Early Renaissance, Acta* 5 (1978): 69–80; id., "'Apologie de la femme' and 'Poésie de la dame' in *La Chasse et le départ d'Amours*," *Fifteenth Century Studies* 2 (1979): 233–40; id., "Poems by 'The Lady' in *La Chasse et le départ d'Amours* (1509)", in *Vox Feminae: Studies in Medieval Woman's Songs*, ed. John F. Plummer (Kalamazoo, Mich.: Medieval Institute Publications, 1981), pp. 179–98.

56. Among the twenty-eight rondeaux with a woman's point of view in *La Chasse et le départ d'amours*, the following were set to music and have survived: *C'est mal cherché vostre advantage* / Alexander Agricola (see Brown, *Florentine Chansonnier*, no. 64); *D'ung aultre aymer mon cueur s'abesseroyt* / Johannes Ockeghem and Basiron (see Atlas, *Cappella Giulia*, vol. 1, nos. 97–98); *J'en ay dueil que je n'en suis morte* / Ockeghem (see Martin Picker, *The Chanson Albums of Marguerite of Austria* [Berkeley: University of California Press, 1965], MS. 228, no. 14); *Je ne me puis veoir à mon aise* / Heinrich Isaac (see Brown, *Florentine Chansonnier*, no. 129); *La despourveue et la banye* / Ockeghem (see Laborde Chansonnier, fol. 61^v, in Library of Congress, Washington, D.C., among other manuscripts); *Le souvenir de vous my tue* (four settings): one by Robert Morton (see Dragan Plamenac in *Annales musicologiques* 2 [1954]: 146–47), one by Arnolfo Giliardi (see Atlas, *Cappella Giulia*, vol. 1, no. 53), and two by Johannes Tinctoris (see his *Opera Omnia*, ed. William Melin [n.p.: American Institute of Musicology, 1976], pp. 135–38); *Nulle plus dolente que moy* / anonymous (see MS. 517, fol. 129^v, Bibliothèque publique, Dijon); *Par voz sermens tous pleins de decevance* / Johannes Prioris (see Richard Wexler, "The Complete

Works of Johannes Prioris," Ph.D. diss., New York University, 1974, pp. 376, 386–87, 539–43); and *Vostre oeil s'est bien tost repenty* / Prioris (see ibid., pp. 376, 388–89, 556–58). The rondeau *Joye me fuit et douleur me court seure* / Antoine Busnois, which is apparently related to the rondeau *Joye me laisse et dueil m'a espousée* in *La Chasse et le départ d'amours*, appears in the musical settings from a woman's point of view. Its revision in *Jardin de Plaisance*, no. 389, changes the gender of the speaker to male. Such revisions are not uncommon in poetic anthologies of the time.

57. Florence, Biblioteca Nazionale Centrale, MS Banco rari 229. Its contents are listed in Becherini, *Catalogo . . . Biblioteca Nazionale di Firenze*, pp. 22–29. See also Anne-Marie Bragard, "Un manuscrit florentin du quattrocento: Le Mgl. XIX.59 (B.R. 229)," *Revue de musicologie* 52 (1966): 56–72. See Brown, *A Florentine Chansonnier*, for a modern edition of Florence 229, with an extensive introduction and complete bibliographical information for each piece.

58. There has been extensive debate in recent years over the nature of medieval "courtly love," and several scholars, led by D. W. Robertson, have even attacked the validity of the term. Roger Boase, *The Origin and Meaning of Courtly Love* (Manchester: Manchester University Press, 1977), summarizes the debate and provides an extensive bibliography.

59. See Strozzi, *Lettere di una gentildonna fiorentina*, p. 464.

60. Complete English translations of all these poems appear in Brown, *Florentine Chansonnier*. I am grateful to Brian Jeffery for furnishing me with prose translations.

61. On this point, see Craig Wright, "Performance Practices at the Cathedral of Cambrai, 1475–1550," *Musical Quarterly* 64 (1978): 308–11. On Isabella d'Este's search to replace soprano Carlo di Launoy (Colinet de Lannoy), who left Mantua without permission, with another male soprano, see Stefano Davari, "La musica in Mantova," *Rivista storica mantovana* 1 (1885): 63–64.

5

Courtesans, Muses, or Musicians? Professional Women Musicians in Sixteenth-Century Italy

ANTHONY NEWCOMB

In sixteenth-century Europe the issue of women's place in society was a live one, and Italy took the lead in trying to broaden the limited, stereotyped roles assigned to women by tradition.[1] The most famous poem of sixteenth-century Italy can testify to the concerns of its culture. The twentieth canto of Ariosto's *Orlando furioso* (published 1516, final revised edition 1532) opens with a veritable manifesto on women's place in the arts:

> Le donne son venute in eccellenza
> di ciascun'arte ove hanno posto cura;
> e qualunque all'istorie abbia avvertenza,
> ne sente ancor la fama non oscura.
> Se'l mondo n'è gran tempo stato senza,
> non pero sempre il mal influsso dura;
> e forse ascosi han lor debiti onori
> l'invidia o il non saper degli scrittori.

> Ben mi par di veder ch'al secol nostro
> tanta virtù fra belle donne emerga,
> che può dare opra a carte et ad inchiostro,
> perchè nei futuri anni si disperga,
> e perchè, odiose lingue, il mal dir vostro
> con vostra eterno infamia si sommerga. . . .

> (Women have arrived at excellence
> in every art in which they have striven;
> in their chosen fields their renown is apparent
> to anyone who studies the history books.
> If the world has long remained unaware of their achievements,
> this sad state of affairs is only transitory;

perhaps envy concealed the honors due to them,
or perhaps the ignorance of historians.

In our own day I can clearly see
such virtues evident among fair ladies
that pen must be set to paper
to record it all for posterity
and to drown in perpetual shame
the calumnies of evil tongues.)[2]

From the same poem Rinaldo's spirited response upon learning that
Guinevere is condemned to die after being accused of adultery sounds
surprisingly like a modern proclamation of women's rights:

S'un medesimo ardor, s'un desir pare
inchina e sforza l'uno e l'altro sesso
a quel suave fin d'amor, che pare
all'ignorante vulgo un grave eccesso;
perchè si de' punir donna o biasmare,
che con uno o piú d'uno abbia commesso
quel che l'uom fa con quante n'ha appetito,
e lodato ne va, non che impunito?

Son fatti in questa legge disuguale
veramente alle donne espressi torti;
e spero in Dio mostrar che gli è gran male
che tanto lungamente si comporti.

(If the same ardor, the same urge
drives both sexes
to love's gentle fulfillment, which to
the mindless crowd seems so grave an excess,
why is the woman to be punished or blamed
for having done with one or several men the very thing
a man does with as many women as he will,
and receives for it not punishment but praise?

This unequal law does
obvious injustice to women;
and by God I hope to show how criminal it is
that it should have survived so long!)[3]

Indeed, Ariosto begins his entire epic with an audacious reworking
of the opening phrase of Virgil's *Aeneid*, in which the arms and men
of Virgil are outflanked by women and love: *Arma virumque* (Arms
and the man) becomes *Le donne, i cavallier, l'arme, gli amori* (Ladies, knights, arms, loves); *arma virumque canto* (I sing of arms
and the man) becomes *Le donne, i cavallier, l'arme, gli amori, / le*

cortesie, l'audaci impresi io canto (I sing of ladies, knights, arms, loves, / courtesies, daring exploits). Even in his expansion into two lines, Ariosto continues to insist on the balance between what were, in the sixteenth century, the areas of society appropriate to women and to men, between le cortesie and l'audaci impresi.

The place of women in society was, then, a live issue to the sixteenth-century Italian, and Ariosto took his stand firmly in favor of a much expanded recognition of women's activity in some aspects of public life. In a more restricted way, Castiglione did so, too, in his vastly influential treatise on manners, Il Cortegiano. Even Vasari, in his life of the early sixteenth-century artist Properzia de' Rossi, gives a disquisition on the achievements of women in the arts, and he ends by quoting part of the passage by Ariosto that opens this essay.[4]

That such influential figures were riding with them does not mean that sixteenth-century women, like Ariosto's Marfisa and Bradamante, won virtually every battle.[5] Another quotation—this one from a man who in his time was as influential a patron as Ariosto was a poet—will give an idea of the violence of the feelings aroused by these matters and of the difficulty with which old opinions were dislodged even in the relatively progressive and sophisticated environment of the north Italian courts. Duke Alfonso d'Este of Ferrara, having just established a pioneering group of singing ladies within his court, took them with him on a visit in mid-1581 to the Gonzaga court in nearby Mantua. Duke Guglielmo Gonzaga's reaction was recorded by a resident ambassador who was admitted to some of the festivities.

[Duke Alfonso,] having with great ceremony caused His Excellency [Duke Guglielmo] to hear the music of these ladies, was expecting to hear them praised to the skies. Speaking loudly enough to be heard both by the ladies and by the duchesses who were present [Duke Guglielmo] burst forth, "Ladies are very impressive indeed—in fact, I would rather be an ass than a lady." And with this he rose and made everyone else do so as well, thus putting an end to the singing.[6]

Duke Guglielmo's outburst was more than an indecorous indulgence of ill temper. It was the violent reaction of a brittle, conservative old man to changes that he sensed in courtly society. The role of women, especially their participation in the arts, was changing there, and Guglielmo did not approve—to no avail. In spite of the old man's animadversion, music as an honorable profession, especially within the confines of the court, became much more accessible to women during the sixteenth century. This easily observable change was important not only socially but also musically, for the increased

participation of women in professional music-making had wide repercussions in the monuments of late sixteenth- and early seventeenth-
century music that have come down to us. Madrigals written at the
end of the century with two or three difficult parts in the treble clef
apparently call for trained women's voices; operas of the early seventeenth century have women's parts written with trained women's
voices in mind. The crucial steps in this change occurred around
1580 in the closely connected courts of Florence, Mantua, and
Ferrara.

The first part of this essay will deal with the what, where, and
when of the change—relatively straightforward matters that one
can approach through a summary of documentary evidence for the
events around 1580, with some instances, some anecdotes, and some
salaries. Here we are on fairly sure ground (although someone may
eventually prove that the same things happened slightly earlier in
the princely households of Rome). The second part of the essay will
raise the broader question of the preparation for the change—its how
and its why. Here the terrain is less well explored; a lot of interesting
work remains to be done.

The change itself was not a subtle one. A situation in which
women were an obscure and unrecognized part of the profession became one in which they were at its apex.[7] All this took place in
twenty-five years or, perhaps, less. By 1600 the change was virtually
complete: a woman could actually aim for a career in music (or be
aimed there by an ambitious relative) as an alternative to a career as
an unpaid handmaiden of the Church or as the manager of her husband's household.[8] In 1580, the year of the foundation of the *concerto di donne* (the group of singing ladies) at the court of Ferrara,
the decisive part of the change seems just to have begun.

Even such a relatively rapid and dramatic change began, not
with a grand gesture, but with a subtle sideways movement. Laura
Peverara, Anna Guarini, and Livia d'Arco—the initial members of
the concerto di donne—found their prestigious places in the musical
establishment of one of the most important courts of the age, not
directly through acceptance into the public *cappella di musica*, but
obliquely through infiltration into what was variously called the
musica privata, *musica reservata*, or *musica secreta* of the ruler—
that is, through infiltration into the informally constituted group
that provided the court with its chamber music. Peverara, Guarini,
and d'Arco were entered in the court rolls, not as musicians, but as
ladies-in-waiting to the duchess. A bit later, in 1583, they were joined
by Tarquinia Molza, who had officially the same function. Yet the

documents surrounding the hiring of all four women make clear that they were brought in and paid richly by the court because of the beauty of their voices, and that they were expected to sing regularly upon demand.[9]

Such seems to have been the path to an honorable place in the profession of music for the Italian woman in the late sixteenth century: she gradually shaded over from an expression of the generalized ideal of the woman courtier—who was expected, among other things, to be able to sing—to the more specialized role of the woman musician within the confines of the inner court, a woman who was hired to realize with particular excellence only one part of the generalized ideal of the woman courtier. Only after this subtle shift had occurred do we see the widespread appearance of the woman musician who was expected only to perform and not to be at least an out-of-balance reflection of the complete courtier—women such as Ferdinando de' Medici's young girl of 1589 mentioned below or the young girl being trained for Enzo Bentivoglio's musica secreta in Rome in 1609.[10]

I have called the three ladies of the Ferrarese group of 1580 early examples of the highly prestigious professional woman musician. Although they served as professional musicians, custom suggested that the title not yet fit the role. That the Ferrarese court of 1580 was aware of this equivocation is demonstrated by the case of the one man, Guilio Cesare Brancaccio, who served for three years in the new Ferrarese musica secreta. Brancaccio wanted to be what he was called and what he had been all his life—a courtier and a cavalier. He resisted the idea that the privilege depended on his service as a musician and that he had to sing for the court and for influential guests when asked to do so. This brought him too close to the status of a professional musician, a situation the old man's pride could not permit. Finally, in 1583, he refused on the spot to sing for the Duke de Joyeuse and was sent packing.[11]

The ladies of the 1580s—younger, more flexible, and doubtless used to hypocrisies much stronger and rather harder to bear—indulged in no such tantrums. Indeed, we have no hint that they did not genuinely like their positions. Rather than being sensitive about the socially degrading implications of their specialized function at court, they were happy that their specialized abilities caused them to be welcomed and honored there. The fervent attachment of the duke and duchess of Ferrara to music and musicians doubtless helped to smooth this passage.

A summary of the documentation surrounding the formation of

this first concerto di donne at Ferrara can demonstrate more fully the points raised above: that the ladies owed their positions in court primarily to their gifts as musicians, that their positions were of great honor and prestige, and that the question was a novel and delicate one, whether or not the members of the concerto were in fact serving as musicians.

The first trace of the group is found in March 1580 in a dispatch of the Florentine resident in Ferrara. He says that the idea for the new group was Duke Alfonso d'Este's and that the duke had been strongly enough moved by a certain singer that he went outside his own duchy to recruit her from among the subjects of the duke of Mantua: "When His Excellency [Duke Alfonso] was at Mantua he saw a young lady who was rather beautiful and, in addition, had the virtue of singing and playing excellently. He thereupon conceived the desire of having her at Ferrara and, upon his return here, he had the Duchess send to obtain her as one of her ladies in waiting, which was done by special messenger." [12] The reference is to Laura Peverara, who was, in time and in prestige, the prima donna of the new group. She was joined in its formative stages by the young Ferrarese woman Anna Guarini and by the aging Neapolitan minor nobleman, warrior, braggart, and bass Giulio Cesare Brancaccio, who was mentioned as a fine solo singer and amateur actor in various courts of Italy from the 1540s onward.

The documents surrounding Brancaccio's acceptance into the Ferrarese court demonstrate both that the duke was taking these people into his court specifically to serve him as musicians and that the correspondent, once again the Florentine resident in Ferrara, found the situation, especially the part played by the ladies, to be novel and a bit puzzling. "[The Duke] tells me also that he expects Signor Giulio Cesare Brancaccio to enter his service within ten days, but that he has made a pact with him that he is not to talk of his miracles of war. He is rather to take part now and then in a *musica secreta*, which is being prepared by some ladies of the court." The new group began to perform regularly during carnival season in early 1581. The Florentine resident observes, in the midst of a general description of the season's entertainment, that "there is consistently some private entertainment (*trattenimento ritirato*), most of the time with the musica secreta of some ladies of the court (especially Peverara) and Brancaccio, whom the duke called into his service principally to take advantage of this skill of his." The resident goes on to analyse Brancaccio's position in some detail. He mentions again the pact concerning Brancaccio's interminable discourses on the art of war; and he notes that, although he had understood Brancaccio was supposed to serve as a musician, he cannot say that he really does so, since he acts like a member of the court (*cavalliere*), is so treated by the duke, and "sings only *in secreta* in the company of ladies."

The resident later reports that Brancaccio "beyond the 400 scudi per year of salary, had a furnished house, and horses as many and whenever he wishes." Peverara, we learn in a letter on the occasion of her marriage in early 1583, did even better. The duke furnished 10,000 scudi of dowry, beyond which she received 300 scudi per year, as did both her husband and her mother. The family was to have the apartments in the ducal palace that had formerly belonged to Leonora d'Este, the duke's late sister, plus all the rooms on the floor below once held for Count Ottavio Landi.

Tarquinia Molza of Modena was the last woman to join the duke's concerto di donne. A chronicler reported on her trial appearance with the group in December 1582: "Every evening there is the usual music by the ladies, from 6:30 to 9:30. The Signora Tarquinia Molza also took part in it, and I hear that the Duke's praise for her was such that one could not imagine higher." Tarquinia was a widow who did not need to be provided with husband and dowry, but her salary and fringe benefits were scarcely less rich than Peverara's. The same chronicler reported, in early 1583, that "Signora Tarquinia is also joining the service of the duchess, with a salary of 300 scudi per year, plus the rooms where Signor Lucio Pagantio had formerly lived." The chronicler concludes tartly that in the Ferrarese court "one needs to know how to sing."

One appreciates the meaning of these salaries (and of the chronicler's remark) more fully when one knows that Ippolito Fiorino, the *maestro di cappella* of the court, and Luzzasco Luzzaschi, its most influential musician, received approximately 125 and 135 scudi per year respectively. (Luzzaschi was also given some rooms in the palace and a farm outside of the city.)

In reading the chronicles and dispatches of the 1570s and 1580s at Ferrara, one comes to realize that the duke's passion for music and poetry, and for their meeting in the madrigal had led him to a new idea, which then led to a subtle but important shift in the function of music for women within the court. First the duke, driven by his desire for excellence in the performance of madrigals, formed within the court a specialized group of madrigal singers. He did so by hiring women singers under the guise of ladies-in-waiting to put with the most appropriate male chamber singers from his cappella di musica

(for this was the exclusive source of male singers in the musica secreta after Brancaccio left—no more male *cantori secreti* were hired).
He thus took one of the traditional abilities of the courtier—like
dancing and telling witty stories, an ability designed for the courtier's own recreation and for the entertainment of his fellows—and
pushed it, by his increasing demands for both time and virtuosity,
into a specialized realm, where the ability became split off from the
whole courtier. At the same time, the audience was separated from
the performer within the music-making of the inner court. Instead
of members of the audience often becoming performers and vice
versa, as had previously happened in courtly chamber music, now
the performers were always the same, and the audience remained
only an audience. Each group settled into its specific role, and among
the performers was a group of highly prestigious women.

Duke Alfonso's idea was an unqualified success. It succeeded in
both senses he could have hoped for: it brought him pleasure at
home, and it brought him prestige abroad. The duke's unfeigned, almost excessive, enjoyment of his new musica secreta is reported by
almost everyone who visited Ferrara in these years. A typical dispatch, of June 1581, relates:

Cardinal Madruzzo was entertained on the day of his arrival with the usual
music of the ladies, which takes place every day without fail. The Duke is
so inclined to and absorbed in this thing that he appears to have placed there
not only all his delight but also the sum total of his attention. One can give
him no greater pleasure than by appreciating and praising his ladies, who are
constantly studying new inventions.

The duke regularly used his singing ladies to impress visitors from
outside the duchy. In July 1583, upon the visit of the Duke de Joyeuse to Ferrara, a chronicler reported the following scene:

In the morning the Duke went to find His Highness at his rooms, and they
remained there together for a while. Then they heard Mass in the small
chapel and then went to eat, with music as usual by trombones, cornetts,
and other instruments. After dining they retired [to their chambers] with
great ceremony, the one wanting to accompany the other, and they stayed
there until about 4:00 P.M. Then the Duke [of Ferrara] took [the Duke de
Joyeuse] to the rooms of the Duchesses, who were together, and after a few
ceremonies and without sitting down, they went into the first room where
Luzzaschi was, with the harpsichord. La Turcha [Peverara's married name],
La Guarina, and the other one, d'Arca [neither of the last two was yet mar-
ried], came in as well, and all three sang very nicely—alone, in duets, in
trios all together; they sang echo dialogues and many other beautiful and
delicious madrigals. His Highness had put in the hands of His Excellency a

book with all the things that the ladies were singing. As a result they were greatly praised by that Prince and by the other gentlemen.[13]

The duke's new concerto di donne brought to the court of Ferrara a propaganda victory of the first order. Visitors to Ferrara sang the group's praises in the courts of Italy and southern Germany; imitations, which sprang up with astonishing rapidity, testified to its wide prestige. In 1582 the court of Mantua tried to form a concerto di donne for Prince Vincenzo (Duke Guglielmo's heir apparent and the brother of the duchess of Ferrara) upon the occasion of Vincenzo's ill-fated marriage to Margherita Farnese. It aimed to lure from a convent, as the star of the new group, a Bolognese woman of angelic voice, Laura Bovia by name. This first Mantuan attempt (like Vincenzo's marriage to Margherita) was never consummated. Two years later, in 1584, however, a second concerto di donne was ready in Florence to help celebrate Vincenzo's second attempt at marriage—this time to Leonora de' Medici. This Florentine concerto, which stayed at the court of Francesco de' Medici and Bianca Cappello, was directed by Giulio Caccini. When Grand Duke Francesco and Bianca Cappello died in 1587 and Ferdinando de' Medici came to take power in Florence, the concerto was dissolved, apparently because Ferdinando hated on principle everything Francesco and Bianca had liked.

Although Ferdinando grumbled in the first months of his reign that he had no taste for Francesco's "little chamber groups," he soon was forming a concerto di donne of his own, with a largely different cast. And in 1589 he announced that he had brought back from Rome a girl of eleven with a stupendous voice, who was to be trained in Florence and would become, Ferdinando was sure, one of "the finest women in music." This is an important stage in the evolution of the professional woman musician: in this case, attention was no longer paid to the virtues of an all-around woman of the court. Because of the young woman's undeveloped talent as a musician, she was taken in by the court and trained specifically to become one of "the finest women in music." Thus, the disguise of the woman courtier seems already by 1589 to have slipped from the woman musician in court.

Meanwhile, other similar groups were being formed. In late 1587, Vincenzo Gonzaga immediately hired a group of women musicians for his musica secreta upon becoming the duke of Mantua. The sister of Duke Alfonso d'Este, Lucrezia d'Este, the duchess of Urbino, who was estranged from her husband and living in Ferrara, had by 1589 formed her own concerto di donne, the second in the *palazzo estense*.[14] And in 1590 the young ladies in the circle of Maria de' Medici and the wife of Virginio Orsini, Flavia Peretti, were assembling a concerto di donne of their own in Rome.

Although there were doubtless new concerti di donne formed in the 1590s and new women were hired to fill them, the crucial decade was the 1580s. At its beginning, the chroniclers and ambassadors at the Ferrarese court were surprised and a bit puzzled by the new musical group that performed in the private apartments of the ruling couple, and they were struck by its novelty. By the end of the decade, the concerto di donne was a courtly cliché in northern Italy. Every princely household had to have at least one.

Nor were the musicians only singers, even though at the beginning they may have been primarily so. Although the women of the first Ferrarese concerto played instruments appropriate for accompanying themselves in solo song (lute, viol, harp), they were praised almost exclusively as singers. The same is not true of two of Vincenzo Gonzaga's musicians, who were specifically praised as players of the cornett. And at least one of Lucrezia d'Este's musicians was described, not as a singer, but as a player of the *viola bastarda*.[15]

What was the social background and education of the women who were drawn into this lucrative and prestigious profession? In a few cases we know at least a small amount about one or the other of these matters. Laura Peverara was the daughter of a well-to-do Mantuan merchant, who had provided her with the education appropriate to a woman being groomed for courtly society.[16] Anna Guarini, one of seven children of the poet and court secretary G. B. Guarini, also was taught music as part of her education as a courtly lady. Her mother, Taddea Bendidio Guarini, came from an ancient and wealthy Ferrarese family, and Taddea's sisters Vittoria and Isabella were among the most able of the amateur singers at the Ferrarese court in the 1570s. Thus Anna was musically educated in an artistically, even a musically inclined family, which was closely connected with a major court. Tarquinia Molza was the niece of the poet Francesco Maria Molza. She, like Peverara and Guarini, was educated according to the ideal of the courtly lady expressed in *Il Cortegiano* and a few other treatises of the time.[17] Indeed, she fulfilled that ideal better than any other of the musicians who concern us here, for she was known at least from the early 1570s as an accomplished poetess as well as a ravishing singer. Livia d'Arco was the daughter of a minor Mantuan nobleman who was not in easy financial circumstances. Ironically, although a noblewoman, she was the only one of the four ladies who came to the court without a thorough lady's education, that is, without musical training. She had to spend almost two years working under Luzzaschi before she was allowed to sing with the concerto di donne. This young noblewoman comes as close as any of the first Ferrarese singers to the case of Ferdinando de' Medici's girl later in the decade: she was brought into the court because of the undeveloped beauty of her voice (the documents describing her recruitment make this clear), and she was specially trained there to fulfill her designated function as a singer within the court.[18]

The pattern of family background is varied then, but not widely so. The musicians mentioned tended to come from what we would now call upper middle-class families of either important artists or wealthy merchants, where the place of music in the traditional education of the ladies aspiring to courtly life uncovered and developed their talent for music and eventually prepared them for their careers. Another such instance is sketched in the dedication to the book of four-voice madrigals by Vittoria Aleotti (quoted in chapter 6 below), a dedication written in 1593 by Vittoria's father, Giovanni Battista Aleotti, the Ferrarese ducal architect and stage designer.[19] Vittoria Aleotti had been taught keyboard playing and probably some theory before electing "to dedicate herself . . . to the service of God" in the convent of San Vito. The dedication of this bit of juvenilia (she was presumably in her mid-teens) to Hippolito Bentivoglio may suggest that the young composer (and her father) would not have been displeased by a summons from the convent to the princely household similar to the one received ten years earlier by Laura Bovia.

We know that several early women musicians were members of musicians' families, although we cannot be sure that this is where they received their relatively intense musical training. Caterina Willaert and Virginia Vagnoli, who were active in Venice around 1560 (see below), both came from musicians' families. The Pelizzari sisters hired by Vincenzo Gonzaga in late 1587 or 1588 were sisters of a musician who had worked for the Accademia Olimpica of Vicenza at least since 1581. Vittoria Archilei, a well-known singer in Roman courts and one of the members of the first concerto di donne at Florence in 1584, was the wife of a singer and lutenist in the service of cardinals Alessandro Sforza and Ferdinando de' Medici in Rome.[20] Another member of the first Florentine concerto di donne was Caccini's wife. Claudia Cattaneo, a singer at the Mantuan court who married Monteverdi in 1599, was the daughter of another member of the Mantuan *cappella di musica*. The daughters of Giulio Caccini, who began their musical careers in the first years of the seventeenth century, are other well known examples of this type (see chapter 6 below).

It seems that encouragement from a family involved in the profession was an important factor in the formation of women artists in several fields in the sixteenth century. This is suggested not only by the above cases, but also, in the visual arts, by the case of the Anguissola sisters, who are discussed at several places by Vasari,[21] and by that of Isabella and Virginia Andreini in the theater (see below).

Thus were the subtle forces of chance and custom that prepared women for the musical profession in the 1580s and 1590s. There are indications that by about 1600 it was possible for a father of quite modest background to educate his daughter directly for a career in music, without the pretense that music had entered simply as part of the education of the aspiring woman courtier. The examples of Caterina Martinelli and Adriana Basile suggest this. Yet the career of woman musician had lost none of its prestige. We have only to read of the lengths to which Vincenzo Gonzaga went to persuade Adriana Basile to come to Mantua in 1610 to realize how much importance he attached to having such a singer in his court. From the friendly and familiar tone of Ippolita Recupita's letters to Enzo Bentivoglio (and of her references in them to her employer, the powerful Cardinal Montalto) we can infer the honored and intimate position that such a favored musician held in important households of the time.[22]

By 1610 such women were at the apex of their profession, and they appear to have been trained and considered purely as women musicians, not as specialized kinds of courtiers. The process begun with Laura Peverara, Livia d'Arco, Tarquinia Molza, Anna Guarini, and Vittoria Archilei in the early 1580s was completed with Adriana Basile and Ippolita Recupita in the first decade of the seventeenth century. I should like now to look backward instead of forward from the early 1580s and to ask what had prepared this large change in the relation of women to the profession of music—what had made Italy so quick to provide and accept the professional woman musician at the end of the sixteenth century.

The first and most important element is one already mentioned in sketching the training of some early women musicians: the ideal of the cultivated and well-bred woman courtier, the *donna di palazzo*. (The important place of music in this ideal during the fourteenth and fifteenth centuries is sketched in chapter 4 above.) The ideal at the beginning of the sixteenth century, given a classic statement in Castiglione's *Il Cortegiano*, is summarized as follows: "And, to repeat in part and with few words what has been said thus far, I want this lady to know something of letters, of music, of the visual arts, and to know how to dance and be festive."[23] This ideal encouraged ladies who aspired to the courtly condition to train themselves in music, and prepared them to slip over to the role of musicians in court when the audience of patrons separated itself from the patronized courtier-performer. The almost ubiquitous influence of Castiglione's ideal extended to the famous (if not always socially prestigious) *cortegiane oneste* of the period—to Tullia d'Aragona, Veronica Franco, and others. Although musical proficiency was an important and often cited part of the arsenal of delights manipulated by these women, they were not professional musicians. They were, rather, imitations of the ideal donna di palazzo.[24]

Although Castiglione's ideal encouraged women to become proficient amateurs, it did not make accessible to them the highest ranks of the profession. A prominent new figure in late sixteenth-century Italian society did, however, help to prepare the way for the professional woman musician—the musician who was no longer a disguised courtier. This new figure was the professional actress. Virtually from the beginning, around mid-century, of the *commedia dell'arte* (which means, literally, *theater by professionals* as opposed to *theater by amateurs*), at least some of the stable troupes of *comici* had women members, although some others used men to play the female roles. From the 1550s onward, the roster of actresses in Italy contains figures of great fame and, at least in some cases, great prestige. Vincenza Armani, who is reported in performances of the 1560s and who was poisoned in 1569, was the subject of an elaborate printed encomium in 1570.[25] The author, Adriano Valerini of Verona—following the carefully chosen hierarchy in Castiglione's summary quoted above: letters, music, then visual arts—says that Vincenza spoke Latin at age fifteen, and "by herself wrote madrigals, set them to music, and sang them; she was a most graceful player of various instruments, a worthy sculptress in wax, fluent and profound in conversation, and a very fine actress." Here again were the characteristics of the sixteenth-century donna di palazzo, with one important difference: she was not a courtier, she was an actress. The fame of the lady was considerable, as was the passionate adulation she aroused;[26] the prestige of her social position is a little less clear. With Signora Armani we may be closer to the world of the courtesan than to the respectable world of Laura Peverara.

This is not so in the case of Isabella Andreini, who seems to have been the most famous woman of the Italian stage from her debut in the late 1570s until her death in 1604. Though she came of humble origins, she rose to see the king of France as godfather to one of her children. The list of her admirers and patrons is impressive:

Vincenzo Gonzaga; Carlo Emmanuele of Savoy; Francesco, Ferdinando, and Maria de' Medici; Henri IV of France; and Cardinal Cin-
zio Aldobrandini. She was, most exceptionally, welcomed into the
masculine world of the prestigious academies, not only as a visitor,
but as a member (of the Accademia degli Intenti in Pavia). Poems
were written to her by Tasso, Chiabrera, and Marino. Her pastoral
Mirtillo and her *Rime* were published and widely praised. As an
actress she played the *prima donna* (sometimes called the *innamo-
rata*); she was thus, on stage at least, another emulation of Castiglione's donna di palazzo. She seems to have been so in real life as
well, with impressive abilities as a poet, a fine singing voice, and a
"soavissimo tocco nella musica" (a very gentle touch at the instrument). Beyond this she had an unblemished reputation as a *"donna
di salda virtù"* (a woman of solid virtue). Yet she was a woman pursuing a professional career onstage, before a paying audience, and independent of any single court or protector.[27] She was not, however, independent of any man. She was married to Francesco Andreini, the
director of the famous company of actors called *I Gelosi*,[28] and it
may have been Francesco who trained Isabella and carved out her
place in the theater.

The same was not true of another actress of the early commedia
dell'arte, Vittoria Piisimi, who was widely famous at least by the
time of the visit Henri III of France paid to Venice in 1574. K. M. Lea,
in her history of the commedia dell'arte, considers it a noteworthy
moment in the evolution of woman's place in the theater when, in
1575, an entire company was referred to simply as *"la compagnia
della Vittoria."*[29] Vittoria went on to manage and direct several companies over the next twenty years. I have not seen her name linked to
that of a man, as either husband, constant companion, protector, or
stable sponsor. The stage seems to have offered Vittoria the opportunity for a free and independent professional career as a woman. She
might prove to be one of the most interesting figures for a study of
female artists in sixteenth-century Italy. What remains unclear again
is her social prestige. Because she was unmarried (if she was unmarried), was she considered no better than a courtesan—a remarkable renegade to be looked at, applauded, but not included in polite
society?

Whatever Vittoria's social status, the general point remains: the
rise of famous, important, and much praised actresses in the commedia dell'arte of the 1560s and 1570s taught the aristocratic world
to see women before it as professional performers and to think of and
admire women as performers, even as singers.[30] The hypothesis that

the connection between the rise of the professional actress and the rise of the professional woman musician was a close one is strengthened by the fact that the patrons and localities that most fervently supported the rising commedia dell'arte—Venice, Ferrara, Mantua, and the Florentine court at the end of the century—were the same that seem first to have sponsored the rise of the professional woman musician. What is more, many of the prime donne of the commedia dell'arte were in fact skilled musicians, as is demonstrated by the famous case of Virginia Ramponi-Andreini, the wife of Isabella's son and the prima donna in his company, who was chosen to substitute in the part of Arianna in Monteverdi's operatic tragedy when Caterina Martinelli fell fatally ill just before the projected performance.[31]

Women's education as influenced by the sixteenth-century ideal of the donna di palazzo and the professional activity of the actresses of the commedia dell'arte were the two elements that, I suggest, prepared Italian society to provide and accept women into the top ranks of the musical profession from the 1580s onward. Beyond these two elements there is a third, which we may not yet have seen clearly because we are blinded by the brilliance of the divas of the end of the century. However shadowy, there are nonetheless traces of professional women musicians in Italy well before 1580. This is an area less explored by scholars than the ideal of the cultivated sixteenth-century woman courtier or the personnel of the early commedia dell'arte troupes.

Near the beginning of the preceding chapter in this volume, the evidence for such musicians up to the early sixteenth century is summarized. The evidence is difficult to evaluate, especially with regard to the professional status of the women involved and, to a lesser degree, with regard to their social status. It becomes a bit clearer as the sixteenth century progresses. In a book on Girolamo Parabosco by Giuseppe Bianchini, we learn of a woman of the second and third decades of the century, a certain Giulia, daughter of Giovanni Francesco *ab alpicordis* (no one is quite sure what this means) and a *virtuosa di sonar, di parlar, e di scriver* (a person skilled in playing, speaking, and writing). Here we have the account of a contemporary witness whose words have been preserved because Giulia's husband instituted a proceeding against her for alleged infidelity.[32] Testimony given in the case disclosed that Giulia taught harpsichord to the daughters and sons of rich families, that she received a certain young man repeatedly for lessons, that they sang together, and that she played for his friends. Giulia's charms apparently gave her considerable influence in important circles, for her husband, while objecting to the music-lesson tête-à-tête, admitted that his wife's intervention had got him his present position in the local administration. While music was doubtless an important part of Giulia's activity, it is probably wrong to think of Giulia as a professional musician. The testimony in the case makes her sound more like a courtesan for whom music was simply an accessory necessary for her trade.

Clearer is the case of a woman listed simply as *madonna Laura musica*, who formed part of the musica secreta of Pope Paul III from 1 January 1538 at least until the extant records cease on 1 January 1545. We know her surname, Ruggeri, because her salary (on the same level as that of the four men in the musica secreta) was collected by her husband Francesco Ruggeri for the first six months or so of her employ. That she was consistently listed as *musica* and not as *cantore* like one of the other musicians on the rolls, seems to indicate that part, at least, of her duties included the playing of an instrument. Whether she was instrumentalist or singer, or both, she was clearly a professional musician earning a fair salary in a stable position.[33] Some households of princes of the Church in Rome may have maintained such women musicians even from the time of the music-loving Leo X at the beginning of the century right through to the time of Vittoria Archilei around 1580. The history of secular music and of musica secreta in sixteenth-century Rome has yet to be written. Indeed, the research is just beginning.

In Venice, the other urban center where patronage was not overwhelmingly concentrated in one court, we catch glimpses of a few additional prestigious women musicians in the middle of the century. That these women were respected and prestigious is clear; that all of them were truly professional is not. An early example rather well known to modern music historians is Polissena Pecorina, who once owned the manuscript source for Willaert's *Musica nova* and who seems to have given her name to the collection, at least in some circles.[34] By the early 1530s La Pecorina already lived in Venice, in the circles around Willaert; for she is placed there in a letter written in Venice on 17 March 1534 by Ruperto Strozzi, who says in particular that La Pecorina "*canta sul leuto benissimo, ed in su' libri*" (sings very well to the lute, and also from part books).[35] Antonfrancesco Doni testifies anew to Pecorina's divine singing in a letter of 1544.[36] By 1570 she was dead. There is no positive indication anywhere that Polissena was a professional musician (that is, that she made her living from music), and I do not believe it likely that she was. Neither is there any indication that she was one of Venice's numerous courtesans, whose ability as singers was so often praised by Doni and his circle. I think it most likely that she was simply one of the cultivated upper-class donne di palazzo—doubtless a particularly gifted one musically—who frequented at least one and perhaps several Venetian salons in the 1530s, 1540s and 1550s.

An idea of the social position of such an upper-class woman in the liberal, intellectual world of the Venetian salons (called *ridotti* or *trebbi*) can be formed by reading the sizable literature grown up around the poet Gaspara Stampa.[37] Gaspara was the daughter of a well-to-do Paduan jeweler, who gave her the education of a courtly lady. Her father died while she was still rather young, and in 1530 her mother moved to Venice with her three young children. There she set up a ridotto, into which the brightest lights of Venice's bookish world were soon eager to be accepted. Although Gaspara, who never married, had at least two well-documented liaisons, she seems to have been considered a respectable woman by all around her. Even evil-tongued gossips, such as Aretino, did not slander her. Gaspara was an accomplished musician, too, though perhaps not in the exalted class of La Pecorina.[38]

The case of Madalena Casulana shows a different and apparently much rarer type of Venetian woman musician. To judge from surviving dedications between 1568 and 1570, she was at this time a young woman, probably in her late twenties or early thirties, who was approaching the profession of music as many men approached it in the same years. She published madrigals, first in anthologies then in collected books, and sought through her publications to attract the patronage of a highly placed sponsor.[39] One such sponsor was Antonio Molino, presumably the same Antonio Molino who was a successful Venetian merchant, the founder of a musical academy in his home, a well-known performer in the nascent commedia dell'arte, and a poet of lyrics and mock epics in dialect.[40] In the dedication of his first book of madrigals (1568) to Madalena, Molino remarks on the strangeness of a man's starting to publish music when already as old as he was (he was over 70). He explains the phenomenon by "considering that the earliest instruction in this science was imparted to me by you [Madalena], whose ability is such that it would kindle in the hoariest intelligence a new desire for glory."[41] Madalena herself composed madrigals that were published in two Venetian anthologies of 1566 and 1567, and she saw two books of her four-voice madrigals published in 1568 and 1570. In addition, a secular Latin piece of hers was played by Lasso at the prolonged festivities for the marriage of

Archduke Wilhelm of Bavaria in 1568, together with a piece by "madonna Caterina, daughter of the famous messer Adriano Willaert."[42]

From all the documents now known concerning Madalena we can put together a picture of a young woman active as composer, teacher, and singer in the most prestigious musical circles of Venice in the late 1560s—a woman whose fame as a composer even crossed the Brenner. That she remained a prestigious musician in the Venetian area at least into the early 1580s is indicated by Gardano's dedication to her of Monte's first book of three-voice madrigals (1582). Gardano, in enlisting Madalena's help in his crusade to revive the traditional three-voice madrigal, refers to her reputation as "the Muse and Siren of our age."[43] Her madrigal book of 1570 and her publications of 1583 may testify to a spreading reputation in Milan and on the Venetian mainland as well.[44] The change of name on the publication of 1583 (Madalena Mezari detta Casulana Vicentina) also suggests that she may have married at some time after 1570 and settled in Vicenza.

Madalena's activity as a teacher and her relatively widely published efforts as a composer cause her to conform to the role of professional musician according to the male model more thoroughly than any other woman discussed here. Yet we know tantalizingly little about her. Present evidence suggests a woman of modest lineage born around 1540. The editor of the new edition believes her to have come from a small town between Florence and Siena, but the evidence is equivocal. In any case, the circumstances of the beginning of her career in 1566–70 (her inclusion in anthologies assembled by Giulio Bonagionta, the dedications from Molino) place her firmly in the Venetian musical world. She may have tried in these years to find a place for herself as a musician in the world of Venetian ridotti—singing in them, teaching their patrons, composing for them. This would have been a natural place for such a bold experiment because of the relatively tolerant attitude of this environment toward the active and independent woman. Yet the experiment seems not to have been an unqualified success. Her publications suggest that after 1570 she may have married, gone to Milan for a time, and pulled back from her intense professional involvement with music, for there are no surviving books between 1570 and 1583; and when the last book appeared in 1583 (with a dedication to Mario Bevilacqua of Verona, which is much less direct in its appeal for patronage than were the dedications of 1568–70), she had acquired a new surname and a new home town.[45] Not until around

1600 do we encounter women musicians (Cesarina Ricci, then Francesca Caccini, and Barbara Strozzi) who were not only performers but also composers and teachers. Was Madalena, then, a bold exception in her own time, or is it just the accident of surviving evidence that makes her seem unusual? [46]

Some information survives concerning a certain Virginia Vagnoli, whose career, at least in its beginnings, was remarkably similar to that of Madalena Casulana. Virginia came to Venice from Sienese territory, probably around 1555, some ten years before Madalena. Like Madalena she found acceptance in prestigious Venetian ridotti.[47] Her career also came to the same end that I have hypothesized for Casulana: she married and retired from professional involvement in music.

But there were important differences between the two careers. First, as far as we know, Virginia was only a performer. Like Polissena Pecorina she sang, accompanying herself on the lute. Second, she seems to have lived and worked with her father, who was also a musician. When she served the court of Urbino from c. 1566 to 1570, her father served there with her; should an offer come from the Imperial Court in Vienna, it was stipulated in her contract with the Urbinate court that her father was to decline or accept on her behalf. The suggestion is that Virginia found her way into the profession of music under her father's protection and that, however much she herself may have been valued, it was considered more decorous to treat her officially as an adjunct of her father.[48] Nonetheless, it is clear that Virginia was, in fact, a professional musician, at least during the late 1560s. She was hired by the court at Urbino to sing and play instruments, probably for the musica secreta of the court, and she was well paid for her work there. (Father and daughter together received 200 scudi per year paid in monthly salary and title to property worth another 200 scudi per year in income, which bears comparison with Peverara and Molza's salaries in Ferrara some fifteen years later.)

Before Virginia went to Urbino she may have met in Venice some musicians from the Imperial Court in Vienna, for she apparently came to Urbino expecting an eventual summons from north of the Alps. Such a summons did, in fact, come in 1570. In the offer from the Imperial Court, she is still placed under the protection of a man: although she was to serve the court as a singer, part of the offer stipulated that she come there as the wife of the young cornettist Luigi Zenobi, who was at the time in the service of Emperor Maximilian II.[49] It is not clear that this deal was ever concluded, for by 1575 Virginia was certainly in Florence as the wife of Alessandro Striggio, and their first son is usually said to have been born in 1573. After her marriage, we hear of no further professional activity. Striggio was intimately involved with the new concerto di donne set up at Florence in 1584 and, presumably, also with that set up by Vincenzo Gonzaga, his new employer, in 1587. But no Virginia is mentioned as a singer in connection with either concerto.[50]

The occasional appearance of shadowy figures, such as Madalena Casulana, Laura Ruggeri, Virginia Vagnoli, and Caterina Willaert, suggests that perhaps only ignorance prevents us from pointing to an increasingly common, prestigious and stable group of professional women musicians in Italy leading up to the famous singers of the 1580s. "Perhaps envy concealed the honors due to them, / or perhaps the ignorance of historians." Ariosto may still be right about the ignorance, perhaps even about the envy, of historians. No doubt much remains to be discovered concerning women musicians in sixteenth-century Venice and Rome, perhaps in all of sixteenth-century Italy. Yet it seems unlikely that the outline of the situation as we now see it will be much changed.

During the early and middle decades of the sixteenth century, women musicians in Italy existed in a shadowy half-world; theirs was a profession that hesitated to declare itself clearly. With the sudden rise of the famous groups of singing ladies in the 1580s, this situation changed dramatically, first opening the way for highly prestigious women performers and then, if always to a lesser degree, for women composers as well. The social basis that allowed women to accept this professional performing and creative activity was probably established by the famous and socially prestigious actresses of the 1570s and, perhaps, by the (relatively) liberated women of the Venetian intellectual salons of the middle of the century as well. Women were musically prepared to accept these roles once they were offered by society because of the place of musical training in the long-standing tradition of the courtly lady in Italian society.

NOTES

1. See Ruth Kelso, *Doctrine for the Lady of the Renaissance* (Urbana: University of Illinois Press, 1956), esp. chap. 2. In the quotations and citations throughout the book, Italians—represented most frequently by dialogues of the Ferrarese poet Tasso—almost invariably take the progressive position.

2. Lodovico Ariosto, *Orlando furioso,* ed. Lanfranco Caretti (Turin: Einaudi, 1971), canto 20, stanzas 2–3, pp. 567–68. The translation is mine.

3. Ibid., canto 4, stanzas 65–66. The translation is mine.

4. Baldassare Castiglione, *Il Cortegiano*, bk. 3; Giorgio Vasari, *Le vite*, 9 vols. (Milano: Club del Libro, 1962–66), 4:336–41.

5. Giovanni Bruto, in *La Institutione di una fanciulla* (Antwerp: Jehan Bellere, 1555), opposes even a liberal-arts education for women, not on the grounds that women were not able enough for it, but on the grounds that it was inappropriate for them; quoted in Kelso, *Lady of the Renaissance*, p. 59.

6. Archivio di Stato, Firenze; Archivio Mediceo, fol. 2900, dispatch of Orazio Urbani dated 26 June 1581. For the original Italian, with full citation of primary sources, see Anthony Newcomb, *The Madrigal at Ferrara, 1579–1597*, 2 vols. (Princeton: Princeton University Press, 1979), app. 5, doc. 13. Where possible, further references to documents quoted will be to this modern edition.

7. For the obscurity of professional women musicians in fifteenth-century Italy, see chap. 4 above.

8. The issue of a particular woman's marital status is not germane here. What is important is whether she was a professional musician, that is, whether she made her living through her training and gifts as a musician. All of the women musicians whose marital status I know were either married or widowed, but the husband was of secondary importance. In some cases the marriage occurred after the woman had gained her enviable position, as part of the reward for her attainments; in some cases the husband was a professional partner; in other cases, the husband seems to have been part of his wife's retinue, almost a high-class valet.

9. See below, pp. 95–96. For a fuller version of the documents, see Newcomb, *Madrigal at Ferrara*, 1:183–84, 187–88.

10. See Anthony Newcomb, "Girolamo Frescobaldi, 1608–1615," *Annales musicologiques* 7 (1977): 120–34.

11. For the story of Brancaccio's dismissal, see Newcomb, *Madrigal at Ferrara*, 1:26, 185–86. That Count Alfonso Fontanelli felt the same kind of ambivalence toward the use of his musical talents in the Ferrarese court is discussed in Anthony Newcomb, "Alfonso Fontanelli and the Seconda Pratica Madrigal," *Studies in Renaissance and Baroque Music in Honor of Arthur Mendel* (Kassel: Bärenreiter, 1974), p. 56.

12. Quoted in Newcomb, *Madrigal at Ferrara*, 1:11. For the documents discussed below surrounding Brancaccio and Molza's acceptance into the court and Duke Alfonso's pride at his new group, see ibid., chap. 2; for salaries of the various musicians, see ibid., app. 1.

13. This is the same Duke de Joyeuse who is famous in music history as the promulgator of the *Ballet comique de la reine* in 1581. The duchesses referred to in the passage are, first, the wife of the duke of Ferrara and, second, the sister of the duke of Ferrara, the duchess of Urbino, who was living at the time in the Ferrarese court. For a fuller version of the passage quoted, with original text, see ibid., 1:26–27.

14. Fuller documentation on the imitations of the new concerto can be found ibid., chap. 5. Concerning, in particular, Ferdinando's concerto di

donne of 1589, together with my speculation that the girl of eleven may have been Ippolita Recupita, see ibid., 1:92–93. Concerning Vincenzo Gonzaga and Lucrezia d'Este's musicians, see ibid., 1:99–100, 102–3.

15. For a group of remarkable instrumentalists who were nuns in the Ferrarese convent of San Vito, see chap. 6 below.

16. Peverara's social background would seem to have been rather like that of Gaspara Stampa, who is discussed below.

17. See Kelso, *Lady of the Renaissance*, chap. 7.

18. For fuller documentation on these women, see Newcomb, *Madrigal at Ferrara*, app. 1, pt. 2.

19. The dedication to Vittoria Aleotti's book of madrigals can be found in Emil Vogel, *Bibliothek der gedruckten weltlichen Vocalmusik Italiens*, 2 vols. (1892; reprint, Hildesheim: Olms, 1962), 1:14–15. For further information on the importance of Vittoria's father, see the *Dizionario biografico degli italiani* (Rome: Treccani, 1960–), 2:152–54.

20. On the Pelizzari sisters, see Antonio Magrini, *Il Teatro Olimpico* (Padua, 1847), p. 63, as quoted in Leo Schrade, *La Représentation d'Oedipo tiranno au Teatro Olimpico* (Paris: C.N.R.S., 1960), p. 50. Both the Pelizzari sisters and Archilei are discussed in chapter 6 below.

21. See especially the life of Benvenuto Garofalo in Vasari, *Le Vite*, 6:353–56.

22. For the backgrounds of Basile and Martinelli, see Alessandro Ademollo, *La bell' Adriana* (Città di Castello: S. Lapi, 1888): chap. 1 for Basile; pp. 36ff. for Martinelli. For Recupita, see Newcomb, "Girolamo Frescobaldi," pp. 135–39.

23. Bk. 3, chap. 9. "E, per replicar in parte con poche parole quello che già s'è detto, voglio che questa donna abbia notizia di lettere, di musica, di pittura, e sappia danzar e festeggiare." The translation is mine.

24. For a recent study of the famed and accomplished courtesans of sixteenth-century Italy, see Georgina Masson, *Courtesans of the Italian Renaissance* (New York: St. Martin's, 1975).

25. Adriano Valerini, *Oratione d'Adriano Valerini Veronese: In morte della Divina Signora Vincenza Armani, Comica Eccellentissima. . . . Con alquante leggiadre e belle Compositioni di detta Signora Vincenza* (Vicenza, 1570).

26. The entry in the *Dizionario biografico degli italiani* (cf. n.19 above) suggests that she was poisoned by a rival in love.

27. See Vito Pandolfi, *Isabella comica gelosa: avventure di maschere* (Roma: Edizioni Moderne, 1960), a historical novel of some 350 pages designed for young readers, which explores the growth of the professional actress's consciousness in Isabella. For Isabella's origins and qualities, see Francesco Bartoli, *Notizie istoriche de' comici italiani che fiorirono intorno all'anno 1550 fino a' giorno presenti*, 2 vols. (Padua, 1782). Benedetto Croce has written on Isabella as poet in his *Poeti e scrittori del pieno e del tardo Rinascimento* (Bari: Laterza, 1952), vol. 3.

28. Francesco Andreini was also the author of *Le bravure del Capitano*

Spavento (Venice: Giacomo Antonio Somosco, 1607), one of the earliest sources on the commedia dell'arte.

29. Kathleen M. Lea, *Italian Popular Comedy*, 2 vols. (1934; reprint, New York: Russell & Russell, 1962), 1 : 114.

30. Indeed, some aristocratic ladies seem to have taken part themselves in theatrical performances, playing side by side with men whom we consider professional musicians and pioneers of the early commedia dell'arte. In a description of the intermezzi done for a performance of a comedy by Alessandro Piccolomini in Naples in 1558 (see Erasmo Percopo, "Di una stampa sconosciuta delle 'stanze' del Tansillo," *Rassegna critica della letterature italiana* 19 [1914]: 85–87) we read of one intermezzo, called *La nave di Cleopatra*, in which, after Cleopatra's boat was hauled on stage, a woman stood up and delivered a series of stanzas "in a manner midway between singing and reciting. . . . The sweetness and novelty of the singing transported everyone to Paradise. . . . The queen Cleopatra was Phomia, whose singing cannot be compared to terrestrial matters, but to the heavenly harmonies." Phomia is given no title here, but she is almost certainly the same as the ravishing singer to whom Antonio Allegretti dedicated his *Fumia la pastorella*, a poem that was set to music by Monteverdi and others. In the index of Dionigi Atanagi's *De le rime di diversi nobili poeti toscani, libro primo* (Venice, 1565), the Fumia of the poem is said to be Madonna Eufemia Jozola, a *gentildonna napoletana*. Since there is no unequivocal indication that Eufemia was a professional and since the title *gentildonna* seems to make it unlikely, I am assuming that she was but another musically cultivated donna di palazzo. It is possible, however, that she was a professional performer. Among her fellow performers in the intermezzo of 1558 were the professionals Giovanni Leonardo dall'Arpa and Scipione delle Palle, Caccini's teacher.

31. For the complicated circumstances surrounding this performance, see Stuart Reiner, "La vag'Angioletta (and others)," *Analecta Musicologica* 14 (1974): 53ff.

32. Giuseppe Bianchini, *Girolamo Parabosco*, Miscellanea di storia veneta, ser. 2, vol. 6 (Venice, 1899), p. 332. Cited in Enrico Paganuzzi, "Il cinquecento," in *La Musica à Verona* (Verona: Banca Mutua Popolare di Verona, 1976), p. 130, where some details are added to Bianchini's account.

33. My attention was first drawn to *madonna Laura* by Nino Pirrotta's section of the article on Rome in *Die Musik in Geschichte und Gegenwart* 9 (1963): col. 705. All of the above information is drawn from L. Dorez, *La cour du Pape Paul III à Rome* (Paris: Ernest Leroux, 1932), which is in turn based on registers of the privy expenditures of Paul III during the periods November 1535 to November 1538 and November 1543 to January 1545. (In 1932 the registers were in private hands.) Laura received the same salary (8 scudi per month) as a certain *messer Galeazzo musico*; she received more than one male singer, but not as much as two other male musicians. Five musicians are listed in the registers; her husband is not among them.

34. For a recent review of the documents surrounding La Pecorina, see

Anthony Newcomb, "Editions of Willaert's *Musica Nova*: New Evidence, New Speculations," *Journal of the American Musicological Society* 26 (1973): 132–44.

35. Ruperto Strozzi to Benedetto Varchi (at Florence), 17 March 1534. The letter is printed in *Raccolta di prose fiorentine: Tomo quinto contenente lettere* (Venice: Domenico Occhi, 1735), *Parte terza*, vol. 1, p. 61. My attention was called to this letter by Professor Gary Tomlinson. It reads in part: "I received the madrigals you sent me, and they made quite a success. Now that I am asked to make another in praise of the said Madonna Pulisena, I must turn again to you, having no other recourse. And certainly I do it with the same warmth, as if I were to have to ask from my beloved. . . . [Omission in the transcription of 1735?] Still, I beg you, just as you served me magnificently the first time, do no less the second. Make it in praise of said Pulisena, who sings very well to the lute and also from part books, and put her name in it, and make the last two lines both eleven syllables long and rhyming. Her name should come after the middle of the madrigal. I wanted to tell you all the details so that you would not complain, as you did the last time, that I had not explained it to you. Now you can see very well what is the wish of the lady. I will leave it to you, who know better how to do than I to say. I shall not tell you not to speak of this to anyone at all, because I know I would offend you, seeming thus to have little faith in you, which would certainly be false, because I have more faith in you than the Hungarians have in their swords. The sooner I have the poem the better." The translation is mine. For a full translation of the letter, see R. J. Agee, "Ruberto Strozzi and the Early Madrigal," *Journal of the American Musicological Society* 36 (1983): 1–2.

36. The apposite part of Doni's letter is quoted in translation in Armen Carapetyan, "The *Musica nova* of Adriano Willaert," *Journal of Renaissance and Baroque Music* 1 (1946): 203. The original letter is reprinted in Antonfrancesco Doni, *Dialogo della Musica* (Venice, 1544); modern ed., G. F. Malipiero, *Collana di musiche veneziane inedite e rare*, 7 (Vienna: Universal Edition, 1965), p. 5; much of it is printed and translated in Alfred Einstein, *The Italian Madrigal*, 3 vols. (Princeton: Princeton University Press, 1949), 1:198–99.

37. A recent summary is found in Maria Bellonci, intro. to *Rime*, by Gaspara Stampa (Milano: Rizzoli, 1976).

38. No study has yet concentrated on women's role in the Venetian ridotti of the sixteenth century.

39. The fullest biographical and bibliographical information on Casulana is to be found in Beatrice Pescerelli, *I madrigali di Maddalena Casulana*, Studi e testi per la storia della musica, 1 (Florence: Leo S. Olschki, 1979), pp. 5–20. In chapter 6 below Jane Bowers speculates on the difficulty women like Casulana had in finding professional positions in music.

40. See P. Fabbri, "Fatti e prodezze di Manoli Blessi," *Rivista italiana di musicologia* 11 (1976): 182–96.

41. The relevant part of Molino's dedication is printed in Vogel, *Biblio-*

thek (cf. n. 19 above), 1:473. The entire dedication may be found in Pesce-relli, *I madrigali di Casulana*, p. 10.

42. *Dialoghi di Massimo Troiano* (Venice: Bolognino Zaltieri, 1569), fols. 123^v–24^v; cited in Wolfgang Boetticher, *Orlando di Lasso und seine Zeit* (Kassel: Bärenreiter, 1958), p. 340; quoted in chap. 6 below, where Jane Bowers also suggests that Caterina may not have been Willaert's daughter.

43. The dedication is printed in Pescerelli, *I madrigali di Casulana*, pp. 16–17.

44. See ibid., pp. 14–19.

45. Note that the women of letters cited by Howard Brown at the beginning of chap. 4 above, whose careers are described in the essay by Margaret L. King cited in his note 2, suffered a similar fate: marriage and withdrawal from creative artistic activity.

46. Throughout Castiglione and the few other treatises on the ideal woman of the sixteenth century, the decorative, recreational, and inspirational role of women in society is stressed—their role as *muse*—not their independent and creative role. This ideal tended to make women musicians into performers, not composers; but it would seem to leave room for women as teachers. One would think there would have been a sizable demand for women as teachers of music for the aspiring women courtiers of the century: as the examples of Giulia ab alpicordis and Girolamo Frescobaldi (see Newcomb, "Girolamo Frescobaldi," pp. 122–34) show, male-female teacher-student relationships were fraught with danger. Yet the few specific instances of which I know do not indicate that women were chosen to teach music to women and men to men. Quite the opposite was true. Antonio Molino was taught by Madalena Casulana; the Este princesses in the 1580s were taught by Paolo Virchi (see Newcomb, *Madrigal at Ferrara*, 1:181); Enzo Bentivoglio's young Angiola was taught by Frescobaldi (Newcomb, "Girolamo Frescobaldi," pp. 122–34); Giulia ab alpicordis was teaching a young man when she ran into trouble.

47. All my information on Vagnoli's career through 1575 is taken from Alfredo Saviotti, "Un' Artista del cinquecento: Virginia Vagnoli da Siena," *Bulletino senese di storia patria* 26 (1919): 105–34. I thank Jane Bowers for drawing my attention to this article. The similar careers in Venice of these two early women musicians again suggest that a detailed study of women's place in sixteenth-century Venetian intellectual ridotti will be rewarding. In this instance, Virginia may have been Madalena's direct predecessor in the same ridotto. In Antonio Molino's ridotto around 1560 there was a Virginia who sang and played most wonderfully. Her praises are sung in Manoli Blessi [Antonio Molino], *I fatti, e le prodezze di Manoli Blessi* (Venice: Giolito, 1561), and in three of his *Grechesche*, settings of which by various Venetian musicians were printed by Antonio Gardano in 1564. The poems to Virginia are numbers 9, 14, and 30–31 in the modern edition: id., *Grechesche [sic]*, ed. Siro Cisilino, Celebri raccolte venete del cinquecento, 1 (Padua: Zanibon, 1974); the settings are by Annibale Padovano, Andrea Gabrieli, and

Gioseffo Guami. The links that might be seen to connect the Venetian Virginia of c. 1560 with the Virginia Vagnoli at Urbino in 1566–70 are suggested in Saviotti, "Un'Artista del cinquecento," pp. 116–18.

48. This case recalls other daughters of famous sixteenth-century artists who were among the early female members of their professions. The daughters of Titian and Tintoretto are cases in point.

49. For further details concerning Zenobi, see Newcomb, *Madrigal at Ferrara*, 1:181–83.

50. See ibid., 1:53–56, 90–91, 99–100.

6

The Emergence of Women Composers in Italy, 1566–1700

JANE BOWERS

When four madrigals composed by Madalena Casulana appeared in the anthology *Il Desiderio* in Venice in 1566 alongside madrigals by such illustrious composers as Cipriano de Rore and Orlando di Lasso, they were the first compositions by a woman to be published anywhere. By the end of the sixteenth century four other women composers had seen their musical works appear in print, while several others had earned reputations as composers. During the course of the seventeenth century, eighteen more Italian women had their music published, some in remarkable quantities, while many others were reported to have composed music that was not published and has not survived.

More women emerged as composers in Italy between 1566 and 1700 than in any previous period in Western music history—indeed, than in all of that history taken together. During those years women also composed in a greater variety of musical genres than their predecessors, and their music circulated to a larger extent than that of any women before them. These advances seem to deserve both enthusiastic heralding and detailed documentation.

Yet, how significant in reality were these advances? Did they signal a new equality of creative opportunity and activity? When the compositional activities of women are compared with those of men during this period, striking differences become apparent. While the number of women who composed was revolutionary in one sense, it was tiny when compared with the number of men who composed, and most women wrote fewer compositions and in a more limited number of musical genres than men. The social milieu in which women composers emerged also differed markedly from that which produced men composers.

How can we explain these two very different phenomena—the emergence of women composers in apparently larger numbers than in any earlier era, and the vastly different nature of women and men's relationship to musical composition? Some approaches are offered by the work of recent scholars in the field of women's history, among them Joan Kelly-Gadol, who points out that major structural changes in society have had different effects upon women than they have had upon men. She states, "The activity, power, and cultural evaluation of women simply cannot be assessed except in relational terms: by comparison and contrast with the activity, power, and cultural evaluation of men, and in relation to the institutions and social developments that shape the sexual order."[1]

Along these lines, I propose to undertake two tasks. The first will be to illustrate the nature of women's achievements in musical composition and to analyze the changes that took place in Italian musical and social life that permitted women to make unprecedented progress as composers between 1566 and 1700.[2] The second will be to identify the traditions, restrictions, and sharp divisions between the sexes that existed in Italian society which excluded women from benefiting from many of the advances in music-making made during that period and determined their slighter achievements in musical composition.

I

Composing Activities of Italian Women

As Anthony Newcomb has pointed out in the preceding chapter, the appearance of Madalena Casulana's madrigals in *Il Desiderio* in 1566 was quickly followed by the publication of two complete books of her four-voiced madrigals in 1568 and 1570 and the performance by Orlando di Lasso of a five-voiced secular Latin work of hers in Munich around the same time. Though Casulana's composing activities seem to have diminished after this initial period, her work nevertheless continued to reach the public in collections issued in 1583 and 1586, giving the first woman composer to appear in print a not inconsiderable oeuvre.[3] Soon madrigals by other women began to be issued: Paola Massarenghi of Parma (1585), Vittoria Aleotti of Ferrara (1591, 1593), and Cesarina Ricci di Tingoli (1597). In 1593 the first collection of polyphonic sacred music by a woman, the Fer-

rarese nun Raffaella Aleotti, appeared. Thus, by the end of the sixteenth century, Italian women had publicly entered the spheres of
both secular and sacred musical composition.

During the course of the seventeenth century, these initial ventures of women into music publishing were multiplied many times
over. Between 1609 and 1616, some sacred pieces with basso continuo by the nuns Caterina Assandra of Pavia and Claudia Sessa of
Milan appeared,[4] and in 1611 the first known solo monody by a
woman, Lucia Quinciani, was published. Then in 1618 came a publication of unusual importance, the *Primo libro delle musiche a
una e due voci* of Francesca Caccini.[5] The daughter of Giulio Caccini and a celebrated singer employed at the Medici court in Florence, Francesca Caccini had already been active as a composer for
some time. Over a period of about twenty years she produced music
for numerous dramatic court entertainments, a *sacra rappresentazione*, and *ottave*, madrigals, and canzonettas.[6] Aside from her
Primo libro and a balletto, *La Liberazione di Ruggiero dall'isola
d'Alcina* (1625), however, most of her works were never printed; and,
with a few minor exceptions,[7] those that did not reach print have
disappeared.

Following Caccini's *Primo libro*, several nuns—Sulpitia Cesis of
Modena (1619), Lucretia Orsina Vizana of Bologna (1623), and Claudia Rusca of Milan (1630)—as well as two Roman women, the poet
Diacinta Fedele (1628) and Francesca Campana (1629), brought out
one collection of music each. Between 1640 and 1650 Chiara Margarita Cozzolani, a nun in the convent of Santa Radegonda in Milan,
brought out four books of sacred music; and in 1659 another Milanese nun, Maria Cattarina Calegari, is said to have published some
solo motets, which were to have been followed by madrigals and canzonettas, masses, and vespers,[8] although none of these can now be
traced.[9]

Between 1644 and 1664, however, Venetian-born Barbara Strozzi,
the adopted daughter of the poet and dramatist Giulio Strozzi, published an unprecedented eight books of vocal music—all but one
secular. As Ellen Rosand points out in the next chapter, Strozzi was
one of the few known women among the many aria and cantata composers of seventeenth-century Italy. She was also the first woman
who seems to have sought a career as a professional composer outside the confines of a court, and she achieved substantial public recognition.[10] Another first for women composers occurred in 1665
when Marieta Prioli published her *Balletti et correnti a due vio-

lini. . . , the earliest known instrumental works by a woman. According to Prioli's dedication, her pieces were "the early fruits of a youthful talent," however, and the mature woman, already a mother when she published them, seems to have produced nothing further.[11]

During the latter part of the seventeenth century, the patterns established earlier continued to hold sway. Most women produced just one collection of music each, as did the nuns Maria Xaveria Peruchona of Galliate (1675), Rosa Giacinta Badalla of Milan (1684), and Bianca Maria Meda of Pavia (1691). Badalla, however, also composed at least two unpublished secular cantatas.[12] Maria Francesca Nascimbeni of Ancona described her only collection, the *Canzoni, e madrigali morali, e spirituali* of 1674, as the product of the "studies of a sixteen-year-old girl."[13] Somewhat more prolific as a composer was the painter Angiola Teresa Muratori Scanabecchi of Bologna, who wrote the music for four oratorios that were performed in that city between 1689 and 1696, the first such works known to have come from the pen of a woman. Never printed, Muratori Scanabecchi's scores have not survived.[14]

In the work of the extraordinarily productive Isabella Leonarda, a nun in the Collegio di Sant' Orsola in Novara, however, the culmination of more than a century of work on the part of women composers was reached. Two of Leonarda's motets had appeared as early as 1640 in Gasparo Casati's *Terzo libro de sacri concenti*. It is not certain when her first two books of pieces were published,[15] but after 1670 her works appeared on a frequent basis, sometimes even in yearly succession. By 1700, the year in which she turned eighty,[16] she had produced an astonishing twenty books of music, including solo motets, motets and sacred concertos for two to four voices, litanies, masses, psalm settings, and music for vespers. In 1693 she also was the first woman to publish trio sonatas for violins and basso continuo (as well as a single solo sonata).[17]

Supplementing the information provided by publications about the activities of women composers in late sixteenth- and seventeenth-century Italy are a few manuscripts that preserve music by women and a variety of contemporary reports that point to women who composed, although their works have not survived. From the early part of this period, Massimo Troiano's account of the celebrations that took place in Munich in February 1568 for the marriage of Guglielmo VI and Renata of Lorraine describes music composed for that occasion not only by Madalena Casulana but also by Caterina Willaert:

In the evening then at the sumptuous dinner among the other entertainments and most pleasing concerts of music that were presented there, at the confections course the most famous Orlando Lasso had a work for five voices by the Signora Madalena Casulana sung, which was heard with the greatest attention. . . . And after the above piece was finished another work for five voices was sung, composed by the virtuous lady Caterina, daughter of the most famous gentleman Adriano Viulaert, and the same [Nicolò] Stopio wrote the verses in praise of Her Serene Highness Anna of Austria, Duchess of Bavaria.[18]

But Troiano probably erred in saying that Caterina Willaert was the daughter of the renowned composer and chapel master Adrian Willaert, since that musician is not known to have had any children. Caterina may thus have been his niece or sister.[19]

Giovanni Battista Spaccini's chronicle of Modenese life in the late sixteenth and early seventeenth centuries describes the twenty-two-year-old Faustina Borghi, a nun in the convent of San Geminiano, as being "exceedingly virtuoso in counterpoint [and] in playing the cornetto and organ,"[20] from which we may surmise that Borghi either improvised very well or composed. The same source also reveals that Sulpitia Cesis, whose works were not published until 1619, wrote a motet that was performed at the doors of San Geminiano on the occasion of a religious procession in 1596.[21] Atanasio Pisticcio's *Motetti a due voci*, op. 7 (1637), cites Cecilia Torniella, a nun in the convent of Giesù in the town of Asti, as a "composer of music and celebrated organist," and a *status personalis* of Francesca Caterina Cellana, a nun in the Ursuline convent in Galliate, describes her in similar terms.[22]

Further activities of women composers are suggested by the presence of some lute songs in a manuscript at the Biblioteca Estense in Modena (Miscellanea MS. Mus. C. 311). Compiled by Cosimo Bottegari, a musician at the Modenese court, this manuscript contains two songs for voice and lute that may have been composed by the noblewomen Isabella de' Medici (1542–76) and Leonora Orsina, duchess of Segni (d. 1576), although the attributions to them are puzzling.[23] Gerber states that another sixteenth-century woman, a Signora Baglioncella from Perugia, was famous for the composition of many songs and madrigals, but I have been unable to locate further information about her.[24]

Many women who were well known as singers are reported to have composed music for their own use, though much of it may never have been written down.[25] One is Laura Bovia, who was acclaimed "most skilled in composing" by Camillo Cortellini in the dedication of his *Primo libro de' madrigali a cinque voci* published in 1583.[26] Others include Vittoria Archilei and Settimia Caccini, who, according to Jacopo Cicognini's description of the *Mascherata di ninfe di Senna* produced in Florence in 1611, composed some of the pieces they sang upon that occasion:

> The music of the above-mentioned *ottave* was composed by the same women who sang them: the first was sung by the Roman Signora Vittoria Archilei, with her usual grace and angelic voice; the second with supreme delicacy by Signora Settimia; the third, with her customary spontaneity, and to the admiration of all by Signora Francesca, both of these last named being daughters of that renowned Giulio Romano.[27]

Several pieces with basso continuo by Settimia Caccini, in fact, have been preserved in two related manuscripts,[28] along with works by her husband Alessandro Ghivizzani.

The compositional activities of Adriana Basile and her sisters Vittoria and Margherita are attested to by various contemporary accounts.[29] Those of Leonora Baroni, the daughter of Adriana Basile, were reported by the Frenchman André Maugars in 1639: "Finally I had the good fortune to hear her sing on several occasions more than thirty different airs, with second and third stanzas, which she composed herself."[30] The recitative-writing skills of the daughter of a theorbo master of Padua, Domenico Bassano, who "played and sang to nine several instruments," were reported by the Englishman John Evelyn in 1645,[31] Finally, the Baroness Del Nero, who sang in some private performances in Rome in 1678, is reported to have composed occasional musical works.[32]

What factors contributed to all this compositional vigor on the part of women musicians in late-sixteenth- and seventeenth-century Italy?

The Development of Careers for Women Singers

Probably first in importance among the factors that contributed to the emergence of women composers was the rather sudden development of singing careers for women that took place in late sixteenth- and early seventeenth-century Italy. According to Newcomb,[33] the decisive steps in this development took place shortly after 1580 at the court of Ferrara with the formation of a new ensemble of women singers. Although these musicians had not been trained from childhood for independent careers in music and were not entered in the court roles as musicians, they were brought into the court and richly paid because of the beauty of their voices, and they performed regularly in daily concerts. Competing ensembles were soon formed at other courts, and though not long-lived, these ensembles firmly established women's position in the profession of courtly singing. They also affected changes in the training of women musicians; for the first time girls were sought out and brought to courts specifically to be trained to serve as musicians.

By shortly after 1600, women singers had reached the apex of the profession; they were vigorously sought after, highly paid, and widely acclaimed for their appearances in chamber music and dramatic productions. Like "the famous Vittoria" Archilei at Florence, who had "almost originated the true method of singing for females" according to Vincenzo Giustiniani,[34] they were explicitly entered on court payrolls as musicians rather than given appointments as ladies-in-waiting as the Ferrarese singers had. Although Archilei's salary was lower than those of the singers in the concerto di donne at Ferrara, in 1603 she received ten scudi a month while her husband Antonio received eleven; in addition, they were paid four scudi a month from the grand duke's own purse, so that their total income was 300 scudi a year.[35] It may be of some significance that Archilei, as a fully acknowledged professional singer, is known to have written songs for her own use (as in the *Mascherata di ninfe di Senna* mentioned above), while the ladies of Ferrara are not.

At Mantua the virtuosa Adriana Basile developed some reputation as a composer. In 1620 she sent one of her canzonettas to Isabella of Savoy, and in 1616 she may have written her own part for a Mantuan entertainment. She also engaged in a comparison test with Francesca Caccini in Rome in 1623, in which both singers were asked to improvise on a poem of Gian Battista Marino.[36] Primarily, however, Basile was known as an outstanding singer. Having initially established herself as the idol of Neapolitan society with the excellence of her singing, she was hired in 1610 for the Mantuan court after long and arduous negotiations. Paid a fabulous salary (2,000 scudi a year), if an anonymous letter written at Milan in 1611 can be believed, she was also given many expensive presents by both the duchess and duke, and with her husband received the baronial title and fief of Piancerreto. She remained in the employ of the Mantuan court until 1624, when she returned to her native Naples before moving to Rome with her daughter Leonora Baroni around 1633. She gave up singing only in 1637, when she was around sixty years of age, and she is thought to have died in 1640 or a little later.[37] Of the two daughters she raised to be singers, Leonora and Catarina Baroni, the former distinguished herself as much as her mother,[38] and she was also known as an improviser or composer.

The career of one further singer, Francesca Caccini, suggests more strongly than that of any other woman that access to professional singing careers directly influenced women's creativity in music. Francesca was born on 18 September 1587 to the singer, teacher, and composer Giulio Caccini and his wife Lucia, who was also a singer. Her father trained Francesca in singing and composition at an early age, and she also learned to play the harpsichord, lute, and "chitarineta" well. She performed at the Florentine court as early as 1600 and was married to another singer there in 1607. In succeeding years she sang regularly in theater pieces, sacred music, and intimate concerts. By 1623 she had become the most highly paid singer at court; in fact, in that year and the next she earned more than anyone else (240 scudi) with the exception of the duke's secretary.[39]

The first indication that Caccini was composing music comes from two letters she wrote in 1606 to Michelangelo Buonarroti the Younger regarding canzonetta texts. Had her compositional efforts remained confined to the setting of such texts, they would not have exceeded those of many singers of her time. But they extended much further. Beginning in 1608 Caccini was given the charge of setting to music *invenzioni*—short fanciful dramatic works with something of an improvisatory character.[40] In 1611 she composed not only an ottava to sing herself in the *Mascherata di ninfe di Senna*, but also a trio for herself, her sister Settimia, and Vittoria Archilei, in which she combined a "most charming and delicate style" with "beautiful *fughe* and passages."[41] By 1612 she had probably begun to set religious texts to music.[42] Letters from Caccini to Buonarroti in December 1614 indicate that one of her invenzioni had been a big success at court and that she was also composing music for the intermedios of a comedy the ladies would perform for carnival.[43] During the same year she taught and trained an ensemble of singers, probably made up primarily of her own pupils, an activity in which she would remain involved for a number of years.[44]

Caccini's first major work mentioned in court chronicles by name is the *Ballo delle zigane* performed at the Pitti Palace on 24 February 1615. In 1618 she brought out her *Primo libro*, and in 1619 she and Marco da Gagliano set to music Michelangelo Buonarroti's play *La Fiera*. She and Giovanni Battista da Gagliano provided the music for *Il martirio di Sant'Agata*, a *sacra rappresentazione* by Jacopo Cicognini, which was given its first performance in 1622; the *avvertimento* to the libretto printed in 1624 states that Caccini was universally known and admired as a composer.[45] Her most important court commission, *La Liberazione di Ruggiero dall'isola d'Alcina*, set to a text by Ferdinando Saracinelli, was composed a few years later for the visit of Prince Ladislas Sigismund of Poland to Florence. It was performed on 2 February 1625 in the loggia of the Medici Villa di Poggio Imperiale and proved to be both Caccini's crowning success and the apparent end of her activity as a court composer. Although she seems to have been reworking an older work called *La Stiava* in 1626, nothing appears to have come of it. She stopped collecting pay as a singer at the end of May 1627, and aside from some rumors that circulated about her involvement in an intrigue at court in 1628, nothing further was recorded about her activities. A contemporary *ricordo* said that she remarried a Luccan and noted that she died of cancer of the mouth. The date of her death is unknown, but it must have occurred before 1640.[46]

Caccini's outstanding achievements in so many areas of music, particularly in composition, undoubtedly depended upon the convergence of a variety of factors. First, of course, was her birth into a family of musicians, one of whom—her highly renowned father—took a great interest in her musical upbringing and carefully groomed her for a musical career. Second, the great admiration she developed for him, as well as the example he set for her as a composer, performer, and teacher, may well have been an important inspiration for her own prodigious undertakings in music.[47] Third, of course, were her own extraordinary talents, which gained her a court position of her own that in turn gave her access to literary figures like Buonarroti, with whom she was able to establish long-term working relationships. But, most crucial of all, perhaps, was her position, which provided her with the services of many other musicians, actors, and dancers, and allowed her to compose works of a sort that she surely would never have written under other circumstances.

Thus Caccini's career strikingly demonstrates the influence of the professionalization of singing for women on the emergence of women composers. Although Caccini composed both more voluminously and over a longer period than her counterparts, other women singers of the time also devoted attention to composition.[48] Even though the training of women singers may generally have included less instruction in composition than that of men,[49] for those who were trained and gifted in composition, professional positions offered important incentives for the creation of musical works. The expectations of and opportunities for composition that went along with professional singing careers meant that women singers were able to develop their compositional talents more than most other groups of women.

The Cultivation of Polyphonic Music in Convents

Perhaps second in importance among the factors that contributed to the emergence of women composers was a dramatic growth in the performance of polyphonic music that began to take place in Italian convents in the late sixteenth century. In a number of different cities, convents became known for the excellence of their music, and visitors from near and far attended services to hear the nuns sing and play.[50] Particularly in Milan convents were distinguished for their music. In 1595 Paolo Morigia wrote:

I shall go on to say how in this our city almost all the convents of nuns devote themselves to music, both with the sound of many kinds of musical instruments and with singing; and in some convents there are voices so fine they seem angelic, and like sirens they allure the nobility of Milan to come to hear them. But among the others there are two that are worthy of praise, that are inferior to no others in their musical excellence; one is the Convent of Santa Maria Maddalena near Sant' Eufemia, the other is that of the Assonta detto del Muro; these venerable religious, besides their holy observance of the apostolic life, are also exceedingly skilled and experienced in music, both in playing and in singing, and one hears select voices that are concordant in harmony, and minglings of divine voices with instruments, so that they seem to be angelic choirs that please the ears of the listeners and are praised by connoisseurs.[51]

Another Milanese convent that fostered nun musicians was the Monastero Maggiore; there Corona Somenza was held in the greatest esteem, according to Antonio Campi, "because of the holiness of her life, and because of her many virtues, and particularly because of her excellence in music of every sort."[52]

The convent whose musicians earned the highest praise in the late sixteenth century was, however, San Vito in Ferrara. In *Il Desiderio* (1594), Hercole Bottrigari states that he had heard the musical ensemble of San Vito on many occasions; his visits probably took place during the period in which he resided in Ferrara (1576–87). Because his description tells us much about the constitution of the ensemble, the way in which it functioned, and its high degree of skill, I shall quote it at some length:

They are indubitably women; and when you watch them come in . . . to the place where a long table has been prepared, at one end of which is found a large clavicembalo, you would see them enter one by one, quietly bringing their instruments, either stringed or wind. They all enter quietly and approach the table without making the least noise and place themselves in their proper place, and some sit, who must do so in order to use their instruments, and others remain standing. Finally the Maestra of the concert sits down at one end of the table and with a long, slender and well-polished wand . . . , gives them without noise several signs to begin, and then continues by beating the measure of the time which they must obey in singing and playing. . . .

. . . . It is not at all new. If I were to speak of tens and twenties of years I would not be mistaken. Because of this, in great part, can one understand how the great perfection of their concordance comes about. Neither Fiorino nor Luzzasco, though both are held in great honor by them, nor any other musician or living man, has had any part either in their work or in advising them; and so it is all the more marvelous, even stupendous, to everyone who delights in music. . . .

If I remember rightly, there are twenty-three of them now participating in this great concerto, which they perform only at certain times—for most solemn feasts of the Church, or to honor the Princes, their Serene Highnesses, or to gratify some famous professor or noble amateur of music at the intercession of Fiorino or Luzzasco, or by the authority of their superiors; but never extemporaneously nor in haste, nor do they play all compositions, but only . . . those works judged to be prepared.[53]

Giovanni Maria Artusi, another strong advocate of the musical ensemble at San Vito, indicated in 1600 that it included cornetti, trombones, violins, *viole bastarde*, double harps, lutes, cornamuses, recorders, harpsichords, and voices.[54]

That the cultivation of polyphony in Italian convents tended to foster the development of composers is first suggested by the fact that the earliest printed collection of sacred music by a woman, Raffaella Aleotti's *Sacrae cantiones* for five, seven, eight, and ten voices of 1593, was the product of one of San Vito's holy sisters. Though the names of no other nun composers from San Vito are known, Marcantonio Guarini, who wrote about the convent in 1621, said that some years earlier it had had "excellent composers" as well as "rare instrumentalists" and "very refined singers," one of the latter being "Alfonsa Trotti singular and stupendous bass."[55]

In addition, over half the women whose musical works were published in Italy during the period in question were nuns, and other nuns were also known as composers, as we have already seen. At Maria Annunciata in Milan, the singer and instrumentalist Claudia Sessa drew such crowds on feast days that many people were compelled to remain outside. Among the great potentates who are said to have visited the convent to hear Sessa were Queen Margaret of Austria, the *serenissimo* of Savoy, Archduke Albert and Infanta Isabelle, cardinals Aldobrandino, San Giorgio, and Piato, the count of Fuentes, and the *contestabile* of Castile and his wife. Evidently Sessa's music-making at Maria Annunciata motivated her to compose, for not only are two monodies of hers extant, but also Girolamo Borsieri wrote in 1619, "She died young, and just when she had begun to compose those same musical works that she then sang at the feasts."[56]

Later in the century, convents located in various other Italian cities including Rome, Venice, Bologna, and Lucca also became known for the excellence of their music.[57] Milan, however, retained its lead, and Santa Radegonda across from the Duomo captured the greatest fame. The publication of Cozzolani's four books of sacred music including motets, a mass, and some eight-voiced psalms between 1640 and 1650 offers the first evidence of the development of its musical ensemble. Then in 1670 Filippo Picinelli wrote that "the nuns of Santa Radegonda of Milan are endowed with such rare exquisiteness in the realm of music, that they have been recognized as the first singers in Italy." Just a little later Carlo Torri stated that its "veiled singers" were so excellent that "even Rome, [which] glories in nurturing new Orfeos, must surrender the honor to these Lombardic Pierides." In 1684 a second nun composer, Rosa Giacinta Badalla, emerged from this stimulating atmosphere with the publication of some solo motets. Apparently the excellence of Santa Radegonda's music continued for many years, since in 1737 it was still praised by Serviliano Latuada.[58]

In the 1660s the convent of Santa Margarita in Milan also attracted attention through the singing and playing of Maria Cattarina Calegari, who, according to Donato Calvi, rendered "all tongues tired in celebrating her outstanding qualities, acclaimed as a heavenly singer, a composer of angelic harmonies, and in organ playing a divine Euterpe."[59]

Not all nun composers were well known as singers or instrumentalists, and not all convents that produced composers had distinguished musical reputations, however. Little or nothing is known about the performing skills of the composers Caterina Assandra, Bianca Maria Meda, Lucretia Orsina Vizana, Claudia Rusca, Isabella Leonarda, and Maria Xaveria Peruchona, or about the musical ensembles in the convents in which they resided—Sant'Agata di Lomello and San Martino del Leano in Pavia, Santa Maria Nuova in Bologna, Santa Caterina in Brera in Milan, Sant'Orsola in Novara, and Sant'Orsola in Galliate. The most prolific composer of all the nuns, Leonarda, moreover, had lived in the Collegio di Sant'Orsola in Novara for many years before she began to compose regularly; thus it does not seem likely that her prodigious work in composition after 1670 was inspired by the excellence of Sant'Orsola's musical ensemble, barring of course its sudden development just at the time Leonarda began to compose in earnest. At the same time, the collegio undoubtedly afforded her opportunities for the performance of her works, and in one of her publications she especially extolled two of its singers.[60]

What, then, accounts for Leonarda's unusual achievements? As in the case of Francesca Caccini, those achievements undoubtedly depended upon the convergence of a variety of factors. First was Leonarda's birth into an extraordinary noble family, which produced numerous high government and church officials.[61] Second were her own exceptional gifts—presumably coupled with a good measure of ambition, both of which were demonstrated by her rise to the position of mother superior within her religious community. Third, once she had reached a fairly high administrative level within the collegio, she may have been able to devote more time to composing than most nuns who had obligations to perform menial duties at fixed times. Here, however, the dedication of her Opus 10 offers a contradictory view, for she apologizes for the weakness of her works, saying that she wrote them in the hours devoted to rest in order not to neglect her duty to government. Finally, she may have chosen to pursue composition as a vehicle for the expression of intense devoutness. Almost all her works carry an unusual double dedication—one to the Virgin Mary as well as the standard one to a highly placed living person; and in one of the Marian dedications Leonarda states that she wrote music not to gain credit in the world but so that all would know that she was devoted to the Virgin.[62]

Leonarda's special gifts aside, the influence of the cultivation of polyphonic music in Italian convents on the emergence of women composers was profound. In those institutions an atmosphere conducive to women's musical creativity existed that was found in few other places (though see the section below entitled "Restrictions on Music-making in Convents" as well). Just as in the Middle Ages, convents provided religious women with both the stimulus and outlets for artistic creativity that were not available to most other groups of women.

The Growth of Private Music Instruction

A third factor that contributed significantly to the development of women composers in late-sixteenth- and seventeenth-century Italy was the growth of private music instruction. For several centuries, composers had received their principal music instruction in church, monastery, and cathedral schools, sometimes following this with further study in universities.[63] Because women were traditionally excluded from music-making in church, girls were not admitted to ecclesiastical schools, and hence few had access to extensive training in music. During the sixteenth century, however, the educational functions of the ecclesiastical schools were increasingly supplemented and supplanted by private secular instruction in many areas of study, including music. The aristocracy and the patriciate, and whoever else could afford it, frequently employed private tutors for their children.[64]

What little information is available about the music instruction women who composed received in late-sixteenth- and seventeenth-century Italy suggests that private instruction was the norm, although it might well be followed or supplemented by study in a convent. One of the earliest documents to shed light on the subject is Giambattista Aleotti's dedication of his daughter Vittoria's *Ghirlanda de madrigali* (1593). In it Aleotti, an outstanding engineer and architect in the service of the duke of Ferrara, reveals that he had hired such distinguished musicians as Alessandro Milleville and Ercole Pasquini to teach his daughters music and, further, that he had had his eldest daughter instructed in it because she seemed drawn to a monastic life and music was considered one of the Christian virtues, whereas Vittoria was provided with instruction because she manifested such a keen interest while watching her sister learn. At the suggestion of Pasquini, Vittoria was sent to the convent of San Vito for further study, and seeing how successful her work in the theory of music was, her father extracted some poems from G. B. Guarini, so that she might try her hand in setting them to music:

To the most distinguished Signore Hippolito Bentivoglio. . . .

The first of the five daughters . . . that God was pleased to give me took with her from the maternal womb a natural instinct to serve his divine Majesty. Therefore I strove to the best of my ability so that she would be as much adorned as possible with every Christian virtue, and among other things, I had her taught a little music under the guidance of the famous Alessandro Milleville, a man who in his time was endowed with every honored virtue as well as that excellent discipline, and then by Mr. Hercole Pasquino, and it happened that while this daughter was learning, my second daughter and her sister who was called Vittoria was always present (a little child between four and five years old), who affixing her pure mind on the precepts of the Maestro who was teaching the other, learned so much, that (without anyone realizing it) within a year's time nature untied her child's hands so that she began to play the harpsichord in such a way that it amazed not only her mother and me, but also her teacher himself. And that good old man began to teach her with so much dedication, that in two years she made very great progress. Wherefore he asked me with great affection to have her brought up (as I did) in the convent of the never-enough-praised Reverend Mothers of San Vito here in Ferrara, whose perfection and excellence in music surpasses (as Your Distinguished Excellency knows, and as everyone knows) that of all the most famous ensembles of women that have been heard for a long time. And so it came to pass that this daughter when she reached the age of fourteen years wisely elected to dedicate herself in this convent to the service of God. . . . And seeing how much she was devoting herself to the theory of music, I managed to obtain some madrigals by the very distinguished and most excellent Cavaliere Guarini in which one can see all the virtuous and honored qualities shine. And she set them to music. . . .

Gio. Battista Aleotti d'Argenta.[65]

Another document that sheds light on the training of women who composed is the publisher Filippo Lomazzo's dedication of Giovan Paolo Cima's *Partito de ricercari, & canzoni alla francese* to the young Caterina Assandra in 1606:

Knowing therefore how great is the desire of your father that Your Excellency be adorned with all the virtues, maintaining for you teachers of letters, and of music both in singing as well as in playing various sorts of instruments customarily used in church to praise God, I am sure that you will be grateful, that besides the many books of music by excellent authors that he already asked me for in order to give Your Excellency greater occasion to learn, I have added to them now these, and dedicate them to you.[66]

Like the eldest Aleotti daughter, the young Assandra was taught music by private tutors maintained by her father, and her training was also justified by a religious purpose. Indeed, it seems likely that Assandra was being prepared for a religious life at this time, since just three years later, when some motets of her composition appeared in print, she had entered the convent of Sant'Agata di Lomello. Here, she apparently continued her musical studies with Don Bendetto Rè, who was said to be her "Maestro di contraponto."[67]

The musical education of another young woman who composed

is also interesting enough to detain us for a moment. She is Laura Bovia. Although sometimes referred to as the niece of Monsignor Giacomo Bovio, a highly placed church official in Bologna, she was probably his illegitimate daughter.[68] Though Bovia was educated by the nuns of San Lorenzo, she also seems to have been instructed by a number of musicians from outside the convent, since a rumor circulated casting suspicions on her character because of her relations with too many musicians. This rumor, indeed, caused Duke Guglielmo to stop all negotiations to bring Bovia as a singer to the Mantuan court in 1581 until a reliable report came from the canons of San Giovanni in Monte, under whose care the convent of San Lorenzo was, dispelling the suspicions.[69] For several years beginning in 1584 Bovia seems to have formed part of a concerto di donne at the Mantuan court. But after Grand Duke Ferdinando de' Medici came to Florence to take power, she was dismissed from the court in a drastic reduction of the musical ensemble and was told by Ferdinando that she must either marry, enter a convent, or return home.[70] Bovia chose the first alternative; she married Giacomo Basenghi in 1592[71] and thereafter dropped out of sight.

One further composer whose musical education with private teachers is documented is Barbara Strozzi. Adopted into the family of the poet and dramatist Giulio Strozzi, Barbara was provided with the opportunity to study music with "many professors of this beautiful art," particularly Francesco Cavalli, the leading composer in Venice.[72] In addition, her father arranged for her to sing in private concerts in their home, founded the Accademia degli Unisoni, where he installed her as mistress of ceremonies and chief singer, and wrote the texts for the madrigals she published as her first work. Thus Strozzi's formal studies were supplemented by frequent opportunities to exercise her musical talents before audiences of connoisseurs—both apparently part of her father's plan to prepare her specifically for a career in music, possibly even for the profession of composing.[73] This crucial ingredient of being trained for a career in music of course strikingly distinguishes Strozzi from the majority of women composers of the period, and it undoubtedly does much to explain the difference between her productivity as a composer and theirs.

Although little information is available about the musical education of the rest of the composers in question, we do know that many came from noble, patrician, and professional families who could afford private tutors for their daughters; and I think we may assume, in the absence of information to the contrary, that it was through this means that most women who composed were trained in music. Of the forty women I know of who are reputed to have composed, probably at least seventeen, including the four already discussed, came from noble, patrician, and professional families. Only five came from the families of musicians where music instruction was directly available (Francesca and Settimia Caccini, Leonora Baroni, Domenico Bassano's daughter, and possibly Caterina Willaert), while seventeen have unknown origins.[74]

Among those who came from noble and patrician families were Isabella de' Medici, Leonora Orsina, the Baroness Del Nero, Sulpizia Cesis, Isabella Leonarda, Marieta Morisina Prioli, and probably Claudia Sessa.[75] In addition, Claudia Francesca Rusca may well have belonged to the important and noble Rusca family, and Lucretia Orsina Vizana may have come from the noble Vizana family of Bologna, although their names have so far not emerged in biographical and archival material pertaining to those families.[76] The status of the family of Paola Massarenghi was elevated as well, if we can judge from biographical information preserved about her brother Giovanni Battista Massarenghi.[77]

Women composers who came from distinguished professional families included Raffaella Aleotti, the sister of Vittoria, about whose private music study we have direct evidence from the dedication of her *Sacrae cantiones*.[78] Faustina Borghi may also have come from a professional family, since her cousin, the Modenese chronicler Giovanni Battista Spaccini, served for a long time at the ducal court at Modena,[79] and Teresa Muratori Scanabecchi was the daughter of "Roberto eccellentissimo Medico."[80]

We have here, then, a substantial number of women from exceptional families, most of whom probably studied music because it was considered either appropriate for well-bred young girls to do so or suitable for girls going into religious life. This factor was undoubtedly important in determining the rather peripheral and sporadic relationship most of these women appear to have had to composition, especially for those of noble and patrician background; for not only was no one belonging to the nobility and patriciate trained to become a professional musician as a rule, but also women of these classes were primarily educated for marriage or the convent.[81] Of the seventeen women composers who probably came from noble, patrician, and professional families, only Barbara Strozzi seems to have been specifically groomed for a professional career in music, although it is possible that Laura Bovia was as well. Of the other fifteen, nine became nuns, one (Muratori Scanabecchi) became a painter, and the others seem to have had no professions other than those dictated by noble blood or marriage. Thus, even though women of this period were able to acquire some of the skills necessary for composing precisely because they grew up in good families, they were not trained or encouraged to devote themselves seriously and over a long period of time to developing those skills. Nevertheless, the growth of private music instruction in late-sixteenth- and seventeenth-century Italy probably meant that a greater number of women than in any previous period received some formal training in composing.

The Growth of Music Printing and Other Factors

A further factor that influenced women's emergence as composers was the vast development of music printing that took place in sixteenth- and seventeenth-century Italy. Because printed works generally circulated more widely and reached a broader spectrum of musicians than manuscripts, publication offered composers without church, court, or other professional appointments greater opportunities to get their works into the hands of musicians who could perform them. Access to music publication seems to have been another decisive factor in the development of Barbara Strozzi as a composer, for example. Even though she held no musical post which sustained her financially or which offered opportunities for the performance of her works, she was able to get a substantial series of works many of which belong to a type usually left in manuscript by her male colleagues—before an audience through their publication, and she probably also reaped some financial rewards from the highly placed persons to whom she dedicated them. The development of music printing thus offered her some measure of independence as a composer, however slight, that she could not have enjoyed in earlier times. The wider availability of music that music printing brought about must also have provided her as well as other women with a larger number of compositional models for study than had heretofore been available.

Models of another sort, which must have given women with musical talent some encouragement to conceive of themselves as composers, were women artists in other creative fields, particularly poetry and painting—some of whom had begun to work well before women became known as composers. In poetry, figures such as Vittoria Colonna (1490–1547), Veronica Gambara (1485–1550), and Gaspara Stampa (1523–54), and in painting, figures such as Sofonisba

Anguissola (1532/35–1625), Lavinia Fontana (1552–1614), and Artemisia Gentileschi (1593–1652/53), must in some measure have awakened musical women to the possibility of their own creativity.[82]

The issue of female creativity was also indirectly raised by a lively literary debate about the virtues and vices of the female sex that both preceded and paralleled the publication of women's musical works in Italy. While some of the debate literature was strongly misogynist, declared women to be vastly inferior to men, and advocated very limited roles for women in society, the opposing side declared women to be the equals of men, even if their roles in life were decidedly different, and some even argued for the superiority of women.[83] The social tensions and changes reflected in this debate are too complex to be dealt with here. Yet I should like to suggest that the issues it raised must have challenged some educated women to reevaluate their capacities and to take a fresh look at their roles in society. Indirectly, it may thus have encouraged some women who were musical to develop their talents more fully and to assert them more publicly.

II

In spite of the positive forces that contributed to the development of women composers in late-sixteenth- and seventeenth-century Italy, the number of women who composed was tiny when compared with the number of men who composed; most women composers wrote fewer compositions than was the norm for men composers; and few women undertook the composition of instrumental music and large works such as operas, oratorios, and sacred music for large forces. Let us now turn directly to the traditions, restrictions, and sharp divisions between the sexes in Italian society that acted as barriers to women's composing and determined their lesser achievements in the field.

The Scarcity of Professional Musical Posts for Women

Throughout Western music history, productivity in composition has usually been linked to participation in the mainstream of music-making. In Italy during the period in question, nearly all the men who excelled as composers, in whatever field of composition they were active, held posts as professional musicians. One of the

chief factors that seems to have limited women's activities as composers was their much narrower participation in the full range of
musical professions and their consequent isolation from the musical
mainstream. The occupational barriers that excluded women from
most professional positions in music also meant they could not receive the special kinds of on-the-job training men received and that
they did not benefit from the incentives and demands for musical
composition that professional musical posts engendered.

In late-sixteenth- and seventeenth-century Italy, employment
for musicians and composers revolved principally around five types
of institutions—the church, the court, the theater, the private household, and the town. In addition, some musicians were employed in
connection with schools, as for example, the German Jesuit College
in Rome, where the composer Giacomo Carissimi functioned as the
head of musical instruction and chapel master of the college's church,
Sant' Apollinaire. All institutions that hired musicians employed
many more men than women musicians, and some employed no
women at all.

The Church was the largest institution that employed no women
musicians in any capacity, as chapel masters, as singers, or as instrumentalists. Courts, as we have already seen, employed some women
as singers for dramatic productions and chamber music; but since
they did not employ women as singers for chapel music, chapel masters, composers, or instrumentalists (except those women who accompanied their own singing on various instruments or on extremely
rare occasions),[84] women had access to only a fraction of all court
positions. The same situation obtained in the musical establishments maintained by the nobility, patriciate, and high church officials in their private households.

Musical theaters, both public and private, did of course frequently hire women as singers and actresses. Like the courts they
thus provided women with significant opportunities to develop musical careers. These opportunities were limited, however, in Rome
and the papal states, where successive popes, beginning with Sixtus V
in 1588, banned the appearance of women in public theaters. Although some scholars suggest that the papal bans were not strictly
adhered to, others believe they were rarely violated and that castrati
were customarily employed to replace women in Roman theaters up
through the late eighteenth century.[85] Even in cities in which women
were not prohibited from appearing in the theater, they seem to have
been outnumbered by men on the opera stage. Simon Towneley

Worsthorne's lists of singers in Venetian opera productions of the seventeenth century, for example, include a significantly higher number of men than women.[86]

Women's opportunities for employment as instrumentalists in theaters were even more limited. I know of only three women who were hired to play instruments in theaters during the entire period in question, and the two about whom we know the most—the sisters Lucia and Isabella Pellizzari—were part of a family package deal at the time they were employed by the theater of the Accademia Olimpica in Vicenza. After taking part in a solemn Mass celebrated in January 1582 at the church of San Michele for the entrance of the new prince of the academy, the *"due putte sorelle"* (two little sisters) were each awarded a salary of twenty ducats a year on the condition that they, along with their brother Antonio, would provide music for the academy twice a week on a regular basis and at any other times that might be necessary.[87] Although their duties for the academy seem to have included singing and giving singing lessons to several little girls,[88] they were best known for their instrumental abilities, especially on the cornetto and trombone. On several different occasions they were said to have especially amazed the audience at the Teatro Olimpico with their skill on these instruments.[89]

Presumably still fairly young when they transferred their services to the Mantuan court in late 1587 or 1588, they may have formed part of a concerto di donne established there by Vincenzo Gonzaga, singing as well as playing instruments. Although they appear to have continued to work as musicians at the Mantuan court into the early years of the seventeenth century,[90] they no longer seem to have specialized in playing instruments. While as young girls they were hired as instrumentalists, as adult women they were apparently no longer employable in the same capacity. In fact, it appears that their early employment by the Accademia Olimpica was dependent upon their being both part of a larger family group and child prodigies, and that after they grew up and were no longer novelties, they were unable to obtain positions in the area of their specialization.

The only other woman I know of who was paid for instrumental playing in an Italian theater during the entire period in question was a "Sig[ra] Prudenza," who was paid ten lire for playing the "third keyboard instrument" in a performance at the Teatro di SS. Giovanni e Paolo in Venice in 1665.[91] Since the records pertaining to the hiring of instrumentalists for the theater are so sketchy, we don't know whether Signora Prudenza played frequently or was simply drawn into a few performances during one season. Whatever the case, the extreme scarcity of information about women instrumentalists in theaters clearly demonstrates that women were rarely hired in this capacity. Nor do they seem to have been hired by Italian cities and towns for their bands of instrumentalists that entertained the citizenry at regular hours of the day with concerts from the balcony of the town hall or on the market square and performed at public functions and celebrations.[92]

Apparently women were not hired as music teachers by educational institutions either, although there is some evidence that a few women taught music privately or as an adjunct to another musical job. Newcomb points out that Madalena Casulana, for example, taught composition to Antonio Molino, and Francesca Caccini and the Pellizzari sisters gave singing lessons to young girls. But salaried positions as music teachers were apparently not entrusted to women.

For the most part, then, women had no access to professional positions in music except as singers, and even in that field their activities were restricted. Such severe occupational exclusion helps explain the limited number of musical genres to which women contributed during the period in question. To the entire field of instrumental music, for example, only two Italian women (Prioli and Leonarda) are known to have made contributions, and each of them published only one collection of such music. That this late start of women in writing instrumental music was strongly linked to their exclusion from jobs as instrumentalists seems to be demonstrated by the fact that most of the men who composed instrumental music were instrumentalists by profession during at least a portion of their careers. Arcangelo Corelli (1653–1713), for example, a leading composer of solo and trio sonatas for the violin as well as of concerti grossi, began his career in Rome by playing the violin in church and theater orchestras, was later *maestro di musica* for Cardinal Benedetto Pamphili, and finally, as principal violinist, conducted weekly concerts in the palace of Cardinal Pietro Ottoboni, where he also lived. Maurizio Cazzati (c. 1620–77), Giovanni Battista Vitali (1632–92), Marco Uccellini (c. 1603–80), Giovanni Maria Bononcini (1642–78), and Giuseppe Torelli (1658–1709), other important composers of string music, were also string players by profession as well as chapel masters. These men would have absorbed, through their daily activities, the idioms of the kinds of music they then wrote as well as a keen knowledge of the capabilities of the instruments with which they were associated.

Another genre of music to which women composers contributed little was that of sacred music for large forces. Again their relative silence seems largely due to their absence from the kinds of positions held by most men composers of this kind of music—chapel master, singer, and organist in an important church. Giovanni Gabrieli (c. 1555–1612), organist at St. Mark's Church in Venice, and Orazio Benevoli (1605–72), chapel master in various churches in Rome and the Vatican and at the imperial chapel in Vienna, are good examples. Women's minimal contributions to the genre of oratorio also seem to be best explained by their absence from the professions from which oratorio composers emerged—chapel master, singer in a sacred music chapel such as the Papal Chapel, organist, and priest—[93] as well as from their infrequent participation in the performance of oratorios.[94]

Women were also absent from the musical professions in which most male opera composers were active; for, while some opera composers in seventeenth-century Italy were primarily singers, most were not. The occupation of chapel master and others connected with sacred music were common ones for opera composers in Italy. Consider the examples of Claudio Monteverdi (1567–1643), from 1613 until his death chapel master at St. Mark's in Venice; Pier Francesco Cavalli (1602–76), first singer, then organist, and finally chapel master at St. Mark's; and Marc' Antonio Cesti (1623–69), chapel master at the courts of Innsbruck and Vienna and also a singer in the Papal Chapel. Preparation for such positions bespoke a breadth of musical education scarcely available to women, and their attainment placed men composers much more squarely in the mainstream of music-making than women composers. Viewed in this light, neither the different kinds, nor the lesser degree, of activity of women as composers is surprising.

The Disappearance of Women into the Domestic Realm and Negative Attitudes toward Women's Creativity

Women's lack of access to the full range of musical professions in late-sixteenth- and seventeenth-century Italy was but part of a much larger restriction of their public activities during that period. This situation seems to have resulted, at least in part, from a new division between personal and public life that had developed during the preceding period, roughly 1350 to 1530. According to Joan Kelly-Gadol, the reorganization of Italian society along modern lines which had taken place at that time affected women so adversely that

there was no renaissance for women—at least, not during the Renaissance. The state, early capitalism, and the social relations formed by them impinged on the lives of Renaissance women in different ways according to their different positions in society. But the startling fact is that women as a group . . . experienced a contraction of social and personal options that men of their classes either did not, as was the case with the bourgeoisie, or did not experience as markedly, as was the case with the nobility.[95]

Noble women were increasingly removed from public concerns, and patrician bourgeois women disappeared into a private realm of family and domestic concerns, subordinated in a new way to the interests of their husbands and male-dominated kin groups.[96]

The resulting domestic confinement to which women became subject upon marriage effectively suppressed the musical activities of many of them, as we have already seen.[97] But the division between public and private life had still more far-reaching effects on other women who, even before marriage, were prohibited from receiving any musical instruction because it was thought to deflect them from concerns that were more appropriate for their intended roles as wives and mothers. Howard Brown cites the case of Elena Bembo, whose father forbade her to learn to play the clavichord because playing was "a thing for thoughtless and frivolous women" and would distract her from "other more laudable activities."[98]

In a treatise devoted to the education of noble girls published in 1555, the Venetian humanist Giovanni Michele Bruto voiced similar apprehensions regarding the study of music by girls. Although music, said Bruto, if used with laudable and good intentions, was not evil in itself but deserved a place among the other liberal arts, nevertheless, under the honest cover of virtue it opened the door to various vices. Therefore, girls ought to refrain altogether from the use of music.[99] In Bruto's view, the only proper subjects for a girl to study were those that prepared her for her principal vocation—"the government of her household and family."[100]

Although the statements of Bembo and Bruto slightly predate the period in which women composers emerged, various sources suggest that similar ideas persisted in influential circles at least through the end of the seventeenth century. Indeed, they received the official sanction of the Church. On 4 May 1686 Pope Innocent XI issued an edict which declared that "music is completely injurious to the modesty that is proper for the [female] sex, because they become distracted from the matters and occupations most proper for them." Therefore, "no unmarried woman, married woman, or widow of any rank, status, condition, even those who for reasons of education or anything else are living in convents or conservatories, under any pretext, even to learn music in order to practice it in those convents, may learn to sing from men, either laymen or clerics or regular clergy, no matter if they are in any way related to them, and to play any sort of musical instrument."[101] In 1703 Clement XI renewed Innocent XI's edict.[102]

How effective these papal edicts may have been, we do not know. It seems unlikely that they could have effectively stemmed the tide of girls and women studying music satirized by Cesti in a mid-seventeenth-century solo cantata: "Ladies, nuns, old maids, wives, widows, female relations, public women and private women, princesses and young noblewomen; I name no names; I merely point out that oh so many want elaborate material without being able to sing 'lanturlulu'."[103] Yet, since the attitudes the edicts represent persisted for at least a century and a half, the attitudes, if not the edicts, must have limited the musical study of some groups of girls and women, and by extension then must also have impeded the development of women composers.

Negative attitudes toward women's intellectual and creative potential also played a role in impeding women's musical activities. In the dedication of Madalena Casulana's first book of madrigals in 1568 to Isabella de' Medici Orsina, the duchess of Bracciano, the composer both expressed her modest estimate of the worth of her first works and described the disdain men had for women's creative potential:

I know truly, Most Illustrious and Excellent Signora, that these my first fruits, because of their weakness, cannot produce the effect that I would like, which would be not only to give you some testimony of my devotion but also to show the world (to the extent of my knowledge in the art of music) the vain error of men, who so much believe themselves to be the masters of the highest gifts of the intellect, that they think those gifts cannot be shared equally by women.[104]

Some three quarters of a century later, Barbara Strozzi indicated, in the dedication of her first book of madrigals to Vittoria della Rovere, the grand duchess of Tuscany, that she expected her works to be received with slander due to her lack of suitable modesty, as a woman, in publishing them.[105] Since it is unlikely that either Casulana or Strozzi would have expressed her fears to male patrons, we owe these patronesses thanks not only for the financial assistance they must have given the composers but also for permitting these documents, which tell us something about negative attitudes toward women's composing, to be written.

Such attitudes undoubtedly created an environment that was more hostile to women's creativity than to men's. Indeed, they may well have so influenced the self-concepts of some women that they never considered becoming serious composers.[106] I do not intend to suggest that all of women's compositional activities were treated scornfully. We know, for example, that certain works by Francesca Caccini were received with great approbation, and in Paris the compositions of Isabella Leonarda were so highly prized by the bibliophile, encyclopedist, and composer Sébastien de Brossard that he noted in the catalog of his collection of music: "All the works of this illustrious and incomparable Isabella Leonarda are so beautiful, so gracious, so brilliant and at the same time so knowledgeable and so wise, that my great regret is in not having them all."[107] Still, women composers had to contend with negative attitudes toward their work that men did not encounter. Their compositional achievements are bound to have suffered thereby.

Restrictions on Music-making in Convents

In the sacred sphere still other obstacles impeded women's opportunities to develop their musical and compositional abilities. One was the limited amount of time nuns had available for musical activities because of their obligations to perform spiritual duties and housekeeping tasks. But of greater importance were a series of rules and ordinances pertaining to music-making in convents that were promulgated by church officials beginning in the late sixteenth century. As decisions pertaining to nuns adopted by the Council of Trent were implemented and enforced by successive popes and local church officials, some convents were forced to restrict severely their cultivation of polyphonic music.

During the last session of the Council of Trent held in late 1563, the Fathers of the Council adopted certain measures pertaining to religious orders of women. Among other things, they declared that:

The Divine Office should be continued by them in high voice and not by professionals hired for that purpose, and they should answer in the Sacrifice of the Mass whatever the choir is accustomed to answer; but they will leave to the Deacon and Subdeacon the office of chanting the Lessons, Epistles, and Gospels. They will abstain from singing either in Choir or elsewhere the so-called "figured" chant [polyphonic music].[108]

The Fathers also declared themselves in favor of strict enclosure for nuns, and in some localities, bishops carried out this recommendation with great zeal, enforcing enclosure both on nuns under their jurisdiction and on those who had previously been exempt from their jurisdiction. They also placed severe limitations upon the entrance of outsiders into convent grounds.[109]

In 1599 Giovanni Fontana, the bishop of Ferrara, issued the *Constitutioni, et ordinationi generali appartenenti alle monache*, a substantial set of rules and ordinances regarding discipline in the convents of the city of Ferrara. The *Constitutioni* stated that all the rules concerning enclosure commanded by the Holy See were to be observed by both the convents directly under the bishop's authority and those that were subject to regular clergy, and that no nun was to leave her convent without the express license of the bishop, under threat of excommunication.[110] Ordinances directly pertaining to music declared that: (1) Only nuns were to sing the Divine Office; neither lay persons nor ecclesiastics were to assist them. In the principal solemnities of their church or in funeral rites, the nuns could be assisted by deacons and subdeacons in singing the mass, but in all other masses they must sing alone. (2) No one, not even a woman, was to be permitted to enter a convent to teach either *canto figurato* (polyphonic music) or *canto fermo* (plainsong) or to give instructions in playing any kind of musical instrument, even the organ, under penalty of fifty scudi. A nun who knew how to play the organ or was practiced in music, however, could teach other nuns, but she must not teach any instrument other than the organ.[111] (3) Nuns were not to play any instruments except the organ or harpsichord.[112]

When we recall that the musical ensemble at San Vito included many different kinds of instruments, we can immediately appreciate the drastic effect the rules restricting the use of instruments must have had upon it. Indeed, music of the sumptuousness described by Bottrigari and Artusi does not seem to have survived at San Vito beyond the date of Fontana's ordinances, and by 1621 the only instrumentalists who appear to have been active at San Vito were Olimpia Leoni, who played the tenor viola, and Raffaella Aleotti, who was said to be "without equal" in playing the organ.[113] The rules prohibiting music teachers from entering convents must also have contributed to the decline, for most nuns entered the convent at an early age, before they had been able to complete extensive musical educations, and the continuation of their training would thus have been limited by whatever instruction was available within the convent's walls. The enforcement of enclosure must also have had some impact on nuns' music-making, for in Ferrara in 1592 nuns from at least one convent—and three were noted at that time for their music, San Antonio, San Silvestro, and San Vito—[114] took part in *musiche solenni* at the Estense court.[115] It is not very surprising that no composers appear to have developed at San Vito or any other Ferrarese convent after the publication of Fontana's rules, for their enforcement would have removed nuns from contacts with musicians outside the convent, instruction that might have guided them in their work, and the stimulation to compose that might have come from the continued existence of a large and varied musical ensemble.[116]

In Milan, church officials also made vigorous attempts to restrict the study and practice of music in convents. On 31 January 1647 the monasterial vicar A. Rusca sent a notice to the *madres* of all Milanese convents charging them with restoring the complete observance of the *Regole della religione* and setting forth the following rules pertaining to music: (1) no one was to enter a convent for the purpose of teaching *canto figurato*; (2) no one was to teach the playing of any musical instrument, including the organ, in the parlors; and (3) nuns were not to play any instruments other than the organ or clavichord.[117]

But abuses of the regulations pertaining to music-making evidently took place, for on 30 October 1675 the vicar general of Milan, Andreas Abbate de Pilastria, sent out a notice stating that the introduction of singing and playing in the parlors and at the doors of convents in Milan had come to the attention of the archbishop. Wishing to deter such amusements, by which the sacred virgins were said to be distracted from enclosure and from applying themselves to the service of God, the archbishop commanded that no one—be they nuns, students, or other persons of either sex of any condition or degree, whether ecclesiastical or lay—sing or play, cause to be sung or played, or be present to listen to singing or playing anywhere except in the nuns' interior church during mass and vespers. Anyone who disobeyed the archbishop's orders was subject to excommunication, and any superior who allowed the orders to be disobeyed would be excommunicated ipso facto.[118]

Records of visitations made to Milanese convents to ascertain whether the rules and regulations that had been issued for their governance were being followed reveal attempts to regulate music-making in those institutions at an even earlier date. In 1622 the convent of Maria Annunciata, where Claudia Sessa had been famous as a singer, was visited by Athanasio da Napoli and Don Ascanio da Verona. After their investigation, these visitors issued a list of orders for "the destruction of vices and maintenance of virtue" at the convent. Two focused directly on music:

1. There was to be no singing or playing in church except in sung masses and in the divine offices of the principal feasts com-

manded by the Holy Church; they were not to take place at the request of or for the satisfaction of any person of whatsoever position or rank. If the Madre Abbess permitted such singing or playing, she would be suspended from her office for three months, and those who sang and played would be deprived of the veil and of singing and playing in perpetuity.

2. There was to be no singing or playing in the parlors or at the grates, either among the nuns or with other people from outside the convent, not even under the pretext of learning or teaching. If the Madre Abbess permitted these activities to take place, she would be suspended from her office, and those who sang or played would be deprived of the veil and of the privilege of the grates for three months.[119]

The Milanese convent of Santa Margarita was also visited right around the time Maria Cattarina Calegari seems to have been active there. Orders given after a pastoral visit in 1663 stated that, because of all the scandals and corruption of morals, it would be necessary to remove music from the convent altogether for at least three years, because otherwise it would be impossible as well as inconvenient to check the abuses.[120]

The convent of Santa Radegonda, where Cozzolani and Badalla resided, was also visited on a number of occasions during the years 1660–93. While the matters investigated were quite varied in nature—they included, for example, the presence of heretical beliefs, what the nuns wore, who celebrated the Mass, and how the novices and students were taught—some were specifically musical in nature. On various occasions the visitors forbade singing and playing in the parlors, in the guest quarters, and at the doorways without the permission of both the abbott and abbess; and in 1660 it was stated that if vespers were not finished by 11:00 P.M. on festive days, music was to be prohibited altogether.[121]

That Santa Radegonda long continued to be a thorn in the side of the Church in matters of music-making emerges from a document issued by Pope Benedict XIII on 19 September 1728 stating that although the nuns had professed adherence to an old regulation forbidding them to perform instrumental music and "figured chant," they had departed from this norm for some years, on feast days and on the more solemn occasions.

In such instances at Mass and at Vespers, they are accustomed to sing music of figured type, and to introduce, besides the organ, instruments of various types, which introduce secular melodies. Because of this practice, time is taken to learn this music, and whole days are taken away from prayer, to the detriment of the spiritual life of many of the nuns. . . . But the worst part of the whole thing is that those nuns who are skilled in the art of music spend much time with persons of the same city speaking about the art of music, and the techniques of the same. Their superiors have forbidden this but all exhortations to the contrary are ignored. . . .

. . . . Thus, in order that this abuse might be cut at the very roots . . . we set these rules concerning music. Never more, and at no time in the future may anyone for any reason, cause, or excuse make use of figured music, or dare to introduce musical instruments into the church and choir. Anyone who might do such a thing or dare to disobey this edict will suffer the punishment of interdict of the Church, under the disabilities and threats of excommunication *latae sententiae*. . . .[122]

It seems significant that the Milanese convent that most clearly violated the Church's rules regarding the performance of polyphonic music produced two known composers, one of whom wrote secular cantatas as well as sacred motets. Clearly, the cultivation of polyphonic music in Italian convents contributed in an important manner to the development of women composers. Yet the restrictions of music-making in convents that resulted from the Council of Trent must have checked that development to a significant degree. In those convents under the authority of strong and vigilant bishops, nuns would have had very limited access to musical instruction, different kinds of instruments, and new musical ideas and styles. Few incentives or opportunities for the composition of anything besides plainchant would have emerged. Thus, the measures taken by the Church to restrict nuns' study and practice of music must have been responsible in some measure for the limited oeuvre they produced.

How, finally, should we assess the activities and achievements of women in music-making in late-sixteenth- and seventeenth-century Italy? When we compare and contrast women's contributions with those of men, we find that they equalled men's only in the realm of amateur music-making and that in all other areas their contributions and even the advances they made over their former achievements were consistently smaller than those made by men. In sum, the achievements of women in music-making during this period, particularly in composing, seem to have been flawed. As Margaret L. King has pointed out for women humanists of an earlier period, the deficiency lay not so much in what women did in fact achieve, but in what they failed to achieve.[123] Only a few women continued to write music after their years of youth, and the remarkable accomplishments of Francesca Caccini, Barbara Strozzi, and Isabella Leonarda must be recognized as exceptional for their age.[124]

Yet, a new sort of climate did appear, and the emergence of more women composers than in any previous period in Western history was to have repercussions elsewhere. Still, it would take far more sweeping changes in society before the obstacles that stood in the way of women's creative work in music would be sufficiently reduced—albeit still far less than for men—to permit relatively large numbers of women to become serious composers who worked over a long period of time and produced a significant body of musical works.

NOTES

1. Joan Kelly-Gadol, "The Social Relation of the Sexes: Methodological Implications of Women's History," *Signs* 1 (1976): 812, 817.

2. See the appendix for a listing of all known publications by Italian women composers dating from this period.

3. For the titles of the works in which all of Casulana's known compositions appear, see the appendix to this essay. In Beatrice Pescerelli, *I madrigali di Maddalena Casulana*, Studi e testi per la storia della musica, 1 (Florence: Leo S. Olschki, 1979), Pescerelli points to the listing of two books of four-voiced spiritual madrigals by Casulana in a catalog of music available through the Venetian publisher Giacomo Vincenti, and she suggests that Casulana pursued her composing activities after 1586 with this new orientation (p. 20). Vincenti's catalog, however, indicates that these works were originally published by the firm of Girolamo Scotto, who had issued Casulana's two books of four-voiced secular madrigals in 1568 and 1570; since no other evidence points to Casulana's composition of spiritual madrigals, it seems likely that Vincenti simply erroneously labeled these books "spirituali." For the Vincenti catalog, see Geneviève Thibault, "Deux catalogues de libraires musicaux: Vincenti et Gardane (Venise, 1591)," *Revue de musicologie* 10 (1929): 177–83.

4. Since the motets by Assandra issued in 1609 were labeled Opus 2, they may have been preceded by an earlier work that has disappeared. Possibly the two motets by Assandra that were copied into an early seventeenth-century manuscript in German organ tablature (Regensburg, Fürstlich Thurn und Taxissche Hofbibliothek, F. K. Musik 22, II. Abteilung) came from such an earlier publication; see Eckart Tscheuschner, "Die Neresheimer Orgeltabulaturen der Fürstlich Thurn und Taxisschen Hofbibliothek zu Regensburg," Ph.D. diss., Erlangen, 1963, pp. 55–56, 107.

5. For a discussion of this publication, see Carolyn Raney, *Francesca Caccini, Musician to the Medici, and her "Primo Libro" (1618)* (Ann Arbor,

Mich.: University Microfilms, 1971); id., "Francesca Caccini's *Primo Libro,*" *Music and Letters* 48 (1967): 350–57.

6. An excellent discussion of Caccini's life and works is presented by Maria Giovanna Mascra, in "Una musicista fiorentina del seicento: Francesca Caccini," *La rassegna musicale* 14 (1941): 181–207, 237–44, and 15 (1942): 249–66. See also Doris Silbert, "Francesca Caccini, called La Cecchina," *Musical Quarterly* 32 (1946): 50–62; Carolyn Raney, *Francesca Caccini; Dizionario biografico degli italiani* (Rome: Istituto della Enciclopedia Italiana, 1973), s.v. "Francesca Caccini," 16:20; *The New Grove Dictionary of Music and Musicians* (1980), ed. Stanley Sadie, s.v. "Francesca Caccini," 3:581.

7. The aria *Dispietate guancie amare* (Florence, Biblioteca Nazionale, Magliabecchi Classe XIX, MS. 66, no. 107), and an "Egloga Pastorale Tirsi e Filli della Sig.ra Fra.ca Caccini" (Rome, Biblioteca Alessandrina, MS. 279, fols. 11r–69v) cited in *Dizionario biografico degli italiani,* s.v. "Francesca Caccini," 16:20.

8. See Donato Calvi, *Scena letteraria de gli scrittori bergamaschi. . . . Parte seconda* (Bergamo: Figliuoli di Marc' Antonio Rossi, 1664), p. 61.

9. Some manuscripts of Calegari's music that were supposed to have remained in the convent after her death were said to have been given out little by little and ultimately to have disappeared without trace. See Don Mariano Armellini, *Bibliotheca benedictino casinensis sive scriptorum casinensis congregationis alias S. Justinae Patavinae. . . . Pars Altera [II]* (Assisi: Andreae Sgariglia, 1732), pp. 93–94; Johann Simon Mayr, *Biografie di scrittori e artisti musicali bergamaschi nativi ad oriundi. Raccolte e pubblicate con note dal prof. Ab. Antonio Alessandri. . . . Con aggiunta degli scrittori musicali bergamaschi del p Vaerini, Biblioteca Musica Bononicnsis,* Sezione III, N. 29 (1875; reprint, Bologna: Forni, 1969), pp. 143–45.

10. On Strozzi, see also Ellen Rosand, "Barbara Strozzi, *virtuosissima cantatrice*: The Composer's Voice," *Journal of the American Musicological Society* 31 (1978): 241–81.

11. The complete dedication is printed in Claudio Sartori, *Bibliografia della musica strumentale italiana stampata in Italia fino al 1700* (Florence: Leo S. Olschki, 1952), pp. 432–33.

12. *O fronde care,* Paris, Bibliothèque nationale, Vm7 23; and *Vuò cercando quella speme,* London, British Library, Harley 1273, fols. 44r–45r.

13. See the dedication to this work printed in Gaetano Gaspari, comp., *Catalogo della biblioteca musicale G. B. Martini di Bologna,* ed. Napoleone Fanti et al, 4 vols. (1890–1905; reprint, Bologna: Forni, 1961), 2:469–70.

14. The oratorios were entitled *Il Martirio di S. Colomba, Li Giochi di Sansone, L'Esterre,* and *Cristo morto.* See Ugo Sesini, ed., *Catalogo della biblioteca del Liceo Musicale di Bologna,* vol. 5, *Libretti d'opera in musica* (Bologna: Cooperativa Tipografia Azzoguidi, 1943), 1:329.

15. See app., 1665?

16. According to the Atti di battesimo, libro 7, fol. 262v, in the Archivio

storico diocesano di Novara, fondo duomo, Anna Isabella, the daughter of Antonio Leonardi and Apolonia Sali, his wife, was born and baptised in Novara on 6 September 1620. According to a document in the private archives of the Leonardi family, Famiglia e feudo, I, no. 252A, Isabella died on 25 February 1704. I am indebted to Marchese Nicolò Leonardi for supplying me with a copy of the latter document as well as copies of other documents that pertain to Isabella Leonarda.

17. For further information about the works of Isabella Leonarda, see the excellent dissertation by Stewart Carter, *The Music of Isabella Leonarda (1620–1704)* (Ann Arbor, Mich.: University Microfilms, 1981).

18. *Dialoghi di Massimo Troiano: Ne' quali si narrano le cose piu notabili fatte nelle nozze dello illustriss. & eccell. prencipe Guglielmo VI. conte palatino del Reno, e duca di Baviera; e dell' illustriss. & eccell. madama Renata di Loreno* (Venice: Bolognino Zaltieri, 1569), fols. 123v–24v. I wish to thank Donatella Stocchi for her help with many of the translations in this article.

19. See Marco Minghetti, *Le donne italiane nelle belle arti al secolo XV e XVI* (Florence, 1877), p. 38; René Lenaerts, "Notes sur Adrien Willaert maître de chapelle de Saint Marc à Venise de 1527 à 1562," *Bulletin de l'Institute Historique Belge de Rome* 15 (1935): 112–13.

20. Giovanni Battista Spaccini, *Cronaca modenese (1588–1636)*, 2 vols., ed. G. Bertoni, T. Sandonnini, and P. E. Vicini, Monumenti di storia patria delle provincie modenesi, Serie delle cronache, 16–17 (Modena: Giovanni Ferraguti e C., 1911–19), 16:34.

21. Ibid.

22. A superscription to the motet *O virgo speciosa* in the Pisticcio collection reads, "Nella festivita di S. Cecilia—alla Molto Reverenda Madre Suor Cecilia Torniella Monacha di Santa Chiara Musicha Compositrice & Organista Celebre, nel Monastero del Giesù nella città d'Asti Patrona mia osservandissima." I am indebted to Keith Larson for supplying me with this information. The *status personalis* of Cellana is quoted in Graziano Sanvito, "Organi, organisti, organari della diocesi di Novara nel secolo XVII," *Novarien* 12 (1982): 135.

23. On fol. 25v the song *Lieta vivo et contenta* carries the heading "di Autore Incerto—idest Sᵗᵃ Isabella Medici," and Isabella's name also appears in an index of authors of music on a page attached to fol. IVv. Nevertheless, it is not clear whether the attribution to Isabella refers to the text of the song, the music, or both. See Carol MacClintock, ed., *The Bottegari Lutebook*, Wellesley Edition, 8 (Wellesley, Mass.: Wellesley College, 1965), table of contents and pp. 77–78, where a transcription of the song also appears. On fol. 5v the song *Per pianto la mia carne* carries the heading "Della Illusᵐᵃ et Eccᵐᵃ Sᵗᵃ Leonora Orsina Duchessa di Segni." While Leonora's name appears in an index of authors of music drawn up in recent times (fols. I–IV), it does not appear in the index on the page attached to fol. IVv, where it does, however, appear in a list of dedicatees of songs. Dr. Ernesto Milano (director of the Biblioteca Estense) to this author, 11 September 1978, states that it

cannot be ascertained whether the heading at the top of the page refers to an attribution or to a dedication; thus it is impossible to tell whether the song was written by Leonora or dedicated to her. Leonora's song appears in MacClintock, *Bottegari Lutebook*, pp. 16–17; it has also been transcribed in id., *The Solo Song* (New York: W. W. Norton, 1973), pp. 7–8.

24. Ernst Ludwig Gerber, *Historisch-biographisches Lexikon der Tonkünstler*, 2 vols. (Leipzig: J. G. I. Breitkopf, 1790–92), 1:98.

25. For a discussion of this question, see Rosand, "Barbara Strozzi," pp. 254–56.

26. The complete dedication is printed in Gaspari, *Catalogo*, 3:63.

27. Federico Ghisi, "Ballet Entertainments in the Pitti Palace, 1608–25," *Musical Quarterly* 35 (1949): 426. See also Alois M. Nagler, *Theater Festivals of the Medici, 1539–1637* (New Haven: Yale University Press, 1964), pp. 116–18; Robert Lamar Weaver and Norma Wright Weaver, *A Chronology of Music in the Florentine Theater 1590–1750: Operas, Prologues, Finales, Intermezzos, and Plays with Incidental Music*, Detroit Studies in Music Bibliography, 38 (Detroit: Information Coordinators, 1978), pp. 94, 97.

28. Bologna, Civico Museo Bibliografico Musicale, Q49, and Prague, Národní Muzeum, Hudebni Oddělení, II La 2; see esp. Paul Nettl, "Über ein handschriftliches Sammelwerk von Gesängen italienischer Frühmonodie," *Zeitschrift für Musikwissenschaft* 2 (1919–20): 85, 87, 90, 92; Nigel Fortune, "A Florentine Manuscript and Its Place in Italian Song," *Acta Musicologica* 23 (1951): 126, 130–33; *New Grove Dictionary*, s.v. "Settimia Caccini," 3:581. One of Settimia's works, *Già sperami*, is printed in Robert Haas, *Die Musik des Barocks*, Handbuch der Musikwissenschaft, ed. Ernst Bücken (Wildpark-Potsdam: Akademische Verlagsgesellschaft Athenaion, 1928), p. 49.

29. Rosand, "Barbara Strozzi," p. 254.

30. Walter H. Bishop, trans., "Maugar's *Response faite à un curieux sur le sentiment de la musique d'Italie*," *Journal of the Viola da Gamba Society of America* 7 (1971): 13.

31. John Evelyn, *Diary and Correspondence of John Evelyn, F.R.S. . . . ,* ed. William Bray, rev. ed., 4 vols. (London: Henry Colburn, 1850–52), 1:215.

32. See Alessandro Ademollo, *I teatri di Roma nel secolo decimosettimo* (Rome: L. Pasqualucci, 1888), pp. 155–57, who quotes from the *Avvisi* of Tommaso Tomasi: "Rome 5 febbraio 1678. Giovedì sera fu recitata l'opera in musica della Baronessa cantata da diversi Cavalieri," and "12 detto. La Regina di Svezia è intervenuta due volte con alcuni signori Cardinali e Prelati alla Commedia di Antonio Maissì. . . . Si è recitata più volte questa settimana quella della Baronessa."

33. See chap. 5 above, and Anthony Newcomb, *The Madrigal at Ferrara, 1579–1597*, 2 vols. (Princeton: Princeton University Press, 1980). Sixteenth-century Italian women musicians are also discussed by Carl Gustav Anthon, in "Music and Musicians in Northern Italy during the Sixteenth Century" (Ph.D. diss., Harvard University, 1943), chap. 3, pp. 60–79. For an early sixteenth-century singer and actress not cited by either of these authors,

Barbara Salutati, see Wolfgang Osthoff, *Theatergesang und darstellende Musik in der italienischen Renaissance, 15. und 16. Jahrhunderts*, 2 vols. (Tutzing: Hans Schneider, 1969), 1:219–22.

34. Vincenzo Giustiniani, *Discorso sopra la musica*, trans. Carol Mac-Clintock, Musicological Studies and Documents, 9 (n.p.: American Institute of Musicology, 1962), pp. 70–71.

35. See C. Lozzi, "La musica e specialmente il melodramma alla corte medicea," *Rivista musicale italiana* 9 (1902): 314; Masera, "Una musicista fiorentina," pp. 188–89, for the date of the documents cited by Lozzi. See also Frederick Hammond, "Musicians at the Medici Court in the Mid-seventeenth Century," *Analecta Musicologica* 14 (1974): 154, 157, 159, 167, for information about Archilei's salary. For further information about Archilei's career, see Alessandro Ademollo, *La bell' Adriana, ed altre virtuose del suo tempo alla corte di Mantova* (Città di Castello: S. Lapi, 1888), pp. 137–42; Emil Vogel, *Bibliothek der gedruckten weltlichen Vocalmusik Italiens. Aus den Jahren 1500–1700*, 2 vols. (Berlin: A. Haack, 1892), 1:330, 383–85, and 2:122; Angelo Solerti, *Le origini del melodramma* (Torino: Fratelli Bocca, 1903), pp. 51, 109–10, 137, 164; id., *Musica, ballo e drammatica alla corte medicea dal 1600 al 1637* (Florence: R. Bemporad & Figlio, 1905), passim; Nigel Fortune, "Italian 17th-Century Singing," *Music and Letters* 35 (1954): 209–10, 213; *Enciclopedia dello spettacolo* (1954), s.v. "Vittoria Archilei," vol. 1, cols. 789–90; Claude Palisca, "Musical Asides in the Diplomatic Correspondence of Emilio De' Cavalieri," *Musical Quarterly* 49 (1963): 345–46; Nagler, *Theater Festivals*, pp. 76–77, 87, 89, 95, 116–17; Newcomb, *Madrigal at Ferrara*, 1:90–93; *New Grove Dictionary*, s.v. "Vittoria Archilei," 1:551–52.

36. Rosand, "Barbara Strozzi," p. 254.

37. The principal source on Adriana Basile is Ademollo, *La bell' Adriana*. See also *Enciclopedia dello spettacolo*, s.v. "Adriana Basile," vol. 2, cols. 11–12; *New Grove Dictionary*, s.v. "Andreana Basile," 2:238.

38. On Leonora Baroni, see Alessandro Ademollo, *I primi fasti della musica italiana a Parigi (1645–1662)* (Milan: R. Stabilimento Musicale Ricordi, n.d.), pp. 7–15; id., *La Leonora di Milton e di Clemente IX* (Milan: R. Stabilimento Musicale Ricordi, [1885]); id., *La bell' Adriana*, pp. 315–18; Solerti, *Le origini del melodramma*, p. 164; Romain Rolland, "Le Premier Opéra joué à Paris: 'L'Orfeo' de Luigi Rossi," *Musiciens d'autrefois* (Paris: Librairie Hachette, 1908), pp. 57–59; Henry Prunières, *L'Opéra italien en France avant Lulli* (Paris: Librairie Ancienne Honoré Champion, 1913), pp. 40–42, 51–55, and passim; *Enciclopedia dello spettacolo*, s.v. "Leonora Baroni," vol. 1, cols. 1544–46; *New Grove Dictionary*, s.v. "Leonora Baroni," 2:171–72.

39. For Francesca Caccini's life, see the sources mentioned in nn. 5 and 6 above as well as Solerti, *Musica, ballo e drammatica*, passim. See Michelangelo Buonarroti, *Descrizione delle felicissime nozze della cretianissima maestà di madama Maria Medici regina di Francia e di Navarra* (Florence: Giorgio Marescotti, 1600), [fol. 22v,] for the earliest performance—

that of Giulio Caccini's *Rapimento di Cefalo*, in which Francesca is known to have taken part, along with other members of the family—"un suo figliuolo, e . . . quattro donne di sua famiglia di voce angeliche." For Francesca's wedding date, see Raney, "Francesca Caccini's *Primo libro*," p. 352; for her salary in 1623–24, see id., *Francesca Caccini*, pp. 61–62.

40. Masera, "Una musicista fiorentina," p. 250.

41. Ghisi, "Ballet Entertainments," p. 426.

42. In Angelo Grillo to Francesca Caccini, n.d., which was published among the poet's letters in 1612, Grillo states that he had sent Caccini some religious madrigals to set to music; see Silbert, "Francesca Caccini," p. 56.

43. Masera, "Una musicista fiorentina," pp. 197–98. See also id., "Alcune lettere inedite di Francesca Caccini," *La rassegna musicale* 13 (1940): 175–78. One of these letters appears in an English translation in Carol Neuls-Bates, ed., *Women in Music: An Anthology of Source Readings from the Middle Ages to the Present* (New York: Harper & Row, 1982), pp. 56, 60.

44. See Masera, "Una musicista fiorentina," p. 198; id., "Lettere di Francesca Caccini," pp. 175–78; Solerti, *Musica, ballo e drammatica*, pp. 151–55.

45. Masera, "Una musicista fiorentina," p. 203. Cicognini's testimony reads, "e per lodarle [Caccini's music] basti solo l'aver nominato chi ne fu il compositore, che come donna eminente e singolare ormai dal mondo per tale è conosciuta e ammirata."

46. Ibid., pp. 239–40.

47. See Maria Giovanna Masera, *Michelangelo Buonarroti il giovane* (Torino: R. Università di Torino, 1941), p. 97, for a letter attesting to Caccini's admiration for her father.

48. Francesca Caccini's younger sister Settimia (1591–c.1638?), an outstanding singer who held positions in Florence, Mantua, Lucca, and Parma, is another example. On Settimia's career, see *Descrizione delle feste fatte in Firenze per le reali nozze de Serenissimi sposi Ferdinando II. Gran Duca di Toscana, e Vittoria Principessa d'Urbino* (Florence: Zanobi Pignoni, 1637), p. 34; Paolo Emilio Ferrari, *Spettacoli drammatico musicali e coreografici in Parma dell' anno 1628 all' anno 1883* (Parma: Luigi Battei, 1884), p. 9; Ademollo, *La bell' Adriana*, pp. 72–79; Solerti, *Le origini del melodramma*, pp. 136–37; N. Pelicelli, "Musicisti in Parma nel secolo XVII," *Note d'archivio per la storia musicale* 10 (1933): 238; Masera, "Una musicista fiorentina," pp. 195–97, 240; Silbert, "Francesca Caccini," p. 55; Nagler, *Theater Festivals*, pp. 116–17, 154, 161, 173; *New Grove Dictionary*, s.v. "Settimia Caccini," 3:581. A further composer who may also have been a singer was Francesca Campana Romana, whose *Arie* were published in 1629: it is possible that she was one of "le Campane" who were said by della Valle to be famous singers in Rome around 1640. See Solerti, *Le origini del melodramma*, p. 165.

49. In 1608 Jacopo Peri wrote to the duchess of Mantua about a little girl whom he was having trained as a singer for the court; her training included reading in all the keys, singing from notation, and singing with and

playing on a keyboard instrument; see Ademollo, *La bell' Adriana*, p. 82. By way of contrast, a young male singer in the Cappella Giulia at St. Peter's under Virgilio Mazzocchi in the 1630s was obliged to spend an hour singing difficult and tiring things, an hour practicing trills, an hour practicing *passaggi*, an hour studying letters, an hour being trained in and practicing singing within the hearing of a teacher and in front of a mirror, a half-hour studying theory, a half-hour improvising counterpoint on a cantus firmus, an hour writing counterpoint *sopra la Cartella*, and the remainder of the day practicing the harpsichord and composition; see *Die Musik in Geschichte und Gegenwart*, vol. 11 (1963), col. 717, s.v. "Rom," where Giovanni Angelini Bontempi's *Historia musica* of 1695 is quoted.

50. The increased performance of polyphony in convents depended in part upon a large influx of girls from well-to-do families, some of whom had already acquired considerable musical training before entering the convent. The reasons for this influx were primarily economic and political. Dowries paid to convents were much lower than those required for suitable marriages, and families no longer needed to concern themselves with the economic requirements of their daughters once they had entered convents. By choosing a religious life for their daughters, wealthy families were able to protect the familiar patrimony and to safeguard their positions of economic and political preeminence. Convents thus became numerous and well populated. Some, though by no means all, were well off financially and had large landholdings from which they derived considerable income, or they received a certain degree of financial support from princes and potentates. For information relevant to the economic and political reasons women entered convents, see Mario Fanti, *Abiti e lavori delle monache di Bologna in una serie di disegni del secolo XVIII* (Bologna: Tamari, 1972), pp. 8–10; M. Giovanna Cambria, *Il monastero domenicano di S. Agnese in Bologna: Storia e documenti* (Bologna: Tipografia SAB, 1975), pp. 18–19; Patricia H. Labalme, "Women's Roles in Early Modern Venice: An Exceptional Case," in *Beyond Their Sex: Learned Women of the European Past*, ed. Patricia H. Labalme (New York: New York University Press, 1980), pp. 137, 148n.

51. Paolo Morigia, *La nobilità di Milano* (Milan: Pacifico Pontio, 1595), pp. 186–87.

52. Antonio Campi, *Cremona fedelissima citta et nobilissima colonia de romani* (Cremona: Auttore, 1585), Libro Terzo, p. 1. Campi calls Somenza a "Cremonese sacred virgin" and says that she was the daughter of the senator Agostino Somenzo, who was on the Secret Council of Francesco Sforza, duke of Milan. According to Luigi Lucchini, in *Cenni storici sui più celebri musicisti cremonesi* (Casalmaggiore: Contini Carlo, 1887), p. 7, Somenza was also a composer, but his assertion seems to be based on an erroneous interpretation of Campi. Lucchini gives Somenza's death date as 12 April 1609, following the registers of the convent.

53. Hercole Bottrigari, *Il Desiderio; or, Concerning the Playing Together of Various Musical Instruments*, trans. Carol MacClintock, Musicological Studies and Documents, 9 (American Institute of Musicology,

1962), pp. 58–60. The musicians mentioned in the quoted text are Ippolito Fiorino, the chapel master of Duke Alfonso d'Este, and Luzzasco Luzzascho, organist, composer, and leader of the concerted music at the Estense court. See also Neuls-Bates, *Women in Music*, pp. 43–49.

54. Giovanni Maria Artusi, *L'Artusi, overo delle imperfettioni della moderna musica* (Venice: Giacomo Vincenti, 1600), fols. 1v–4v.

55. Marcantonio Guarini, *Compendio historico dell' origine, accrescimento, e prerogative delle chiese, e luoghi pii della città, e diocesi di Ferrara* (Ferrara: Heredi di Vittorio Baldini, 1621), pp. 375–76. A further source of information about the music at San Vito is Gasparo Sardi, *Libro delle historie ferraresi del sig. Gasparo Sardi. Con una nuova aggiunta del medesimo Autore. Aggiuntivi di più quattro libri del Sig. Dottore Faustini* (Ferrara: Giuseppe Gironi, 1646), pp. 88–89 and 179–80.

56. Girolamo Borsieri, *Il supplimento della nobiltà di Milano raccolto da Girolamo Borsieri* (Milan: Giovanni Battista Bidelli, 1619), pp. 51–54.

57. For convents in Rome, see Solerti, *Le origini del melodramma*, p. 166, and Richard Lassels, *An Italian Voyage; or, A Compleat Journey through Italy*, 2d ed. (London: Richard Wellington & B. Barnard Lintott, 1697), p. 150; for convents in Venice, see Denis Arnold, "Music at the Scuola di San Rocco," *Music and Letters* 40 (1959): 229, and Francesco Sansovino, *Venetia citta nobilissima, et singolare con le aggiunte di Giustiniano Martinioni* (Venice: Steffano Curti, 1663), p. 90; for convents in Bologna, see Lodovico Frati, *La vita privata di Bologna dal secolo XIII al XVII* (Bologna: Ditta Nicola Zanichelli, 1900), pp. 98–99, and Giulio Cesare Arresti, *Messe a tre voci*, op. 2, which was dedicated to a nun musician, Giulia Maria Vittoria Malvezzi, at Santa Maria Nuova in Bologna (the dedication is printed in Gaspari, *Catalogo*, 2:24); and for convents in Lucca, see Luigi Nerici, "Storia della musica in Lucca," *Memorie e documenti per servire alla storia di Lucca* 12 (1880): 100–101.

58. Filippo Picinelli, *Ateneo dei letterati milanesi* (Milan: Francesco Vigone, 1670), p. 147; Carlo Torre, *Il ritratto di Milano* (Milan: Federico Agnelli, 1674), p. 360; and Serviliano Latuada, *Descrizione di Milano*, 5 vols. (Milan: Giuseppe Cairoli, 1737–38), 1:150. See also pp. 144–45 below.

59. Donato Calvi, *Scena letteraria*, p. 61.

60. On Peruchona, however, see Sanvito, "Organi, organisti, organari della diocesi di Novara," pp. 136–38, where she is said to have been an esteemed singer and excellent "maestra di musica." For some recently published information on music in Leonarda's convent, see Emilia Dahnk Baroffio, "Ricerche sulla musica sacra nel Novarese," *Novarien* 12 (1982): 257–60; id., "La Compositrice Isabella Leonarda," ibid., 13 (1983): 75–92. In 1658 eleven nuns were said to sing very well and two fairly well. For Leonarda's praise of the two collegio singers, see in her Opus 13 the dedications of *O cor humanum* and *Paremus nos fideles* to Chiara Margarita Gattica and Flaminia Morbida.

61. For the most comprehensive account of Leonarda's family as well as of Leonarda herself, see Baroffio, "La Compositrice Isabella Leonarda."

62. Dedication to the Sonate à 1. 2. 3. e 4. istromenti . . . , op. 16: "Beatissima Vergine. . . . In queste mie fatiche io non hebbi altro fine, che d'honorare il vostro Figlio, e Voi. . . . Protesto ò Santissima Madre, ch'io non dò alle Stampe queste Musiche per accreditarmi al Mondo, mà acciò da tutti si sappia esser io vostra Divota. Non vi sdegnate ò gran Regina, se mi usurpo di dire, che son troppo interessata ne' Vostri honori. Con questi miei concerti penso dar motivo à Vostri divoti di moltiplicar le Vostre glorie. Se queste Musiche non piaceranno al Mondo, me basterà che piaccino a Voi, che più dell' ingegno gradite il cuore."

63. For a general overview of music education, see *Die Musik in Geschichte und Gegenwart*, vol. 9 (1961), cols. 1105–20, s.v. "Musikerziehung. A. Geschichte der Musikerziehung bis um 1800." For fifteenth-century Italian composers, see the beginning of chapter 4 above.

64. Anthon, "Music and Musicians," p. 65.

65. For the complete dedication, see Gaspari, *Catalogo*, 3:19.

66. For the complete dedication, see ibid., 4:38–39.

67. Title-page of Assandra's publication of 1609.

68. In an annotated copy of Pompeo Scipione Dolfi, *Cronologia delle famiglie nobili di Bologna* (Bologna: Gio. Battista Ferroni, 1670), at the Biblioteca Comunale dell' Archiginnasio, Bologna, a marginal note next to the name of Giacomo Bovi reads: "He had a bastard daughter named Laura whom he married to Giacomo Basenghi in the year 1592" (p. 221). In a family tree of the Bovio family at the Archivio di Stato, Bologna (MS Gozz. 73–16), "Giacomo, Primicerio di S. Petronio," is shown to have had two children—"Giulio Francesco Mantichelli Bovio. Spurio [illegitimate]. Cavaliere di S. Steffano," and "Laura naturall."

69. On Bovia, see Canal, "Della musica in Mantova," pp. 700–701; Anthon, "Music and Musicians," pp. 77–78; Newcomb, *Madrigal at Ferrara*, 1:90–93, 98–99; Iain Fenlon, *Music and Patronage in Sixteenth-Century Mantua* (Cambridge: Cambridge University Press, 1980), 1:134–35, 196.

70. Newcomb, *Madrigal at Ferrara*, 1:92.

71. See n. 68 above.

72. See the dedication of Strozzi's opus 2, *Cantate, ariette, e duetti* (1651), published in Lorenzo Bianconi, "Weitere Ergänzungen zu Emil Vogels 'Bibliothek der gedruckten weltlichen Vokalmusik italiens, aus den Jahren 1500–1700' aus italienischen Bibliotheken," *Analecta musicologica* 7 (1970): 185.

73. For fuller information on Strozzi's upbringing, see chap. 7 below.

74. The fact that Chiara Margarita Cozzolani, Bianca Maria Meda, and Cesarini Ricci di Tingoli were referred to as "Donna" or "Madonna" on the title-pages of their works may suggest some slightly elevated origins for them as well, but this is far from certain. And while the anonymous letter referred to above (see p. 122) calls Adriana Basile a "Gentildonna Napoletana" (see Ademollo, *La bell' Adriana*, p. 174), her origins and those of her family are virtually unknown, according to Ademollo and to *New Grove Dictionary*, s.v. "Andreana Basile," 2:238.

75. Sulpizia Cesis was the daughter of a count, according to Spaccini, *Cronaca modenese*, 16 : 34. The noble Leonardi family is still in existence, and Isabella's father was also a "Dottor di Legge Collegiato," according to her younger sister Orsola Margarita's baptism record (Archivio storico diocesano di Novara, Fondo duomo, Atti di battesimo, libro 8, p. 247). Prioli was designated a "nobile veneta" (noblewoman of Venetia) on the title-page of her *Balletti et correnti*. Sessa's biography appeared in Borsieri, *Supplimento della nobiltà di Milano*.

76. Particularly Pompeo Litta, *Famiglie celebri italiane*, 11 vols. (Milan: Giusti, 1819–85?), vol. 11, for the Rusca family; and the Vizana family archives in the Archivio di Stato, Bologna.

77. According to Nestore Pelicelli, "Musicisti in Parma nei secoli XV–XVI," *Note d'archivio per la storia musicale* 9 (1932): 126–27, Giovanni Battista Massarenghi cultivated Greek letters, studied law at the Collegio Borromeo at Pavia under the protection of Duke Ranuccio, published both poetry and music, and was on his way to serve at the Court of Rome when he was robbed and murdered.

78. "Hae igitur sunt Sacrae Cantiones, nonnullae à me (cum à divinis vacarem) & nonnullae ab Hercule Pasquino in hac scientia praeceptore meo compositae."

There is still some confusion surrounding the identities of Raffaella and Vittoria Aleotti. Giambattista Aleotti's will in the Archivio di Stato in Ferrara (Archivio notarile antico di Ferrara, Notaio Mainardo Guarini, Matricola 852, Pacco 23, Anno 1631, fols. 217–22) mentions only four daughters—Raffaella, Cinthia, Beatrice, and Arnanda—although his dedication of Vittoria's *Ghirlanda* states that he had five. Luigi Napoleone Cittadella, in "Memorie intorno alla vita ed alle opere dell' architetto Giambattista Aleotti Argentano," published in *Dell' interrimento del Po di Ferrara . . . discorso inedito di Giambattista Aleotti Argentano* (Ferrara: Domenico Taddei, [1847]), pp. 5–57, gives the same four names (with minor spelling differences) as well as that of a Valeria who was a nun at San Vito and died in 1625, six years before Giambattista's will was made. It seems likely that Valeria and Vittoria were the same person, although I have not been able to check the archival document to which Cittadella ascribes Valeria's death date. According to Cittadella, Beatrice also entered the convent of San Vito, but since her father's will states that she was the widow of Orazio Nigrelli, she must not have remained a nun. Both Cinthia and Arnanda married.

Since Giambattista states in the *Ghirlanda* dedication that his eldest daughter had a natural instinct for serving God, the first daughter must have been either Beatrice or Raffaella. But it is not clear in the phrase, "my second daughter and her sister who was called Vittoria," whether the second daughter was Vittoria or another daughter in between the eldest and Vittoria in age. I think it likely that both Beatrice and Raffaella were older than Vittoria, Raffaella because the dedication of her *Sacrae cantiones* does not hint at her youthfulness as her father's *Ghirlanda* dedication in the same year hints at Vittoria's. Since Beatrice, according to Cittadella, was born in 1574 and by 1588, at age fourteen, had become a nun at San Vito, she too must have been older than Vittoria, because if she were younger, in 1593 when Vittoria's madrigals were published Vittoria would no longer have been as young as their dedication hints. I think it thus likely that the "sister who was called Vittoria" was the third Aleotti daughter who received musical training. I am grateful to Richard Shindle for suggesting that the second daughter and Vittoria were two different people.

Although the matter is certainly confusing, it seems clear that Raffaella and Vittoria were not the same person, as various writers have proposed. In the first place, both the *Sacrae cantiones* and the *Ghirlanda de madrigali* came out in 1593, and it is unlikely that the same person would have had works published under two different names in the same year. In the second place, Giambattista says that Vittoria entrusted the dedication of her madrigals to him since she no longer cared about worldly things, but Raffaella took on herself the responsibility for writing the dedication of her *Sacrae cantiones.*

Raffaella Aleotti probably died shortly after 2 August 1640, since her name last appears in a document pertaining to the convent of San Vito on that date (Curia Arcivescovile di Ferrara, Archivio Residui Beni Ecclesiastici e Congregazioni Soppresse, Fondo S. Vito, Mazzo FF, no. 66); I am deeply indebted to Maestro Adriano Franceschini for supplying me with information about Raffaella Aleotti found in convent documents. Even though Sardi, *Historia ferraresi,* p. 89, states that Aleotti was still living around 1646, though she was very old at the time, the absence of her name from convent documents for so long a period suggests that he erred in this regard.

79. Spaccini, *Cronaca modenese,* 16:34.

80. Marcello Oretti, "Notizie de professori del dissegno cioè pittori scultori ed' architetti bolognesi," vol. 9, p. 22 (Bologna, Biblioteca Comunale dell' Archiginnasio, MS n. B.131).

81. On the latter point, see Ruth Kelso, *Doctrine for the Lady of the Renaissance* (Urbana: University of Illinois Press, 1956), p. 78 and passim. See also Margaret L. King, "Book-Lined Cells: Women and Humanism in the Early Italian Renaissance," in *Beyond Their Sex,* ed. Labalme, pp. 68–69, 85n, who argues that young women, after a period of freedom during adolescence, eventually confronted a choice between two futures: marriage and full participation in social life on the one hand; or abstention from marriage and withdrawal from the world, either to a convent or to a self-imposed solitude at home on the other hand. She cites Giovanni Caldiera as defining the following different conditions of women—virgins destined for marriage, married women, widows, nuns, servants (slaves), and prostitutes—and summarizes, "Since maidens and widows would pass through the condition of matrimony at some time or would already have done so, respectable women, neither servants nor prostitutes, were seen to have only two choices: marriage and the convent."

82. For the poets, see esp. Giuseppe Toffanin, "Petrarchiste del Cinquecento," *Annali della Cattedra Petrarchesca* 8 (1938): 43–66; Ettore Bonora, "Le donne poetesse," in *Storia della letteratura italiana,* 9 vols., ed. Emilio Cecchi and Natalino Sapegno (Milan: Garzanti, 1965–69), vol. 4, *Il Cinquecento* (1965), pp. 241–58. For the artists, see esp. Ann Sutherland Harris and Linda Nochlin, *Women Artists: 1550–1950* (Los Angeles County Museum of Art, 1976), pp. 26–32, 106–8, 111–14, 118–23; Germaine Greer, *The Obstacle Race: The Fortunes of Women Painters and Their Work* (New York: Farrar, Straus & Giroux, 1979), pp. 180–85, 189–214.

83. For an overview of this debate, see Kelso, *Lady of the Renaissance,* chap. 2, pp. 5–37. A helpful analysis of the social groups to which the differing ideas about women correspond is offered by Joan Kelly-Gadol, "Did Women Have a Renaissance?," in *Becoming Visible: Women in European History,* ed. Renate Bridenthal and Claudia Koonz (Boston: Houghton Mifflin, 1977), p. 140. Other useful sources include Joan Kelly, "Early Feminist Theory and the *Querelle des Femmes,* 1400–1789," *Signs* 8 (1982): 4–28; G. Battista Marchesi, "Le polemiche sul sesso femminile ne' secoli XVI e XVII," *Giornale storico della letteratura italiana* 25 (1895): 362–69; Ellen Rosand, "Barbara Strozzi," pp. 247–52 (for a discussion of Venetian feminism and antifeminism); Emilio Zanette, *Suor Arcangela, monaca del Seicento veneziano* (Florence: Leo Olschki, 1961), esp. chap. 6, pp. 211–37. The last source focuses on the feminist writings of Arcangela Tarabotti, a Venetian Benedictine nun, as well as those of two of her predecessors, Modesta da Pozzo and Lucrezia Marinelli.

84. On women who accompanied their own singing, see chap. 5 above. Newcomb, *Madrigal at Ferrara,* 1:102, 184, mentions a Giulia Avogadri, a musician maintained by the duchess of Urbino in the 1590s, who was described as a player of the viola bastarda. But Avogadri, like most women musicians employed by courts during this period, probably both sang and played in the duchess's chamber music, rather than functioning exclusively as an instrumentalist. Id., "Girolamo Frescobaldi, 1608–1615: A Documentary Study . . . ," *Annales musicologiques* 7 (1964–77): 111–58, also describes a Neapolitan lady who played the harp and was given a rather large salary plus other advantages when she entered the service of the Marchese Bentivoglio in Rome in February 1609. She quickly established an excellent reputation: in December 1609 Cardinal Montalto is said to have stated that he was willing to fast in order to hear her play. It seems that the Neapolitan lady, who is never named, was being trained as a musician in the Bentivoglio household, since various letters suggest that she was receiving musical instruction; Frescobaldi was among her teachers, although what he taught her is not specified. No information about her activities after June 1610 has so far come to light.

85. On the papal bans, see Alessandro Ademollo, *I teatri di Roma,* pp. xvi–xxvii, 136–39; *Musik in Geschichte und Gegenwart,* 11:716, s.v. "Rom"; Franz Haböck, *Die Kastraten und ihre Gesangskunst* (Stuttgart:

Deutsche Verlags-Anstalt, 1927), p. 223; Rudolf Ewerhart, "Die Händel-Handschriften der Santini-Bibliothek in Münster," *Händel-Jahrbuch*, 1960, p. 121; id., "New Sources for Handel's 'La Resurrezione,'" *Music and Letters* 41 (1960): 128.

86. Simon Towneley Worsthorne, "Some Early Venetian Opera Productions," *Music and Letters* 30 (1949): 146–52; id., *Venetian Opera in the Seventeenth Century* (Oxford: Clarendon Press, 1954), app. 4, pp. 170–75.

87. Giovanni Mantese, *Storia musicale vicentina* (Vicenza: Istituto S. Gaetano, 1956), p. 32. See also Fenlon, *Music and Patronage*, 1 : 128, 195.

88. Mantese, *Storia musicale vicentina*, p. 34; Anthon, "Music and Musicians," pp. 92–93, 332; Canal, "Della musica in Mantova," pp. 722–23.

89. See Alberto Gallo, *La prima rappresentazione al Teatro Olimpico* (Milan: Edizioni Il Polifilo, 1973), p. 35; Leo Schrade, *La Représentation d'Oepido tiranno au Teatro Olimpico* (Paris: CNRS, 1960), p. 50; Antonio Magrini, *Il Teatro Olimpico* (Padua: Coi tipi del Seminario, 1847), p. 64.

90. Fenlon argues in *Music and Patronage* that a document listing the Pellizzaris, which is dated 1591, actually must date from the early years of the seventeenth century (see app. 2, doc. 64, and pp. 192–93n, on the dating of this document). On the dating of Mantuan pay lists, see also Jessie Ann Owens's review of the Fenlon book in *Journal of the American Musicological Society* 25 (1982): 340–41; Susan Parisi, "The Social and Musical Role of the Virtuoso Performers at the Court of Mantua, 1587–1627: An Archival Study" (Ph.D. diss., University of Illinois, forthcoming). Further information about the Pellizzaris appears in Fenlon, pp. 127–28, 132.

91. Denis Arnold, "*L'Incoronazione di Poppea* and its Orchestral Requirements," *Musical Times* 104 (1963): 177.

92. For information about town musicians in sixteenth-century Italy, see Anthon, "Music and Musicians," chap. 9, pp. 233–52; id., "Some Aspects of the Social Status of Italian Musicians during the Sixteenth Century—II," *Journal of Renaissance and Baroque Music* 1 (1946): 222–34. A full study of Italian women instrumentalists during the period in question would have to include those who studied and performed in the Venetian *Ospedali* or conservatories. Among the many sources pertinent to this subject, see esp. Denis Arnold, "Orphans and Ladies: The Venetian Conservatories (1680–1790)," *Proceedings of the Royal Musical Association*, 89th Session [1962/63], pp. 31–48; id., "Instruments and Instrumental Teaching in the Early Italian Conservatories," *Galpin Society Journal* 18 [1965]: 72–81. See also Eleanor Selfridge-Field, *Venetian Instrumental Music from Gabrieli to Vivaldi* (Oxford: Blackwell, 1975), pp. 42–47; Gastone Vio, "Precisazioni sui documenti della Pietà in relazione alle 'figlie del coro'," in *Vivaldi: Veneziano europeo*, ed. Francesco Degrada (Florence: Leo S. Olschki, 1980), pp. 101–22; M. V. Constable, "The *Figlie del Coro*: Fiction and Fact," *Journal of European Studies* 11 (1981): 111–39. But although some of these instrumentalists seem to have earned their keep by practicing, performing, and teaching music to other girls and, thus, to some extent might be considered professional musicians even though they were bound to

their institutions and led sequestered lives, they certainly functioned out-side the mainstream of institutional musical life in Italy. During the seven-teenth century, moreover, none is known to have gone on to a musical career outside the conservatory or to have become a composer.

During the eighteenth century, however, at least one composer emerged from the conservatory of the Mendicanti—Maddalena Sirmen, who also went on to study violin with Tartini and to concertize in the major capitols of Europe. See Marion M. Scott, "Maddalena Lombardini, Madame Syrmen," *Music and Letters* 14 (1933): 149–63; Jane Berdes's book-length manu-script (currently untitled and being revised) on the life, times, and works of Lombardini-Sirmen, which also includes information about the Venetian conservatories.

93. According to the brief biographies of oratorio composers included by Howard E. Smither in *A History of the Oratorio,* vol. 1, *The Oratorio in the Baroque Era, Italy, Vienna, Paris* (Chapel Hill: University of North Carolina Press, 1977).

94. Ursula Kirkendale, "The Ruspoli Documents on Handel," *Journal of the American Musicological Society* 20 (1967): 236–37, mentions a papal admonition issued to Prince Francesco Maria Ruspoli in 1708 for having em-ployed a female singer, Margherita Durastante, in an oratorio performance.

95. Kelly-Gadol, "Did Women Have a Renaissance?" p. 139.

96. Ibid., pp. 160–61. See the beginning of chapter 4 above for a further discussion of Kelly-Gadol's views. Around 1501 Mario Equicola noted in *De mulieribus* that men unlawfully exercised tyranny over women's natural freedom, kept them in a state of subjugation, and virtually restricted them to the activities of the house; see Conor Fahy, "Three Early Renaissance Treatises on Women," *Italian Studies* 9 (1956): 6–39. Ideas about the subor-dination of women in marriage and their assignment to the home are also treated by Ian Maclean, in *The Renaissance Notion of Woman: A Study in the Fortunes of Scholasticism and Medical Science in European Intellec-tual Life* (Cambridge: Cambridge University Press, 1980).

97. For the idea that marriage may have been responsible for bringing a halt to Madalena Casulana's composing career and Virginia Vagnoli's per-forming career, see chap. 5 above.

98. Two letters of Pietro Bembo deal with the question of his daughter's musical study; see Pietro Bembo, *Opere del Cardinale Pietro Bembo,* 12 vols. (Milan: Società tipografica de' classici italiani, 1808–10), 7:478–80, 8:138–39.

99. Giovanni Michele Bruto, *La Institutione di una fanciulla nata nobilmente* (Antwerp: Jehan Bellere, 1555), pp. 35–37.

100. Ibid., trans. Thomas Salter, under the title *A Mirrhor mete for all Mothers, Matrones, and Maidens* (London: Edward White, n.d.), quoted by Kelso, *Lady of the Renaissance,* p. 59.

101. Ludovico Frati, *La vita privata di Bologna,* p. 98. Although Frati does not cite the source of his quote, the substance of the passage is similar to that of one quoted by Emmanuel Pierre Rodocanachi, in *La Femme ita-*

lienne avant, pendant et après la Renaissance: Sa Vie privée et mondaine, son influence sociale (Paris: Hachette, 1922), p. 245, for which the author gives as the source Archiv. Seg. Vat. Armadio, V, vol. LX, n. 240, 4 May 1686.

102. Rodocanachi, *Le Femme italienne*, p. 245. See also Kast, "Rom," col. 716.

103. See David Burrows, "Antonio Cesti on Music," *Musical Quarterly* 51 (1965): 527.

104. The entire dedication is printed in Pescerelli, *I madrigali di Casulana*, p. 7. Isabella de' Medici Orsina may herself have been something of a composer; see pp. 120 and 148n23.

105. See chapter 7 below for this and other statements in Strozzi's dedications related to her sex.

106. See chapter 13 below for the effects of another sort of discussion about women's compositional capabilities on their activities in another age.

107. Sébastien de Brossard, "Catalogue des livres de musique," p. 155 (Paris, Bibliothèque nationale).

108. Robert F. Hayburn, *Papal Legislation on Sacred Music, 95 A.D. to 1977 A.D.* (Collegeville, Minn.: Liturgical Press, 1979), p. 29.

109. Raimondo Creytens, in "La riforma dei monasteri femminili dopo i Decreti Tridentini," *Il Concilio di Trento e la Riforma Tridentine. Atti del Convengo Storico Internazionale. Trento—2–6 settembre 1963*, vol. 1 (Rome: Herder, 1965), pp. 45–84, gives an excellent account of the council's adoption of the measures pertaining to nuns, the debates about them that were carried on in ensuing years, the extension of the principle of enclosure by successive popes, and the hardships for nuns that resulted from the enforcement of enclosure. See also Joan Morris, *The Bishop Was a Lady: The Hidden History of Women with Clerical Ordination and the Jurisdiction of Bishops* (New York: Macmillan, 1973), pp. 101–2; and Léopold Willaert, "Ordini e congregazioni femminili," *La restaurazione cattolica dopo il Concilio di Trento (1563–1648), Parte I*, vol. 18:1 of *Storia della chiesa dalle origini fino ai nostri giorni*, ed. Eugenio da Veroli (Torino: Editrice S.A.I.E., 1966), pp. 181–200.

110. Giovanni Fontana, *Constitutioni, et ordinationi generali appartenenti alle monache, publicate d'ordine di Monsig. Reverendiss. Vescovo di Ferrara. l'Anno M.D.XCIX.* (Ferrara: Vittorio Baldini, 1599), intro., and p. 91.

111. Ibid., pp. 34–35.

112. "Orders Sent by His Holiness Pope Gregory XIII [1572–85] to be Observed by the Nuns of the City of Ferrara," ibid., p. 99.

113. Guarini, *Compendio historico*, p. 376.

114. Sardi, *Historia ferraresi*, p. 89.

115. See Newcomb, *Madrigal at Ferrara*, 1:201, who quotes a dispatch stating that "*musiche solenni* is made now by ladies, now by refined male singers, and even the nuns take part, because His Highness is completely taken by this entertainment."

116. When the Estense court was forced to move from Ferrara to Modena

in 1598, there must have been a significant reduction in the number of important visitors to San Vito, which may also have contributed to the drastic reduction of its musical ensemble. According to Sardi, *Historia ferraresi*, pp. 88–89, the duke of Ferrara had encouraged the nuns in their study of music, so his removal from the city would undoubtedly have taken its toll as well.

117. Achillis Ratti, ed., *Acta ecclesiae mediolanensis*, vol. 4 (Milan: Typographia Pontificia Sancti Josephi, 1897), cols. 985–87.

118. Ibid., cols. 1259–60.

119. Milan, Archivio di Stato, Fondo di religione, Monastero di Maria Annunciata, busta 1955, O.O.V.V.

120. See Baroffio, "La Compositrice Isabella Leonarda," p. 89n.

121. Milan, Archivio di Stato, Fondo di religione, Santa Radegonda Cassinense Monastero, busta 1660 (annual visitations for the years 1660, 1670–74, 1688–93).

122. Hayburn, *Papal Legislation*, p. 90. I am indebted to Keith Larson for calling my attention to prohibitions of polyphonic music-making in Neapolitan convent churches throughout this same period. In about 1589, the order was given that only *canto fermo* was permitted in convent churches and that the only musical instruments permitted were organs; even organs, however, could be used only outside the perimeter of enclosure (see Carla Russo, *I monasteri femminili di clausura a Napoli nel secolo XVII* [Naples: Università di Napoli, Istituto di Storia Medioevale e Moderna, (1970)], pp. 137–38). Ascanio Filomarino (archbishop of Naples 1641–66) prohibited secular music in convents and punished transgressions of his prohibition with short interdictions. He placed an interdiction in 1658 on the convent of Santa Croce di Lucca because a page of Monsignor Luigi d'Aquino, who was received into the convent to visit his four sisters, brought a lute into the convent parlor. He placed another on the convent of Donnalbina in 1659 for having violated the edict that prohibited the performance of polyphonic music, though it was later removed by the viceroy (ibid., p. 74). See also Baroffio, "La Compositrice Isabella Leonarda," pp. 83–84, for prohibitions by the vicar general Fabio Tempestino in 1591 of all polyphonic music-making in convents in Novara, with the exception of singing a few motets at mass and the Magnificat or other things at vespers. Novarese nuns were also ordered to play no instruments other than the clavichord or "violone da gamba which serves for the bass" and to sing no canzone, madrigals, or secular motets. They were also not to sing in any place where they could be heard by outsiders except in church.

123. King, "Book-Lined Cells," p. 70.

124. The accomplishments of the composer Antonia Bembo, who styled herself a *nobile veneta* (noble Venetian), are also worthy of note here, although they do not fall within the purview of this article, since Bembo both worked in France and produced most of her work after 1700; see especially Yvonne Rokseth, "Antonia Bembo, Composer to Louis XIV," *Musical Quarterly* 23 (1937): 147–69.

Appendix

Compositions by Italian Women Published 1566–1700

1566   Madalena Casulana, *Vedesti Amor giamai, Sculpio ne l'alm'Amore, Morir non può il mio cuore,* and *Se scior si ved'il laccio.* In *Primo libro de diversi eccellent.mi auttori à quattro voci, intitulato Il Desiderio,* ed. Giulio Bonagionta da San Genesi (Venice: Girolamo Scotto, 1566). (1566²) The Casulana madrigals have been republished in a modern edition by Beatrice Pescerelli, in *I madrigali di Maddalena Casulana,* Studi e testi per la storia della musica, 1 (Florence: Leo S. Olschki, 1979), pp. 88–99.

1567   Madalena Casulana, *Amorosetto fiore.* In *Terzo libro del Desiderio. Madrigali à quattro voci di Orlando Lasso et d'altri eccel. musici con un dialogo à otto,* ed. Giulio Bonagionta da San Genesi (Venice: Girolamo Scotto, 1567). (1567¹⁶)

1568   Madalena Casulana, *Il primo libro de madrigali à quattro voci* (Venice: Girolamo Scotto, 1568). 2/(Brescia: Vincenzo Sabbio, 1583) and (Milan: Francesco & Simon Tini, 1583). Includes the five madrigals published in 1566 and 1567 above.

1570   Madalena Casulana, *Il secondo libro de madrigali à quattro voci* (Venice: Girolamo Scotto, 1570). Republished in Pescerelli, *I madrigali di Casulana,* pp. 29–87.

1583   Madalena Mezari detta Casulana, *Il primo libro de madrigali à cinque voci* (Ferrara: Angelo Gardano, 1583).

1585   Paola Massarenghi, *Quando spiega l'insegn'al sommo padre.* In F. Arcangelo Gherardini, *Il primo libro de' madrigali à cinque voci* (Ferrara: Vittorio Baldini, 1585). (1585²⁴)

1586   Madalena Casulana, *Stavasi il mio bel sol'.* In *Il Gaudio. Primo libro de madrigali de diversi eccellen. musici à tre voci* (Venice: L'herede di Girolamo Scotto, 1586). (1586¹²) Republished in Pescerelli, *I madrigali di Casulana,* pp. 100–102.

1591   Vittoria Aleotti, *Di pallide viole.* In *Giardino de musici ferraresi. Madrigali à cinque voci* (Venice: Giacomo Vincenti, 1591). (1591⁹)

1593   Vittoria Aleotti, *Ghirlanda de madrigali à quatro voci* (Venice: Giacomo Vincenti, 1593).

1593   Raffaella Aleotti, *Sacrae cantiones quinque, septem, octo, & decem*

Dates followed by raised numbers and enclosed in parentheses are the identification numbers of collections of music given in the *Répertoire international des sources musicales: Recueils imprimés XVIe–XVIIe siècles* (Munich: G. Henle, 1960), vol. 1.

vocibus decantande. Liber primus (Venice: Ricciardo Amadino, 1593). The complete works of Vittoria and Raffaella Aleotti are being prepared for publication by C. Ann Carruthers-Clement and will be published by Broude Brothers in New York. Five pieces by the two sisters have already been edited by Carruthers-Clement and published by Broude Brothers in its series, Nine Centuries of Music by Women. See also C. Ann Carruthers-Clement, *The Madrigals and Motets of Vittoria/Raphaela Aleotti* (Ann Arbor: University Microfilms, 1982).

1597   Cesarina Ricci de Tingoli, *Il primo libro de madrigali à cinque voci. Con un dialogo à otto* (Venice: Angelo Gardano, 1597).

1609   Caterina Assandra, *Motetti à due, & trè voci, per cantar nell' organo con il basso continuo. . . . Opera seconda* (Milan: L'herede di Simon Tini, & Filippo Lomazzo, 1609).

1611   Lucia Quinciani, *Udite lagrimosi spirti.* In Marc' Antonio Negri, *Affetti amorosi. . . . Libro secondo* (Venice: Ricciardo Amadino, 1611). (1611[16])

1613   Claudia Sessa, *Vattene pur lasciva orechia humana* and *Occhi io vissi di voi.* In *Canoro pianto di Maria Vergine sopra la faccia di Christo estinto. . . . Posta in musica da diversi auttori. . . . A una voce da cantar nel chitarone o altri instromenti simili* (Venice: Bartholomei Magni, 1613). (1613[3])

1616   Caterina Assandra, *Impetum fecerunt* and *O dulcis amor Jesu* (from Opus 2). In *Siren coelestis duarum, trium et quatuor vocum, quam novavit e principibus, etiam nec dum Vulgatis auctoribus legit, pro temporum dierumque. . . . 2/ Siren coelestis centum harmoniarum. . . . Editio altera correctior & melior* (Munich: Berg Witwe, 1622). (1622[3])

1618   Francesca Caccini ne' Signorini, *Il primo libro delle musiche à una, e due voci* (Florence: Zanobi Pignoni, 1618). Transcriptions of seven of these pieces appear in Carolyn Raney, *Francesca Caccini: Musician to the Medici and her "Primo Libro" (1618)* (Ann Arbor, Mich.: University Microfilms, 1971).

1619   Sulpitia Cesis, *Motetti spirituali* (Modena: Giulian Cassiani, 1619).

1621   Francesca Caccini, *Dove io credea* (from *Il Primo Libro*). In *Ghirlandetta amorosa, arie, madrigali, e sonetti, di diversi eccellentissimi autori, à uno, à due, à tre, & à quattro. . . . Opera settima. Libro primo,* ed. Fabio Costantini Romano (Orvieto: Michel' Angelo Fei & Rinaldo Ruuli, 1621). (1621[14]) The original strophic variations of this aria have been replaced in this collection by an exact repetition of the music for all four verses.

1622 Caterina Assandra, *Impetum fecerunt* (from Opus 2). In *Promptuarii musici, concentus ecclesiasticos II. III. & IV. vocum, e diversis. . . . Pars prima,* comp. Joanne Donfrido (Strasbourg: Pauli Ledertz, 1622). (1622²)

1623 Lucretia Orsina Vizana, *Componimenti musicale de motteti concertati à una e piu voci* (Venice: Bartholomeo Magni, 1623).

1625 Francesca Caccini ne' Signorini, *La Liberazione di Ruggiero dall' isola d'Alcina. Balletto . . .* (Florence: Pietro Cecconcelli, 1625). Republished in a modern edition, edited by Doris Silbert, in the Smith College Music Archives, no. 7 (Northampton, Mass.: Smith College, 1945).

1628 Diacinta Fedele, *Scelta di vilanelle napolitane bellissime con alcune ottave siciliane nove, con le sue intavolature di quitarra alla spagniola* (Vicenza: Francesco Grossi, 1628).

1629 Francesca Campana Romana, *Arie à una, due, e tre voci. . . . Opera prima* (Rome: Gio. Battista Robletti, 1629).

1629 Francesca Campana Romana, *Pargoletta vezzosetta, Donna se l' mio servir.* In *Le risonanti sfere da velocissimi ingegni armonicamente raggirate. . . . Con il primo mobile del basso continuo* (Rome: Gio. Battista Robletti, 1629). (1629⁹)

1629 Francesca Caccini Fiorentina, *Ch' io sia fedele.* In *Le risonante sfere* (see above).

1630 Claudia Rusca, *Sacri concerti à 1. 2. 3. 4. e 5. voci con salmi e canzoni francesi a 4. varii motetti, magnificat* (Milan, 1630). This title appears in Robert Eitner, *Biographisch-bibliographisches Quellen-Lexikon der Musiker und Musikgelehrten,* 2. verbesserte Auflage, 11 vols. (Graz: Akademische Druck & Verlagsanstalt, 1959–60), 8:363; the work is now missing.

1640 Chiara Margarita Cozzolani, *Prima vera di fiori musicali concertati nell' organo a 1, 2, 3 e 4 voci,* Opus 1 (Milan, 1640). This title appears in *Zur Feier des Wohlthätenfestes im Berlinischen Gymnasium zum grauen Kloster* (Berlin, 1856), p. 7; the work is now missing.

1640 Isabella Leonarda, *Ah domine Jesu* and *Sic ergo anima.* In Gasparo Casati, *Il terzo libro de sacri concenti à 2. 3. e 4. voci. . . . Opera terza* (Venice: Bartolomeo Magni, 1640).* (1640³) Reprinted by Magni in 1642 and 1644 and by Gardano in 1650. For additional reprints see Stewart Carter, *The Music of Isabella Leonarda (1620–1704)* (Ann Arbor, Mich.: University Microfilms, 1981), p. 290.

1642 Chiara Margarita Cozzolani, *Concerti sacri à una, due, tre, et quattro voci con una messa à quattro. . . . Opera seconda* (Venice: Alessandro Vincenti, 1642).

1644 Barbara Strozzi, *Il primo de' madrigali . . . à due, tre, quattro e cinque voci* (Venice: Alessandro Vincenti, 1644).

1648 Chiara Margarita Cozzolani, *Scherzi di sacra melodia à voce sola. . . . Opera terza* (Venice: Alessandro Vincenti, 1648).

1649 Chiara Margarita Cozzolani, *O dulcis Jesu* (from Opus 2). In *Corollarium geistlicher collectaneorum, berühmter Authorum,* ed. Ambrosio Profio (Leipzig: Timotheum Ritzsch, 1649). (1649[6])

1650 Chiara Margarita Cozzolani, *Salmi à otto voci concertati et due magnificat à otto con un Laudate pueri à 4. voci, & doi violini, & un Laudate dominum omnes gentes à voce sola, & doi violini, motetti, et dialoghi à due, tre, quattro, e cinque voci. . . . Opera terza* [sic] (Venice: Alessandro Vincenti, 1650).

1651 Barbara Strozzi, *Cantate ariette, e duetti. . . . Opera seconda* (Venice: Gardano, 1651).

1654 Barbara Strozzi, *Cantate ariete à una, due, e tre voci. Opera terza* (Venice: Gardano, 1654).

1655 Barbara Strozzi, *Sacri musicali affetti. . . . Libro primo. Opera quinta* (Venice: Gardano, 1655).

1656 Barbara Strozzi, *Quis dabit mihi.* In *Sacra corona, motetti à due, e trè voci di diversi eccelentissimi autori moderni,* ed. Bartolomeo Marcesso (Venice: Francesco Magni, 1656). (1656[1]) 2/(Antwerp: Héritiers P. Phalèse, 1659). (1659[2])

1656 Barbara Strozzi, *Risoolvetovi pensieri* and *Chi brama in amore.* In *Arie a voce sola di diversi auttori,* comp. Francesco Tonalli (Venice: Alessandro Vincenti, 1656). (1656[4])

1657 Barbara Strozzi, *Ariette à voce sola. . . . Opera sesta* (Venice: Francesco Magni, 1657). Includes the two arias published in Tonalli's *Arie* above.

1659 Barbara Strozzi, *Diporti di Euterpe overo cantate & ariette à voce sola. . . . Opera settima* (Venice: Francesco Magni, 1659).

1659 Maria Cattarina Calegari, *Mottetti à voce sola.* This title appears in Donato Calvi, *Scena letteraria di gli scrittori bergamaschi. . . . Parte seconda* (Bergamo: Figliuoli di Marc' Antonio Rossi, 1664), p. 61. Calvi asserts that Calegari's *Madrigali, & Canzonette à voce sola* and *Madrigali à due voci* were also being published, and that her *Messe à sei con istromenti, & un Vespro* would later appear, but none of these works can be traced in modern times.

1664 Barbara Strozzi, *Arie. . . . Opera ottava* (Venice: Francesco Magni detto Gardano, 1664). Republished in facsimile by the Antiquae

Musicae Italicae in the series Monumenta veneta, no. 2 (Bologna: A.M.I.S., 1970).

1665   Marieta Morisina Prioli, *Balletti et correnti à due violini, & violone, agionta la spineta* (Venice: Francesco Magni detto Gardano, 1665).

1665? Isabella Leonarda, *Motetti à tre voci, libro primo* (Milan, 1665). This title appears in François-Joseph Fétis, *Biographie universelle des musiciens et bibliographie générale de la musique,* Deuxième édition, vol. 5 (1884), p. 276; the work is not extant. Fétis claims that Leonarda gave her age as twenty-four in the preface to these motets; her birthdate was 1620 rather than 1641, however (see n.16 above). Franz Giegling, in "Leonarda, Isabella," *Die Musik in Geschichte und Gegenwart* 8 (1960): col. 634, suggests that this work might have been Leonarda's Opus 2 and a reprint of an earlier edition. The fact that Lazzaro Agostino Cotta, in *Museo novarese . . . accresciuto di nuove biografie d'illustri novaresi e di altre notizie* (Novara: Francesco Merati, 1872), p. 269, mentions 1642 as the date of Leonarda's earliest publication invites speculation that this was the year of her Opus 1. (I thank Stewart Carter for this observation; see *Isabella Leonarda,* p. 22n.) Opera 1 and 2 of Leonarda, as well as her opera 5, 6, and 9, are now missing.

1670   Isabella Leonarda, *Sacri concenti à una, due, tré, et quattro voci. . . . Opera terza* (Milan: Fratelli Camagni, 1670).*

1674   Maria Francesca Nascimbeni, *Sitientes venite.* In Scipione Lazarini, *Motetti à due, e tre voci. . . . Opera seconda* (Ancona: Claudio Percimineo, 1674). (1674[1])

1674   Maria Francesca Nascimbeni, *Canzoni, e madrigali morali, e spirituali. A una, due, e tre voci* (Ancona: Claudio Percimineo, 1674).

1674   Isabella Leonarda, *Messa, e salmi, concertati, & à capella con istromenti ad libitum. . . . Opera quarta* (Milan: Fratelli Camagni, 1674).

1675   Maria Xaveria Peruchona, *Sacri concerti de motetti à una, due, tre, e quattro voci, parte con violini, e parte senza. . . . Opera prima* (Milan: Francesco Vigone, 1675).

1676   Isabella Leonarda, *Mottetti à voce sola. Parte con istromenti, e parte senza. . . . Opera sesta* (Venice: Gardano, 1676).*

1677   Isabella Leonarda, *Mottetti à una, due, tre, e quattro voci. Parte con istromenti, e parte senza. Con le litanie della Beata Vergine. . . . Opera settima* (Bologna: Giacomo Monti, 1677).

*Transcriptions of selected works from each of the starred collections appear in Stewart Carter, *The Music of Isabella Leonarda (1620–1704)* (Ann Arbor, Mich.: University Microfilms, 1981).

1678   Isabella Leonarda, *Vespro à cappella della Beata Vergine, e motetti concertati.* . . . *Opera ottava* (Bologna: Giacomo Monti, 1678).*

1684   Isabella Leonarda, *Motetti à quatro voci con le littanie della B. V.* . . . . *Opera decima* (Milan: Fratelli Camagni, 1684).* The Marian antiphon, *Ave regina caelorum,* from this collection has been edited by Stewart Carter and published by Broude Brothers (New York, 1980) in the series Nine Centuries of Music by Women.

1684   Rosa Giacinta Badalla, *Motetti à voce sola* (Venice: Giuseppe Sala, 1684).

1684   Isabella Leonarda, *Motetti à voce sola.* . . . *Opera XI* (Bologna: Giacomo Monti, 1684).*

1686   Isabella Leonarda, *Motetti à voce sola.* . . . *Opera duodecima* (Milan: Fratelli Camagni, 1686).

1687   Isabella Leonarda, *Motetti à una, due, e tre voci, con violini, e senza.* . . . *Opera decima terza* (Bologna: Giacomo Monti, 1687).*

1687   Isabella Leonarda, *Motetti à voce sola.* . . . *Opera decima quarta* (Bologna: Giacomo Monti, 1687).

1690   Isabella Leonarda, *Motetti à voce sola.* . . . *Opera decimaquinta* (Bologna: Pier-Maria Monti, 1690).

1691   Bianca Maria Meda, *Mottetti à 1. 2. 3. e 4. voci, con violini, e senza* (Bologna: Pier-Maria Monti, 1691).

1693   Isabella Leonarda, *Sonate à 1. 2. 3. e 4. istromenti.* . . . *Opera decima sesta* (Bologna: Pier-Maria Monti, 1693).* The twelfth sonata (the only solo sonata in the set) has been republished in Isabella Leonarda, *Sonata Duodecima from Opus 16* (1693), edited by Barbara Garvey Jackson, Baroque Chamber Music Series, no. 16 (Ottawa: Dovehouse Editions, 1983).

1695   Isabella Leonarda, *Mottetti à voce sola.* . . . *Opera decimasettima* (Bologna: Pier-Maria Monti, 1695).*

1696   Isabella Leonarda, *Messe à quattro voci concertate con stromenti, &* *motetti à una, due, e trè voci, pure con stromenti.* . . . *Opera decima ottava* (Bologna: Pier-Maria Monti, 1696).* The first mass in this collection has been recorded by the Schola Cantorum of the University of Arkansas, conducted by Jack Groh, on *Music for the Mass by Nun Composers,* Leonarda LPI 115 (1982).

1698   Isabella Leonarda, *Salmi concertati a 4. voci con strumenti.* . . . *Opera decimanona* (Bologna: Marino Silvani, 1698).*

1700   Isabella Leonarda, *Motetti à voce sola, con istromenti.* . . . *Opera vigesima* (Bologna: Marino Silvani, 1700).

7

The Voice of Barbara Strozzi

ELLEN ROSAND

Barbara Strozzi was a singer and the author of eight volumes of vocal works published in Venice between 1644 and 1664.[1] All but one of her extant publications are secular; their contents—madrigals, arias, and cantatas—place her directly within the cantata tradition of the mid-seventeenth century, along with such major figures as Luigi Rossi, Giacomo Carissimi, and Antonio Cesti, as well as a host of less well-known composers.[2] She stands apart from these composers because of her sex. Indeed, she is one of the few known women among the many aria and cantata composers of seventeenth-century Italy, and with the notable exception of her somewhat older contemporary, Francesca Caccini (1589–c.1640), she seems to be alone in having pursued a career as a composer and in having achieved substantial public recognition.

Although this historical distinction attracted attention to her works early in the present century, when the music of most of her male contemporaries still remained relatively ignored, appreciation of her style was predictably limited to an isolation of its supposedly feminine qualities, "great spontaneity, exquisite grace, marvelously fine taste, and characteristics of true femininity."[3] If such an appreciation appears irrelevant as well as polemical in its incompleteness, we are now in a better position—with regard to both historical knowledge and social awareness—to attempt a fuller consideration and more just evaluation of a figure like Barbara Strozzi, to measure her achievement within the contexts, social and aesthetic, in which she created. This study is an attempt to explore some aspects of the milieu in which Strozzi lived and worked and to consider some of the connections between her life and her art.

Born in Venice in 1619, Barbara lived, apparently for many years, in the home of Giulio Strozzi, a renowned poet and leading figure in the Venetian intellectual community. First mentioned in a will signed by Giulio in 1628, she was identified as Barbara Valle, daughter of one Isabella Garzoni, Giulio's longtime servant and heir-designate. In his final will, signed twenty-two years later, Giulio named Barbara his chief heir, referring to her as "Barbara of Santa Sofia, my elective daughter [*figliuola elettiva*], however, commonly called Strozzi." Giulio's expression *elettiva* may be interpreted as *adopted*, and very likely it was also a euphemism for *illegitimate*. Whatever their actual relationship may have been, Barbara's presence in Giulio's household had significant consequences for her career; it guaranteed her an early and full exposure to Venetian musical and literary society.[4]

Although Giulio Strozzi was a member of an illustrious Florentine family, he was born in Venice in 1583 and by 1620 had become a figure of considerable importance in the cultural life of that city. The founder and an active member of a succession of academies, a prolific poet and dramatist, he was an energetic supporter of theatrical entertainments. He provided librettos for many of the operas performed on Venetian stages during the 1630s and 1640s, collaborating with every composer active in this earliest and most important phase of Venetian opera, including Claudio Monteverdi and Francesco Cavalli. His theatrical involvement also included managerial responsibilities for several seasons.

Through Giulio, then, Barbara Strozzi became acquainted with the intellectual elite of Venice. Indeed, by virtue of her adoption, if not her birth, she was enabled to enter a world that was apparently closed to other members of her sex. A comparative glance at the background of the most prominent and successful woman composer of the period, Francesca Caccini, the daughter of professional musicians, who was exposed *per forza* to music from infancy, suggests that such an environment may have been essential for the development of a female composer.

For most of Barbara's career—first as a singer and later as a composer—the guiding and sustaining hand of her father is perceptible in the background. From at least as early as 1635 (when Barbara was sixteen) Giulio arranged for her to sing informally at his home, where she was evidently heard and appreciated by various *letterati* and musicians. One composer, Nicolò Fontei, was inspired to write two volumes of songs for her (1635, 1636), a project most likely encouraged by Giulio, who supplied most of the texts himself.[5]

Soon thereafter, in 1637, Giulio institutionalized her performances with the creation of an academy, the Accademia degli Unisoni, designed primarily—it would seem—to exhibit her talents to a wider audience. A publication of that academy, *Le Veglie de' Signori Unisoni* (1638), which is dedicated to Barbara, lists the members by name and describes three of their meetings.[6] The meetings consisted of discourses by the various academicians, rhetorical exercises on typical debating subjects that all seem to have concerned love. Barbara apparently functioned as mistress of ceremonies, suggesting subjects on which the members were to display their forensic ingenuity, judging the discourses, and awarding prizes to the best of them; she also performed songs during the course of the meetings. In addition, on at least one occasion, she read both sides of an argument written by two of the academy's most illustrious members. The subject of this debate, to which we shall return, concerned whether tears or song be the more potent weapon in love, and it seems to have been explicitly designed for Barbara herself.[7]

The members of the Unisoni listed in the *Veglie* were all notable figures in the cultural life of Venice. Moreover, almost without exception they belonged, as well, to another older and much larger Venetian academy, the Accademia degli Incogniti. Indeed, the Unisoni seem to have functioned as a musical subgroup of the Incogniti, whose own meetings do not appear to have included music. The Accademia degli Incogniti had been founded in 1630 by the patrician Giovanni Francesco Loredano. Nearly every intellectual of any importance in Venice and many from other Italian cities as well belonged to the group, which represented a major political and cultural force in mid-seicento Venetian society. The Incogniti were united by a libertine philosophy that derived in part from the teachings of the Aristotelian Cesare Cremonini at the University of Padua.[8]

The academy comprised poets, philosophers, historians, and clerics—all of them prolific writers—and their publications included a large number of popular novels and romances, poetry of various kinds, letters, historical and religious tracts, academic discourses, and opera librettos. In fact, the Incogniti membership roles listed nearly every name associated with the opera libretto in Venice of the 1640s—i.e., the decade that witnessed the establishment of opera as a regular, seasonal occurrence, a central part of Venetian life.

The nature of Barbara Strozzi's relationship to the Incogniti is somewhat ambiguous. Although her contact, through the Unisoni, with various Incogniti is documented, she was evidently not considered an official member of the academy. Whether this was because she was a woman or a musician is uncertain, since neither of these minority groups seems to have been represented among the elite membership.

Despite the fact that there were no women academicians among the Incogniti, the academy itself, which was involved with all the controversial moral and intellectual issues of the day, was manifestly interested in questions of feminism. Academic concern with the position of women in society had been sparked by the appearance of a series of antifeminist and profeminist tracts, pseudoscientific and intentionally polemical pamphlets that argued, for example, whether women had souls or even belonged to the human race. The Incogniti fueled the fire of this debate by encouraging the publication of these and other similar pamphlets and by writing some of their own. This activity must be viewed as part of their fundamental desire to explode accepted dogma, a feature of their libertine posture. For a number of them the problem of women cloistered in nunneries took on special importance; these *monache* (nuns) represented ideal objects of interest for the Incogniti, a natural fusion of their anticlerical and licentious predilections.[9]

In addition to being fashionable, the feminist issue, both pro and con, suited well the Incogniti's particular brand of salacious iconoclasm. The intentional ambiguity inherent in the issue for them, as well as its centrality to their concerns, is epitomized by their adoption of the motto *Ignoto Deo* (Unknown Deity) for the emblem of the academy. This motto, one of several invented justifications for the origin of their name, appears on the title page of one of Loredano's many lascivious volumes, the *Sei dubbi amorosi* (1647). It is inscribed at the base of a veiled female statue, which Loredano identifies as the unknown woman whose questions provided the *raison d'être* of his book. In his characteristically irreverent manner, he equates her with the unknown god worshiped by the Athenians, as reported by St. Paul. Similarly veiled women, although unaccompanied by the motto, grace the title pages of several subsequent works by Loredano as well.[10] That the symbolic god of the Incogniti should be a veiled woman seems quite appropriate. Their objectives and ideals, their infusion of irreverence into serious moral issues, their insistent association of religion and sex all seem quite properly symbolized in the worship of such an idol.

The rhetorical stances assumed by the academy as a group toward the female sex did not, however, preclude respectful intellectual relationships with women. The correspondence of Loredano with the controversial nun Arcangela Tarabotti, for example, indicates that he took seriously both her abilities as a writer and her position as an ardent and angry feminist. Barbara Strozzi may well have enjoyed a similar respect. She was, in any case, clearly an initiate into their occult world, for her third publication, Opus 3 (1654), prominently displays the academy's trademark, the inscription *Ignotae Deae* (in the feminine), in the center of the page normally reserved in her other publications for the dedication.

Compared to the ambiguity surrounding her relationship to the Incogniti, Barbara's position within the Unisoni would seem rather clear: she was publicly acknowledged as its hostess and guiding spirit. Yet this position evidently raised questions in the minds of her contemporaries. To at least one seventeenth-century Venetian observer, Barbara's function seems to have evoked the traditional association between music-making and sexual license so well documented in cinquecento Venice; for an anonymous series of satires describing meetings of the Unisoni finds numerous opportunities to impugn every aspect of the academy, including the virtue of its hostess. Among the slurs against Barbara Strozzi's virtue is a comment made following a description of her distribution of flowers to the academicians: "It is a fine thing to distribute the flowers after having already surrendered the fruit." And her relationship with a castrato is offered as the explanation for her never having become pregnant.[11]

To be sure, a strong link between courtesans and music-making did exist in the traditions of Venice, and music was not considered a particularly suitable occupation for a well-brought-up woman. We might quote Pietro Aretino's remark that "the knowledge of playing musical instruments, of singing, and of writing poetry on the part of women is the very key which opens the gates of their modesty."[12] That a similar connection still existed in the seventeenth century is illustrated by the colorful histories of a number of female singers who were notorious for their combination of amorous and musical exploits.[13]

It may be unfair to venture an opinion on the morals of Barbara Strozzi on the basis of the slanderous (even if jesting) remarks in some anonymous satires against her and the traditional yet general association between courtesans and music-making—unfair and, perhaps, irrelevant. Nevertheless, in view of the nature of Strozzi's music, her choice of texts, her subject matter, and her concentration on love themes, it is not inconceivable that she may, indeed, have been a courtesan, highly skilled in the art of love as well as music.

If, on the one hand, the anonymous satires impugned Strozzi's virtue, her talents are celebrated, on the other hand, by a number of different observers. She is praised for her bold and graceful manner of singing; her voice is likened to that of Amphyon and Orpheus, and to the sound of the harmonies of the spheres. Although these compliments provide little in the way of precise qualitative critical description, they do at least document her activity as a singer. Contemporary references to her as a composer, however—by far the more remarkable aspect of her career—are rare, indeed, and hardly more specific. The *Veglie*, for example, refer to the high quality of the music performed at the Unisoni meetings; but although Strozzi herself must have written at least some of it, no composer is ever mentioned. Only Loredano, in an undated letter to a friend, mentions her music, commenting that "had she been born in another era she would certainly have usurped or enlarged the place of the muses."[14] The main evidence of her activity as a composer is, of course, the music itself. Yet the very preservation of her compositions represents a highly unusual phenomenon.

Although numerous contemporary reports and descriptions bear witness to the existence of highly skilled female singers who graced the courts and theaters of seventeenth-century Italy, we know few compositions by secular women of the period. It is difficult to believe, however, that none of the most celebrated female singers wrote music—at least for their own use. There seems no reason to assume that, in this respect, they would have differed in ability from the ubiquitous, highly esteemed, and famous male singer-composers of the early part of the century. Yet the fact remains that we have very little of their music.

For singers—female as well as male—creating at least some of the music they performed may well have been such an integral aspect of their activity that it was simply taken for granted, viewed as a normal part of the performer's task. If such music has not survived, part of the reason must lie in the fact that it was neither printed nor copied in manuscripts. It may have been partly or totally improvised and thus never committed to paper, even originally. For whatever reason, it was apparently not prized as an object independent of its performance.

These female musicians were vigorously sought after and generously rewarded by the highly sophisticated and competitive courts of seventeenth-century Europe. But composition was evidently merely an adjunct to performance. As women they were celebrated for their physical attributes, their beauty, their voices. As musicians they were appreciated for their public, ornamental value, for their abilities as performers.[15]

Against this background Barbara Strozzi's determination to publish her works assumes a special significance. Despite the precedent of Francesca Caccini, Strozzi herself must have been well aware of her unusual position as a publishing composer, for she alluded rather self-consciously to her femininity in the prefaces of several of her publications. In Opus 1 (1644), dedicated to the grand duchess of Tuscany, Vittoria della Rovere, she wrote, "I must reverently consecrate this first work, which as a woman I publish all too boldly, to the Most August Name of Your Highness so that, under an oak of gold it may rest secure against the lightning bolts of slander prepared for it." In Opus 2 (1651) she declared, "The lowly mine of a woman's poor imagination cannot produce metal to forge those richest golden crowns worthy of august rulers." With all their conceit, these statements have the modest, even self-deprecating tone typical of dedicatory messages. Yet by Opus 5 (1655), four years later, Strozzi could explicitly dissociate her creative efforts from the condition of her sex. Her dedication of that volume concludes, "and since feminine weaknesses restrain me no more than any indulgence of my sex impels me, on lightest leaves do I fly, in devotion, to bow before you." She makes no mention of her femininity at all in her last three dedications. Perhaps by then she had gained recognition for her works. Indeed, there is evidence to suggest that she had achieved a new peak of success between the publication of her Opus 5 in 1655 and Opus 6 in 1657. Compositions by her appear along with those of her most important contemporaries, including Francesco Cavalli, in two collections published in 1656, one by "diversi eccellentissimi autori moderni," the other by "sogetti eminenti nella musica." [16]

Barbara Strozzi's public stature as a composer distinguishes her career from those of other female singers who also, but rather incidentally, may have composed. And this seems to have been the professional goal Giulio Strozzi envisioned for his daughter. From the beginning he saw that she received proper training in composition, for it was undoubtedly he who arranged for her to study with the leading composer in Venice, Francesco Cavalli. Giulio's active encouragement of Barbara can be gauged by her first volume of music (1644), for which he himself provided the texts.

Although Giulio clearly stood behind Barbara's Opus 1, by the time of her second publication, five years later, his influence had receded considerably. Of its twenty-six texts only two are definitely by him, and these were not written specifically for her but were taken from opera librettos performed several years earlier. When Giulio died the following year, in March 1652, although Barbara was his sole heir, she inherited very little. He did not even leave enough money to cover the cost of his burial or to satisfy his own charitable wishes. In fact, his testament indicates that Barbara herself had some money of her own; and he requested that she use it on his behalf, "remembering," he says, "how much I have done for her by raising her and setting her on the path of virtue."[17]

The source of Barbara's financial support, if it was not Giulio Strozzi, is uncertain. The next phase of her career shows clear signs of her efforts to secure a living as a professional composer. The dedication of her Opus 2 to Ferdinand II of Austria on the occasion of his marriage to Eleanor of Mantua in 1651 may in fact have been an attempt—apparently fruitless—to secure employment or some more permanent patronage. The Austrian court was, after all, renowned as one of the chief European importers of Italian music and musicians. Her publication of several more volumes in rapid succession—five in as many years—dedicated to a variety of important, well connected personalities (including one future doge of Venice, Nicolò Sagredo), suggests that she was still in search of support. Five years separate her final two publications, and nothing at all is known of her activities after the appearance of her Opus 8 in 1664.

From the evidence presently available, Barbara's career seems to have survived Giulio Strozzi by scarcely more than a decade; it might well be argued, in fact, that were it not for Giulio, Barbara would never have enjoyed a career at all. His own precarious financial situation may have prevented him from providing her with the dowry required for marriage. (And the monastic alternative, even if he possessed the requisite funds, seems highly unlikely for the daughter of a man with Giulio's libertine proclivities.) Yet he seems to have been actively committed to another kind of life for her. Indeed, he appears to have been a champion of female achievement in general, for among the unpublished writings listed in a bibliography of his works printed in 1647 is a volume entitled "Elogii delle donne virtuose del nostro secolo."[18] His legacy to Barbara was clearly more than financial. He provided her with opportunities that only a man of his interests and connections could have provided for a daughter— the possibility of aspiring to a career, the possibility of becoming a professional composer.

Barbara Strozzi's eight published volumes contain just over one hundred pieces, most of them cantatas and arias for solo voice and basso continuo. This output places her among the most prolific contributors to secular chamber music of the seicento—along with such significant figures, mentioned earlier, as Giacomo Carissimi, Luigi Rossi, and Antonio Cesti. Qualitatively as well, her works compare favorably with the best cantatas of these composers.

But several important features distinguish her contribution from theirs. Perhaps most immediately striking is the fact that nearly all of her known cantatas were published, in monographic prints that she herself apparently planned and saw through the press. In contrast, although Carissimi and Rossi both wrote more cantatas than she did, very few of them (approximately three percent) ever appeared in print. Strozzi actually published more cantatas than any other seventeenth-century composer.

Barbara Strozzi's works stand out in a more fundamental way, however. For most mid-seventeenth-century composers vocal chamber music represented just one aspect of their production, which usually also included music for the theater, the church, or both. In this context the dimensions of Strozzi's activity—her exclusive concentration on arias and cantatas—appear particularly limited. Furthermore, her work is not only restricted virtually to a single genre, but even within that genre it is confined primarily to the expression of a single affect: the suffering caused by unrequited love, sometimes treated highly ironically, even humorously, but more often treated with great seriousness and intensity. In this respect, of course, Strozzi's cantatas are not atypical of the genre. Because she wrote little other music, however, the restrictive affective content of her cantatas assumes particular significance within her oeuvre, as a defining characteristic of her style. Nevertheless, despite these restrictions, Barbara Strozzi emerges as a composer of considerable skill and highly individual eloquence.

The texts she set are, for the most part, limited to the Marinistic love poetry that flowed with such apparent ease from mid-seicento pens. These poems are characterized by a basic similarity of form, language, and subject matter. Marked by preciosity and built upon elaborate conceits, they often carry such topical headings as *Moralità amorosa* (*Amorous Morality*) or *L'Amante bugiardo* (*The Lying Lover*). The composer herself identified a number of her poets. Among the sixteen names she mentioned, six, including Giulio Strozzi, were well-known opera librettists of the time, and at least two others happened also to be involved with opera but in the capacity primarily of patrons or theater owners. Moreover, a number of them were also members of the Accademia degli Incogniti.

Aside from the early madrigals of her Opus 1, Strozzi's compositions fall into the two general categories I have already mentioned, aria and cantata, depending on the structure of their texts. The arias are usually brief pieces, often strophic or else enclosed by a refrain at beginning and end; whereas the cantatas are normally lengthier, more varied works, containing multiple sections and a mixture of vocal styles. But these terms are inadequate to describe the formal variety of her works. Indeed, from the outset of her career she displayed a strong interest in formal exploration.

In her early volumes Strozzi favored simple strophicism or strophic variation, but formal flexibility often distinguishes her settings. She occasionally obscured textual strophicism by varying the successive strophes so much that they contrast with one another, creating sectional but nonstrophic forms. Although she continued to make use of strophic texts in her later volumes, the later texts are usually longer and more complicated than the earlier ones, many of them containing one or more lengthy refrains, and her treatment of them is correspondingly freer and more varied. Indeed, some of the later arias comprise so many long sections of such extreme contrast that they approach, and even surpass, some of the cantatas in both length and musical variety; the only real clue to their identity as arias lies in the strophic structure of their texts.

Strozzi's formal solutions in the cantatas are even more varied than in the arias. In part because of their texts, few of these works display the regular alternation between declamatory recitative and lyrical aria that was soon to become standard procedure in the Italian cantata. Dramatic texts with story lines, which would most naturally call for clear-cut narrative and lyrical portions, are indeed unusual in Strozzi's oeuvre; only three of her published cantatas fall into this category. These works, however, surely rank among her most inspired compositions. One of them is particularly outstanding. Its text is a vivid account of an actual, recent historical event: the execution, in 1642, of the courtier Henri de Cinq-Mars, who was condemned by Louis XIII for his participation in a plot against Richelieu. Strozzi's setting creates a miniature drama in which the hero's progress unfolds in a carefully calculated series of musico-dramatic events: both narrator and victim speak in recitative, arioso, half-aria, and aria. And the drama ends abruptly with a real *coup de théâtre*: the heroic victim is decapitated and the Seine reverberates in sympathetic shock[19] (see figure 7).

Dramatic or narrative cantatas of this kind are, as I have suggested, decidedly in the minority among Strozzi's works. Her preferred mode of expression appears more lyrical than dramatic; she seems to have been especially concerned with direct communication to an audience without the aesthetic distance imposed by a narrator. Accordingly, secco recitative is virtually absent from most of her cantatas, which consist, rather, of alternation between free, affective lyrical passages (i.e., arioso) and more highly structured, usu-

Figure 7
Il lamento, conclusion

Men - tre_il Re col suo pian - to del - le sue fret - te il

pen - ti - men - to ac - cen - na tre - mò Pa - ri - gi, tre - mò Pa -

ri - gi, e tor - bi - dos - si, tor - bi - dos - si Sen - na.

While the king with his weeping
betrayed his repentance for his haste,
Paris trembled and the Seine became agitated.

Source: Barbara Strozzi, *Cantate ariete a una, due e tre voci*, Opus 3
(Venice: Gardano, 1654)
Translation by Ellen Rosand

ally less affective formal arias. Some cantatas even lack formal arias altogether, containing instead a series of open-ended arioso passages usually held together by a refrain.

In cantatas as well as arias, then, Strozzi's primary formal procedure is contrast, usually combined with some kind of refrain idea: it is always a textual event that provokes a change in the musical setting. In the arias a particular word might initiate a new section, or a rhymed couplet or refrain line might engender its musical separation from the rest of the text. In the cantatas more emphatic distinctions of meter, rhyme scheme, or meaning between sections of text elicit distinct changes in musical treatment.

In general, Strozzi's music reflects the influence of her training in the *seconda prattica* tradition. The style of her esteemed teacher, Cavalli, is recalled in her easy shifts between unmeasured and measured passages, between duple and triple meter, and in her occasional use of the *stile concitato*—all in response to her faithful adherence to her texts. Indeed, her musical language is especially fluent and expressive in those less formal passages where she can follow the text flow most closely and freely. (See figure 8. Note especially the treatment of the words *passeggiando* [walking], *vaccillante* [unsteady], and *fiamme* [flames].)

The arias, on the other hand, are less natural and spontaneous, frequently leaving the impression of having been more problematical to the composer. Here, where the text does not easily suggest a succession of fleeting images, Strozzi relies almost exclusively on the idea of repetition of units of different sizes: brief melodic-rhythmic patterns repeated sequentially—occasionally extended beyond the limits of interest—and reiteration of longer phrases on different scale degrees. The opening phrases of some arias are immediately repeated and extended in motto style; and, almost without exception, final phrases in arias as well as arioso passages are repetitions of penultimate phrases transposed to end on the tonic.

Although Strozzi's music evokes the spirit of Cavalli, her style is more lyrical than his, more dependent on sheer vocal sound. To be sure, this kind of distinction reflects fundamental differences between the genres in which master and pupil worked. The uninterrupted narrative flow, the momentum so crucial to Cavalli's dramatic realism has only limited relevance in the context of chamber music. Strozzi's expressive goals were clearly very different from Cavalli's.

If, like him, she displays special sensitivity to nuances of text expression—indeed, indulging wherever possible in word painting—she treats her texts more freely, repeating and extending individual words and phrases much more frequently and to greater lengths than his more austere and functionally narrative style allowed. Where Cavalli, the musical dramatist, heir to Monteverdi, reserved text repetition purely for affective words or as a means of rounding out or closing a recitative passage or aria, Strozzi, the singer, the miniaturist, frequently repeated neutral words over and over again, sometimes creating a lengthy and complex, even bipartite, aria out of four or five short lines of text.

The disproportion resulting from the combination of a short text with a lengthy musical setting presages later seventeenth-century operatic developments, although on a much smaller scale. But frequent, even routine, repetition of neutral words and phrases is not the only

Figure 8
A pena il Sol, conclusion

In ques-ta gui - sa ap - pun-to, sù la ri - va del fiu-me pas-seg-gian - do, gri-da va, gri - da-va Eu-ril - lo quan-do per so - ver-chio do-lo - re ha-vend' il pie-de al pa-ri del pen-sie - ro vac-cil-lan - - te, e non es-sen-do as - ciu - to dal-la rug-gia-da an-cor l'hu - mi-do suo-lo, sdru-cio-lan - - do nell' ac-que s'af-fo-gò co-sì, co - sì, co - sì d'a - mo-re, co - sì d'a-

mo - re le fiam - me, le fiam - - -

- me, le fiam - - - me, le

fiam - - - me̲ a-mor - zò.

In this manner, walking on the river bank, did Eurillo shout, when, because of his excessive suffering, his foot, like his thoughts, unstable, and the damp ground not yet dry from dew, he slipped into the water and drowned; thus were the flames of love extinguished!

Source: Barbara Strozzi, *Diporti di Euterpe overo cantate e ariette a voce sola*, Opus 7 (Venice: Magni, 1659)
Translation by Ellen Rosand

suggestion of incipient musical domination of text in Strozzi's works. More significant is the dissociation of word and music that permits her to accompany repeated lines of text with entirely new music, or, vice versa, to repeat a musical section to a new text.

The most striking evidence of this dissociation, and most indicative as far as Strozzi's personal language is concerned, is offered by her melismatic passages, which, although generally set into motion by the meaning of a specific word, are so frequent and lengthy that an unusually large proportion of her music remains virtually without any text at all. Freed from the intermediary of words, yet text-inspired and often filled with the standard techniques associated with affective text interpretation—pungent chromaticism, awkwardly large leaps, persistent syncopation, sudden interruptions—these passages allow the voice to speak for itself; Strozzi exploits the superior eloquence of the naked human instrument. (See figure 9.)

Figure 9
Che v'hò fatto

What have I done to you, oh eyes, tell me,
you who torment me always.

Source: Barbara Strozzi, *Diporti di Euterpe overo cantate e ariette a voce sola*,
Opus 7 (Venice: Magni, 1659)
Translation by Ellen Rosand

Strozzi's concern for the nuances of text expression manifests itself further in the numerous performance indications—for tempo, dynamics, and ornamentation—scattered throughout her scores. The subtlety and care with which she provided such indications, and their close connection with specific aspects of text interpretation, suggest that for Strozzi the mode of performance was intimately linked with the meaning of each piece.

Like the monodies published by so many singer-composers earlier in the century, as well as most mid-century cantatas, Strozzi's music is emphatically singer's music, conceived for the voice of the composer. Strozzi's own voice, to judge from those works explicitly written for her in 1635 and 1636, must have been a rather light soprano possessed of sufficient flexibility for rapid passage work, yet possibly more comfortable in sustaining long legato lines. And her own compositions call for similar vocal qualities. Nearly three-quarters of her works are scored for solo soprano and continuo; indeed, she published only two solo works for voices other than soprano. Her remaining compositions are ensembles: duets, trios, quartets, and quintets, most of which involve at least one soprano. Strozzi could have performed almost any of these pieces with or without other singers, on occasions such as those described in the *Veglie de' Signori Unisoni*, which mention ensemble performances as well as solo songs by her. Like most singers of the time, she probably accompanied herself, perhaps on a lute or theorbo.

Many of the texts of her works indicate that they were written especially for her: the *Barbara-barbaro* conceit occurs prominently in many different pieces. In even more of her compositions, the chief subject is singing and the protagonist is specifically a singer. Although a woman is clearly the speaker in only a few instances, in several other cases the gender is not explicit, allowing us to believe that the voice is feminine. One cantata in particular, which bears an unusually specific dedication to one Giovanni Antonio Forni, is so clearly a direct address—the text begins with the refrain "I am not afraid of you" ("Non pavento io di te")—that it is difficult not to hear the voice of Barbara Strozzi herself, the woman, the persona of the composer merging with that of the singer.

To whom, indeed, did Barbara Strozzi sing her songs? What function did they serve? One assumes that her cantatas, like those of her contemporaries, were performed in intimate surroundings, in drawing rooms, and as entertainment in academies. Unfortunately we have no specific record of Strozzi's own performances after those that took place at Unisoni meetings in the late 1630s. Nonetheless it is probable that she continued to perform in similar circumstances.

Her identity as a performer clearly remains central to her works. Indeed, I would like to suggest the possibility—even the necessity—of viewing Strozzi's compositions within a specific personal context, as the efforts of a singer to reconcile those two terms that had provided the Accademia degli Unisoni with such an appropriate subject for debate in 1638: the *paragone* of tears and song (*pianto* and *canto*). In that controversy—of which, we must remember, Barbara was the mouthpiece—a relationship between the two means of amorous persuasion was articulated, a relationship that ultimately lies at the heart of her own compositions. In the opening argument tears were claimed the stronger of the two, because they were natural, whereas song was artificial. But the opposition then declared that art was the superior force, because it harnessed and directed nature's power. Barbara herself came down firmly, if somewhat ironically, on the side of music, concluding the debate thus: "I do not question your decision, gentlemen, in favor of song; for well do I know that I would not have received the honor of your presence at our last session had I invited you to see me cry rather than to hear me sing."

The affective force of music—especially of Strozzi's own music—does indeed depend, at least in part, upon its ability to imitate or borrow the power of tears. Strozzi's exploration of the affect of suffering, the concentration of so much of her art on the expressive, the plaintive, the tearful, on the lamenting singer-lover, seems to offer a deliberate demonstration of those opposed yet related powers. If her music can be seen in some sense as a reconciliation, a fusion of the power of tears and song, surely as the end product of such a synthesis it would be superior in power to either of its constituents, more powerful, that is, to incite love. When she sang her songs at academic meetings for the pleasure of the gentlemen present, she may indeed have intended them to inspire love—in the venerable tradition of the Venetian courtesan.

In this context I should like to introduce a painting from the Gemäldegalerie of Dresden that was on view in the United States in 1978 in the traveling exhibition, The Splendor of Dresden. (See plate 10.) The painter is Bernardo Strozzi (no relation to Barbara Strozzi insofar as we know, although the similarity of names is certainly a curious coincidence). It was painted in Venice, probably in 1637. Its label offers a straightforward descriptive title, *Female Musician with Viola da Gamba*.[20] This representation, which is distinguished by a highly individualized physiognomy, is clearly the portrait of a specific young woman rather than a generalized personification of Music; her pensive, indeed almost melancholic, expression speaks directly and movingly to us. In contrast with the pathos of her face, however, is the seductive looseness of her costume, which so provocatively displays her ample breasts. The flowers in her hair make explicit reference to her role as courtesan, as *Flora meretrice*; and her musical attributes confirm this invitation to love.[21] There are two instruments in the picture: her own viola da gamba and a violin on the table in the lower left corner. As in so many paintings of women and music—from Titian to Vermeer—the second instrument seems to be awaiting the arrival of its player. In Bernardo Strozzi's picture, the music depicted in the songbook above the violin is indeed a duet; its performance requires the participation of another.

Although I am not able to demonstrate that the music is by Barbara Strozzi, I am intrigued by the possibility that the Dresden *Female Musician* is her portrait. Circumstantial evidence, along with the picture's expressive tone, seems to point toward such an identification. The painter, Bernardo Strozzi, left his native Genoa in 1630 for Venice,[22] where he was evidently involved in the same cultural circles we have been discussing. Among those who posed for portraits by him were Claudio Monteverdi and, more important for us, Giulio Strozzi—whose image, dated 1635, is among the rare dated works of the artist's Venetian period. Finally, along with Giulio's portrait, the Dresden picture of a female musician can be traced back to the collection of Niccolò Sagredo, one of Barbara's most important patrons, who became doge of Venice in 1675.[23] It is tempting to reconstruct the circumstances surrounding the execution of this painting. In the very years in which Giulio Strozzi was launching his daughter's career, we may imagine that he himself could have commissioned this image.

Whatever the social position of Barbara Strozzi and whatever the function of her art, her life and work distinguish her from her contemporaries. Whereas other composers sought (and found) a public forum for their affective expression—in theater or in church—her world remained, rather, private. Although she demonstrated her potential abilities as a dramatic composer—particularly in her single political cantata—the narrative mode, with its distancing of pathos, was evidently not the one she preferred. Her voice remained small, addressing itself to a more intimate audience and expressing, we sense, less the feelings of fictive characters than her own. She herself confessed in the preface to her Opus 7, "These harmonic notes are the language of the soul and instruments of the heart."

Plate 10
Bernardo Strozzi, *Female Musician with Viola da Gamba*

Source: Dresden, Staatliche Kunstsammlungen

The Voice of Barbara Strozzi

Such an interpretation is encouraged, if not actually documented, by the apparent paradoxes of her life. Barbara Strozzi was a singer in Venice surrounded by librettists and impresarios when the main cultural interest of a large segment of the society was opera, yet she apparently never sang in opera. She was an unusually gifted composer who studied with the foremost opera composer of the day, yet she never wrote an opera. Despite the fact that those around her were deeply involved in public activity, her sphere seems enclosed, insular, and self-contained. Her academic performances and her eight published volumes are all we know of her career.

The date of her death is unknown. Barbara Strozzi disappears from history with the last of her publications in 1664; she left no testament or monument other than that impressive body of works. As an inscription for her unknown tomb we might borrow the epitaph written by two Incogniti for an unnamed musician:

> Although I always bore bitter misfortune
> And was unhappy until death,
> In this one thing was fate kind to me:
> Others cry of their sufferings.
> I sang of mine.[24]

NOTES

This essay contains material previously published in Ellen Rosand, "Barbara Strozzi, *virtuosissima cantatrice*: The Composer's Voice," *Journal of the American Musicological Society* 31 (1978): 241–81, and David Rosand and Ellen Rosand, "Barbara di Santa Sofia and Il Prete Genovese: On the Identity of a Portrait by Bernardo Strozzi," *Art Bulletin* 63 (1981): 249–58, which appears here with the permission of the original publishers.

1. Strozzi's works include the following prints: [op. 1:] *Il primo de' madrigali . . . a due, tre, quattro e cinque voci* (Venice: Vincenti, 1644); op. 2: *Cantate, ariette e duetti* (Venice: Gardano, 1651); op. 3: *Cantate ariete a una, due e tre voci* (Venice: Gardano, 1654); op. 5: *Sacri musicali affetti* (Venice: Gardano, 1655); op. 6: *Ariette a voce sola* (Venice: Magni, 1657); op. 7: *Diporti di Euterpe overo cantate e ariette a voce sola* (Venice: Magni, 1659); op. 8: *Arie* (Venice: Magni [detto Gardano], 1664). Although François-Joseph Fétis, *Biographie universelle des musiciens* (Paris: 1870), 7:161, listed an Opus 4, *Cantate a voce sola*, no such volume has been mentioned since then. The few copies of the other seven volumes to have survived makes it plausible to regard Opus 4 as lost; yet the appearance of Opus 3 and Opus 5 in consecutive years suggests that Opus 5 may possibly have been Opus 4 misnumbered by Gardano, and that Fétis may have been mistaken.

This confusion may be related to another problem, raised by Sir John Hawkins in his *General History of the Science and Practice of Music* (London: Payne & Son, 1776), p. 594. In discussing Barbara Strozzi, Hawkins mentions a volume entitled *Cantate, Ariette e Duetti* published by her in 1653, in the preface of which she claims to have invented the "commixture [of air and recitative]" "given to the public by way of trial." Since none of her known works was published in 1653 and she makes no similar claim in any of her known prefaces, perhaps we are dealing here with another (or the same) lost work.

Works by Strozzi are also found in several anthologies. A three-voice motet, *Quis dabit mihi*, appears in Bartolomeo Marcesso, ed., *Sacra corona, motetti a due, e tre voci di diversi eccelentissimi autori moderni* (Venice: Magni, 1656; reprint, Antwerp: Heirs of P. Phalèse, 1659). Two arias, *Rissolvetevi pensieri* and *Chi brama in amore* (both from op. 6), are published in Francesco Tonalli, ed., *Arie a voce sola di diversi auttori* (Venice: Vincenti, 1656).

Manuscript works ascribed to Strozzi include: *Aure giacchè non posso*, in Modena, Biblioteca Estense, MS P (from op. 8); *Presso un ruscello algente*, Venice, Conservatorio Benedetto Marcello, Collezione Correr 2, no. 43; *Rissolvetevi pensieri*, London, British Library, MS. 59 (1681), fol. 31b (from op. 6); *Havete torto* and *Un amante doglioso*, Kassel, Landesbibliothek, MS collection of cantatas, fol. 34, from Robert Eitner, *Biographisch-bibliographisches Quellen-Lexikon*, 10 vols. (Leipzig: Breitkopf & Härtel, 1898–1904), 9: 315. Although a manuscript collection, *Diporti d'Euterpe overo madrigali a due voci col basso* (1660), attributed to her (Venice, Biblioteca Marciana, class 4, cod. 726 [10364]), bears the title, approximate date, and name of the same dedicatee as her Opus 7, it is not her work. Its contents are inconsistent with her style and probably date from a considerably later period.

Among the few works of Strozzi that have appeared in modern editions, the most accessible are: *Chiamata a nuovi amori* (op. 2), in Vittorio Ricci, ed., *Antiche gemme italiane* (Milan: Ricordi, 1949); *Non c'è più fede* (op. 2), in Francesco Vatielli, ed., *Antiche cantate d'amore* (Bologna: F. Bongiovanni, n.d.); *Soccorrete, luci avare* and *Spesso per entro al petto* (op. 2), in Knud Jeppesen, ed., *La flora* (Copenhagen: Wilhelm Hansen, 1949), vol. 2; *Lagrime mie* (op. 7), in Carol MacClintock, ed., *The Solo Song* (New York: W. W. Norton, 1973); *Con le belle non ci vuol fretta* and *Consiglio amoroso* (op. 1), ed. Carolyn Raney, in the series Nine Centuries of Music by Women (New York: Broude Brothers, 1977). A facsimile of Opus 8 was published in the series Monumenta veneta (Bologna: A.M.I.S., 1970) but is not readily available. A volume devoted to her music will appear in the forthcoming series, The Italian Cantata of the Seventeenth Century, to be published by Garland Press. Selections from her cantatas have been recorded by Judith Nelson on *Barbara Strozzi virtuosissima cantatrice: Cantate*, Harmonia Mundi HM 1114 (1983).

2. These include, among others, Benedetto Ferrari, Nicolò Fontei, Filiberto Laurenzi, Francesco Luccio, Francesco Manelli, Martino Pesenti, and Giovanni Felice Sances.

3. Arnoldo Bonaventura, "Le donne italiane e la musica," *Rivista musicale italiana* 37 (1925): 524.

4. The documentary support for these and other relevant details of the biographies of both Giulio and Barbara Strozzi are found in Ellen Rosand, "Barbara Strozzi, *virtuosissima cantatrice*: The Composer's Voice," *Journal of the American Musicological Society* 31 (1978): 241–81.

5. See Nicolò Fontei, *Bizzarrie poetiche* (Venice: Magni, 1635) and *Bizzarrie poetiche libro secondo* (Venice: Magni, 1636).

6. *Veglia prima de' Signori academici Unisoni havuta in Venetia in casa del Signor Giulio Strozzi. Alla Molto Illustre Signora la Sig. Barbara Strozzi* (Venice: Sarzina, 1638). The volume contains three *veglie* (descriptions of meetings), each with its own title page; but the title pages bear the same date and dedication to Barbara Strozzi. A general title page, *Veglie de' Signori Unisoni*, without either date or dedication, opens the volume.

7. The text of this debate was printed twice in the same year by the same publisher as the *Veglie*. See *La contesa del canto e delle lagrime. Discorsi academici. Recitati dalla Sig. Barbara Strozzi nell'academia de gli Unisoni* (Venice: Sarzina, 1638); Giovanni Francesco Loredano, *Bizzarrie academiche* (Venice: Sarzina, 1638), pp. 182–202.

8. For general information on the Incogniti, see Michele Battagia, *Delle accademie veneziane* (Venice: Orlandelli, 1826), pp. 41–43; and Michele Maylander, *Storia delle accademie d'Italia*, 5 vols. (Bologna: L. Cappilli, 1926–30), 3:205. Biographies of 106 of the members, including a portrait of each, are printed in *Le glorie degli Incogniti . . .* (Venice: Valvasense, 1647). For a more specific discussion of seventeenth-century libertinism, see Giorgio Spini, *Ricerca dei libertini. La teoria dell' impostura delle religioni nel seicento italiano* (Rome: Universale di Roma, 1950), pp. 139–63. Further bibliography on various aspects of the academy is found in Lorenzo Bianconi and Thomas Walker, "Dalla 'Finta pazza' alla 'Veremonda': Storie di Febiarmonici," *Rivista italiana di musicologia* 10 (1975): 418n.

9. For a discussion of the polemics of feminism during the seventeenth century, in addition to Spini, *Ricerca dei libertini*, see Emilio Zanette, *Suor Arcangela monaca del seicento veneziano* (Venice: Istituto per la collaborazione culturale, 1961), pp. 211–37.

10. For a full discussion of the iconography of the Incogniti emblem, see Lionello Puppi, "Ignoto Deo," *Arte veneta* 23 (1969): 169–80.

11. The satires appear in a manuscript located in the Biblioteca Marciana, Venice. For a fuller discussion of these satires, see Rosand, "Barbara Strozzi," nn. 31–37.

12. See Rita Casagrande, *Le cortigiane veneziane nel cinquecento* (Milan, 1968), pp. 189, 199, for a brief discussion of some of the Venetian courtesans who were particularly well known for their musical abilities.

Aretino's statement is quoted and translated in Alfred Einstein, *The Italian Madrigal*, 3 vols. (Princeton: Princeton University Press, 1949), 1:94–95.

13. See Bianconi and Walker, "Dalla 'Finta pazza,'" pp. 441–42.

14. See Loredano, *Lettere* (Geneva: Widerhold, 1669), 2: 249. The relevant text from this letter is given in Rosand, "Barbara Strozzi," n. 48.

15. Several female singers, in addition to Strozzi and Caccini, are known to have written music. These include Adriana Basile and Leonora Baroni. See Rosand, "Barbara Strozzi," pp. 254–55 and nn. 49–54; see also chap. 6 above.

16. These are Marcesso, *Sacra corona, motetti a due, e tre voci*, and Tonalli, *Arie a voce sola*; see n. 1 above.

17. For the text of this passage in Giulio's will, see Rosand, "Barbara Strozzi," n. 67.

18. The work was probably never printed in its entirety. The only part of the "Elogii" known to us is Strozzi's eulogy of the singer Anna Renzi, "Elogia di Giulio Strozzi, tratto dal libro secondo de' suoi Elogii delle donne virtuose del nostro secolo," in *Glorie della Signora Anna Renzi Romana* (Venice: Surian, 1644), pp. 5–12.

19. This cantata was published twice, in Opus 2 and Opus 3.

20. *The Splendor of Dresden: Five Centuries of Art Collecting*, exhibition catalogue (New York: Metropolitan Museum of Art, 1978–79), no. 522. See also Luisa Mortari, *Bernardo Strozzi* (Rome: De Luca, 1966), p. 103.

21. For the meanings of Flora, see Julius S. Held, "Flora, Goddess and Courtesan," in *De Artibus Opuscula XL: Essays in Honor of Erwin Panofsky* (New York: New York University Press, 1961), pp. 201–18.

22. The basic biography of Bernardo Strozzi is Raffaello Soprani, *Vite de' pittori, scultori, ed architetti genovesi*, 2 vols., ed. Carlo Giuseppe Ratti (1674; Genoa: Casamara, 1768–69), 1:184–96.

23. Ratti (ibid., p. 195n) cites a letter of Francesco Algarotti (1751), who acquired the picture along with others for Augustus III of Poland. In an earlier letter, of 1743, Algarotti had described three pictures by Bernardo Strozzi in the Sagredo collection: the female musician, a half-length figure of *David*, and—not mentioned by Ratti—a portrait of Giulio Strozzi; see Hans Posse, "Die Brief des Grafen Francesco Algarotti an den sächsischen Hof und seine Bilderkäufe für die Dresdener Gemäldegalerie 1743–1747," *Jahrbuch der preussischen Kunstsammlungen* 52 (1931), supp., pp. 43–44. For the portrait of Giulio Strozzi, which was mistaken for an image of the painter and used by Ratti to illustrate the biography of Bernardo Strozzi, see Mortari, *Bernardo Strozzi*, p. 143, fig. 358.

24. Loredano and Pietro Michiele, *Il Cimiterio, epitafi giocosi* (Venice: Guerigli, 1654), *centuria seconda*, epitaph 34.

8

Musiciennes of the Ancien Régime

JULIE ANNE SADIE

When, in 1732, Titon du Tillet apportioned the places of honor on Mount Parnassus, one woman, Elisabeth-Claude Jacquet de la Guerre (c. 1666–1729), was included with Blamont, Campra, Destouches, Lalande, and Marais among the composers of the seventh row; only Lully was ranked higher.[1] But the lives and careers of many other accomplished women—singers, harpsichordists, and poets among them—were mentioned, if only briefly, in the text of his *Parnasse françois*. Titon du Tillet was looking back nostalgically at a time when the hierarchy of distinguished musicians and men of letters had already made way for a younger generation in which women were allowed greater opportunity. Indeed, by 1753 D'Aquin de Château-Lyon could write that "women today distinguish themselves in every manner," calling them "true Muses, such as are imagined only on Parnassus."[2] Appropriately, when it came to a new edition in 1760, Titon du Tillet invited many of these women to assume places in the newly conceived lower rungs of his artistic hierarchy reserved especially for aristocratic amateurs.[3]

The rise, if not the recognition, of amateur musicians among the French aristocracy had begun much earlier. In the seventeenth century, musically inclined noblewomen sang and played the lute or the harpsichord for their private amusement and occasionally retained small staffs of musicians—perhaps even including a composer—for their more formal entertainments. Between 1653 and 1659 the novelist and intellectual Mademoiselle Madeleine de Scudéry and her confidant, Mademoiselle [Anne or Marguerite] Bocquet (died after 1660), who was a lutenist and composer,[4] held a *salon précieux*.

The lute and the harpsichord by their nature were sufficient unto themselves or could serve to support the player's own voice. Playing these instruments thus represented a suitable accomplishment for a young lady and was doubtless an asset in procuring a husband. The best musicians were hired to teach them the rudiments; if they excelled at an early enough age, they might be invited to play before the king and queen. To play an instrument or to sing was, then, a social grace, and to do so well could lead to special favor. As more people came to value musical training, the demand grew for teachers, instruments, and printed music. From the turn of the century onward, dozens of collections of chamber music composed by aspiring young music masters were dedicated to their aristocratic female pupils, and individual pieces were often named after them.[5]

The increased participation of women in music-making is reflected in the art of the period. Seventeenth-century engravers, such as Nicolas Arnoult, Abraham Bosse, and the artists of the Bonnart family atelier, produced many prints of young ladies and *dames de qualité* playing the harpsichord, the organ, the lute, the mandolin, and even the viol; sometimes the ladies are identified.[6] Often such pictures may be the only source of information for the lady's musical accomplishments, as is the case with André Bouy's engraving (1702) of François de Troy's portrait of Catherine de Loison (plate 11). Other artists, among them the eighteenth-century painters Bernard Picart, Antoine Watteau, Carle Van Loo (whose wife was a fine singer), and Louis Carrogi de Carmontelle, included women musicians in settings bearing such designations as *concert champêtre* or *concert intime* (plate 12).[7]

Although many noble women doubtless could not consider becoming professional singers because of their position in society, the *lettres patentes* granted to Pierre Perrin in June 1669 for the establishment of *académies d'opéra* specifically allowed the participation of ladies and members of the nobility. This represented an important encouragement for women of lesser rank and means who wished to make a profession of singing. Their cause was aided by the abhorrence felt by the French public for the Italian castrati. The best sopranos came to enjoy a glamorous star status rivaled in the eighteenth century only by the fame of the *haute-contre* Pierre de Jélyotte. Those of the first generation were rigorously trained by Lully; later the older artists taught those coming after them. Besides singing with the Académie Royale de la Musique, the most popular singers sang in church services, at court, and, later, in public concerts, notably the *Concert Spirituel* (inaugurated in 1725).[8] At some point in their careers, most of these women became the mistresses of princes, dukes, or counts; some received royal pensions that enabled them to live

Plate 11
François de Troy, *Catherine de Loison* (holding a piece of
her own composition), engraving by André Bouy (1702)

Source: Paris, Bibliothèque nationale,
Département des Estampes

Plate 12
Louis Carrogi de Carmontelle, *M. et Melle Pitoin*

Source: Chantilly, Musée Condé
Photograph by Giraudon, Paris

grandly as long as their voices and physical beauty found favor. It is a sad commentary that they often died in poverty and oblivion.

Women who wished to become professional instrumentalists made their way only slowly into the ranks of the court musicians; the few that succeeded were mostly the daughters of prominent musicians like François Couperin-le-Grand and François-Joseph de Caix. As with the singers, their number grew with the increasing opportunities created by the Concert Spirituel; many supplemented their playing careers by teaching.

It is less easy to know to what extent women were encouraged to compose. Was it through their music masters' connections or their fathers' determination that a number of young ladies succeeded in publishing pieces in the monthly collections of *airs sérieux et à boire*? The naïvety of their efforts at composition contrast markedly with the mastery of Elisabeth-Claude Jacquet de la Guerre.[9] Her skill in improvisation at the keyboard blossomed into a compositional technique that enabled her to produce an opera (1694) and collections of suites (1687), sonatas (1707), and cantatas (1708, 1711, 1715). She was patronized by the king, although she never enjoyed a royal appointment. Not until later in the century did another woman, Julie Candeille, make a substantial mark as a composer.

It was a sign of the times that by then women were not only teaching, performing, writing methods, and composing, but also advertising their skills in the *Almanach Musical*. Music-making had become a socially less self-conscious pursuit. Increasingly, women were taking on professional engagements as singers and instrumentalists and, like men, were composing pieces to display their own artistry. Evidence of the general broadening of society's attitudes toward musiciennes in the course of the eighteenth century may be found in the tributes to their lives and reviews and accounts of their compositions and performances that follow.

The most powerful women in France, the wives and mistresses of the Bourbon kings, were among the most ardent lovers of music. Their tastes and habits were widely imitated. Anne of Austria, the mother of Louis XIV, maintained a private musical entourage; when she herself took up the lute under the tutelage of Ennemond Gaultier, she set a precedent that was widely followed at court. Both Madame de Montespan and Madame de Maintenon organized chamber music concerts in Louis XIV's private apartments. In the declining years of his reign, the king's daughter-in-law, the Duchesse de

Maine, gave lavish musical entertainments which drew many courtiers and musicians to her château at Sceaux, near Versailles.[10]

Marie Leszcinska, upon her marriage to Louis XV in 1725, inaugurated the *concerts chez la Reine* at Versailles, organized by the opera composer Destouches. These often took the form of repeats of performances earlier heard at the Concert Spirituel (which the queen was unable to attend in Paris). The queen herself played many instruments, though without particular distinction, and she encouraged her children to do likewise. According to the Duc de Luynes, she often participated in the evening chamber music and was obligingly joined by some of the leading musicians of the day, including the greatest of all the castrati, Farinelli.[11] Her musical endeavors were to be curtailed with the growing attachment of the king to the Marquise de Pompadour. At court from 1745, Madame de Pompadour spent much of her time between 1747 and 1753 producing and taking part in private performances of the latest pastorales and excerpts from operas with her friends, like the Duchesse de Brancas and the Duc d'Ayen. The performances, open only to those invited by the king, were held in the Théâtre des petits cabinets that Madame de Pompadour had specially built in the château.[12] The Duc de Luynes, who was often present, never failed in his memoirs to praise her singing and acting—though perhaps he could hardly do otherwise.[13]

Before becoming Louis XVI's wife, Marie-Antoinette of Austria was well schooled in French language and culture. She sang and played the harpsichord and the harp. Installed at Versailles as the dauphine in 1770, she continued daily music lessons and organized small private concerts in which she herself took part.[14] She loved opera—comic or serious, Italian or French. She patronized not only Gluck but also Piccinni, Sacchini, and Grétry, and as a result often found herself enmeshed in intrigues, which her vision of a more diversified musical life for France enabled her for a time to mitigate.[15]

Throughout the period under discussion, court music—as opposed to the music heard in Paris (at the homes of nobles and musicians and at the Palais Royal during the Regency)—was notoriously conservative. For a long time French music was reckoned as official and Italian music was considered almost subversive. But it is clear that the royal patronesses at Versailles were eager to hear and perform the latest music from Paris, of whatever kind. It seems that Louis XIV's cousin, the Duchesse de Guise, even commissioned the first cantata and the first sonata to be composed in France (these were genres of Italian origin) from Charpentier.[16]

For the precocious and well-born, music instruction began in childhood. The daughters of noble families became pupils of the most eminent seventeenth-century harpsichordists: Chambonnières, D'Anglebert, and the Couperins, for example. François Couperin (*L'Art de toucher le clavecin*, 1717) even observed that female hands had a natural advantage over male hands for playing the harpsichord. Jacquet [de la Guerre], whose father was a musician, was only one of the particularly talented children who were brought to play before Louis XIV.[17] At the age of seven Jacquet amazed her royal audience by singing even difficult works at sight, accompanying tastefully, and composing in all keys.[18] At twelve she was hailed as *"la merveille de notre siècle"*[19] and at nineteen, according to the Marquis de Dangeau, she composed all the airs for a *petit opéra*.[20] At twenty she published her first book of *Pièces de clavessin*. The breadth of her skill indicates that she must have had excellent instruction. Louis XIV was enchanted by the child and Mme de Montespan took her under her wing. For his own daughter by Louise de la Vallière the king appointed D'Anglebert to teach the harpsichord; in return D'Anglebert dedicated to her his first book of *Pièces de clavecin* (1689).[21] Other children of Louis XIV by Mme de Montespan (two girls and two boys) were taught by Lalande and Couperin.

Many ladies, noble and bourgeois, could claim the distinction of having been students of Couperin, among them Anne-Elisabeth Bouret (born 1693), the daughter of a lawyer and later the wife of the Marquis de la Mézangère.[22] She herself also taught the harpsichord, and in turn one of her students, Simon Simon, became *"maître de clavecin de la Reine & des Enfans de France."* La Borde reckoned her Couperin's best pupil and a gifted composer.[23] Couperin's daughter Marguerite-Antoinette (1705–78) was sufficiently accomplished to be appointed in 1736 to succeed to her father's position as the royal chamber harpsichordist; she was the first woman to gain such a distinction, though the position was downgraded to a *commission d'ordinaire*; one doubts it was strictly a matter of her sex or her lesser abilities, but rather because she was simply less experienced and certainly less eminent.[24] In addition, she was chosen by Louis XV to teach his daughters the harpsichord.[25] Couperin's other daughter, Marie-Madeleine [Marie-Cécile] (1690–1742), was a nun and may have been organist of the royal abbey at Maubuisson.

There were, inevitably, those who were cynical about the musical ambitions of women. One among them, the Abbé Carbasus, penned a satire in 1739 on a marquise who is made proudly to proclaim:

I play the harpsichord; I perform the *pièces* of Couperin; I bang out those of Rameau, whose *Traité d'harmonie* with Campion's octave rule I possess. I perform and transpose at sight, a half tone higher, a half tone lower, or otherwise, every kind of French and Italian music; I double and triple it [i.e., embellish it]. The art of composition is so familiar to me that I can improvise for an hour in three, four, and five parts, on any subject for a fugue, double fugue, and counter fugue [!] submitted to me.[26]

Few men could make good such a claim.

That singing and playing music were often merely preoccupations of young women may explain why the careers of so many promising young musiciennes did not extend beyond the time of their marriages. Le Blanc noted this in 1740 and attributed it to the fact that they were taught to play solo pieces rather than to accompany. In his opinion marriage should not deter women from music-making; he even went so far as to say there were women who "surpassed in facility the best-trained young people in Paris."[27] Michel Corrette echoed this sentiment in the preface to *Le Maître de clavecin pour l'accompagnement* (1753) and attempted to remedy the deficiency in current harpsichord instruction:

As the harpsichord is now a part of the proper education of young noble women who, as I have noted, no longer give it up on marriage if they have once mastered accompaniment, I have long been endeavoring to write for them a short and easy method to simplify the alleged difficulties that the foes of good harmony are at pains to propagate.

The frontispiece to the edition shows a violinist accompanied by a lady at the harpsichord.

Intermarriage between musical families insured that some women would in some measure continue their musical careers. Two such were Henriette-Angélique Houssu and Marie-Rose du Bois, the wives of Antoine Forqueray and his son Jean-Baptiste Antoine Forqueray; both accompanied their husbands on the harpsichord.[28] D'Aquin extolled the talents of Marie-Rose in particular and described her union with Forqueray as *"un mariage conclu sur le Parnasse"*[29] (this could not be said of Henriette-Angélique's stormy marriage to the elder Forqueray, which ended in divorce). Marie-Louise Mangot, the wife of Rameau, was well known for the performances she gave of her husband's pièces de clavecin at the home of La Pouplinière.[30] Anne-Jeanne Boucon, whose harpsichord playing in the financier Crozat's private concerts was praised by Titon du Tillet (along with that of Mademoiselle Guyot), became the wife of Mondonville in 1748.[31]

There were, on the other hand, women like Lully's mistress, Marie-Françoise Certain (died 1711), who gathered around themselves a circle of like-minded musicians. Titon du Tillet wrote of her, "As she gave extremely fine concerts in her home, the very best composers brought along their music, which was always performed with considerable success."[32] He went on to praise the precision of her playing and her command of repertory. Her library included more than a hundred volumes of music—ballets and operas by Lully, motets and airs, and books of harpsichord pieces by everyone from D'Anglebert to La Guerre. She owned two harpsichords, a recorder, a guitar, a theorbo lute, two treble viols, two bass viols, and an Italian *basse de violon* (cello).[33] Le Blanc portrayed her as an important mediator between French and Italian tastes.[34] Like Certain, La Guerre also gave concerts at her home near St. Louis-en-l'Ile, where "all the great musicians and fine connoisseurs went eagerly to hear her."[35]

The exigencies of spinsterhood and widowhood led many women to give private lessons, particularly later in the eighteenth century. The *Almanach Musical*, published in the late 1770s and early 1780s, contains the names of numerous women teachers of the harpsichord and the fortepiano, the organ, the harp, singing, and even composition. A certain Mademoiselle Simon of the Saint André-des-Arts quarter advertised that "she takes young women as boarders, teaches them vocal music, the harpsichord, the harp, and geography. She spends the winter in Paris and the summer on the outskirts: price 800 *livres*."[36] Madame Ravissa of Turin was another who, in 1778, advertised herself as a professor of the harpsichord, harp, composition, singing, and the *gout italien*; it must surely be significant that the same issue carried a favorable review of her *Six sonates pour le clavecin ou le forte-piano* (opus 1) in which the reviewer also noted her high character and her success as a teacher.[37] With Hélène de Nervo de Montgeroult (1764–1836) widowhood initiated a more public musical career.[38] Provincial and of noble birth, she was taught to play the piano by Hüllmandel and, in 1786, by Dussek. She was briefly married to the Marquis de Montgeroult, who died a prisoner of the Austrians in 1793. Two years later she was appointed to the piano faculty of the newly founded Conservatoire de Paris. While she remained there only two years, she went on to publish two collections of *Trois sonates pour le forte-piano* and a *Cours complèt pour l'enseignement du forte-piano*, which ran to two editions.

For one woman in particular, skill at the keyboard was but one of many talents. While only a child, Amélie-Julie Candeille (1767–1834),[39] distinguished herself as a singer, pianist, harpist, and (like her father Pierre Candeille) composer; after singing for several years at the Opéra she joined the Comédie Française, where she took tragic roles in productions of Racine while also excelling as a comic actress. She made her debut as fortepiano soloist at the Concert Spirituel on 15 August 1783 playing a concerto by Clementi; the critic of the *Journal de Paris nationale* wrote that "she demonstrated a most brilliant and assured technique."[40] On 20 May of the following year she played a concerto of her own composition (Opus 2, repeated on 1 November), which was reported by the *Mercure de France* in a notice whose opening words must indicate what the writer and his readers thought most interesting:

> Miss Candeille, who has a very pleasing face and figure, brings to a special talent for the fortepiano, acquired as a composer, new claims to applause. The concerto, which she performed very well, is charmingly cast, and she cannot be too much encouraged in the cultivation of an art in which she promises so well.[41]

Playing the harpsichord and, later, the fortepiano was, then, a favored pursuit for young French women during the ancien régime, and their needs—particularly those of young women of good families—provided employment for numerous teachers, just as they also stimulated composition and publication. For most such women, a musical profession was beneath them; but it is clear from the remarks of Couperin, Le Blanc, and the Duc de Luynes—to name only three—that many women amateurs achieved a very high standard. Those who, like Jacquet and Candeille, came from bourgeois musical families stood the best chance of making their way in the musical life of Paris; Mlle Couperin's unprecedented court appointment, it must be admitted, was opened to her only because of her father's unique prestige. The absence in the profession of women lacking such family connections can only mean that a middle-class woman, unlike her male counterpart, had no entrée on the grounds of talent alone.

Singing, in contrast to instrumental playing, was an admirable profession for a talented young woman even before the reign of Louis XIV. The social and financial rewards were more than sufficient to attract ambitious bourgeois women. And, from the beginning, women who performed in the *ballets de cour* and later the *tragédies lyriques* also sang in the Easter services at the convents. The boundaries between sacred and secular music so sharply defined at court seem not to have inhibited the most popular sopranos of the day.

Loret wrote of the Tenebrae services in 1656 at the Paris convent of the Feuillants, where the singing of Anne de la Barre excited "*grand ravissement*," that of Hilaire Dupuy captivated "*toute la Compagnie*," and the voice of Anne Fonteaux de Cercamanan approached "*celuy d'un ange*."[42] These women were already well-known for their performances in ballets and in the *musique du petit coucher*; they later became *filles ordinaires de la musique de chambre*. La Barre (1628–88), daughter of the royal organist Pierre de la Barre, had sung in the Paris production of Luigi Rossi's *Orfeo* in 1646 and in the early 1650s spent about three years touring northern Europe.[43] With the popular Italian soprano Anna Bergerotti, she sang at Cardinal Mazarin's bidding for many court functions.[44] Lully cleverly capitalized on their fame in his *Ballet de la Raillerie* (1659) with a bilingual dialogue between "La Musica italiana" and "La Musique françoise." But the participation of popular opera singers was liable to turn a religious gathering into a circus, as Le Cerf de la Viéville pointed out:

> In their honor, the price that would be charged at the Opera is charged for a seat at the church. People recognize Urgande and Arcabonne [characters in Lully's *Amadis*] and clap their hands. (I have even heard applause at the Tenebrae and Assumption services, although I cannot now recall whether it was for La Moreau or Madame Cheret.)[45]

At Versailles the women who sang solos in the grand motets were the wives, sisters, and daughters of court musicians. One who could claim all three connections was Anne-Renée Rebel, whose father and brother were violinists—the latter was leader of the Vingt-quatre Violons—and whose husband was Michel de Lalande (the king paid the dowry and wedding expenses of July 1684). She sang at court as early as 1673, and her two daughters, Jeanne and Marie-Anne, sang for the king in 1704 and were invited to sing regularly at his Mass; for that they were awarded a pension of 1,000 livres. (Sadly, both girls died in the smallpox epidemic of 1711.)[46] The cousin of François Couperin, Louise Couperin (died 1728), also sang in the king's service; her name appears beside some of the motet *versets* in Couperin's published collections of 1702, 1704, and 1705, composed " by order of the king." It may have been one of these that the two Couperins, joined by the colorful Mlle de Maupin, performed for the Mass of the Duc d'Orléans on 8 July 1702.[47]

Serious music-making was also pursued in the convents. The musicians at the Abbey of Longchamps were praised in the *Mercure Galant* of October 1678:

The beautiful voices employed in the concert compel admiration by their variety and their exactness. The orchestra which accompanies them is marvelous. It performs with a delicacy responsive to the search for perfect tuning; and it may be said that as many mistresses' hands make it up as play the viol or the harpsichord. The blend of voices and instruments that form this charming music is so meticulously prepared that the best connoisseurs are in accord that nothing so beautiful is to be heard in any other convent.[48]

It was at the request of the nuns at Longchamps that François Couperin composed his *Leçons de Ténèbres* around 1714.

Singing was also cultivated in the school for young women, the Maison Royale de Saint-Louis at Saint-Cyr, presided over by Mme de Maintenon. The girls sang psalms and motets for the services on holy days and were occasionally allowed to rehearse dramatic music. Nivers and Clérambault wrote collections of motets especially for the girls.[49] In 1688 Mme de Maintenon commissioned Racine to write for Saint-Cyr a sacred dramatic work, for which Moreau composed the music. The result, *Esther*, was performed before the king on 5 February 1689.[50]

During the ancien régime, women sang extensively in sacred and secular spheres and were duly rewarded. The salaries of those who sang at the Académie Royale de Musique were on a par with those of male singers. Among those who devoted themselves to opera, the most famous singer of the seventeenth century was Marthe le Rochois (c. 1658–1728). Titon du Tillet's description of her portrayal of Armide in 1686 reveals the extent to which singers were actors of consummate skill:

When she began to move and sing, she dominated the stage. What rapture to see her in the fifth scene of the second act—sword in hand, ready to pierce Renaud's breast. . . . Rage animated her features, love took possession of her heart; first one then the other acted upon her in turn. . . . What true and beautiful poses! How many different movements and expressions in her eyes and on her face during this monologue of twenty-nine lines.[51]

Even when she was at her country house in Certrouville-sur-Seine, she was sought out for her advice and instruction by both musicians and actors.

Le Rochois's finest protégée was Marie Antier (1687–1747), who made her debut in the 1711 revival of La Barre's *La Vénitienne* (1705).[52] During the next thirty years she sang at least five major roles in new productions as well as revivals each season. In 1720 she became *première actrice* of the Académie Royale de Musique and significantly, in the following year, a *musicienne de la chambre du Roi*. She was for a time the mistress of the Prince de Carignan. She married in 1726 and the next year was involved in a scandalous affair with the financier La Pouplinière. Her career was evidently undisturbed by these liaisons; at the same time she took on many solo engagements at the Concert Spirituel and the Concert Français in addition to her commitments at the Académie.

The careers of all the major French opera singers of the eighteenth century—among whom Catherine-Nicole le Maure, Marie Pélissier, Marie Fel, Sophie Arnould, and Anne-Antoinette Clavel Sainte-Huberty must be counted—were varied and colorful, but none more so than that of the deep-voiced Mlle Maupin (1673?–1707). The Marquis de Dangeau described her voice as the most beautiful in the world.[53] The legends surrounding her opera career mention a fondness of masquerading as a man, an ability to duel to the death, passionate lesbian tendencies, and corpse-snatching. Although married, she was the mistress of many men including the elector of Bavaria. Théophile Gautier wrote a colorful fictional account of her life in 1835–36.

Seventeenth-century noblewomen, heeding the example of the Queen Mother, took up the lute and, to judge from contemporary paintings, the guitar. In the mid-eighteenth century the *vielle* (hurdy-gurdy) became a popular instrument among the aristocracy (even Marie Lesczinska briefly took it up). With the generation of Marie-Antoinette came the vogue of harp playing. Next to her, the most important female exponent of that instrument was Stéphanie-Félicité du Crest de Saint-Aubin, later comtesse de Genlis (1746–1830), an immensely gifted woman who distinguished herself as a teacher and an author of over sixty volumes,[54] as well as a musician (see plate 13). In her youth she sang and played the harpsichord, the *pardessus de viole*, and the guitar; but it is as a harpist that she is mainly remembered.[55] She published a method around 1802 and revised it several years later. In addition to devising a deceptively simple method for mastering the instrument, Mme de Genlis claimed to have invented a portable three-string practice harp: "One can carry this little instrument in a carriage or on a walk, during which one can rehearse noiselessly without being detected; and this practice, often repeated, produces great progress and usefully fills an infinitude of idle moments in the service of art."[56] The unkind remarks of the baroness of Oberkirch may however indicate a certain eccentricity: "This mas-

Plate 13
Jules Porreau, engraver, *Stéphanie-Félicité du Crest
de Saint-Aubin, Comtesse de Genlis*

Source: Paris, Bibliothèque nationale,
Département des Estampes

culine woman makes herself colossally absurd with her harp. She takes it everywhere, she talks of it when she doesn't, she plays on a crust of bread and practices on a string."[57] Considered one of the most intelligent and beautiful women of her day, Mme de Genlis was governess to the family of the Duc de Chartres, mistress of the Duc d'Orléans (Philippe-Egalité), and much in demand as a subject by the most eminent painters.

Playing bowed string instruments was less appealing as a pastime. Still, the unladylike position required for playing the bass viola da gamba and the cello—Abbé Carbasus observed that "decency, modesty, and the hoopskirt fashion effectively prohibit the fair sex from playing the viol"[58]—did not deter several viol players' daughters and several princesses.[59] To judge from the Bonnart engravings, seventeenth-century *dames de qualité* played both treble (see plate 14) and bass viols.[60] As early as 1692 the name of Mlle Mengey was included by Du Pradel in his list of viol teachers in *Le Livre commode des adresses de Paris*.[61] Marie-Louise de Cury (1692–1775), daughter of a royal surgeon and later the second wife of Lalande, played the viol.[62] Fewer women appear to have taken up the cello. Corrette, in his *Méthode pour apprendre à jouer de la contrebasse* (1781), blamed the necessity to shift frequently and the greater degree of string resistance for the cello's lack of feminine patronage. Mindful of the difficulties presented by an outsize instrument, the *Annonces* of 1763 offered a "small violoncello appropriate for a woman or a young man."[63]

As in other musical spheres, the daughters of professional viol players—Sainte-Colombe, Marais, and Caix—achieved the highest acclaim as performers. Titon du Tillet tells how Sainte-Colombe and his two daughters performed music for three viols in concerts at their home, and how one of Marais's daughters was as fine a player as her brothers Roland, Vincent, and Nestor.[64] In 1738 Marie-Anne Ursule de Caix (died 1751) was appointed to Louis XV's chamber music as a bass viol player; but, unlike her brothers, she could never hold an appointment in the royal chapel.[65]

Many more eighteenth-century women took up the smallest member of the viol family, the *pardessus*;[66] indeed, that instrument's leading exponents were women. Mme Levi of Rouen, whose compositions for the instrument are lost, was perhaps its best player; she performed on eleven consecutive occasions at the Concert Spirituel in 1745;[67] Ancelet noted that "she is a talented teacher and makes . . . her instrument equal to the violin through the beauty of her playing."[68] One may assume that most of her pupils were female.

Plate 14
Nicolas Bonnart, engraver, Woman accompanying
herself on the viol (1670)

Chez N. Bonnart. ruë St Jacques 'a l'aigle . auec priuil. du Roy . 1670 .

Dame qui joüe de la Viole en chantant .

Elle sçait marier fort agreablement   Et peut auec cét art obliger un Amant
La beauté de sa Voix, auec sa Viole ;   De se faire Ecolier d'une si douce Ecole .

Source: Paris, Bibliothèque nationale,
Département des Estampes

206

Three of Louis XV's daughters—Adélaïde, Victoire, and Sophie—studied the pardessus with Barthélemy de Caix;[69] Adélaïde, Victoire, and Henriette (another of Louis's daughters) also studied the bass viol with F.-J. de Caix and J.-B.-A. Forqueray;[70] Adélaïde also took up the cello. Both Adélaïde and Victoire played the harpsichord and the violin and amused themselves with the guitar and the musette. Their large music library is now in the Bibliothèque nationale. When the eight-year-old Wolfgang Amadeus Mozart visited Paris, he dedicated to Victoire his first opus, *Sonates pour le clavecin avec l'accompagnement de violon* (1764).

Only a few ambitious women played the violin professionally. The most prominent during the first half of the eighteenth century was Elisabeth de Haulteterre, who was also a composer. She played Leclair's sonatas at the Concert Spirituel in 1737 "with all imaginable intelligence, vivacity, and precision."[71] Her own *Premier livre de sonates* for the violin (1740, engraved by her husband Levésque), to which a discussion of bow strokes is appended, was dedicated to Leclair. She may have played a concerto of her own composition at the Concert Spirituel on 9 June 1737; the *Mercure de France* of January 1744 announced the publication of such a work, dedicated to Princess Adélaïde. Unfortunately, none of her concertos and sonatas for the violin have survived.

Two other women played violin concertos at the Concert Spirituel: an Italian, Maddalena Laura Lombardini Sirmen (1735–after 1785) and Mlle Deschamps (later Mme Gauthcrot).[72] Mmc Sirmcn, a student of Tartini, made her debut with her husband, the violinist-composer Lodovico Sirmen, playing a concerto of his for two violins on 15 August 1768. When she returned on 5 May 1785, she performed a concerto of her own.[73] In the meantime Mlle Deschamps (born 1763) made her debut in 1774 playing two violin concertos. On 26 March 1777 she performed a concerto by Giornovichi [Jarnowick], of which she gave at least twelve further performances before the end of 1787. Her other appearances there included the première and four subsequent performances of a new concerto by Viotti between 1787 and 1790.

Many more women must have played and studied the violin. The number of professional players and collections of sonatas for violin and keyboard published in the eighteenth century would have provided ample instruction and amusement for a young woman, particularly if a mother or sister played the harpsichord. So, while female instrumentalists were barred from the orchestras, the most talented could perform as soloists and scrape up a living by teaching; the rest had to be content to remain amateurs.

Musical composition in the seventeenth century and most of the eighteenth century lay for the most part within the realm of the accomplished performer, who composed almost exclusively to fulfil an obligation to a patron. Since a woman rarely had the opportunity to develop her talent to a high level or to enter a patron's service, the need—one may even say the urge—to compose would have been less manifest. It is clear that most of the efforts at composition by French women were undertaken at a young age, under the guidance of a music master, before marriage and family responsibilities intervened. Most of the published music by women is therefore slender; indeed, much of it is restricted to simple airs for soprano and continuo. (Most of the airs composed by men from the turn of the seventeenth century and the cantatas that began appearing shortly thereafter are also scored for high voice, although, of course, they were often transposed.)

Mlle de Ménétou,[74] in 1691, was the first woman to publish an entire collection of airs; most women were content to contribute—often anonymously—single songs to monthly publications such as Ballard's *Recueil[s] d'airs sérieux et à boire*. But from 1695 on, the names of mademoiselles Bataille, Herville, and Coco appear several times in those collections. Mlle Guédon des Presles (died c. 1754), a professional singer and actress, and Mlle Buttier, among others, contributed to the *Meslanges de musique latine, française et italienne* also issued by the Ballard firm between 1727 and 1729. Numerous other collections of airs published first in Paris and later in Amsterdam contain single works by women whom we would not otherwise realize had been composers.[75]

The *Mercure de France* appears to have been an appropriate and sympathetic place to publish single pieces. In September 1728, the text of a cantata, *Le Jugement d'Imole* by Mlle L'Hériter, was printed (the music is lost); in the 1740s a number of unaccompanied airs by Mlle Guédon des Presles were printed there, followed in the 1750s by those of Mme Pellecier-Papavoine.[76] The June 1776 issue included an air for soprano, harp, and a bass instrument by the fifteen-year-old Mlle Duv***, "who charms distinguished gatherings."[77]

The cantata and later the *cantatille* (a short cantata) offered composers dramatic and expressive possibilities within a suitably limited framework of airs and connecting recitatives. Jacquet de la

Guerre, best known for her harpsichord pieces and violin sonatas,[78] was the first French woman to compose in this genre and the only one known to have published whole books of cantatas. The cantatas of her first two books are based on the Scriptures, in keeping with the increasing emphasis on sacred music at Versailles at the time; the third, dedicated to the elector of Bavaria, includes three extended cantatas that may have been intended for stage performance. The texts she selected and the manner in which she chose to set them were far from decorous, in accord with the religious spirit of the times. The sense of brutality conveyed in the first air of *Esther* (in book 1) is arresting: "Oh! What dreadful image traces itself in her spirits! Such tears! Such cries! What horrible carnage!"

Equally graphic are the instrumental parts of *Le Passage de la Mer Rouge* (also in book 1). There are also examples of the popular tempest scene in *Jonas* (in book 1) and in the *Sommeil d'Ulisse* (in book 3). Sensuality is to be found in the first air of *Jacob et Rachel* (in book 1), where the music sensitively mirrors the text (see figure 10).

Julie Pinel's *Nouveau recueil d'airs sérieux et à boire* (1737) (apparently not the first collection this composer produced, although we know of no other)[79] contains *brunettes*, a pastorale, and a cantatille for two voices and accompaniment. One of its *airs sérieux* entitled *Printems*, for soprano, flutes, and continuo, is particularly charming (see figure 11). The embellished flute part introducing the voice typifies the style favored in the concertante airs of contemporary cantatas. A remark in the dedication to the Prince de Soubise implies that Pinel intended to publish a collection of cantatas, but none is known.

Hélène-Louise Demars (born c. 1736), daughter of the organist and harpsichordist Jean Odo Demars, dedicated to Mlle de Soubise a cantata entitled *Horoscope* (Paris, Bibliothèque nationale, Rés. R. 436), the text of which was published after the cantata was performed for its dedicatee on 21 November 1748.[80] Mlle Demars also published two cantatilles, *Hercule et Omphale* and *Les Avantages du buveur*. A talented harpsichordist, Demars participated in the concerts given by La Pouplinière, through whom she became Mme de Genlis's teacher.[81] In 1759 she married Jean-Baptiste Venier, a violinist and music dealer; and as Mme Venieri [*sic*] she was advertised as a harpsichord teacher in the *Tableau de Paris* for that year.[82]

Another composer of cantatilles was Mme Pellecier-Papavoine (c. 1720–90). Appended to *Le Cabriolet*, which was published in

Figure 10
Vien cher objet de mes desirs, from the cantata *Jacob et Rachel*
Elisabeth-Claude Jacquet de la Guerre

Come dear object of my desires,
Come share my tender bonds.

Source: Mademoiselle de la Guerre, *Cantates françoises sur des sujets tirés
de l'Écriture*, book 1 (Paris: Christophe Ballard, 1708), p. 27. Paris,
Bibliothèque nationale, Vm⁷ 159
Translation by Julie Anne Sadie

Figure 11
Printems
Julie Pinel

Ros-sig- nols vous chan- tez les dou- ceurs du prin- tems

Nightingales, you sing of the sweetness of springtime.

Source: Julie Pinel, *Nouveau recueil d'airs sérieux et à boire* (Paris: The author,
Mme La Veuve Boivin, and Mr Le Clerc, 1737), p. 1. Paris, Bibliothèque nationale,
Vm⁷ 629
Translation by Julie Anne Sadie

1755, was a list of seven cantatilles to her credit;[83] and she wrote at
least one more, *La France sauvée; ou, Le Triomphe de la vertu.* Her
husband was also a composer.

Since there would have been no point in composing an opera
without the assurance of a performance by the Académie, few women
took up that challenge. Only Jacquet de la Guerre produced a five-
act *tragédie lyrique.* But in 1736 Mlle Duval composed a *ballet-
héroïque*, and in the second half of the eighteenth century Mme
Bayon-Louis, Henriette-Adélaïde Villard de Beaumesnil, Lucile Grétry,
and Julie Candeille wrote one- and two-act *opéras-comiques.*

As a young woman Jacquet de la Guerre accompanied dramatic

productions (she played the harpsichord in a 1678 production en-titled *Andromède* given in the home of Louis de Mollier);[84] doubt-less this helped her to develop her ideas. In 1691 she wrote an *opéra-ballet* for the king entitled *Les Jeux à l'honneur de la victoire*. The music is lost but a manuscript libretto survives (Paris, Bibliothèque nationale, MS frç. 2217); its dedication to the king reveals how con-scious the composer was of the significance of her achievement.[85] Her tragédie lyrique *Céphale et Procris* was performed by the Aca-démie on 16 March 1694. Like so many French operas of this period, the music owed all too much to Lully and was not flattered by the comparison. But Jacquet de la Guerre found a champion in Sébastien de Brossard, the Paris-loving provincial ecclesiastic who collected and composed music. After the Paris production of *Céphale et Pro-cris*, Brossard mounted his own with the Strasbourg Académie de la Musique (which he had founded), reinforced with supplementary in-strumental parts of his own composition.[86] Perhaps discouraged by her opera's reception in Paris or unable to obtain a further commis-sion, Jacquet de la Guerre restricted herself thereafter to the cantata genre. She also contributed music to the pastiche productions given at the fairs of Saint Germain-des-Près, of which the recitative and duet entitled *Raccommodement comique de Pierrot et de Nicole*, concluding her last collection of cantatas, is an example.[87]

Little can be deduced about the life of Mlle Duval,[88] whose ballet *Les Génies; ou, Les Caractères de l'amour* the Académie premiered on 18 October 1736. From the dedication of the ballet we learn that the Prince de Carignan was Duval's protector. The Parfaict brothers wrote of the opening night in detail:

> The public saw with astonishment and pleasure the youngster who had composed the music for this ballet accompanying on the harpsichord in the orchestra from the beginning to end. From this work it is easy to be per-suaded of her talents, which seemed varied and extremely well developed in many regards. In general, the recitative was applauded; the scenes seemed well treated, some violin airs well done and quite lively, some choruses . . . greatly pleasing.[89]

Unfortunately the libretto came under sharp criticism and the work had only nine performances. We know even less about the sixteen-year-old Mlle Guerin, who according to a letter in the *Mercure de France* of November 1755 composed an opera entitled *Daphnis et d'Amalthée*, which was performed in her native city of Amiens.[90]

On 22 August 1776 a two-act comedy by Mme Bayon-Louis, *Fleur-d'épine*, was performed by the Comédiens Italiens. The success of the music may be measured by the numerous surviving sources. A full score was published in 1776; one air, *On ne doit compter* (see figure 12), was published in various versions for accompanied voice.[91] In one collection devoted to "Airs detachés de *Fleur-d'épine*" (Paris, Bibliothèque nationale, Y. 522) all the tunes were transposed into the treble clef and were given without accompaniment.

A second career as a composer awaited Henriette-Adélaïde Villard de Beaumesnil (1758–1813), who in 1766 made her debut as a singer at the Académie, and within a month performed cantatas by Mouret at the Concert Spirituel.[92] The *Almanach Musical* of 1782 reported her retirement on 1 May 1781 and characterized her as a pleasant singer and clever actress.[93] After studying harmony and accompaniment with Clement,[94] she composed a one-act opera *Tibule et Délie; ou, Les Saturnales*, which was performed by the Académie on 16 February 1784. On 8 December of the same year, her oratorio *Les Israélites poursuivis par Pharaon*—the only known oratorio of the century by a French woman—was given at the Concert Spirituel.[95]

Angélique-Dorothée-Lucie Grétry (15 July 1772–25 August 1790)—the daughter of André-Ernest-Modest Grétry and known as Lucile after one of her father's greatest successes—was only thirteen when she composed *Le Mariage d'Antonio*, a one-act *divertissement*, which was performed with great success at the Théâtre de la Comédie Italienne on 29 July 1786. Her father may have assisted her, for the work was published at least once under his name.[96] But some of the most popular airs, extracted and arranged, appeared under her own name in a number of collections for accompanied voice.[97] *Toinette et Louis* (1787), a similar but less successful work, was to be her last major composition. She was honored, shortly before her untimely death, by Marie-Antoinette, who named her *Filleule de la Reine de France*.[98]

In the late eighteenth century the only woman who moved with assurance in the professional, men's world of music was the thrice married Julie Candeille. Her diverse talents were never more evident than when she composed the words and music for the highly successful comedy *Catherine; ou, La Belle fermière* (1792), then sang while accompanying herself on the piano or harp during its 154 performances at the Théâtre de la République.[99] After its première on 27 December 1792, the *Journal de Paris nationale* reported that its "success must gratify the author" and that "it entirely reflects the merit of the work."[100] It was to receive "numerous and incessant revivals" through the first quarter of the nineteenth century. Candeille attempted to repeat her success in 1793 with *Bathilde; ou, Le Duc*

Figure 12
On ne doit compter
Mme Bayon-Louis

One only lives when one loves.

Source: Mme Louis, *Fleur d'épine: Comédie en deux actes* (Paris, n.d.),
act 1, scene 4. Paris, Bibliothèque nationale, Rés. F. 358
Translation by Julie Anne Sadie

by singing the principal role and joining the actor Baptiste *l'aîné* (the elder) in a piano duet, but the work had only five performances. *Catherine* was to be her only unqualified operatic success. Critics were eager to attribute this in part to the assistance of her father (who was a composer) and to her liaison with the writer Vergniaud.[101] As a performer she had suffered from the jealousy of her contemporaries; so, too, as a composer and an author. This uncommonly gifted woman's courageous spirit is revealed in a compelling letter of 30 January 1795 addressed to the editor of the *Journal de Paris*:

> When persecution pursues me, when injustice and calumny seek my ruin, I must, for my supporters—and myself—repel the treacherous insinuations of those who would still wish to rob me of public esteem after having cheated all my efforts to give pleasure.
>
> No insensitive pride, no arrogant pretension, has ever guided me in the service of the arts. Submissiveness and necessity led me to the theatre; a propensity for such work and a love of it emboldened me to write. These two resources, united, are my sole means of survival; the need to support my family, other more onerous responsibilities, my present requirements, and especially the uncertainty of the future—these are my reasons for asserting them.[102]

Her later opéras-comiques, *La Bayadère* (1796) and *Ida; ou, L'Orpheline de Berlin* (1807)—inspired by Mme de Genlis's adoption of Cazimir Baecker—failed miserably. Mme de Genlis in turn wrote sympathetically of her contemporary in her memoirs:

> This interesting person, by thirty years of virtue, has atoned for the error of her parents, who placed her in her earliest youth in a hazardous career unworthy of her. Mrs. Simons-Candeille brings to the seductive art of declamation in a grand genre a talent for writing which she has never abused, because all her works charmingly express a moral, pure and noble in feeling; she is an excellent musician, she plays the piano expertly, and through her we have become acquainted with many pieces that did honor to a great composer.[103]

As the eighteenth century progressed, the social class of the women who composed and what they chose to compose changed. Whereas seventeenth-century noble women wrote simple songs for their families and friends to perform, the daughters of musicians and composers—Jacquet de la Guerre, Pinel, Demars, Grétry, and Candeille—gradually began composing in more ambitious genres: sacred and secular cantata and cantatille, opera, ballet, comic opera, and even oratorio. It is noteworthy that so little sacred music is known: the convent libraries may yet yield music composed by resident nuns. As with their male contemporaries, composition was usually only one of several professional musical activities. There was, however, a difference of kind. Whereas men could hold a variety of appointments and teach extensively, several of the women discussed here (Candeille and Mme de Genlis in particular) were active over a different range of fields, as well-known actresses and prolific authors.

The first person to interest himself in the phenomenon of the *"femmes-compositeurs"* of the ancien régime was Maurice Bourges, who published a two-part article in 1847.[104] He concluded his informative overview by likening the cause of women composers to that of the lower classes of eighteenth-century French society, more in keeping with his point of view than theirs. The first serious studies of individual musiciennes were made by Lucien-Adolph Jullien, who wrote monographs and articles about Mme de Pompadour, Marie-Antoinette, Mlle Le Maure, and Mme Saint-Huberty in particular. Around the turn of the nineteenth century Antoinette-Christine-Marie Bobillier [Michel Brenet, pseud.] published articles on Jacquet de la Guerre, Mme de Montgeroult, and Mme de Genlis; many of her other works, notably *Les Concerts en France sous l'Ancien Régime*,[105] touch upon the careers of women musicians.

More recently the series La Vie musicale en France sous les Rois Bourbon, including works by Norbert Dufourcq, Marcelle Benoit, Albert P. de Mirimonde, and the contributors to *"Recherches" de la musique française classique*, undertaken by the publishers A. & J. Picard, has added greatly to our understanding of family relationships and the relative social and economic status of musicians. The archival work in this series provides a myriad of isolated facts about dozens of women that need further amplification and synthesis. This work has helped to insure that many of these women have entries in *The New Grove Dictionary of Music and Musicians*.

Any further study must take serious account of the historical and social climate in which the women mentioned here—and their numerous musically less distinguished contemporaries—patronized, performed, and composed. Only then can the significance of their achievements be assessed. This is especially so in view of the fact that in many cases little more can ever be gleaned about the lives of individual musiciennes. Some of the more intriguing questions raised by these isolated pockets of information could, in such a broader context, be more profitably addressed.

NOTES

1. Evrard Titon du Tillet, *Le Parnasse françois* (Paris: J.-B. Coignard fils, 1732), p. 35.

2. Pierre-Louis d'Aquin de Château-Lyon, *Siècle littéraire de Louis XV; ou, Lettres sur les hommes célèbres. Première partie* (Paris: Duchesne, 1753), p. 145.

3. Titon du Tillet, *Description du Parnasse françois exécuté en bronze à la gloire de la France et de Louis le Grand. . . . Première partie* (Paris: J.-B. Coignard fils, 1760), p. 20.

4. Mlle Bocquet's manuscript preludes for lute have been edited and published in Monique Rollin and A. Souris, *Oeuvres des Bocquet* (Paris: C.N.R.S., 1972).

5. See Anne Chastel, "Etude sur la vie musicale à Paris à travers la presse pendant le règne de Louis XVI," *"Recherches" sur la musique française classique* 17 (1977): 118–49, which consists of a table of dedicatees, many of whom were musiciennes; notable among them are Mme de Genlis, Mlle Grétry, and Marie-Antoinette.

6. See especially the Bonnart series of "Costumes du règne de Louis XIV" (Paris, Bibliothèque nationale, Département des estampes, series Oᵃ 48–65).

7. See Albert P. de Mirimonde, *L'Iconographie musicale sous les Rois Bourbons*, 2 vols. (Paris: A. & J. Picard, 1975–77).

8. The official documents pertaining to over eighty musiciennes are published in Marcelle Benoit, *Musiques de cour: Chapelle, chambre, écurie, 1661–1733* (Paris: A. & J. Picard, 1971). The index to Constant Pierre, *Histoire du Concert Spirituel, 1725–1790* (Paris: Heugel et Cie., 1975), names all the women who performed there.

9. For a fuller account of Jacquet de la Guerre, see Edith Borroff, *An Introduction to Elisabeth-Claude Jacquet de la Guerre* (Brooklyn: Institute for Mediaeval Music, 1966).

10. Renée Viollier, "La Musique à la cour de la Duchesse du Maine de Châtenay aux Grandes Nuits de Sceaux (1700–1715)," *La Revue musicale*, vol. 20, no. 193 (Aug.–Nov. 1939): 96–105.

11. Norbert Dufourcq, *La Musique à la cour de Louis XIV et de Louis XV d'après les mémoires de Sourches et Luynes: 1681–1758* (Paris: A. & J. Picard, 1970), p. 150 (21 July 1752).

12. See Lucien-Adolphe Jullien, *Histoire du théâtre de Madame de Pompadour dit Théâtre des petits cabinets* (Paris: J. Baur, 1874); Winston Haverland Kaehler, *The Operatic Repertoire of Madame de Pompadour's "Théâtre des petits cabinets" (1747–1753)* (Ann Arbor, Mich.: University Microfilms, 1971).

13. Dufourcq, *La Musique à la cour*, p. 130. Mme de Pompadour studied the harpsichord and singing with Jélyotte.

14. Lucien-Adolphe Jullien, *La Ville et la cour au XVIIIe siècle.*

Mozart—Marie-Antoinette—Les Philosophes (Paris: Edouard Rouveyre, 1881), p. 67.

15. See Lucien-Adolphe Jullien, "La Musique et la politique à la cour de Louis XVI. Marie-Antoinette et Sacchini, d'après des documents inédits extraits des archives de l'Etat," *Le Correspondant*, 25 December 1875, pp. 1184–1213, and 25 February 1876, pp. 662–703; id., *La Cour de l'opéra sous Louis XVI: Marie-Antoinette et Sacchini, Salieri, Favart, et Gluck* (Paris: Didier, 1878).

16. See Julie Anne Sadie, "Charpentier and the Early French Ensemble Sonata," *Early Music* 7 (1979): 330–35.

17. The Marquis de Sourches wrote of little Mlle Roland's performance at court in August 1685 (Dufourcq, *La Musique à la cour*, p. 12); Marin Marais later dedicated to her his 1692 edition of *Pièces en trio*. The Marquis de Dangeau wrote of the playing of another child, Mlle de Ménétou (the daughter of the Duc de la Ferté) in August 1689 (Chantal Masson, "Journal du Marquis de Dangeau, 1684–1720. Extrait concernant la vie à la cour," *"Recherches" sur la musique française classique* 2 [1962]: 203). Couperin included a piece entitled *La Ménétou* in his second book of harpsichord pieces (1716–17); at one time Mlle Ménétou must have been his pupil. Marie Leszcinska also took a serious interest in musical prodigies; on 9 August 1746 the ten-year-old daughter of the director of the Opéra de Bordeaux played the harpsichord and sang while the queen dined (*Mercure de France*, August 1746, p. 157).

18. *Mercure Galant*, July 1677, pp. 107–9.

19. Ibid., December 1678, p. 26.

20. Masson, "Journal du Marquis de Dangeau," p. 198.

21. See Marcelle Benoit, *Versailles et les musiciens du roi, 1661–1733: Etude institutionelle et sociale* (Paris: A. & J. Picard, 1971), p. 33.

22. Dornel dedicated to her his *Sonates à violon seul et suites pour la flûte traversière avec la basse* (1711). Couperin included a piece entitled *La Mézangére* in his second book of harpsichord pieces.

23. Jean-Benjamin de la Borde, *Essai sur la musique ancienne et moderne*, 4 vols. (Paris: E. Onfroy, 1780), 3:454.

24. See Charles Bouvet, "Les Deux D'Anglebert et Marguerite-Antoinette Couperin," *Revue de musicologie*, 12e année, vol. 9 (May 1928): 86–94; and Benoit, *Versailles*, pp. 199, 263.

25. Titon du Tillet, *Le Parnasse françois*, pp. 665–66; see also Dufourcq, *La Musique à la cour*, p. 74.

26. Abbé Carbasus, *Lettre de Monsieur l'Abbé Carbasus . . .* (Paris: La Veuve Allouel, 1739), p. 12.

27. Hubert Le Blanc, *Défense de la basse de viole contre les entreprises du violon et les prétentions du violoncel* (Amsterdam: Pierre Mortier, 1740), pp. 5–6. Le Blanc remarks several times on the superior level of playing among women harpsichordists.

28. Lionel de la Laurencie, "Deux violists célèbres: Les Forqueray," *Bul-*

letin français de la Société internationale de musique 4 (1908): 1251–58, 1267–74.

29. D'Aquin, *Siècle littéraire*, p. 127. Clement dedicated his *Sonates en trio pour un clavecin et un violon* (1743) to them.

30. Georges Cucuel, *La Pouplinière et la musique de chambre au XVIIIe siècle* (1913; reprint, New York: Da Capo Press, 1971), pp. 191, 313, 340; see also Cuthbert Girdlestone, *Jean-Philippe Rameau* (London: Cassell, 1957), p. 474. Dr. Hughes Maret described Marie-Louise as also having *"un bon goût pour le chant"* in his *Eloge historique de M. Rameau* (Dijon, 1766) (cited by Girdlestone, p. 8).

31. La Laurencie, "Les Débuts de la musique de chambre en France," *Revue de musicologie* 15 (1934): 164. Rameau named one of his *Pièces de clavecin en concerts* (1741) after her.

32. Titon du Tillet, *Le Parnasse françois*, p. 637.

33. Michel le Moël, "Chez l'Illustre Certain," *"Recherches" sur la musique français classique* 2 (1962): 71–79.

34. Le Blanc, *Défense de la basse de viole*, pp. 70–71.

35. Titon du Tillet, *Le Parnasse françois*, p. 636.

36. *Almanach Musical* 5 (1779): 188.

37. Ibid., 4 (1778): 175 (*maître de clavecin*), 187 (*maître de harpe*); see also Cucuel, *La Pouplinière*, p. 188.

38. See Michel Brenet, "Quatre femmes musiciennes," *L'Art* 59 (1894): 142–47.

39. See esp. Arthur Pougin, "Une Charmeuse: Julie Candeille," *Le Ménestrel* 49 (1883): 356, 365–66, 372–73, 380–81, 388–89, 403–5, 413–14.

40. *Journal de Paris nationale*, 17 August 1783, p. 947.

41. *Mercure de France*, May 1784, p. 220. Another woman before her, Mlle Le Chantre, demonstrated her skills as both performer and composer at the Concert Spirituel, where in 1768 she was the first woman to play on the fortepiano (Pierre, *Histoire du Concert Spirituel*, entry 830). A year earlier she had made her debut playing an organ concerto, and on 22 April 1770 she presented two organ concertos of her own composition (ibid., entries 790 and 870).

42. Brossard, "La Vie musicale," p. 138 (22 April 1656).

43. See Julien Tiersot, "Une Famille de musiciens français: Les de la Barre," *Revue de musicologie*, 12e année, vol. 9, no. 25 (February 1928): 1–11, 68–74.

44. Brossard, "La Vie musicale," p. 151 (5 February 1656).

45. Quoted by James R. Anthony, *French Baroque Music from Beaujoyeulx to Rameau*, 2d ed. rev. (New York: W. W. Norton, 1978), p. 204.

46. Titon du Tillet, *Le Parnasse françois*, p. 615.

47. *Mercure Galant*, July 1702, p. 366.

48. François Robert, "La Musique à travers le *Mercure Galant*," *"Recherches" sur la musique française classique* 2 (1962): 184.

49. Anthony, *French Baroque Music*, p. 207.

50. See Marie Bert, "La Musique à la Maison Royale de Saint-Louis de Saint-Cyr," *"Recherches" sur la musique française classique* 3 (1963): 55–71.

51. Anthony, *French Baroque Music*, p. 83.

52. See my article in the *New Grove Dictionary of Music and Musicians* (London: Macmillan, 1980), s.v. "Antier, Marie," 1:469.

53. Masson, "Journal du Marquis de Dangeau," p. 212.

54. Her writings include memoirs, theater pieces, novels, children's books, a *Manuel de voyageur* (written while in exile in 1799), a *Dictionnaire critique et raisonné des étiquettes de la cour* (1818), an essay in a *Discours sur la suppression des couvents de religieuses et sur l'éducation publique des femmes* (1790), a tract *De l'influence des femmes sur la littérature française comme protectrices des lettres et comme auteurs; ou, Précis de l'histoire des femmes françaises les plus célèbres* (1811) (see Louis Chabaud, *Les Précurseurs du féminisme: Mme de Maintenon, Mme de Genlis, Mme Campan: Leur rôle dans l'éducation chrétienne de la femme* [Paris: Plon-Nourrit et Cie, 1901]), and a *Manuel de la jeune femme, guide complet de la maîtresse de maison* (1829). As "Dame d'honneur de la Duchesse de Chartres" she had charge of the education of both the future king Louis-Philippe and Mme Adélaïde. For them she wrote *Théâtre à l'usage des jeunes personnes* (1779, 1780), *Annales de la vertu* (1781), *Adèle et Théodore* (1782), and *Les Veillées du château* (1782).

55. François-Joseph Fétis, *Biographie universelle des musiciens et bibliographie générale de la musique*, rev. ed., 8 vols. (Paris: Firmin-Didot et Cie, 1881–84), 3:450.

56. Stéphanie-Félicité du Crest de Saint-Aubin, Comtesse de Genlis, *Nouvelle méthode pour apprendre à jouer de la harpe* (Paris: Madame Duhan, 1811), p. 15.

57. Quoted by Michel Brenet, "Mme de Genlis, musicienne," *Revue internationale de musique* 7 (15 February 1912): 7.

58. *Lettre de Monsieur l'Abbé Carbasus*, pp. 25–26.

59. Dufourcq, *La Musique à la cour*, p. 131.

60. See Mary Cyr, "Solo Music for the Treble Viol," *Journal of the Viola da Gamba Society of America* 12 (December 1975): 5–13.

61. Du Pradel, *Le Livre commode des adresses de Paris pour 1692*, ed. Edouard Fournier, 2 vols. (Paris: Paul Daffis, 1878), 1:209.

62. Titon du Tillet, *Le Parnasse françois*, p. 615.

63. *Annonces* (1763), p. 3, quoted in Sylvette Milliot, *Documents sur les luthiers parisiens du XVIIIe siècle* (Paris: Heugel et cie., 1970), p. 117.

64. Titon du Tillet, *Le Parnasse françois*, pp. 624, 627.

65. Dufourcq, *La Musique à la cour*, p. 147. Louis de Caix d'Hervelois (possibly her uncle) named after her a piece in his fifth book of *Pièces de viole* (1748), which he dedicated to one of Louis XV's daughters. See Benoit, *Versailles*, pp. 252–63; here Benoit describes the positions women held in the royal musical establishment through the reign of Louis XIV and the

early years of the reign of Louis XV, touching upon the careers of the most successful.

66. See Michel Corrette, *Méthode pour apprendre facilement à jouer du pardessus de viole* (Paris: Boivin, Leclerc, 1748).

67. See the *Mercure de France*, February 1745 and March 1745; see also Pierre, *Histoire du Concert Spirituel*, entries 296–306, 308, 397. Mlle Levi's sister Mme Haubaut performed on the pardessus at the Concert Spirituel (Pierre, *Histoire du Concert Spirituel*, entries 397, 399, 405; see also D'Aquin, *Siècle littéraire*, p. 145). Another pardessus player, Mlle Lafond ("all but a child"), performed there in 1762 (Pierre, *Histoire du Concert Spirituel*, entry 674).

68. Ancelet, *Observations sur la musique, les musiciens, et les instrumens* (Amsterdam: Aux dépens de la Compagnie, 1757), p. 24. In 1775 a Monsieur Doublet advertised himself as a "maître de pardessus de viole" in the *Almanach Musical* 1 (1770): 117, claiming to be the "only pupil of the celebrated Mme Levi."

69. It was probably to Adélaïde that Caix dedicated his *VI Sonates pour deux pardessus de viole à cinq cordes*, op. 1 (Paris: Boivin, Le Clerc; Lyon: de Bretonne, n.d.).

70. The Forqueray *Pièces de viole* of 1747 were dedicated to Henriette; Jean-Marc Nattier's portrait of Henriette playing the bass viol, completed two years after her death (1752), hangs today in the bedroom of her father at Versailles.

71. *Mercure de France* (April 1737); quoted in Ernest Thoinan, *Les Hotteterre et les Chédeville: Célèbres joueurs et facteurs de flûtes, hautbois, bassons et musettes des XVIIe et XVIIIe siècles* (Paris: Edmond Sagot, 1894), p. 46.

72. See the index of Pierre, *Histoire du Concert Spirituel*.

73. For a review of her performance, see *Mercure de France*, May 1785, p. 76; for an account of her life and a frank assessment of her music, see Marion M. Scott, "Maddalena Lombardini, Madame Syrmen," *Music & Letters* 14 (1933): 149–63.

74. See n. 17 above.

75. Their names are to be found throughout *Recueils imprimés, XVIIIe siècle* (Munich: G. Henle, 1964), the volume of *International Inventory of Musical Sources (RISM)* devoted to eighteenth-century collections.

76. See RISM. *Einzeldrucke vor 1800* (Kassel: Bärenreiter, 1971–), A/I/3: 392, and A/I/6: 410–11.

77. *Mercure de France*, June 1776, pp. 62–67.

78. See Carol Henry Bates, *The Instrumental Music of Elisabeth-Claude Jacquet de la Guerre* (Ann Arbor, Mich.: University Microfilms, 1978).

79. See Michel Brenet, "La Librairie musicale en France de 1653 à 1790 d'après les registres de privilèges," *Sammelbände der internationalen Musikgesellschaft* 8 (1906–7): 437. Julie Pinel may have been related to François Pinel (died 1709), "*joueur de théorbe de la chambre*," and the

"Mlle. Pinet [sic] la fille" who published an air in Ballard's Recueil of 1710.

80. Mercure de France, March 1749, pp. 40–41.

81. Cucuel, La Pouplinière, p. 226.

82. Brenet, "Madame de Genlis," p. 4. Brenet tells us that Demars's Christian name was Hélène-Louise; David Tunley, in The Eighteenth-Century French Cantata (London: Dobson, 1974), p. 229, gives it as Henriette; and RISM, Einzeldruck, A/I/2: 344, calls her Thérèse and attributes to her a number of romances and airs with harp and fortepiano accompaniment.

83. The others are Les Arrêts d'amour (c. 1754), the text of which appears in Mercure de France, June 1755; La Tourterelle, Les Charmes de la voix (c. 1754), La Fête de l'amour, Issé (c. 1754), Le Joli rien (c. 1754), and Le Triomphe des plaisirs (1755); all of which, except for the last, were published under the name of Mlle Pellecier.

84. Robert, "La Musique à travers le Mercure Galant," p. 189.

85. Quoted in Borroff, An Introduction to Elisabeth-Claude Jacquet de la Guerre, p. 13.

86. Julie Anne Sadie, The Bass Viol in French Baroque Chamber Music (Ann Arbor, Mich.: UMI Research Press, 1980), p. 41.

87. The Raccommodement was performed in 1715 at the Théâtre de la Foire as part of a larger work entitled La Ceinture de Vénus.

88. The identity of the composer has been confused with those of other eighteenth-century mademoiselles Duval, at least two of whom were singers, one a dancer, and another the composer of the air Tout ce que je vois me rapelle, which appeared in the Mercure de France in June 1776.

89. Claude and François Parfaict, "Histoire de l'Académie Royale de Musique," Paris, Bibliothèque nationale, n.a.frç., 6543, 2:83.

90. Mercure de France, November 1755, pp. 215–16.

91. See RISM, Recueils imprimés, XVIIIe siècle, index.

92. Pierre, Histoire du Concert Spirituel, entries 785, 786, 796, 798, 799, 802.

93. "Retraite de Mlle. Beaumesnil du 'Théâtre de l'Opéra'," Almanach Musical (1782), p. 112.

94. Fétis, Biographie universelle, 1:286.

95. This (lost) oratorio, which requires three soloists, was repeated on 24 December 1784 and on 18 March 1785 (see Pierre, Histoire du Concert Spirituel, entries 1140, 1145).

96. It appears, reprinted from the 1786 edition, as no. 23 of a Collection des opéras de Grétry en grandes partitions (Paris, Bibliothèque nationale, D. 5042), to which there is appended a note saying that "the vocal part is by Lucile Grétry, one of the daughters of the composer."

97. See RISM, Recueils imprimés, XVIIIe siècle, index.

98. Jullien, La Ville et la cour, p. 93.

99. See Pougin, "Une Charmeuse," p. 373.

100. Journal de Paris nationale, 29 December 1792, p. 360.

101. Pougin, "Une Charmeuse," p. 381.

102. *Journal de Paris*, 30 January 1795, p. 530; see Pougin, "Une Charmeuse," pp. 388–89.

103. Pougin, "Une Charmeuse," p. 413.

104. Maurice Bourges, "Des Femmes-compositeurs," *Revue et gazette musicale de Paris* 14, nos. 38–39 (September 1847): 305–7, 313–15; see also Adrien de la Fage, "Supplement," ibid., no. 40: 323–25.

105. Michel Brenet [Antoinette-Christine-Marie Bobillier], *Les Concerts en France sous l'Ancien Régime* (1900; reprint, New York: Da Capo Press, 1970).

9

Women and the Lied, 1775–1850

MARCIA J. CITRON

Although women have been composers since the Middle Ages—
Hildegard of Bingen in the twelfth century, Barbara Strozzi in the
seventeenth century, Elisabeth Jacquet de la Guerre at the turn of
the eighteenth century, to name a few—the advent of the nineteenth
century witnessed a marked increase in the number of female musicians who utilized their creative talents, with a parallel rise in recognition from contemporary musicians, journalists, and audiences.
The greater participation of women in a field traditionally associated
exclusively with men is largely attributable to certain political and
social currents wafting across Europe in the early- to mid-eighteenth
century; but significant and far-reaching developments in music itself—most notably the invention of the piano and its concomitant
solo and chamber literature—also played a decisive role in creating
a musical climate conducive to a greater involvement of women as
composers.

The lied, that very special musicoliterary genre that emerged
shortly after 1750, attracted female composers, resulting in many
fine pieces of music written by women. From its inception the lied
constituted a type of chamber music and as such fit comfortably in a
domestic environment, a setting in which women had long been accepted as performers,[1] in clear contrast to the public arena, whose
large-scale operas, sacred music, and orchestral music were off limits
to women.[2]

In the period from 1775 to 1850 in Germany several major female composers of lieder rose to prominence. The singer-pianists
Corona Schröter (1751–1802), Maria Theresia Paradis (1759–1821),
and Luise Reichardt (1779–1826) were three lights within the early
generation. In the nineteenth century Fanny Mendelssohn Hensel

(1805–47), Josephine Lang (1815–80), and Clara Schumann (1819–96) each produced a sizable output of lieder, much of it first-class music. Emilie Zumsteeg (1796–1857) and Annette von Droste-Hülshoff (1797–1848) round out the picture as two very interesting yet less significant figures. The creative achievement of these eight composers is uneven, as is that of their male contemporaries, but among the hundreds of lieder they produced are pieces equal to the best of the lieder composed in that era. Why did these musicians compose lieder? What are the individual and common elements of their background that prompted them to create? This study will explore the sociological conditions affecting these composers, the nature of their creative response to these conditions, and the style and quality of their lieder.

Women's increased activity in bourgeois music-making in the late eighteenth century reflected contemporary sociopolitical trends that theoretically granted women equal status in legal rights and education.[3] As a result, society gradually began to enlarge its concept of appropriate musical education and activities for women. The more enlightened social climate offered a clear contrast to the prevailing attitudes present in the early part of the century, for then only a few voices, notably those of Condorcet and Montesquieu,[4] had spoken out in favor of substantive changes for women. On the other side of the political spectrum in this regard stood the influential Rousseau, who made the following statement at mid-century about the relative position of the sexes:

The education of women should always be relative to men. To please, to be useful to us, to make us love and esteem them, to educate us when young and to take care of us when grown up, to advise, to console us, to render our lives easy and agreeable—these are the duties of women at all times and what they should be taught in their infancy.[5]

Rousseau also expressed strong views regarding women's creative deficiencies:

Women, in general, possess no artistic sensibility . . . nor genius. They can acquire a knowledge . . . of anything through hard work. But the celestial fire that emblazens and ignites the soul, the inspiration that consumes and devours . . . , these sublime ecstasies that reside in the depths of the heart are always lacking in women's writings. These creations are as cold and pretty as women; they have an abundance of spirit but lack soul; they are a hundred times more reasoned than impassioned.[6]

Rousseau's writings reached across national borders and therefore must have been influential, at least to some extent. The last remark was cited in an article from the *Musikalisches Wochenblatt* of 1793, in which the author wondered why no first-class female composers had appeared: "Is this art [composing] too high, too difficult for the female capacity—which, in other respects, is not below ours—or does composing presuppose too much learning? Or is the situation more dependent upon other circumstances?"[7]

Throughout most of the eighteenth century many prominent writers believed that women did not possess the intellectual and emotional capacity to learn and that, furthermore, it was unnecessary and even dangerous for women to acquire knowledge, as such knowledge could only detract from women's true calling of wife and mother. A woman's role would be especially undermined if she applied her knowledge in a professional pursuit, as Johann Campe stated with regard to female composers: "Among a hundred praiseworthy female composers hardly one can be found who fulfills simultaneously all the duties of a reasonable and good wife, an attentive and efficient housekeeper, and a concerned mother."[8] His contemporary, Basedow, agreed: "The most talented female dancer, the leading female singer, and the most well read, most accomplished female artist makes a poor wife, a poor housewife, and a poor mother."[9] Even Moses Mendelssohn, one of the most enlightened men of his era, could write to his fiancée shortly before their marriage in 1762 that "moderate learning becomes a lady, but not scholarship. A girl who has read her eyes red deserves to be laughed at."[10]

Despite or perhaps in response to these narrow views of women's proper sphere and their limited capacities for achievement, many writers near the end of the century began to speak out clearly in favor of women's rights. The first German polemic urging an improvement in the status of women was von Hippel's *Über die bürgerliche Verbesserung der Weiber* (1792). In addition, women themselves emerged as advocates of equal education; Esther Gad-Domeier, for example, penned a response to Campe's views in 1798.[11] Amalia Holst expressed herself eloquently on the issue of equal education:

In the name of our entire sex I challenge men to show why they have arrogated to themselves the right to degrade a full half of the human race, to deny them the sources of knowledge. . . . In the first duty of mankind, which requires that all our powers be developed to their highest perfection, we want to be free. Here we share rights equally. . . . Before we are man or woman, citizen or citizeness, husband or wife, we are human beings.[12]

As the nineteenth century progressed, educational opportunities for women proliferated. Singing became an integral part of the female curriculum, stemming from traditional German pedagogy which recognized society's benefits from the well-reared child nurtured on mother's singing. What better way to strengthen family ties and instill basic moral values? [13] Nina d'Aubigny von Engelbrunner, a musician and champion of women's musical education, in 1824 commented upon the changes in female musical education over the past twenty years: "The author has, with pleasure, found much improved upon her return to Europe. . . . Indeed even many private schools concern themselves with singing instruction, and take to heart what is said in these *Letters* regarding the training of good voices." [14]

Yet despite the inclusion of singing in public and private schools and the growing number of female singers and pianists around the turn of the century, relatively few female singers received professional training. Johann Adam Hiller, opera composer and pedagogue of Leipzig, commented in 1774 on the lack of adequately trained professional female singers, [15] a situation he himself attempted to remedy with the opening of his coeducational singing school. One of his first female students was Corona Schröter, who later turned to the composing of lieder. The relative unavailability of high-quality singing instruction for women persisted at least until the end of the century, as can be seen in the following report from the *Allgemeine musikalische Zeitung* of 1798: "Until now only boys have been instructed in singing. But why should girls be excluded from singing? Are not the best voices often found among persons of the opposite sex, who moreover are not subjected to the male change of voice?" [16]

The scarcity of professional singing instruction for women reflected society's views regarding the impropriety of women's performing in a public forum. One notable pathbreaker was the highly successful Elisabeth Schmehling La Mara, a pupil of Hiller who garnered lavish praise from all corners of Europe in the 1770s and 1780s, including plaudits from Burney on several of his visits to the Continent. [17]

Similar prohibitions obtained with regard to professional female pianists. According to some contemporary writers, such a profession might well endanger the morals and character of a lady. [18] Such a view probably deterred Fanny Hensel from performing in public until 1838 at the age of thirty-two. Furthermore, very few avenues were open to women to receive the level of instruction necessary for a concert career. Piano lessons were not offered in public or private schools until sometime after 1800, and thus private instruction became the means to learn the instrument. Contemporary chronicles reported on a shortage of good piano teachers,[19] of whom, not surprisingly, very few were women.[20] Yet, in spite of these obstacles, a few women became noted concert pianists and teachers. The blind Maria Theresia Paradis, who toured for only part of her professional life, stands out in the late eighteenth century.[21]

The conditions preventing women from becoming singers and pianists in the public world played a major role in focusing women's performing and creative abilities on music intended for a private gathering in the home or salon. It was in such a setting that their lieder flourished.

The composers under consideration in this essay (see table 3) exceeded society's conceptions of proper women's activities—that is, they became artistic creators—largely because of their youthful immersion in sophisticated musicoliterary circles.[22] Schröter, Luise Reichardt, Emilie Zumsteeg, Droste-Hülshoff, Lang, and Schumann all had musical parents. Luise Reichardt, for example, was the daughter of Johann Friedrich Reichardt (1752–1814), composer and critic, and Juliane Benda (1752–83), herself a composer of lieder.[23] Emilie Zumsteeg was the daughter of Johann Rudolf Zumsteeg (1760–1802), a well-known lieder composer in Stuttgart. We have accounts of the young Luise Reichardt singing for the illustrious company assembled in her father's home,[24] of the sixteen-year-old Josephine Lang singing before the enthusiastic Felix Mendelssohn,[25] and of the child Annette von Droste-Hülshoff mingling with famous poets.[26] In some cases strong literary influences began at a later stage in life: Schröter encountered Goethe in her teens, Lang married the poet Christian Köstlin in 1841. Clara Schumann was influenced by the effusive outpouring of lieder by her husband Robert shortly after their marriage in 1840. Fanny Hensel, born into one of the most intellectually and culturally gifted families of the early nineteenth century, was influenced by the constant stream of notables passing through their Berlin salon.[27]

Although singing gradually became a part of female educational programs in the early nineteenth century, none of these lieder composers—with the exception of Schröter studying at Hiller's school and Hensel at the newly opened Berlin Singakademie—received musical instruction in school. Each came from a family of at least moderate means who provided private music teachers. The early training

Table 3
Biographical Summary of Composers

Composer*	Chief Location	Occupation**	Famous Associations	Principal Musical Output
Corona Schröter (1751–1802) S	Leipzig, Weimar	s, a, c, pe	Goethe, J. A. Hiller, J. F. Reichardt	2 Lieder collections, incidental music
Maria Theresia Paradis (1759–1824) S	Vienna	pi, s, c, pe	Mozart	Pieces in many current genres, including lieder
Luise Reichardt (1779–1826) S	Hamburg	c, s, pe	Parents, various poets, musicians of father's circle	At least 14 collections of lieder, including sacred
Emilie Zumsteeg (1796–1857) S	Stuttgart	pe, pi, s, c	Father	6 Lieder collections
Annette von Droste-Hülshoff (1797–1848) S	Westphalia region	po, c, s	Father and uncle, Robert and Clara Schumann	Almost exclusively vocal, including an arrangement of the *Lochamer Liederbuch*
Fanny Mendelssohn Hensel (1805–47) M/1	Berlin	pi, c	Brother Felix, poets and musicians of Berlin salon	Prolific output of lieder, piano music, also other genres
Josephine Lang (1815–80) M/6	Tübingen, Munich	c, s, pi, pe	Father, various poets, Felix Mendelssohn, Clara Schumann	Prolific output of lieder, including over 30 published collections
Clara Wieck Schumann (1819–96) M/8	Düsseldorf, Frankfurt, Berlin	pi, c, pe	Husband, father, leading contemporary musicians	3 Collections of lieder, piano and chamber music

*Symbols under *Composer*:
 S = single (unmarried)
 M/ = married/no. of children

**Symbols under *Occupation*:
 a = actress   pe = pedagogue   po = poet
 c = composer   pi = pianist   s = singer

centered on the keyboard; Lang, it is reported, started at the tender age of five.[28] Beyond this keyboard training, the quality and nature of musical instruction varied from composer to composer. Some acquired comprehensive skills through a diversified range of musical training. Paradis, for example, studied keyboard with Kozeluch, singing with Righini and Salieri, dramatic composition with Vogler, and theory with Friberth. Droste-Hülshoff's background was especially interesting, as she was reared on the *Generalbass* method written by her uncle, a noted composer in the Westphalia region.[29] Hensel was afforded the same musical training as her younger brother Felix, including theory lessons with Karl Friedrich Zelter, and is reported to have equalled him in musical accomplishment.[30]

Female musicians were well aware of the sharp discrepancy between their high level of musical training and society's negative attitudes toward them as composers, especially as published composers. One of the most telling comments was made by Schröter as part of her announcement in *Cramer's Magazin* of her forthcoming lieder publication:

I have had to overcome much hesitation before I seriously made the decision to publish a collection of short poems that I have provided with melodies. A certain feeling toward propriety and morality is stamped upon our sex, which does not allow us to appear alone in public, nor without an escort. Thus how can I present this, my musical work, to the public with anything other than timidity? The work of any lady . . . can indeed arouse a degree of pity in the eyes of some experts.[31]

A similar lack of professional self-confidence characterizes the comments of the blind Paradis, as related by an anonymous writer in the *Allgemeine musikalische Zeitung* of 1810:

To my question as to why she has not published any of her pieces, she responded in jest: "Would male fellow-artists withdraw from me if I, as a woman—and especially as a blind woman—dared to compete with them?" When I told her that I am already acquainted with her settings of twelve exuberant German lieder and Bürger's *Lenore*, she answered: "Oh, those are the fruits of youth, which are not present in maturity."[32]

Fanny Hensel communicated her disenchantment with composing, as well as her need for encouragement, on several occasions: "If nobody ever offers an opinion, or takes the slightest interest in one's productions, one loses in time not only all pleasure in them, but all power of judging their value."[33] Her doubts were rooted in her father's numerous stern admonitions against her becoming a professional musician, which were predicated on the belief that women must train themselves to excel at domestic concerns rather than turn their attention to their place in the world at large.[34] Felix's good opinion of her as a musician was central to her self-esteem, as shown in the following lines written by Fanny to her brother: "I don't know what Goethe means by the demonic influence, but it's clear that if it exists, you exert it on me. If you seriously suggested that I become a good mathematician, I wouldn't have any special difficulty in doing it; if you thought I was no longer any good at music then I'd give it up tomorrow."[35] Felix's warm encouragement of her creative pursuits and his pride in being the brother of such a good composer stopped short, however, of granting approval for his sister's publishing ventures. In responding to his mother's plea urging Felix to encourage Fanny to publish, Felix clearly stated his opposition to Fanny's becoming a professional composer:

I cannot persuade her to publish anything, because it is against my views and convictions. We have previously spoken a great deal about it, and I still hold the same opinion. I consider publishing something serious (it should at least be that) and believe that one should do it only if one wants to appear as an author one's entire life and stick to it. But that necessitates a series of works, one after the other. . . . Fanny, as I know her, possesses neither the inclination nor calling for authorship. She is too much a woman for that, as is proper, and looks after her house and thinks neither about the public nor the musical world unless that primary occupation is accomplished. Publishing would only disturb her in these duties, and I cannot reconcile myself to it. If she decides on her own to publish, or to please Hensel, I am, as I said, ready to be helpful as much as possible, but to encourage her toward something I don't consider right is what I cannot do.[36]

Felix's discouragement clearly played a decisive role in Fanny's publishing history. The following statement by Fanny appeared in a letter to Felix of 22 November 1836: "In regard to my [plans to] publish, . . . Hensel is for it, you are against it. In any other matter I'd naturally accede entirely to the wishes of my husband, but in this matter alone it's crucial to have your approval; without it I might not undertake anything of the kind."[37] Felix's approval and support, therefore, would probably have resulted in the publication of a much greater percentage of the more than two hundred lieder Fanny composed,[38] instead of only two collections issued in her last year (1846–47) and two more published around 1850.[39] Clara Schumann, a woman with great compositional skill and personal courage, also entertained doubts regarding her creative abilities. In January of 1841 she stated, "I have already made a few attempts on the Rückert poems that Robert noted down for me; however, it is not working—I have no talent whatsoever for composing."[40]

Many of the composers—Reichardt, Hensel, and Schumann—published lieder under male authorship. A few of Reichardt's early songs were included in a collection of her father's lieder, *12 Deutsche Lieder* (Zerbst, 1800).[41] Three of Fanny Hensel's early songs appeared in each of Felix's Opus 8 and Opus 9; the *Allgemeine musikalische Zeitung* claimed that "An des lust'gen Brunnens Rand," a duet composed by Fanny, is the best song in the collection (Opus 8).[42] Three of Clara Schumann's lieder were included in a collection of twelve songs published under the joint names of Robert and Clara Schumann. None of the songs in this publication are assigned a specific attribution; numbers 2, 4, and 11 are by Clara.[43] These three lieder were later published separately under Clara's own name—*Drei Gedichte aus Rückert's "Liebesfrühling,"* opus 12 (Leipzig: Breitkopf & Härtel, [n.d.]). In the case of each of the three composers above, the works are early pieces, and their circumstances of publication probably reflect the composer's lack of confidence in her own compositional prowess. Publishing pieces under alternate authorship staved off rejection of these lieder as mere "women's work" as well as potential criticism of the music itself.

None of these women considered herself a professional composer: composing was neither her chief occupation nor her source of livelihood. Nevertheless most of them—particularly Reichardt, Zumsteeg, and Schumann—made their professional mark in some other sphere of music for at least part of their lives. Teaching, an acceptable form of female activity in the nineteenth century, claimed the principal energies of many of these composers. After Schröter published her second and final collection of lieder in 1794, she spent her last eight years teaching voice and drama.[44] Paradis supported herself after her father's death in 1808 by establishing a school for young girls.[45] Reichardt was one of the most acclaimed musical pedagogues in Hamburg in the early nineteenth century, as attested by numerous favorable notices in the press.[46] Like Paradis she became deeply involved with pedagogy after the death of her father in 1814. Zumsteeg gained fame through teaching piano and voice in Stuttgart. Lang supported her large family after her husband's untimely death in 1856 through teaching voice and piano; she had earlier unsuccessfully attempted to earn a living through the publication of her lieder. Clara Schumann, after her husband's death in 1856, supported herself and her family through performing and teaching. Hensel is the only composer in this group who did not support herself through any of her musical pursuits. Before her marriage to Wilhelm Hensel in 1829 she lived with her well-to-do family, who provided for her material and spiritual comforts; afterward her husband supported her. However, her participation in and eventual leadership of one of the focal Berlin salons in the 1830s and 1840s constituted a musical occupation on a par with her composing and, of course, was the raison d'être for a major portion of her lieder and piano and chamber works.[47]

Several lieder composers gained distinction as vocalists. Schröter, who was granted a lifelong stipend for her singing by Duchess Anna Amalia of Weimar, evoked praise from many esteemed men of her time, including Goethe, Johann Friedrich Reichardt, and Gerber.[48] Emilie Zumsteeg was praised for her lovely alto voice.[49] Felix Mendelssohn encountered Lang when she was sixteen and waxed enthusiastic about her pretty voice.[50] Lang later held a position as singer at the Hofkapelle in Munich.

Schröter and Droste-Hülshoff were celebrated in areas outside music. Schröter's activities in Weimar, where she resided from 1776 to her death in 1802, were divided between acting and singing until approximately the last decade of her life. She appeared in dramatic works both with and without music. A close friend of Goethe, Schröter participated in many of Goethe's *Singspiele*, notably as Dortchen in *Die Fischerin* (1782), for which she also composed the incidental music.[51] Her thespian fame was so great that a major history of the theater, published in 1775, was dedicated to her dramatic abilities.[52] Poetry was the strong suit of Droste-Hülshoff, although she herself considered music and poetry equally important creative spheres. She attained fame as a literary figure and is today acknowledged as one of Germany's chief poets in the nineteenth century. A Droste-Gesellschaft was founded for the dissemination of information about her life and poetry; her musical compositions, on the other hand, are hardly known.

For each of these composers, lieder constitute a principal genre in her overall oeuvre. Paradis, Hensel, and Schumann also wrote pieces in other genres, especially for the keyboard. The fact that Hensel and Schumann composed large-scale orchestral works—even if in small numbers[53]—suggests that by the second quarter of the nineteenth century women had begun to break loose from society's narrowly circumscribed dicta regarding appropriate musical media for female expression. In the late eighteenth century Paradis had been one of the few women to write for orchestra,[54] the other exception being Marianne Martinez (1744–1812)—celebrated singer, and composer of symphonies, piano concertos, and other large-scale works.[55]

Schröter, Droste-Hülshoff, Zumsteeg, Reichardt, and Lang devoted their creative efforts almost exclusively to lieder. Two collections of Schröter's lieder appeared in 1786 and 1794,[56] and her incidental music to Goethe's *Die Fischerin* consists of several vocal numbers that do not depart markedly from her lieder style. None of Droste-Hülshoff's lieder were published.[57] Reichardt composed over one hundred lieder, most of which were published.[58] Even more prolific was Lang,[59] a sizable collection of whose songs was issued in 1880, two years after her death.[60]

A considerable proportion of the published lieder received public recognition through reviews. Two of Reichardt's many collections were reviewed: *12 Deutsche und italienische und romantische Gesänge* (1806), and *Sechs deutsche Lieder* (1827).[61] An interesting comment appeared in the review of the latter: "The melodic devices are not mere imitations of the chief beloved masters of the time, as is the case with almost all female compositions that are known to us, but, rather, they have come from her heart and thus have, some more, some less, their own special qualities."[62] Although the reviewer praised Reichardt's affective style, he unfortunately diminished her achievement by judging her music in terms of a restricted class of composers rather than exclusively on its artistic merits.

Only Schröter's first publication was reviewed.[63] An obituary in the *Allgemeine musikalische Zeitung* included an assessment of her compositional abilities:

Corona had too little proper training in composing, and was not able to discover, nor skilled enough to put on paper, what was in her soul; therefore her works are in no way to be disdained and not at all without traces of spirit; but one had to hear her perform them herself in order to discern precisely what was in them, or how much more should be.[64]

It is revealing that the writer attributes Schröter's lack of success in composing to an inadequate musical education, a situation that faced most gifted women musicians of the period and accordingly renders their creative achievements all the more remarkable.

Both of the lieder collections published before Hensel's death were reviewed. The review of Opus 1 is mixed. Hensel is praised for her compositional dexterity but criticized for a lack of emotional depth.[65] A similar flaw is reported in the review of Opus 7, although the reviewer—Emanuel Klitsch—detects a masculine quality in the

Figure 13
Hoffnung
Luise Reichardt

When the roses bloom,
Be of hope, dear heart,
The searing sorrow
Will burn away quietly and coolly.

Source: Heinrich Reimann, *Das Deutsche Lied*, 4 vols. (Berlin: N. Simrock, 1892–93), 4:78–79
Translation by Marcia J. Citron

overall artistic conception of the lieder. Songs three and six are admiringly characterized as Schumannesque.[66]

The literary sources and musical style of the lieder under consideration do not differ from those of male contemporaries. In the period from about 1775 to 1825—encompassing the lieder of Schröter, Paradis, Reichardt, and Zumsteeg—folklike settings predominate: strophic form, four-bar regularity of phrasing, diatonic melody and harmony, syllabic text setting, and sparse piano accompaniments. This style employs texts by Herder (especially from his *Volkslieder* collection of 1779), Voss, Hölty, and Goethe among others. *Hoffnung* by Luise Reichardt illustrates this *volksthümlich* type (see figure 13). In addition, there appears an Italianate style that features

Figure 14
Morgenfreude, op. 4, no. 2
Emilie Zumsteeg, text by Theodor Körner

I am awake! the young spring day
Bathes me in a rosy shimmer;
It drives me from the narrow room,
The bells of longing beckon me;
Yet the resplendent sun that beams forth
Through the clouds doesn't gladden me,
For me it hasn't risen,
Because it isn't my sun.

Source: Emilie Zumsteeg, *Sechs Lieder mit Begleitung des Pianoforte*, Opus 4 (Mainz: B. Schott Söhne, n.d.). Vienna, Gesellschaft der Musikfreunde
Translation by Marcia J. Citron

more idiomatic piano writing, more flexible text setting and phrase structure, greater structural variety, greater use of melodic and harmonic chromaticism, and the occasional use of non-Germanic texts. These characteristics reside in some lieder of Schröter (1794 collection), Paradis, Reichardt, and Zumsteeg. Zumsteeg's *Morgenfreude* illustrates some of these Italianate features (see figure 14).

From 1825 to 1850 a style significantly different from either the early German or Italian styles became prominent. The lieder of Robert Schumann typified this new approach: greater virtuosity and independence in the piano part, greater harmonic and tonal variety, greater structural diversity, less symmetrical phrasing, and less tonal direction in the vocal part. The lieder of Fanny Hensel and Clara Schumann exhibit these traits to a considerable degree (see figures 15 and 16),[67] as do many of the stylistically more varied lieder of Lang.[68] The poems selected by these nineteenth-century composers are mostly by contemporaries, many of whom were personal friends. Notable, also, are frequent settings of two prominent figures of the late eighteenth century—Goethe and Schiller.

An overall assessment of the quality of these lieder is difficult: they span a seventy-five-year period of stylistic change, exhibit a diversity of geographical provenance, and—most important—represent an amalgam of eight different composers grouped together only on account of sexual commonality. Qualitative distinctions nevertheless emerge.

Especially successful are the lieder of Hensel and Schumann; they merit recognition and inclusion in the standard repertoire. The examples above (figures 15 and 16) exhibit the sensitivity to text and attention to detail that characterize their finest work. Hensel's *Nachtwanderer* (figure 15) displays a sophisticated handling of texture, as in the crossing lines between the upper part of the piano and the entrance of the voice in measure 2, and in the doubling of the voice and piano in measures 7 and 8. Flexibility in phrase structure is evident in the appearance of a three-bar phrase in measures 7 to 9 directly after the two-plus-two structure of the previous phrase. Clara Schumann's *Liebst du um Schönheit* (figure 16) presents an affective use of harmonic color in the change of mode in the second half of measure 5. In measures 7 to 10 we see a sure grasp of contrapuntal interplay among the many strands in the piano; lush sonorities in the accompaniment effectively contrast with the squareness and rhythmic simplicity of the vocal line. The vocal line of *Liebst du um Schönheit*, as that in the songs of Robert Schumann, requires additional musical support to clarify its tonal implications.

Figure 15
Nachtwanderer, op. 7, no. 1
Fanny Hensel, text by Joseph von Eichendorff

I wander through the quiet night,
The moon often creeps stealthily and softly
From its dark cloud cover.
And here and there in the valley. . . .

Source: Fanny Hensel, *Sechs Lieder für eine Stimme mit Begleitung des Pianoforte,* Opus 7 (Berlin: Bote & Bock [1847]). West Berlin, Staatsbibliothek Preussischer Kulturbesitz
Translation by Marcia J. Citron

Figure 16
Liebst du um Schönheit
Clara Schumann

If you love for beauty,
Then don't love me!
Love the sun,
It has golden hair!

Source: Robert and Clara Schumann, *Lieder und Gesänge für eine Stimme mit Begleitung des Pianoforte*, Opus 12 (Leipzig: Breitkopf & Härtel [c. 1873]), no. 2
Translation by Marcia J. Citron

First-rate works can also be found in the oeuvre of almost every other lieder composer under consideration in this essay. *An den Abendstern* from Schröter's 1794 publication provides an evocative rendition of the lyrical poem by Matthesson. Luise Reichardt's *Hoffnung* (see figure 13) succeeds admirably in its naïveté, much like Schubert's *Heidenröslein*, even though *Hoffnung* does not contain the subtle melodic directional changes that appear in the Schubert song. *Morgenfreude* by Zumsteeg (see figure 14) successfully conveys the cheerfulness of the poem, with a tunefulness and rhythmic vitality that resemble an Italian folk dance. The only composer whose output does not include a significant number of successful works is Droste-Hülshoff. The extremely sparse texture, awkward tonal orientation, and disconnected phrase structure of many of her lieder—*Der kranke Aar*, for example—leave the listener with a sense of unease.[69] Her idiosyncratic style lies outside the mainstream of nineteenth-century Germanic art music.[70]

Yet, in spite of the high quality of most of the lieder of female composers of this period, the composers did not carve out names for themselves in the professional world. A remark made by the preeminent Viennese salon hostess Caroline Pichler in her memoirs of 1844 reveals the depth of their obscurity:

There still has not been a woman who has succeeded as a composer. There are successful female artists and female poets, and even though a woman has never excelled in any art or science as greatly as a man, they nevertheless have made considerable progress. Not so in music. And to be sure one would think that this art . . . would be the best means in which the female spirit could express itself.[71]

One might ask why women composers were unknown and therefore unsuccessful. In the first place, their pieces were largely unpublished and thus remained unknown to a widespread musical audience. In the second place, most female composers did not travel extensively; thus, they lacked the opportunity to perform their pieces for a wide audience and to meet the people necessary to catapult their names into professional prominence. These two reasons are related and point to a common sociological source: women's horizons and accomplishments were confined to the home. The wealth of lieder composed by women in this period attests to this link. Such an association stamped an air of dilettantism upon the accomplishments of women composers, even if the compositions exhibit a musical sophistication equal to that of male contemporaries. Reviews of the lieder under consideration tended to isolate "female" musical qualities—clearly implying an inferior or more amateur class of musical works. This lack of professionalism often permeated the sensibilities of talented female composers, who unfortunately belittled their own compositions, and it sometimes fostered a need for an inordinate amount of positive reinforcement.[72] Another result was a confused sense of goals. Hensel, for example, often attempted to balance conflicting tendencies in her life: her strong creative instincts, the knowledge of her responsibilities as a woman, and her musical and personal relationship vis-à-vis her brother Felix. She, in particular, was afforded a deep and penetrating introduction to the world via her comprehensive education and was then denied the opportunity to follow through on her training and participate fully in that world.

The possibilities for women composers gradually expanded after the middle of the nineteenth century. More female musicians—notably Clara Schumann—ventured forth outside the confines of the home on a regular basis; more women engaged in genres that previously excluded them, especially orchestral music. Such a sociological shift laid the groundwork for women's fuller participation in the profession of music—especially as professional composers.

The achievements of female lieder composers between 1775 and 1850 were magnificent and admirable. Overall there is a rich trove of lieder, most of it presently inaccessible to the musical public, awaiting serious, scholarly investigation. Numerous first-rate pieces, ranging from the volksthümlich style of Schröter to the sophisticated piano-vocal textures of Hensel and Lang, await publication and performance. The music of gifted female musicians of this period grew out of the complex sociological conditions facing them and attests to their brilliant responses to that environment. We today could be greatly enriched by their accomplishment.

NOTES

1. As described in "Bericht von Magdeburg," *Cramer's Magazin der Musik* 1 (1783): 173; and *Allgemeine musikalische Zeitung* 3 (October 1800), col. 66.

2. See "Vom Kostüm des Frauenzimmer Spielens," *Musikalischer Almanach* (1784): 85–99; Johann Daniel Hensel, *System der weiblichen Erziehung* (Halle: J. C. Hendl, 1787), p. 20; Friedrich Rochlitz, "Uber die vermeynte Schadlichkeit des Harmonikaspiels," *Allgemeine musikalische Zeitung* 1 (November 1798): 97–99.

3. See Jane Abray, "Feminism in the French Revolution," *American His-

torical Review 80 (1975): 43–62; and Katherine B. Clinton, "Femme et Philosophe: Enlightenment Origins of Feminism," *Eighteenth-Century Studies* 8 (1975): 283–99.

4. David Williams, "Condorcet, Feminism, and the Egalitarian Principle," in *Studies in Eighteenth-Century Culture*, ed. Ronald C. Rosbottom (Madison: University of Wisconsin Press, 1976), 5:151–63.

5. From Rousseau's *Émile* (1762), as quoted and translated in Katherine Anthony, *Feminism in Germany and Scandinavia* (New York: H. Holt & Co., 1915), pp. 42–43.

6. Jean-Jacques Rousseau, *Lettre à M. d'Alembert sur les Spectacles* (Amsterdam: Marc Michel Rey, 1758), p. 193n. (The translation is my own; subsequent translations, likewise, are mine unless otherwise indicated.)

7. [C.S.,] "Zwei Fragen an Aesthetiker," *Musikalisches Wochenblatt*, Heft 1, Stück 11 (1793), p. 8.

8. Johann Campe, *Väterlicher Rat für meine Tochter* (Braunschweig: Schulbuchhandlung, 1789), p. 39. This attitude was opposed by one writer in *Für deutsche Mädchen* (Dresden, 1781), p. 366: "The objection of a few unmusical moralists that these pursuits [composing music] would lead a young lady astray from her natural calling—that is, from domestic duties—is far from the mark. A young girl who goes too far in this direction would do so in other areas."

9. Johann B. Basedow, in *Pädagogische Unterhandlungen*, vol. 1 (Dessau: Erziehungs-Institut, 1777), pp. 10–84.

10. As quoted and translated in Herbert Kupferberg, *The Mendelssohns: Three Generations of Genius* (New York: Charles Scribner's Sons, 1972), p. 51.

11. In an article in C. D. Voss, *Kosmopolit* (June 1798), which is discussed in Hugh W. Puckett, *Germany's Women Go Forward* (New York: Columbia University Press, 1930), p. 60.

12. From Amalia Holst, *Über die Bestimmung des Weibes zu höheren Geistesbildung* (1791; reprint, Berlin: Duncker & Humblot, 1802), as quoted and translated in Puckett, *Germany's Women Go Forward*, p. 61.

13. Peter Villaume, in *Pädagogische Unterhandlungen*, 4 (1780): 394; Hensel, *System der weiblichen Erziehung*, p. 202. For discussions of German educational training for women from medieval times to the mid-nineteenth century, see Annemarie Krille, *Beiträge zur Geschichte der Musikerziehung und Musikübung der deutschen Frau (von 1750 bis 1820)* (Berlin: Triltsch & Huther, 1938), pp. 9–36; Peter Petschauer, "Forum," *Eighteenth-Century Studies* 9 (1975–76): 260.

14. Nina d'Aubigny von Engelbrunner, *Brief an Natalie über den Gesang als Beförderung der häuslichen Glückseligkeit und des geselligen Vergnügens*, 2d ed. (Leipzig: Voss, 1824).

15. Johann Adam Hiller, *Anweisung zum musikalisch richtigen Gesange* (Leipzig: J. F. Junius, 1774), preface.

16. *Allgemeine musikalische Zeitung* 1 (1798), col. 187.

17. Charles Burney, *The Present State of Music in Germany, the Netherlands, and the United Provinces*, 2d ed., 2 vols. (London: T. Becket & Co., 1775), 2:108–13, 207–9.

18. See Krille, *Geschichte der Musikerziehung*, pp. 78–79, for Nina d'Aubigny von Engelbrunner's comments on this position.

19. Hensel, *System der weiblichen Erziehung*, p. 17.

20. See Krille, *Geschichte der Musikerziehung*, pp. 63–72; Gustav Stephan, *Die häusliche Erziehung in Deutschland während des 18. Jahrhunderts* (Wiesbaden: J. F. Bergmann, 1891).

21. "Her memory is astounding. In London she learned a few of the most intricate and complicated Handel organ fugues, alongside other keyboard pieces from Handel's first book of *Lessons*, and in Berlin a *Rondo* from one of the sections of Karl Philip Emanuel Bach's *Sonaten für Kenner und Liebhaber*" (Ernst Gerber, *Historisch-biographisches Lexicon der Tonkünstler*, 2 vols. [Leipzig: J. G. I. Breitkopf, 1790–92], vol. 2, cols. 77–78).

22. A similar background applies to women painters. See Ann Sutherland Harris and Linda Nochlin, *Women Artists: 1550–1950* (New York: Alfred A. Knopf, 1977), p. 41.

23. Juliane Benda Reichardt, the daughter of Franz Benda and the first wife of Johann Friedrich Reichardt, was a singer, keyboard player, and the composer of *Lieder und Claviersonaten*, published in Hamburg by C. E. Bohn in 1782. Contemporary notices appeared in Gerber, *Lexicon*, vol. 2, col. 258; Johann Forkel, *Musikalischer Almanach auf das Jahr 1782* (Berlin: Alethinopel, 1782), p. 91; Johann Carl Friedrich Rellstab, *Über die Bemerkungen eines Reisenden die Berlinischen Kirchenmusiken . . . betreffend* (Berlin: der Verfasser, 1789), p. 17.

24. See the account by the Norwegian philosopher Heinrich Steffens, later Luise's brother-in-law, in *Was ich erlebte*, as quoted in Martin Brandt, *Leben der Luise Reichardt* (Karlsruhe: G. Holzmann, 1858), pp. 13–14; the comment by Karl Loewe in his *Selbstbiographie*, ed. K. Bitter (Berlin: W. Müller, 1870), p. 53; and the 1802 assessment by Goethe, in *Tag- und Jahres-Hefte*, *Goethe's Werke*, 60 vols. in 32 (Stuttgart & Tübingen: J. Cotta, 1827–42), 32:136.

25. In a letter from Felix to his family, 6 October 1831, in Felix Mendelssohn-Bartholdy, *Briefe aus den Jahren 1830 bis 1847*, 2 vols. (Leipzig: H. Mendelssohn, 1864), 1:292.

26. For the fullest account of Droste-Hülshoff's musical activities, see Karl Fellerer, "Annette von Droste-Hülshoff als Musikerin," *Archiv für Musikwissenschaft* 10 (1953): 41–59.

27. Two recent American dissertations contribute substantially to our knowledge about Hensel: Victoria Sirota, "The Life and Works of Fanny Mendelssohn Hensel" (Boston University, 1981); and Carol Quin, "Fanny Mendelssohn Hensel: Her Contributions to 19th-Century Musical Life" (University of Kentucky, 1981).

28. H. A. Köstlin, "Josephine Lang: Lebensabriss," *Sammlung musikalischer Vorträge*, ed. P. Waldersee, ser. 3 (1881), p. 55.

29. Maximilian Friedrich von Droste-Hülshoff (1764–1840) published his *Generalbass* method in 1821.

30. See comments by Henry Chorley ("Mendelssohn's Sister and Mother," in Lampadius, *Life of Felix Mendelssohn Bartholdy* [Boston: Ditson, 1865], pp. 210–11); Goethe (Karl Mendelssohn-Bartholdy, *Goethe and Mendelssohn* [London: Macmillan, 1874], p. 50); and Moscheles (C. Moscheles, *Aus Moscheles' Leben*, 2 vols. [Leipzig: Duncker & Humblot, 1872–73], 1:93).

31. *Cramer's Magazin der Musik* (1785), p. 693.

32. *Allgemeine musikalische Zeitung* 12 (April 1810), col. 472. The published lieder are *Zwölf Lieder auf ihrer Reise in Musik gesetzt . . .* (Leipzig: J. C. I. Breitkopf, 1786).

33. Fanny Hensel to Carl Klingemann, 15 July 1836, in Sebastian Hensel, *The Mendelssohn Family 1729–1847*, tr. Carl Klingemann, 2 vols., 2d ed. (New York: Harper & Bros., 1882), 2:31.

34. "For *you* it [music] can and must only be an ornament." Abraham Mendelssohn to Fanny Mendelssohn, 16 July 1820, in S. Hensel, *Mendelssohn Family*, 1:82. And on 14 November 1828, "You must . . . prepare more earnestly and eagerly for your real calling, the *only* calling of a young woman—I mean the state of a housewife." Id., 1:84.

35. Fanny to Felix, 30 July 1836, unpublished letter in Oxford, Bodelian Library, "Green Books" Mendelssohn letters collection. The author is preparing for Pendragon Press an annotated edition of the letters from Fanny to Felix in this collection, in both English translation and the original German.

36. Mendelssohn-Bartholdy, *Briefe 1830 bis 1847*, 2:88–89, in which the letter is incorrectly dated 2 June 1837. The correct date is 24 June 1837; the original letter is in the New York Public Library collection of Felix's letters to his family.

37. Unpublished letter from the Green Books collection. This influence was explored in Marcia J. Citron, "Felix Mendelssohn's Influence on Fanny Mendelssohn Hensel as a Professional Composer," *Current Musicology*, no. 37 (forthcoming).

38. For a listing of the locations of her manuscripts, see Rudolf Elvers, "Verzeichnis der Musik-Autographen von Fanny Hensel in dem Mendelssohn-Arkiv zu Berlin," *Mendelssohn Studien* 1 (1972): 169–74; and id., "Weitere Quellen zu den Werken von Fanny Hensel," ibid., 2 (1975): 215–20.

39. Fanny Hensel, *Sechs Lieder für eine Stimme*, opera 1 and 7 (Berlin: Bote & Bock, [1846, 1847]). Lieder collections opera 9 and 10 were issued circa 1850 by Breitkopf & Härtel (Leipzig). Opus 1 is recorded on Leonarda LPI 112 (1982). In addition, two single lieder, *Die Schiffende* and *Schloss Liebeneck*, were published in 1837 and 1839 respectively.

40. As quoted in Richard Hohenemser, "Clara Wieck-Schumann als Komponistin," *Die Musik* 5 (July-September 1906): 124.

41. Ernst Gerber, *Neues historisch-biographisches Lexicon*, 4 vols. (Leipzig: A. Kühnel, 1812–14), vol. 3, col. 823.

42. A review of Felix's Opus 8 appeared in the *Allgemeine musika-*

lische Zeitung 29 (June 1827), col. 440; of Opus 9 ibid. (November 1827), cols. 813–15. See also the comments in *Harmonicon* 8 (March 1830): 99.

43. A review of this collection appeared in the *Allgemeine musikalische Zeitung* 44 (January 1842), cols. 61–63. *Liebst du um Schönheit*, one of Clara's lieder, was singled out for praise.

44. See Marcia J. Citron, "Corona Schröter: Singer, Composer, Actress," *Music & Letters* 61 (1980): 15–27.

45. An account of her successful teaching appeared in the *Allgemeine musikalische Zeitung* 12 (April 1810), cols. 472–73; ibid., 13 (July 1811), cols. 475–76. See also Hermann Ullrich, "Maria Theresia Paradis als Musikpädagogin," *Musikerziehung* 14 (1960): 9–15.

46. *Allgemeine musikalische Zeitung* 20 (October 1818), cols. 711, 714–15; 24 (March 1822), col. 212; 27 (August 1825), col. 531.

47. See Marcia J. Citron, "The Lieder of Fanny Mendelssohn Hensel," *Musical Quarterly* 69 (Fall 1983): 570–94.

48. See Goethe's essay on the Leipzig theater (1812), as quoted in Hans Moser, *Goethe und die Musik* (Leipzig: C. F. Peters, 1949), p. 14; J. F. Reichardt's autobiography, as quoted in H. H. Schletterer, *Johann Friedrich Reichardt: Sein Leben und seine musikalische Thätigkeit* (Augsburg: J. A. Schlosser, 1865), p. 103; Gerber, *Lexicon*, vol. 2, col. 455; and Schröter's obituary, *Allgemeine musikalische Zeitung* 5 (April 1803), cols. 471–72.

49. *Allgemeine musikalische Zeitung* 23 (November 1821), col. 816.

50. Mendelssohn-Bartholdy, *Briefe 1830 bis 1847*, 1:292. A description of Mendelssohn's enthusiasm also appeared in Ferdinand Hiller, *Aus dem Tonleben unserer Zeit*, 2 vols. (Leipzig: H. Mendelssohn, 1868), 2:124–26.

51. A copy of the playbill is housed in the Goethe collection at Yale University. The manuscript of the incidental music, consisting of ten numbers, resides in the Nationale Forschungs- und Gedenkstätten in Weimar.

52. Christian Heinrich Schmid, *Chronologie des deutschen Theaters* (Leipzig: E. B. Schwickert, 1775).

53. According to Elvers's lists of extant Hensel manuscripts (see n. 38 above), she composed one overture and five vocal works that include orchestra. Schumann composed only one work for orchestra: a Piano Concerto in A Minor, opus 7.

54. See *Die Musik in Geschichte und Gegenwart*, 16 vols. (Kassel: Bärenreiter, 1949–79), vol. 10, col. 743, s.v. "Maria Theresia Paradis." In this article Hermann Ullrich says that Paradis composed two concertos for piano and orchestra, one in g minor, the other in C major; he also lists three stage works that presumably employ the orchestra: *Ariadne und Bacchus*, *Der Schulkandidat*, and *Rinaldo und Alcina*.

55. A pupil of both Haydn and Porpora, Martinez was praised by Burney, *Present State*, 1:311–14, 345–46, 354. At Burney's first meeting with Martinez, he praised her compositions but was especially pleased with her singing: "Her voice and manner of singing, both delighted and astonished me! I can readily subscribe to what Metastasio [her teacher] says, that it is a style

of singing which no longer subsists elsewhere, as it requires too much pains and patience for modern professors" (ibid., p. 312). See also Karen Lynn Fremar, *The Life and Selected Works of Marianna Martines* (1744–1812) (Ann Arbor: University Microfilms, 1983).

56. *Fünf-und-zwanzig Lieder in Musik gesetzt* (Weimar: Hoffmann Buchhandlung, 1786) and *Gesaenge mit Begleitung des Pianoforte, zweite Sammlung* (Weimar: Industrie Comptoir, 1794). In 1907 a facsimile edition of the 1786 collection was printed, with commentary by Leopold Schmidt.

57. A modern edition of her songs is Annette von Droste-Hülshoff, *Lieder und Gesänge*, ed. Karl Fellerer (Münster-Westfalen: Aschendorff, 1954).

58. The most complete listing of Reichardt's lieder is in Carl Ledebur, *Tonkünstler-Lexicon Berlin's von den ältesten Zeiten bis auf die Gegenwart* (Berlin: L. Rauh, 1861; reprint, Tutzing: Hans Schneider, 1965), p. 443. A more recent, condensed list appears in Nancy Reich's article in *The New Grove Dictionary of Music and Musicians* (London: Macmillan, 1980), s.v. "Louise Reichardt," 15:708. A selection of Reichardt's published lieder has been reissued by Da Capo (1981) with an introduction by Nancy Reich. In addition, nine lieder are recorded on Leonarda LPI 112 (1982).

59. The most comprehensive listing of her output appears in the lengthy article by her son, H. A. Köstlin, "Josephine Lang," pp. 51–103.

60. Josephine Lang, *Liederbuch für eine Singstimme mit Begleitung des Pianoforte*, 2 vols. (Leipzig: Breitkopf & Härtel, 1882). A selection of her published lieder has been reissued by Da Capo (1982) with an introduction by Judith Tick.

61. *Allgemeine musikalische Zeitung* 8 (July 1806), cols. 686–87; 29 (August 1827), cols. 542–44.

62. Ibid., 29, col. 542.

63. *Cramer's Magazin der Musik* (1786), p. 1045. Although the reviewer generally praised the collection, a few of the Herder texts were strongly criticized. Gerber's *Lexicon*, vol. 2, col. 455, also praised the collection.

64. *Allgemeine musikalische Zeitung* 5 (April 1803), col. 473.

65. *Neue Zeitschrift für Musik* 26 (1847): 38.

66. Ibid., 28 (1848): 88.

67. *Liebst du um Schönheit* was deemed the best of the joint Clara and Robert Schumann collection (published as Robert's Opus 37) in the *Allgemeine musikalische Zeitung* 44 (January 1842), col. 62. This song plus six others by Clara are recorded on Leonarda LPI 107 (1981). Hensel's *Nachtwanderer* and five other songs also appear on the same record. Still other songs by Hensel appear on *Fanny Mendelssohn Hensel: Rediscovered*, Northeastern NR 213 (1984).

68. Six of Lang's lieder publications were reviewed. See the *Allgemeine musikalische Zeitung* 43 (December 1841), cols. 1042–43; 48 (January 1846), cols. 36–37; 50 (June 1848), cols. 395–96. Nine of Lang's songs are recorded

on Musica Bavarica, MB 902 [n.d.]; five appear on Leonarda 107 (see n. 67 above).

69. This song is published in the 1954 collection, *Lieder und Gesänge*, edited by Fellerer.

70. Four of Droste-Hülshoff's songs are recorded on *Musik auf historischen Instrumenten*, FSM 123003/4 [n.d.].

71. Karoline Pichler, *Denkwürdigkeiten aus meinem Leben*, 2d ed., 2 vols. (Munich: Georg Müller, 1914), 1:191. Similar comments appear on pp. 295–97.

72. See pp. 230–31 above.

10

Clara Schumann

NANCY B. REICH

In January 1838 a poem entitled "Clara Wieck and Beethoven" appeared in a Viennese paper devoted to art and literature.[1] Written by Franz Grillparzer, Austria's leading dramatic poet, the poem immortalized the performance of an eighteen-year-old girl. Grillparzer had heard Clara Wieck on January 7, at her third Viennese recital.[2] His response to her performance of the Sonata opus 57, the *Appassionata*, reflected the general enthusiasm evoked by the young pianist. From her first concert in December 1837 in the Musikvereinsaal to her last concert in April 1838 before the emperor in the Burg, she was greeted with the admiration and respect usually reserved for artists like Paganini and Thalberg.

The Grillparzer poem was only one of the triumphs of Clara's musical season. She earned several thousand *thaler;* her concerts, even during carnival season and at high prices, were sold out; she played to wild applause and warm reviews from the Viennese musical cognoscenti. Schubert's friend, Benedict Randhartinger,[3] gave her an autograph copy of the composer's *Erlkönig,* inscribing it "To the celebrated artist, Clara Wieck."[4]

A critic wrote of one concert:

Demoiselle Clara Wieck charmed our musical public in a fifth concert; the appearance of this artist can be regarded as epochmaking, for the highest level of artistic skill combined with the greatest genius, as was the case here, is only rarely to be found. . . . In her creative hands, the most ordinary passage, the most routine motive acquires a significant meaning, a color, which only those with the most consummate artistry are able to give.[5]

Clara Wieck's days and nights in Vienna were a whirlwind of activities: courtesy visits, presentations, formal acceptance of gifts, private musicales, public concerts, practice sessions. The Viennese nobility and wealthy music lovers vied in inviting her to their palaces to play. Musicians marveled at her skill in sight-reading. The Viennese publishers requested new music for publication—anything from the pen of Clara Wieck would be sure to sell—but her father regretfully wrote home that there were only two hours when she had time to compose—between nine and eleven in the evening. All her other time was committed.

Franz Liszt, then twenty-eight and at the height of his career as a performing artist, was in Vienna during Clara Wieck's visit. Having heard of her accomplishments from Chopin, he was eager to meet her. After Clara played for and with him, he praised her extravagantly in a letter that was published in the Parisian *Revue et Gazette Musicale* and later, in translation, in the Leipzig journal *Neue Zeitschrift für Musik.*[6]

On 15 March 1838, she received the greatest honor Vienna could bestow: she was named *Königliche und Kaiserliche Kammer-Virtuosin* (Royal and Imperial Chamber Virtuoso), a distinction without precedent for an eighteen-year-old who was, moreover, a Protestant, a foreigner, and a woman. A week later the emperor pronounced her a *"Wundermädchen"* and told her of his personal satisfaction with the award.[7]

Clara Wieck and her father, Friedrich, had set out for Vienna from their native Leipzig in October 1837. Behind Clara were ten years of concertizing in Leipzig and Dresden, a Parisian visit in 1832, and extensive tours in northern Germany. She had appeared in the Gewandhaus in Leipzig almost every year since her first appearance there at the age of nine. Although Clara Wieck Schumann went on to many other triumphs, at eighteen she had the technique, skills, and musical understanding that formed the basis of her enduring artistic career.

Clara Schumann, *"geboren* Wieck" as she often styled herself, was the leading woman pianist of her age and was acknowledged as the peer of Liszt, Thalberg, and Anton Rubinstein. The first pianist to play many of the Beethoven sonatas publicly, she also premiered works of Chopin, Schumann, and Brahms; she was among the first to play without music and to give recitals without supporting musicians. Her programming and her musical standards changed the character of the solo piano recital in the nineteenth century.

When Clara Wieck began her performing career, she was compared to other young women pianists—Marie Blahetka, Anna de Belleville, Marie Pleyel.[8] Many of her widely acclaimed female contemporaries made splashy debuts and brilliant appearances but one after the other gave up careers when they married or found they could not keep up with the stresses of combining family and profession. They eventually disappeared from public view. Clara Wieck Schumann, however, played over 1,300 public programs in England and Europe.[9] Respect for her artistry continued to grow during the century, and on the occasion of her sixtieth jubilee in 1888 she was hailed throughout the musical world. No other pianist of her century, male or female, maintained a position as a performing artist over such a span of time. A study of the names of the 261 pianists (84 of them women) appearing in the famed Leipzig Gewandhaus between 1781 and 1881 shows that Clara Wieck Schumann performed there seventy-four times—far more than any other artist. Only Felix Mendelssohn, who performed as a pianist in the hall forty-seven times, and Carl Reinecke, who appeared as a soloist on forty-six occasions, approached her record.[10]

In this essay we will focus on Clara Schumann as a musician and examine her education and career as performer and composer; we will also look at her as wife and mother and consider her position as an artist and woman. Her relationship with her father, Friedrich Wieck, her first and only piano teacher, is of the utmost significance in understanding her musical development and will be explored briefly. Other aspects of her life and work, such as her musical and personal relationships with the two great composers, Robert Schumann, her husband, and Johannes Brahms, a close friend, must be documented in a longer study.[11]

The story of Clara Schumann has been fictionalized, dramatized, and romanticized; but all studies, serious and otherwise, have been based on the authorized biography by Berthold Litzmann, *Clara Schumann: Ein Künstlerleben*.[12] Litzmann worked within the severe limitations of time, space, and the family sense of propriety. The excerpts he presented were generally faithful to the diaries and letters I have examined, but many significant details were glossed over or omitted. His choice of excerpts was dictated by Marie Schumann, the eldest daughter; the story of Clara Schumann's life was recorded as Marie wished posterity to know it. The Grace Hadow translation of Litzmann is accurate but was written under a severe handicap; in it the three volumes of the original were reduced to two, necessitating even more cuts. The Brahms-Schumann correspondence,[13] also edited by Litzmann and translated by Hadow, is abridged as well. Thus the English reader of this material is at the mercy of the translator in many senses.

Until recently, the literature on Clara Schumann has concentrated on presenting her as (1) a devoted wife and mother, (2) a "consecrated, loyal priestess,"[14] (3) a figure in a great romance with Robert Schumann, or (4) a party to a "passionate friendship" with Brahms.[15] In the Robert Schumann biographies she is, of course, a subordinate figure, sometimes treated with reverence, occasionally with reproach.

Litzmann wrote in the first decade of the twentieth century. Since then documentary sources have been reexamined, and letters and music that shed considerable light on the Schumanns and their circle have been found and published. We have, moreover, gained new perceptions about human behavior as well as the roles of women in the history of music. It is obviously time for a new look at Clara Schumann geboren Wieck, who was neither a priestess nor a passionate friend, neither a saint nor a sinner, but a great artist who has not yet been accorded the dignity of the full-fledged scholarly study she deserves.

Clara's father, Friedrich Wieck (1785–1873) was born in Pretzsch, a small town about forty-five kilometers north of Leipzig. His home was a poor one and music was not encouraged. After completing studies for the ministry at the University of Wittenberg, he worked as a *Hauslehrer* (household tutor). As a young tutor he wrote some thoughtful observations on education that demonstrate his extraordinary gift for pedagogy and his understanding of the learning process.[16] After supporting himself as a tutor for nine years, he turned to his first love, music, in which he was largely self-taught. Ambitious and hard-working, he borrowed money to establish a music-lending library and a piano business in which he sold, rented, and repaired pianos.[17] This enabled him to meet all the musicians who toured through Leipzig, a leading commercial city long known as a music center. Travel on behalf of his business brought Wieck into contact with wider circles: in Vienna, where he bought most of his pianos, he met Beethoven, and he knew and corresponded with Carl Czerny and Andreas Stein. He began teaching piano in Leipzig in 1815 and soon acquired a reputation as an excellent teacher, partly due to the successful public appearances of his wife.

On 23 June 1816 Friedrich Wieck married Marianne Tromlitz[18] (1797–1872), a gifted young woman whose grandfather, Johann George Tromlitz (1725–1805), had been a widely known flutist, teacher, and flute maker. Her father, George Christian Tromlitz (1765–1825), was the *Stadtkantor* in Plauen, a Saxon town south of Leipzig. Marianne, a shadowy figure in the Clara Schumann literature, has received little credit for her contributions to the musical development of her daughter.

How Friedrich Wieck and Marianne Tromlitz met has not been established. Perhaps she studied with him in Plauen or when he first came to Leipzig, but that she was uncommonly talented is clear. In the first year of her marriage, Mme Wieck was singing solo parts in the Leipzig Gewandhaus. A review of a performance of the Mozart Requiem on 15 December 1816 referred to the soprano soloist, Mme Wieck, as the young wife of a local piano teacher and praised her voice and "skill, confidence, and diligence."[19] She sang solo in a performance of the Beethoven Mass in C (op. 86) on 13 March 1817 and in other works on 27 March and 6 April 1817.

On 18 October 1821, two years after the birth of Clara (a first child had died shortly before Clara's birth), Mme Wieck again appeared with the Gewandhaus orchestra, this time as a pianist, playing the Concerto in E-flat Major by Ferdinand Ries. Her career was not interrupted by the birth of a third child, Alwin, in 1821, and another son, Gustav, in 1823. She performed at the Gewandhaus in October 1822 and again in November and December 1823. Another son was born in January 1824.

Four months after the birth of her youngest child, Marianne left the bed and board of Friedrich Wieck. She returned to her parental home, requesting a legal separation in May 1824, when Clara was only four and a half years old. The mother was permitted to keep the daughter with her until four days after the child's fifth birthday, 17 September 1824, when Clara was brought back to her father. Of the other children, the mother could have only the infant-in-arms. A divorce was granted within a year.

Marianne was soon married to Adolph Bargiel,[20] a piano teacher who had been a close family friend. Although she lived in Leipzig for almost a year after her remarriage, she could see her children only at Wieck's pleasure, since they were, according to the Saxon law of the time, the father's property, and his authority over them was practically unlimited.[21]

Wieck himself did not remarry until Clara was nine. For four years she lived in a motherless home under the care of her father and servants. During the early and crucial years of her life she had been in the care of an inarticulate maid while living in an atmosphere of strife and tension. At the age of five she had endured what she must have perceived as abandonment by a grieving mother, and she suffered through the harsh divorce that followed. There is no doubt that this traumatic series of events in many ways affected her later life as a musician, wife, and mother.

Wieck held great hopes for the musical career of his eldest child—a career that would demonstrate to the world the superiority of his pedagogical approach. But to his great disappointment Clara did not speak—not even single words—until she was past four years old, and before that she gave so little evidence of language comprehension it was assumed she was hard of hearing. Despite this obstacle, her father began to give her piano lessons on the day after she returned from her mother. In "Clara's" diary we find this entry:

On 18 September, my father began giving me proper piano lessons; actually, I had already learned to play several simple exercises without moving my hand and even played, by ear, simple dance accompaniments a few months before I left for Plauen with my mother. I could not go much further, however, since I could not speak nor could I understand others. During the four months in Plauen, my mother, at least in regard to this, did not do the slightest thing for me.[22]

This was, of course, written for her by her father.

Friedrich Wieck's unblushing appropriation of Clara's personality in the diary continued until she left home in January 1839. It is no exaggeration to say that Wieck considered Clara an extension of himself. On the title page of her diary he wrote, "My Diary, begun by my Father, the 7th of June 1827 and to be continued by Clara Josephine Wieck."[23] Although most entries are in the first person—as though Clara were writing—Wieck actually kept the diary. The occasional entries Clara was permitted to make were written under his supervision; his emendations and marginal comments are scattered through the journal. She was not able to write freely in her own diary until she was nineteen years old.

Wieck used the diary as a way of educating and communicating with his daughter: information, praise, exhortation, condemnation are all to be found there. In addition, Wieck had his daughter copy into her diary letters he wrote to friends, colleagues, and business associates. Thus the child literally absorbed Wieck's personality and attitudes—toward money, music, and success—through her eyes, ears, and fingers.

The musical training Wieck gave his daughter was thorough and practical; and we would characterize it today as progressive.[24] He planned to develop an all-round musician, not merely a pianist. Although the ambitious father had little formal training and was neither a performer nor a composer, he was equipped with exceptional musical understanding and taste.[25]

In his major written work, *Clavier und Gesang,* a book that still holds great interest for piano pedagogues, he wrote that a piano teacher must understand the art of singing to teach the finest possible touch on the piano: "the piano and singing should explain and supplement each other."[26] Wieck was a brilliant and creative teacher, and his daughter was always grateful for the foundation he bestowed with such scrupulous care. Clara knew the education he lavished on her contrasted sadly with that given his sons; the education of both her brothers was neglected in a most deplorable way.[27]

Wieck described himself as a "man of caustic brevity and bluntness."[28] He had a sense of humor (often coarse) and a keen understanding of human nature, but he also had a stubborn disposition and violent temper that he did not hesitate to vent on his favorite when she dared oppose him.

Clara's general education was meager. When she was six, she attended a neighborhood primary school for a few months; then she went on to a larger institute for eight additional months.[29] Formal lessons in theory, harmony, counterpoint, composition, singing, score reading, and violin began when she was eight and continued for many years. The study of languages was pursued in preparation for future trips to France and England. Several hours a day were reserved for piano lessons (from Wieck), for practicing piano, and for long walks in the fresh air. The Wiecks kept open house in Leipzig for publishers, writers, and visiting musicians; and Clara was invariably present, even as a child, to meet them and to perform new and old works. Almost as soon as piano studies began, she was taken to orchestral and chamber music concerts as well as to productions of drama and opera. Wieck believed that the formation of a concert artist began in early childhood and in his book described the ideal curriculum for the proper development of the would-be virtuoso, the plan he had followed for Clara's education.

Wieck's unique method, his understanding of pedagogy and psychology, his dominating personality, the circumstances in the home—both fortunate and unfortunate—all influenced his daughter's development as a musician and artist. When the break with Clara came, Wieck devoted himself to the career of a younger half-sister, Marie Wieck. But although Marie had a successful career as an artist, she always lived in the shadow of her more famous (and gifted) sibling.[30] Only one of Wieck's sons (Alwin) became a musician, and he never achieved the eminence or respect accorded his sisters.

Wieck gave his daughter Clara all the skills needed by a musician, and he never made excuses for her sex. She did not always share his confidence. In 1857, in a lonely and depressed mood, Clara wrote to Joachim requesting that he not withhold the criticism she needed in her striving for intellectual mastery of the music she performed; she added, "that is, as much mastery as a woman is capable of."[31] The statement reflected the view of the larger society in which she lived—not her father's attitude. Wieck never felt his daughter's femininity was a drawback; he proceeded with his training program systematically, thoughtfully, meticulously, as though he were training a racehorse.

He did not care to have Clara spend her time on the so-called feminine arts. All his piano pupils were advised against sewing, knitting or crocheting, and though Clara's diary records that on her return from Paris she went into the kitchen and cleaned knives,[32] this was not part of her father's program. It was, in fact, severely discouraged.

In a letter to Robert Schumann on 2 June 1838 Clara wrote:

It would be very nice if Therese [Robert's sister-in-law] would be with us during the first weeks of our marriage; she could teach me much that I cannot learn at home, since my father wants to see me only at the piano. How I would like to busy myself now and then with household things, but I would just be laughed at.[33]

In view of Wieck's disposition, ambitions, and, one might say, obsession and total identification with his daughter's career, his position was not surprising. Moreover, female performing musicians were not unknown in Leipzig. Gertrude Mara (1749–1833) and Corona Schröter (1751–1802), both eminent singers and musicians, had trained and worked in Leipzig in the 1760s. Regina Strinasacchi (1764–1823), a violinist, concertized there in 1785. Fourteen women had appeared as pianists at the Leipzig Gewandhaus between 1781 and 1830; one (listed only as Mme A. G. Müller) played solo there seventeen times between 1794 and 1810.[34] Wieck's dream of a girl-child who was to be a brilliant performer (hence her name, Clara), was clearly then not unrealistic in a city with such a tradition. Even Wieck, however, could not foresee a career that would be sustained with honor for so many years.

The Wiecks met Robert Schumann at the home of mutual friends in Leipzig in 1828, when Clara was nine years old and Robert was eighteen. Impressed by Clara's playing, Robert began to study with her father. He moved into the Wieck home as a boarder in October 1830 and saw Clara every day during the year he lived with the family. The close ties continued, and even after he changed his residence there were daily meetings.

Clara's name appeared in his diary with growing frequency. Considering that she was not quite twelve in May 1831, it is remarkable to see the significance she had for him. There are entries, both critical and admiring, about Clara on May 27, 31, June 6, 7, 8, and on and on.[35] They become increasingly personal; on her return from the Paris tour in May 1832, he wrote:

2 May. Clara arrived early yesterday with Wieck. Gustav and Alwin [her brothers] came to let me know immediately. . . . 3 May . . . Clara is prettier and taller, stronger and more skilled and has acquired a French accent when she speaks German—but Leipzig will soon get rid of that for her. . . . 4 May . . . Clara was childishly simple. We went home very late: Clara and I arm in arm. . . .[36]

By 1835 interest and friendship had grown to love: "Daily meetings with Clara—on June 8 [Robert's birthday] a watchband from her. . . . Clara's birthday on September 13. . . . [October] Clara's eyes and her love. . . . The first kiss in November. . . . Lovely hours in her arms in the evenings in Wieck's house."[37]

Clara's first letter to Robert, addressed to "Mein lieber Herr Schumann," written in December 1832, reveals her feelings; it is newsy, but also teasing and flirtatious. Many years later, Eugenie Schumann, the youngest Schumann daughter, found a notation her mother had made in the margin of Philipp Spitta's book on Robert Schumann. To Spitta's comment, "As far as we know, a special affection [between the two] first was apparent in the spring of 1836," Clara had appended, "Already in 1833."[38] The first notes and messages that passed between them reveal a mutual ongoing fantasy centering on childish stories he told her and music they played together, as well as motherly concern and girlish coquettishness on her part and worship and awed respect on his. Her Romance Variée (op. 3), composed at age fourteen, was dedicated to him. He, in turn, wrote his Impromptus sur une Romance de Clara Wieck (op. 5) at about the same time. There is no doubt that Clara, almost fifteen, suffered during the short-lived romance between Robert and Ernestine von Fricken, who came to study with Wieck.

Clara was, of course, an unusually mature girl, certainly as adult and far more gifted and stimulating than Ernestine, who was three years her senior. That her maturity, even at thirteen, was somewhat disturbing to onlookers is evident from the six-page article written about her in the journal *Caecilia* in 1833:

At first glance one could take Clara to be a quite lovable thirteen-year-old girl—and think no more about it—but if she is observed more closely— everything appears otherwise! The delicate, pretty little face with the some- what exotic, slanting eyes, the friendly mouth with the touch of sentiment which now and then draws up in a somewhat mocking or painful way, partic- ularly when she answers. And, moreover, the mixture of grace and care- lessness in her movements—not studied—but it goes far beyond one of her years! All this—I confess it openly—stirred a quite peculiar feeling in me when I saw it and I know of no better way to describe it except as "an echo of Clara's mocking-painful smile." It seems as though the child knew of a long story to tell, a story woven out of joy and pain—and yet—what does she know? Music.[39]

During the years 1832–35, Robert was probably at his most at- tractive and appealing: young and handsome, gifted, energetic, hope- ful, and ambitious. Despite an emotional crisis in 1833, he was pro- ductive: the Impromptus (op. 5), Carnaval (op. 9), the Sonata in F- sharp Minor (op. 11), and Twelve Etudes Symphoniques (op. 13), among his greatest works, were written in these years. In 1834 a large part of his time was taken up with the literary and business responsibilities of the *Neue Zeitschrift für Musik*, the weekly jour- nal he had helped found. Only one of a group of editors during the first year, Schumann was the busiest, conducting most of the cor- respondence, contacting potential contributors, editing articles, writ- ing reviews, negotiating, and maneuvering. He became the sole owner and director in 1835.[40]

During this time Clara, who was nominally a child, concertized actively, but she was in daily contact with Robert when she was in Leipzig. Her father, one of the original editors of the *Zeitschrift*, re- mained Robert's friend and counselor until 1836. Clara, present and performing at the adult gatherings in the Wieck home and a frequent companion of her father and friends on their daily walks, was privy to many of the discussions and decisions made during these years.

Robert Schumann's diary entries indicate much ambivalence to- ward Wieck from the beginning of their association. He had grave doubts about the sincerity of Wieck's attachment to Clara and was convinced that the father was avaricious and cared more about Clara's earning power than he did about the girl herself. A witness to many scenes in the Wieck household, he knew Wieck's temper well. His diary entry for 21 May 1831 reads:

Yesterday I saw a scene whose impression will be indelible. Meister Raro [Wieck] is surely a wicked man. Alwin had not played well: "You wretch, you wretch—is this the pleasure you give your father"—how he threw him on the floor, pulled him by the hair, trembled and staggered, sat still to rest and gain strength for new feats, could barely stand on his legs anymore and had to throw his prey down, how the boy begged and implored him to give him the violin—he wanted to play, he wanted to play—I can barely describe it—and to all this—Zilia [Clara] smiled and calmly sat herself down at the piano with a Weber sonata. Am I among human beings?[41]

The sensitive Robert was shaken, but Clara, though never physically humiliated as her brothers were, had obviously lived through many such scenes. Set apart from birth, she was the most gifted and the most obedient of Wieck's children. The household revolved around her and her needs: she was outfitted with silk gowns for her concert tours, she had her own room, pianos were brought from Vienna for her use. And, although three sons were born after her, Wieck had decided that *she* would carry the Wieck name to every civilized corner of Europe. One son (a half-brother) died at age three; and her brothers Alwin and Gustav, abandoned by their mother at the ages of three and one, were virtually ignored, even mistreated, by their father.

Wieck was totally absorbed in Clara; he was proud of her and gloried in his position and propinquity to her. Clara functioned as a vicarious performer for her father. He wrote her diary, ordered her life, traveled with her, arranged her concerts, collected her fees, enjoyed public acclaim and rubbed shoulders with the great—all through her carefully cultivated gifts.

Looking back, we wonder how Robert Schumann could ever have been so naïve as to expect to be welcomed by the fiery-tempered Wieck. It is obvious that Wieck could not have shared his daughter with any man; and although he admired and promoted Robert's music, he certainly would not have approved a marriage with an impecunious young composer. Yet, with typical youthful arrogance and spirit, Schumann anticipated no problem when he asked for Clara's hand. The ending of the love story is well known. It will suffice to say here that Wieck put every obstacle in their path, behaved in a totally outrageous and (finally) irrational way, and that Robert and Clara were forced to appeal to courts of law for permission to marry. The wedding took place on 12 September 1840, the day before Clara's twenty-first birthday.

The few happy years that Clara and Robert Schumann had together were years in which she gave birth to their children and to his musical creations. While he was composing, Robert did not turn to her; she complained, in fact, during the first year of their marriage, the glorious "year of song," that when he was writing, he was cold to her.[42] But as soon as the work was completed—and more than once he referred to it as childbirth[43]—he gave it to her to present to the world. She was the artist who first played the concerto, the piano sonatas, the quintet, and almost every work in which a piano figured. She was, in fact, jealous if anyone else played his works, even in another city. Almost all the Schumann orchestral works were first presented in conjunction with her piano performances.

Clara also prepared piano reductions of his orchestra scores, copied music for him, rehearsed singers, accompanied the choruses he conducted in Dresden and Düsseldorf (sang, too, when necessary), and acted as his mouthpiece when he was ill and depressed. She stood by him and defended him even when she must have been aware of his shortcomings as a conductor. She kept artistic and family life together during his periodic depressions. Robert valued, respected, and used Clara's talent. Though he was a generous and loving husband, he had ambivalent feelings about her career; and during their marriage there were many conflicts, some expressed, others no doubt hidden.

The problems in the first years of their marriage were similar to those of modern couples, each of whom has a career. There is no doubt that she concertized to help with household expenses. However, we know from the correspondence and diary entries that this was not the primary reason for her concert appearances. Clara never intended to give up her concert career after marriage, and Robert never seriously suggested it. In the love letters written before their marriage, Robert repeatedly referred to the continuance of her work. It is equally clear, however, that he longed for a quiet home and a woman to look after him.[44] Robert hoped for the impossible: "in the house such a housewife, in my heart a beloved and loving wife, for the world an artist such as it does not get every day and whom it will know how to esteem."[45]

Robert Schumann was aware of his wife's needs as an artist, however, and his attitude toward her career was, for a man of his time, unusually enlightened. In 1841 the Schumanns were invited to Bremen and Hamburg—he to be present at the premiere of his first symphony and she to play. They accepted and went together leaving behind their first child, six-month-old Marie. The tour to the north ended with Clara continuing on to Copenhagen while Robert returned home to Leipzig to resume his editorial duties on the *Neue*

Zeitschrift and to keep an eye on the baby, who had been left in the care of a maid. Letters written almost daily during their separation testify to his understanding:

March 24, 1842. May this [separation] be worth the sacrifice and bring you joy as an artist. You are still so young and I cannot blame you if, as an artist, you do not want the hard work of your youth to be forgotten; in a word—that you are happy when you still can give people pleasure through your beautiful talent.[46]

April 14, 1842. Cläre, I beg you, play carefully and with all imaginable care and genius so that this gossip [that her playing did not please the northern audiences] can be discredited. Your honor as an artist is as dear to me as your *honor as a woman*, and I can and must depend on you in all things.[47]

Yet Clara's concert ambitions (and perhaps her successes) and the partings that occurred as a result troubled Robert. During her Copenhagen tour, he wrote in their joint marriage diary:

The separation has once more made me aware of my peculiar and difficult position. Shall I neglect my own talent, in order to serve as a companion on your journeys? Have you, should you allow your talent to lie useless because I am chained to the paper and the piano? Now, when you are young and in full possession of your powers? We found the way out. You took a companion with you and I returned to the child and my work. But what will the world say? Thus I torture myself with thoughts. Yes, it is absolutely necessary for us to find some means by which we can both utilize and cultivate our talents side by side.[48]

Clara had conflicts as well. On the one hand, she believed that Robert's needs, since he was a creative artist, should have priority. In a lonely moment after his death, she wrote in her diary: "For Him, in sacrifice to the dearest one, I could have renounced public artistic activities; my heart would have been completely fulfilled with his art and personality."[49] But she had forgotten the days in which she wept because she could not practice and feared for the loss of her powers as a pianist: "My piano playing is falling behind again—this always happens when Robert is composing. Not even one little hour in the day can be found for me. If only I don't fall too far behind."[50]

When Clara went off to play in Copenhagen without Robert, he was concerned about what the world would say. Clara also gave some thought to that question. The separation occasioned much gossip, which must have been distressing to both. In a remarkably revealing letter, Clara explained to her childhood friend, Emilie List:

Yes, I really did go to Copenhagen alone (that is, without Robert, but with a woman from Bremen), separated from him, although this shall never happen again, if God wills. I will explain the whole thing to you so that you will understand our steps. . . . As the time approached [to leave for Copenhagen], Robert realized more and more the impossibility of leaving his paper in strange hands for perhaps another two months; the three weeks for which he had arranged were over, and so we decided to give up the journey; but I weighed the whole thing—I am a woman, am not neglecting anything at home[!], earn nothing, why shouldn't I use my talent for once to contribute my mite to Robert? Could anyone blame me for this? Or my husband for going home to his child and his business? I proposed my plan to Robert, and it is true that at first he was alarmed, but finally agreed since I presented it so reasonably. It was certainly a big step to take for a woman who loves her husband as much as I do, yet I did it out of love for him and for that, no sacrifice is too big or too hard for me.[51]

For a short time, there were some wild ideas about a tour to America so that Clara might earn a great deal of money that would ensure their future. The plan was to then return to Germany, where Robert would devote himself completely to composing. But, given Clara's need to perform and Robert's personality and creative talents, the scheme was totally impractical and was never realized.

Two years after the Hamburg trip, another extensive European journey was undertaken. Robert agreed rather reluctantly to leave his work and, this time, two babies to join Clara on a big Russian tour. There were several reasons for this decision: (1) Robert had found that he really could not work while Clara was away. (2) The money was alluring. (3) It was a trip Clara had been longing to make for several years. This trip, originally planned for the first year of their marriage, had been postponed, partly because of political developments, but primarily because Liszt was to be in Russia that year and Clara did not "want to be in rivalry with him."[52]

After making arrangements for the two children to stay with Robert's brother, the couple set out on a tour that was to last four months. Robert was ill almost from the beginning of the trip, but probably most destructive to Robert's peace of mind were the honors and applause bestowed on Clara, the performing artist. Although some of his works were performed and he gained increasing notice as a composer, it was she who was named an honorary member of the St. Petersburg Philharmonic Society, she who played privately for the czar and czarina, and she who earned the money for the family treasury. A Russian writer present at a private soirée noted:

Clara Schumann performed the Piano Quartet by her husband, his *Kreisleriana*, and several other things. She made a powerful impression on those listening, although we had already begun to hear women pianists at that time. . . . Schumann was, as usual, silent and uncommunicative during the entire evening. . . . Clara Schumann was a bit more talkative; she answered all the questions for her husband. In her piano playing she showed herself to be a great artist with masculine energy and feminine instincts in conception and execution, although she was just twenty-five or twenty-six years old. Yet, [he added,] one could hardly call her a graceful or sympathetic woman.[53]

Clara Schumann had eight children[54] and one miscarriage;[55] hence she was pregnant some part of each of the fourteen years she and her husband had together. During the last two years of their marriage Robert was confined to a mental institution in Endenich, Bonn, after a suicide attempt in February 1854. At the doctor's request, Clara did not see him again until two days before he died in July 1856.

Although concert tours were curtailed to some extent after her marriage and the births of her children, Clara did appear in public. Between 1840 and 1854, she gave 139 concerts that were noted in the program collection,[56] but there were also many other occasions on which she played. Little mention is made in the diaries and letters of cutting down because of child care or confinements; there are, in fact, expressions of resentment at the possibility.

During the fourteen years of their marriage, the Schumanns lived in Leipzig four years, in Dresden six years, and in Düsseldorf four years. In each of these cities, Clara set up homes with the needs of children, composer husband, and performer-wife in mind. In each she practiced, performed, composed, and taught, despite the demands of her children, the illnesses of her husband, and the discomforts of childbearing. She played even in advanced stages of pregnancy, although this was not customary. For most women of her class pregnancy was not discussed; neither did a woman appear publicly while noticeably pregnant. Litzmann does not even allude to pregnancies as such; those months were referred to as times of "physical sufferings" or "health problems."[57] Clara did, of course, have household help: two and sometimes three servants (three servants were not uncommon for a large middle-class family at that time), but pressures on the artist-mother were immense.

When Robert was first admitted to the hospital at Endenich, Clara was carrying her youngest child. The baby was not born until June 1854, three and a half months after Robert was hospitalized. Yet Clara turned down all offers of financial help from friends, partly because she felt they might reflect on Robert's ability to provide for his family, partly because she knew activity was the best solace for her, and partly because she had a need to play again. She resumed teaching almost immediately after her husband left, but she gave no public performances until after the baby was born. In October 1854 she embarked on a concert tour, leaving her children in Düsseldorf in the care of friends and servants.

Hadow makes the comment that Clara Schumann reared and educated seven children (one child having died in infancy) with the "sympathetic encouragement and the occasional help of devoted friends."[58] This is surely a gross understatement. Clara made as intelligent a dispersal and disposal of her seven children as anyone could under the circumstances, but her mothering contact with them was severely limited. Her letters show constant concern; no matter where she was, the children knew she was thinking of them.

Clara felt especially close to her eldest daughter, Marie. In July 1868 she wrote to her: "I long so dreadfully for you all and for the little house [in Baden-Baden], that if I could, I would turn round at once and joyfully run home. My dear, beloved Marie, if you only knew how dear you are to me, and how my whole soul is united with yours."[59] It soon becomes clear, however, that the individual lives of three of the daughters, Marie, Elise, and Eugenie, were consumed in the effort to maintain their mother's career. Aside from the help of young Brahms in 1854–56, Clara was delegating household and musical tasks as early as was practicable to Marie and Elise. Elise married an American at thirty-four years of age; Julie married at twenty-four (but died of tuberculosis at twenty-seven). Eugenie left home when she was over forty to begin a career as a music teacher in England. Marie remained with her mother to the end of her life.

Homes of devoted friends, boarding schools, pensions, and other living arrangements were used, including Grandmother Bargiel and even Grandfather Wieck, once or twice. Whenever possible, there were reunions; at these times the atmosphere sounds warm and cheerful. An especially pleasant interlude was the period 1863–73, when the Schumann family owned a small house in Baden-Baden. Here they would all gather for summer vacations. But while the children all attended to each other, they also all attended to Clara. She was, in Eugenie's words, "the greatest thing we possessed in the world."[60] Everyone in the family contributed when they were together. One daughter would go ahead to prepare a new accommodation or open the summer house. Another would assist Clara on tour—arrange for pianos, care for her wardrobe, fill in for her at piano lessons.

The sons of Robert and Clara Schumann fared poorly, however. The first son, Emil, died in infancy. Ludwig was mentally ill, probably schizophrenic, and needed many placements. He was finally confined to an asylum in 1870 and died there twenty-nine years later. Felix, the youngest and most gifted, died at twenty-five, of tuberculosis like his sister Julie. Ferdinand died in 1891 of medical complications associated with chronic back pain and subsequent morphine addiction. He left six children for whom his mother assumed financial responsibility.

The concept of motherhood in upper-middle-class German families of the nineteenth century differed from what today is considered to be ideal; but even in her day Clara was not the devoted mother she is often pictured to be. Of paramount importance were her art, the music of Robert Schumann, and her career, which, of course, provided the family income. There is no doubt that she suffered profoundly from the tragedies which felled members of her family: first her husband, then four adult children, one after the other. The heartfelt letters to Brahms and other close friends testify to the depths of her feelings. But her way of coping with pain and sorrow was to turn to work. Her friends were often concerned about the constant traveling that took her away from her children and drained her energy. She and Brahms had a falling-out over a letter (2 February 1868) in which he chastised her for her "unsettled way of living."[61] Many months later she answered with a statement that revealed the soul of an artist:

Your view of my concert tours seems rather peculiar to me. You regard them merely as a means of earning money. I do not! I feel I have a mission to reproduce beautiful works, Robert's above all, as long as I have the strength to do so, and even if I were not absolutely compelled to do so I should go on touring, though not in such a strenuous way as I often have to now. The practice of my art is definitely an important part of my being; it is the very air I breathe. . . . I would rather starve than perform with only half my strength.[62]

Her tours often kept her away from her children, missing confirmations, birthdays, even Christmas. What is more, her children suffered illness, and even death without her. When Julie died, Clara was in Heidelberg on a concert tour. She received the telegram informing her of the death on the day she was to give a concert, but she decided to go ahead with the performance because it would have caused great inconvenience to change it! She did not inform Amalie Joachim, with whom she was touring, or anyone else connected with the concert because, as she wrote a friend later (and marveling at her own strength), "it would have upset them too much."[63]

Her children understood that she was earning their bread by these concert tours. Eugenie wrote, "The thought that Mama had to earn every penny I needed with the work of her hands often troubled me when I was a mere child, and I hated to have to ask for new clothes."[64] Yet Eugenie also wrote that many times she wished her home could be like others; and in her *Memoirs* she recorded: "We knew that in our mother woman and artist were indissolubly one, so that we could not say this belongs to one part of her and that to another. We would sometimes wonder whether our mother would miss us or music most if one of the two were taken from her, and we could never decide."[65]

The composing Clara Schumann began as a child continued throughout her life.[66] A list of her published works, Opus 1 through Opus 23, but without Opus 18 and Opus 19, is given in Hadow, Litzmann, and other sources.[67] The works without opus numbers, some still unpublished, include songs and piano pieces written in her child-prodigy years as well as later works written as gifts for her husband and friends.[68] Following the custom of the time, almost every program given by the young Clara Wieck included an improvisation or an original work. As a young child she studied Czerny's *Anleitung zur Kunst des Phantasierens*, and, as Litzmann put it, grasped this so quickly that she was able to improvise with ease on a given theme and did so every day.

Theoretical understanding combined with technical growth, a concept novel for piano study at that time, was stressed by Wieck. Before Clara could read notes, she was taught to play by ear, to play cadences in all keys, and to transpose simple pieces. Her harmony and counterpoint lessons with Christian Weinlig (1780–1842), cantor of the St. Thomas Church, began in the spring of 1830; and by February 1831 her Quatre Polonaises pour le Pianoforte (op. 1) was published. Her Premier Concert, a large bravura work for piano and orchestra, came out in January 1837. This and several of her other virtuoso compositions appeared on many of her Viennese programs in 1837–38.

After her marriage in 1840, she rarely programmed her own works or improvised, since concert practices had already changed and she preferred to play her husband's music. Most of her creative efforts by this time were confined to special occasions, such as Robert's birthday, and as a result she had little opportunity to grow or develop as a composer. Robert was aware of this problem, and in 1843 he wrote in their joint diary:

Clara has written a series of small pieces, which show a musical and tender ingenuity such as she has never attained before. But to have children, and a husband who is always living in the realms of imagination, do not go together with composing. She cannot work at it regularly, and I am often disturbed to think how many profound ideas are lost because she cannot work them out.[69]

Although Robert, the musical public, and the reviewers took her work seriously and were encouraging, Clara had mixed feelings about her compositions. It is difficult to disentangle the contradictory expressions and to determine why she was so confused about her creative efforts. The only consistent words of self-derogation and mortification in her diary concern her attempts at composition. Yet she also writes of the pleasure she received from the creative act. Her confidence about her abilities as a pianist rarely wavered (though she did admit to increasing nervousness and occasional lack of self-confidence as she got older), but she seemed to be uncertain about her compositions from the first.

In 1839 she confided to her diary: "I once believed that I possessed creative talent, but I have given up this idea; a woman must not desire to compose—there has never yet been one able to do it. Should I expect to be the one? To believe that would be arrogant, something which my Father once, in former days, induced me to do."[70] But shortly before this, she had written, "It is really a sin that I have not composed anything for so long. Father is beside himself, I too am often unhappy about it and generally more dissatisfied with myself than I can say."[71] (This was a month or two after she had completed Trois Romances pour le Piano [op. 11], which was published by Mechetti in autumn 1840 in Vienna.)

To continue with this tale of ambivalence, we must note that she had needed Robert's encouragement to complete the pieces, but she resented any attempt on his part to revise them. The correspondence on the Romances began with her writing on April 18: "Yesterday evening I was very happy. I had a beautiful idea for a little romance, but today I am already dissatisfied with it." On April 23 she wrote: "I have written one quite tiny piece. . . . I have a peculiar fear of showing you any of my compositions. I am always ashamed." However, when Robert returned it with alterations, she answered: "I have received the Idylle, and thank you for it, my dearest; but I am sure you will forgive me if I tell you that there are some things in it which I don't like. You have completely altered the closing, which I liked best and had the greatest effect on everyone to whom I played it. . . . You are not angry with me, are you?"[72]

She had mixed feelings, too, about her Trio (op. 17), which is generally considered her best work: "There is no greater joy than composing something oneself and then listening to it. There are some pretty passages in the Trio, and I believe it is also fairly successful as far as form goes." But, she added immediately, "Naturally, it is still only woman's work, which always lacks force and occasionally invention."[73] A year later she wrote: "I received the printed copies of my trio today, but after Robert's D Minor [Trio] I did not care for it. It sounded effeminate and sentimental."[74]

In the spring of 1853, she had a last spurt of creative activity, inspired by a desire to compose for Robert's forty-third birthday, but the urge carried her far beyond a mere birthday offering. Within a few weeks she composed Variationen über ein Thema von Robert Schumann (op. 20), Drei Romanzen für Pianoforte (op. 21), Drei Romanzen für Pianoforte und Violin (op. 22), and Sechs Lieder aus Jucunde, with texts by Rollett (op. 23). On 22 June 1853 she wrote: "Today I composed the sixth song by Rollett, and with it put together a volume of songs which give me pleasure, and provided many happy hours. . . . There is nothing which surpasses creative activity even if one does it only for those hours of self-forgetfulness when one breathes totally in a world of sound."[75] Nevertheless, this happy composer inscribed the Variations, "To my beloved husband, on 8 June 1853, a weak attempt from his old Clara."[76]

Clara had been given the best possible musical education as a child. She improvised and composed because she knew it was expected of her; as she says, her father led her to it. She had talent and the training, background, and skills many composers could envy. Although her time for composing was limited, she wrote a number of creditable works that were performed, published, and favorably reviewed during her lifetime. Yet the ambivalence seen in the diaries and letters continued to the end of her composing career.

I believe Clara Schumann felt that her primary field of competence was as an interpreter. With her father's encouragement and her husband's support, she defied many of the conventions about what women musicians should and should not do. Her gifts as a composer did not equal her husband's, however, and she realized it, taking refuge, perhaps, in the conventions that proclaimed a woman should not compose. Given more time and fewer pressures, both personal and societal, she probably would have achieved more as a composer and certainly would have felt happier about her work.

During the early years of the nineteenth century, all the details of concert tours were the responsibility of the artist. Professional concert management was not a reality in Germany until the 1880s. When Clara was a child, her father made all the arrangements. He rented the halls and instruments, hired supporting musicians, obtained letters of introduction to wealthy and influential patrons, distributed complimentary tickets to the right persons, and fought off rivals and other hostile people.

In 1839, furious at Clara's attachment to Robert, Wieck sent her to Paris with only a Frenchwoman, Mlle Claudine Dufourd, a stranger, as a chaperone.[77] He hoped she would be discouraged, give up, return home, and accept his continuing control. To his astonishment and, indeed, to her own, she persevered, dismissed the chaperone, and arranged several successful concerts. The intrepid nineteen-year-old girl from Saxony faced the French capitol, managed to support herself in the strange city, presented herself to the French public, found students, composed music, and had her works published. Today we would find this remarkable, but in 1839 it was an amazing act of courage. Clara had inherited her father's steel will and acumen, and from that time on she took charge of her own affairs with Robert's help and support.

With her husband ill and seven dependent children at home, she set out again. Although in 1854 concert managers or agents did not exist, Clara Schumann had friends and contacts throughout Europe who helped her with the scheduling and logistics of concerts; but she, of course, was ultimately responsible for the success of the concert and performance. In the hundreds of letters to friends we can read of all the preparations that had to be made for each performance in every city. She rented the pianos and had them moved and tuned, rented the halls and provided for lights and heat, had tickets printed and distributed, arranged for advertising in newspapers and on posters—and then appeared, beautifully gowned in concert attire, to play, as though this was her sole care.

At the beginning of Clara's career, in 1830, concert programs were a hodgepodge of events, musical and nonmusical. Works by Beethoven or Mozart were rarely played; the reigning favorites were Thalberg, Kalkbrenner, Herz, and Liszt. Wieck admired Chopin and Schumann even when they were young unknowns, but he avoided works which would not win public approval. He allowed Clara to play Schumann privately in Paris and Vienna, but for public occasions he programmed Pixis, Herz, Kalkbrenner, and sometimes Beethoven and Scarlatti.

After her marriage Clara's repertoire changed. With Robert she studied Bach's *Well Tempered Clavier*, Beethoven orchestral scores, and Haydn and Mozart chamber music. Robert believed her playing improved because of these studies, and her concert programs and compositions demonstrate that her musical understanding deepened as a result of them. As she grew older and more self-confident, she chose for her programs what she loved and respected. By 1840 the flashy display pieces were dropped; and her programs included works by Mozart, Beethoven, Chopin, Mendelssohn, Schumann, and—after 1854—Brahms and other more conservative composers of his group.[78]

Clara Schumann was one of the first soloists to plan concert programs without supporting artists. She decided to dispense with an orchestra on her Russian trip in 1843 simply because it was so difficult to arrange. After that experience, she wrote to her father, "I gave all the concerts by myself, without any supporting artists, something I will do from now on; it is the best way."[79]

She also broke with tradition by playing from memory, as her father had taught her; although as she grew older and her memory was not so dependable, she deplored this practice. Her programs, which were always innovative, became shorter to allow for greater concentration on each work. Although Clara Schumann gave solo recitals and played with all the great orchestras of England and the Continent, she also took great joy in playing with chamber groups and in sonata and lieder recitals. Two artists with whom she was closely associated were Joseph Joachim (1831–1907), the violinist, and Julius Stockhausen (1826–1906), the singer.

She first met Joseph Joachim when he came to Leipzig as a boy of twelve to study with Ferdinand David, Mendelssohn's friend and concertmaster of the Gewandhaus orchestra. The friendship between Joachim and the Schumanns deepened in 1853 when Robert Schumann invited Joachim to play at the Niederrheinische Musikfest in 1853. When Robert fell ill, Joachim and Brahms were the two friends on whom Clara most depended. Though she was never on *du* terms with Joachim as she was with Brahms, she felt very close to him.[80] In July 1854, soon after her husband went to the hospital, she wrote in her diary:

Joachim gives me the most pleasant hours here [in Berlin], thanks both to his art and to his friendly words. . . . He is as dear a friend to me as Brahms, and I have the utmost faith in him too. He is so sensitive that he understands my slightest feelings immediately. These two [Brahms and Joachim] seem to have been created to be Robert's friends—but he does not know them yet as I do. Only in tragedy does one learn who his friends really are.[81]

The joint concerts by Clara Schumann and Joachim usually included solos for each artist and sonatas for violin and piano.[82] The two were particularly loved for their playing of Beethoven sonatas. Clara toured extensively with Joachim in England and on the continent from 1854 until the 1880s, when Joachim's (family) problems intervened. Clara also participated in many song recitals with Joachim's wife Amalie, a mezzo-soprano.

When Clara Schumann first heard Julius Stockhausen, her *"herrlicher Sänger,"*[83] sing Robert Schumann's songs, he was twenty-eight years old. Stockhausen, a conductor as well as a singer, was best known for his superb interpretations of Schubert and Schumann lieder. He participated in concerts with Clara Schumann and Joseph Joachim that the artists treasured, although the repertoire was not always popular with the audience. In an era of salon music and brilliant virtuosi, their quiet, serious recitals must have been a rare experience.

Contemporaries of Clara Schumann frequently referred to her as a "classical" pianist. They described her playing as healthy or sober and the music she programmed as serious. Litzmann reports that a music dealer in Budapest, who was helping her with arrangements for a concert there in February 1855, was greatly alarmed about her "grave" program, but that he quieted down when he saw the enthusiasm engendered by her playing of such works as the Schumann Piano Quintet and the Beethoven Sonata in D Minor.[84] Hanslick, always a great supporter, noted the "noble selectivity" of her programming with special approval.[85] Franklin Taylor, an admirer and one of her English students, wrote that "her playing was characterized by an entire absence of personal display and a keen perception of the composer's meaning, and an unfailing power of setting it forth in perfectly intelligible form."[86] Sir George Macfarren, the eminent English composer, hailed her performance of Schumann's Sonata in F-sharp Minor, opus 11, writing:

Let me congratulate you on the pleasure you must have had in feeling your ability to render complete justice to the beautiful work you played last night, and also in perceiving that the delighted multitude appreciated the music and its performance. The world is fortunate in having an unknown masterpiece introduced to them in so clear a light as to make its purpose obvious and to set an example to those who may hereafter attempt to reproduce what they have heard.[87]

Plate 15
Clara Wieck Schumann, Frankfurt-am-Main, 1879

Source: Music Division, New York Public Library at Lincoln Center,
Astor, Lenox, and Tilden Foundations

At the age of fifty-nine Clara Schumann embarked on a new career: she accepted the position of principal piano teacher at the Hoch Conservatory founded in Frankfurt in 1878. Frau Kammervirtuosin Schumann, as she was named in the first *Jahresbericht* of the conservatory, had, of course, taught for many years, including a short stint at the Leipzig Conservatory under Mendelssohn's direction in 1843, but she had never before committed herself to a fulltime teaching position. In Frankfurt, where she was the star, her contract was unusually liberal and allowed her much free time for touring. She taught at the Hoch Conservatory until the end of the school year in 1892, when she was almost seventy-three.

The roster of students who flocked to study with her included men and women from South and North America, England, Scotland, and every country in Europe. Her daughters Marie and Eugenie were pressed into service as her assistants, and both retired when she did. Her students felt they were in a special state of grace when they were admitted to her class. One English pupil, Clement Harris, noted in his diary: "At home I was overwhelmed with congratulations. . . . Telegraphed London, 'It is done, I finally made it. Hurrah. Long live seven hours of daily practice.'" A few days later he wrote: "I am proud to be a Schumann-scholar now. I never would have dreamed how difficult it would be to get accepted to her class. Everyone in my generation is trying for it. I believe that fortune really favored me, but I certainly also worked hard enough to earn it."[88] Harris was one of many English students who congregated in Frankfurt to work with her.[89]

Clara took her teaching duties seriously and longed to mother her students. If it were possible she would, no doubt, have taught them as her father had taught her. But this would have entailed complete planning (and control)—physical, mental, and musical—of their lives; and with her own career, her physical ailments, and her ever-increasing family responsibilities, this kind of devotion was not possible. She followed the careers of her students with great interest. She was proud of their good reviews and indignant at the critical ones. She kept in touch with her American and English students for years after they left her. Among the outstanding students mentioned in her diary are Leonard Borwick, Nathalie Janotha, Ilona Eibenschütz, and Adeline de Lara.

In one of the letters Friedrich Wieck sent from Dresden to his wife, he described an incident in the life of eleven-year-old Clara. She had responded to the applause that followed her playing by qui-

Plate 16
Program for last public concert, 12 March 1891

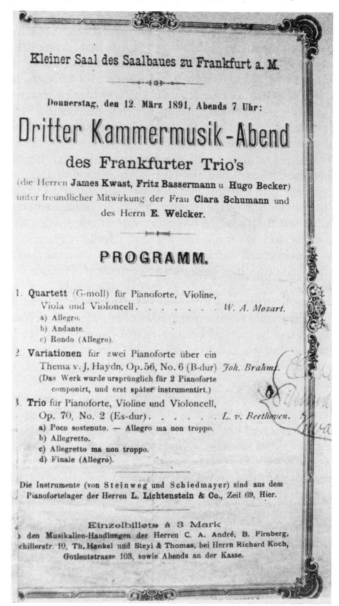

Source: Clara Schumann's personal program collection,
courtesy of Robert-Schumann-Haus, Zwickau, GDR

etly standing up and saying very seriously, "You are clapping and I know very well that I played badly," and she had wept a few tears.[90] Clara Schumann had a sense of proportion and humility about her own playing. She was a born performer: audiences always brought out the best in her. In her diary we often read that she played better than she had expected. Despite her great triumphs, she, like so many performers, had a need for the demonstrations of affection and approval her playing brought her. "Thank your aunt for the kind words about my artistry," she wrote Ernst Rudorff in 1866. "I am one of those persons who, perpetually dissatisfied with oneself, is never able to achieve complete self-confidence, and so a kind word to me as an artist, as well as to me as a person, is often necessary."[91]

In her late forties, Clara Schumann began to suffer great pain from neuralgia and rheumatism, and in her last years she was afflicted with growing deafness. But in spite of her debilities, she played as long as she could physically manage it. Her last public appearance was in March 1891 in Frankfurt, where she played Brahms's Variations on a Theme of Haydn for Two Pianos with a colleague from the conservatory. (See plate 16.) After her retirement from the Hoch Conservatory, she continued to teach in her own home until shortly before her death in 1896.

Clara Schumann was unique among the women of her time. She thought of herself as an artist first and as a woman and mother second. In 1860 she wrote Joachim that she wanted to sign the militant declaration against the New Germans (i.e., Liszt and Wagner, for whom she had a great antipathy), which was signed by Brahms, Joachim, Julius Otto Grimm, and Bernhard Scholz, and was published in a Berlin newspaper. Although the declaration appeared prematurely without her name among the signatories, it is clear that she was ready and willing to take a stand with her fellow artists.[92]

Always accepted by her male colleagues as one of them, Clara Schumann nevertheless remained sensitive to prevailing attitudes toward women. In 1870, for example, she wrote to ask Joachim's advice on a delicate issue. She had been invited to participate in the Beethoven centennial celebrations in Vienna but did not want to go because Liszt and Wagner would be conducting. She was reluctant to make a bold public statement to that effect and wrote to Joachim, "I am turning to you with a request for advice; what shall I do? . . . I, as a woman, cannot act as you do. It would seem arrogant if I, as contrasted with men, were to express my opinion openly. I must invent a lie! But what shall I say?" Joachim's reply sums up what he and many others felt about her: "I find that the fact that you are a woman has nothing to do with it, or it may be the very reason for you to stay away. In any case, you are, as far as art is concerned, 'man enough.'"[93]

Clara Schumann was a woman and an artist and did not see the two as antithetical. For this she had her father to thank—he had trained an artist and that is how she perceived herself. "People have no idea that if anything significant is to be achieved in art, one's entire education, one's entire course of life must differ from that of people in ordinary situations," she wrote to La Mara, the Liszt biographer.[94]

Clara Wieck Schumann was no ordinary person. She had the strength to persevere despite her own illness and pain, the loss of her husband, and the illnesses and death of four of her children. She had the courage to maintain a position that was irregular in the world in which she lived. She ordered her life in a way that enabled her to reach the summits of musical artistry.

NOTES

The author wishes to acknowledge the assistance of the Penrose Fund of the American Philosophical Society, the German Academic Exchange Service, and the National Endowment for the Humanities in the research and preparation of this essay.

1. A translation of the poem, which appeared on 9 January 1838 in the *Wiener Zeitschrift für Kunst, Literatur, Theater, und Mode*, can be found in Berthold Litzmann, *Clara Schumann: An Artist's Life Based on Material Found in Diaries and Letters*, 2 vols., trans. Grace E. Hadow (London: Macmillan, 1913), 1:136.

2. According to the program, the piano works performed were the Sonata opus 57 by Beethoven; the B Major Notturno by Chopin; the *Hexentanz*, from Quatre pièces caractéristiques pour le Piano-forte (op. 5), by Clara Wieck; two works by Adolph Henselt; and the Concert-Variationen über die Cavatina aus Bellini's "Pirata" (op. 8) by Clara Wieck.

3. Benedikt Randhartinger (1802–93), who sang in a concert of Clara's in Vienna on 21 December 1837, had received this version of *Erlkönig* from the composer himself.

4. This holograph, now in the Dannie and Hettie Heinemann Collection in the Pierpont Morgan Library, is inscribed: "Franz Schubert's Handscrift, Der gefeierten Künstlerin Clara Wieck überreicht von Schubert's Freunde [sic] B. Randhartinger. Wien, den 15 Jänner 1838." See Rigbie Turner's preface and the facsimile edition of Schubert's *Erlkönig* (New York: Pierpont Morgan Library, 1978).

5. In Friedrich Wieck, *Briefe aus den Jahren 1830–1838*, ed. Käthe

Walch-Schumann (Köln: Arno Volk-Verlag, 1968), p. 87. This translation and all others in this chapter are my own.

6. The journal edited by Robert Schumann.

7. Diary, 8 March 1838, 3:201, Zwickau, GDR, Robert-Schumann-Haus, Signatur 4877, 1–4. The diaries, bound in four volumes, are numbered as follows: 1:1–247 (1827–32), 2:1–181 (1833–35), 3:1–207 (1836–38), 4:1–217 (1838–40). The original diary and the transcription by Martin Schoppe, director of Robert-Schumann-Haus, were used. I would like to acknowledge the cordial assistance and gracious hospitality of Dr. Schoppe and Dr. Gerd Nauhaus, musicological associate, on my visits to the archives of Robert-Schumann-Haus.

8. Marie Leopoldine Blahetka, 1811–87; Anna Caroline Belleville-Oury, 1808–80; Marie (also known as Camilla) Moke Pleyel, 1811–75.

9. Her personal *Program-Sammlung* (program collection) in Robert-Schumann-Haus, Signatur 10463, 1–5, includes 1,299 printed programs, from 1828 to 1891, in which she was the primary soloist. There were, of course, countless other occasions on which she performed.

10. See Alfred Dörffel, "Statistik der Concerte im Saale des Gewandhauses zu Leipzig," in *Geschichte der Gewandhausconcerte zu Leipzig vom 25. November 1781 bis 25. November 1881* (Leipzig, 1884).

11. See Nancy B. Reich, *Clara Schumann: The Artist and the Woman* (Ithaca, N.Y.: Cornell University Press, 1985).

12. Berthold Litzmann, ed., *Clara Schumann: Ein Künstlerleben nach Tagebüchern und Briefen*, 3 vols. (Leipzig: Breitkopf & Härtel, 1902–8). The eighth edition of volume 1 (1925), the seventh edition of volume 2 (1925), and the sixth edition of volume 3 (1923) attest to the great popularity of this work. The later editions contain only minor changes. References to Litzmann in this essay are to the first edition. The Hadow translation (see n. 1 above) is widely available. For further discussion of Litzmann, see Nancy B. Reich with Anna Burton, "Clara Schumann: Old Sources, New Readings," *Musical Quarterly* 70 (Summer 1984): 332–54.

13. Berthold Litzmann, ed., *Clara Schumann, Johannes Brahms, Briefe aus den Jahren 1853–1896*, 2 vols. (Leipzig: Breitkopf & Härtel, 1927). Translated by Grace Hadow, under the title *Letters of Clara Schumann and Johannes Brahms 1853–1896*, 2 vols. (London: Edward Arnold, 1927).

14. Franz Liszt, as quoted in Litzmann, *Clara Schumann*, 2:351. See also Franz Liszt, *Gesammelte Schriften*, ed. L. Ramann (Leipzig: Breitkopf & Härtel, 1882), 4:187–206, for the complete essay on Clara Schumann written in 1855. Liszt's designation, one of many referring to her as a priestess, was probably based on her stern, serious manner, her total dedication to her art, and her lack of ostentation, both in her personal appearance and in her demeanor at the keyboard.

15. See, for example, Marguerite and Jean Alley, *A Passionate Friendship: Clara Schumann and Johannes Brahms*, trans. Mervyn Savill (London: Staples Press, 1956), an English translation of the French translation of the

original German letters! The study *Clara Schumann* by Joan Chissell (London: Hamish Hamilton, 1983) is the first biography to have focused on the woman and her accomplishments.

16. Friedrich Wieck, "Wöchentliche Bemerkungen über seinen Schüler Emil von Metzradt," in Victor Joss, *Der Musikpädagoge Friedrich Wieck und seine Familie* (Dresden: Oscar Damm, 1902), pp. 106–14. Excerpts translated into English may be found in Florence May, *The Girlhood of Clara Schumann* (London: Arnold, 1912), pp. 4–6.

17. It has been mistakenly assumed by many biographers that Wieck manufactured pianos. This was not the case.

18. Family records, Robert-Schumann-Haus, Signatur 2174 A3 u. A3b.

19. *Allgemeine musikalische Zeitung* 19 (26 February 1817), col. 158. See also ibid. (6 April and 21 May 1817) for other reviews.

20. Adolph Bargiel (1783–1841) and Marianne Bargiel were the parents of Woldemar Bargiel (1828–97), the composer, conductor, and piano teacher. I would like to thank Frau Herma Stamm-Bargiel for information on the Bargiel family.

21. Rudolf Huebner, *A History of Germanic Private Law*, trans. Francis S. Philbrick (Boston: Little, Brown, 1918), pp. 657, 664.

22. Litzmann, *Clara Schumann*, 1:4.

23. Diary, title page. Litzmann mistakenly writes May 7.

24. His educational plan is reminiscent of the Suzuki approach to the violin with its emphasis on ear-training. See Elizabeth Mills and Therese Cecile Murphy, eds., *The Suzuki Concept* (Berkeley, Calif.: Diablo Press, 1973).

25. Wieck composed some polonaises, *écossaises*, and other short works, published between 1815 and 1824, designed mainly for pedagogical purposes.

26. Friedrich Wieck, *Clavier und Gesang: Didaktisches und Polemisches* (Leipzig: F. Whistling, 1853), p. v. Translated by Mary P. Nichols, under the title *Piano and Song* (Boston: Lockwood, Brooks, 1875; reprint, New York: Da Capo, 1981); and by H. Krueger, under the title *Piano and Singing* (Aberdeen: H. Krueger, 1875).

27. Eugenie Schumann, *Robert Schumann: Ein Lebensbild meines Vaters* (Leipzig: Koehler & Amelang, 1931), p. 248.

28. Wieck, *Clavier und Gesang*, p. iv.

29. Diary, 1:7–8.

30. See Marie Wieck, *Aus dem Kreise Wieck-Schumann*, 2d ed. (Dresden: von Zahn & Jaensch, 1914).

31. Litzmann, *Clara Schumann*, 3:22.

32. Ibid., 1:48.

33. Ibid., 214.

34. See Dörffel, "Statistik der Concerte im Saale des Gewandhauses," p. 90.

35. Robert Schumann, *Tagebücher*, 3 vols. to date, ed. Georg Eismann (Leipzig: Deutscher Verlag für Musik, 1971–), 1:334 ff.

36. Ibid., 382–84.

37. Ibid., 421.

38. Eugenie Schumann, *Robert Schumann*, p. 227.

39. Litzmann, *Clara Schumann*, 1:67–68. The author of this description, which originally appeared in Johann Peter Lyser's *Caecilia* (Hamburg) 1 (1833): 253–58, is not known. Wieck suspected it might have been Heinrich Heine, who was living in Paris in 1832.

40. See Leon B. Plantinga, *Schumann as Critic* (New Haven: Yale University Press, 1967), chap. 1, for a discussion of the beginnings of the journal.

41. Schumann, *Tagebücher*, 1:364.

42. Litzmann, *Clara Schumann*, 2:15.

43. Ibid., 28: "I am like a young wife just delivered of a child—so light, so happy, and yet so ill and weak." Also see Robert Schumann, *Jugendbriefe*, ed. Clara Schumann (Leipzig: Breitkopf & Härtel, 1886), pp. 151, 155.

44. Litzmann, *Clara Schumann*, 1:299.

45. Ibid., 1:194–95.

46. Wolfgang Boetticher, *Robert Schumann in seinen Schriften und Briefen* (Berlin: Hahnefeld Verlag, 1942), p. 366. Boetticher's work must be used with extreme care because of his Nazi bias. There is every reason to believe, however, that these particular quotations are given accurately.

47. Ibid., p. 368. The emphasis is mine.

48. Litzmann, *Clara Schumann*, 2:43.

49. Ibid., 3:70.

50. Ibid., 2:15.

51. Ibid., 42–43.

52. Ibid., 37.

53. Quoted in Georg Eismann, *Robert Schumann: Ein Quellenwerk über sein Leben und Schaffen*, 2 vols. (Leipzig: Breitkopf & Härtel, 1956), 1:144.

54. Marie, 1841–1929; Elise, 1843–1928; Julie, 1845–72; Emil, 1846–47; Ludwig, 1848–99; Ferdinand, 1849–91; Eugenie, 1851–1938; Felix, 1854–79.

55. Litzmann, *Clara Schumann*, 2:271, notes one miscarriage in September 1852; there may have been more.

56. See n. 9 above.

57. See, for example, Litzmann, *Clara Schumann*, 2:39.

58. Hadow, *Letters of C. Schumann and J. Brahms*, intro., 1:x.

59. Litzmann, *C. Schumann*, 3:220.

60. Eugenie Schumann, *Memoirs of Eugenie Schumann*, trans. Marie Busch (London: William Heinemann, 1927), p. 9. The American imprint of this translation of Eugenie Schumann, *Erinnerungen* (Stuttgart: J. Engelhorn, 1925) is titled *The Schumanns and Johannes Brahms: The Memoirs of Eugenie Schumann* (New York: Dial Press, 1927).

61. Litzmann, *C. Schumann–J. Brahms Briefe*, 1:576.

62. Ibid., 599.

63. Litzmann, *Clara Schumann*, 3:278n. Hadow does not include this information in her translation.

64. E. Schumann, *Memoirs*, p. 47.

65. Ibid., p. 152.

66. See Reich, *Clara Schumann*, pp. 297–306, for a catalog of the complete works.

67. Among brief studies of her published compositions are: Richard Hohenemser, "Clara Wieck-Schumann als Komponistin," in *Die Musik* 20 (1905–6): 113–26, 166–73; Paula and Walter Rehberg, "Clara Wieck-Schumann als Komponistin," in *Robert Schumann*, 2d ed. (Zurich: Artemis Verlag, 1969), pp. 662–71. See also J. A. Fuller-Maitland, "Joseph Joachim and Clara Schumann," in *Masters of German Music* (London: Osgood, McIlvaine, 1894), pp. 228–36. Chissell, *Clara Schumann*, gives short descriptions of most of the published works. Pamela Susskind, "Clara Schumann as Pianist and Composer: A Study of Her Life and Works" (Ph.D. diss., University of California–Berkeley, 1977), includes extensive discussion and analysis of some of the compositions.

68. Some seventeen works remain unpublished; see Reich, *Clara Schumann*, pp. 303–5.

69. Litzmann, *Clara Schumann*, 2:21.

70. Diary, 26 November 1839, 4:117.

71. Litzmann, *Clara Schumann*, 1:355–56.

72. Ibid., 352–53.

73. Ibid., 2:139–40.

74. Ibid., 140.

75. Ibid., 274.

76. Autograph, Robert-Schumann-Haus, Signatur 5989–A1, June 1853.

77. Diary, 8 January 1839, 4:42.

78. The works studied and the repertoire from 1824–91 are given in Litzmann, *Clara Schumann*, 3:615–24; Hadow, *Clara Schumann*, 2:442–52. See also Pamela Susskind Pettler, "Clara Schumann's Recitals, 1832–50," *Nineteenth Century Music* 4 (Summer 1980): 70–76; Reich, *Clara Schumann*, pp. 258–81.

79. Litzmann, *Clara Schumann*, 2:62. This resolve was not carried out. She continued to play with other musicians and supporting artists.

80. As evidence of the close ties, note the extensive correspondence between Clara Schumann and Joachim in Johannes Joachim and Andreas Moser, eds., *Briefe von und an Joseph Joachim*, 3 vols. (Berlin: Julius Bard, 1911–13). Translated and abridged by Nora Bickley, under the title *Letters from and to Joseph Joachim* (London: Macmillan, 1914).

81. Litzmann, *Clara Schumann*, 2:321.

82. The program of 20 November 1854, for example, included Mozart, A Major Sonata for Violin and Piano; Bach, Adagio and Fugue; Schumann, *Jagdlied* from *Waldszenen* and *Schlummerlied* from *Albumblätter*; Beethoven, *Les Adieux* Sonata; Beethoven, *Kreutzer* Sonata for Violin and Piano.

83. Clara Schumann to Julius Stockhausen, 13 April 1855, in which she

dubbed him *herrlicher Sänger* and asked him to sing for Robert Schumann in Endenich. Frankfurt-am-Main, Universitäts-Bibliothek, Musik abteilung.

84. Litzmann, *Clara Schumann*, 2:401.

85. Eduard Hanslick, *Music Criticisms 1846–99*, ed. Henry Pleasants (Baltimore: Peregrine Books, 1963), p. 51.

86. Franklin Taylor, as quoted in Sir George Grove, *Grove's Dictionary of Music and Musicians*, 3d ed., s.v. "Clara Schumann," 4:647.

87. Sir George MacFarren to Clara Schumann, London, 18 March 1884. West Berlin, Staatsbibliothek Preussischer Kulturbesitz, Musikabteilung.

88. Claus Victor Bock, "Pente Pigadia und die Tagebücher des Clement Harris," *Castrum Peregrini* 50 (1961): 15. I would like to thank Professor Peter Cahn of Frankfurt-am-Main for bringing this article to my attention.

89. Clara Schumann was especially beloved in England. Between 1856 and 1888 she made nineteen channel crossings and toured throughout the British Isles.

90. Wieck, *Briefe . . . 1830–1838*, p. 27.

91. Clara Schumann to Ernst Rudorff, Baden-Baden, 10 June 1866. Rudorff-Archiv: Privatarchiv v. Gottberg, D-3216 Salzhemmendorf-2.

92. Joachim, *Briefe von Joseph Joachim*, 2:85–86.

93. Ibid., 3:42–43.

94. Litzmann, *Clara Schumann*, 3:434.

11

Luise Adolpha Le Beau: Composer in Late Nineteenth-Century Germany

JUDITH E. OLSON

Luise Adolpha Le Beau (1850–1927) enjoyed a long and remarkable career as a pianist, music critic, and prolific composer. Her works number over sixty-six (thirty-five of them published) and include many for large musical resources. Le Beau lived in Karlsruhe, Munich, Wiesbaden, Berlin, and Baden-Baden; but her influence extended to Vienna, Salzburg, Leipzig, and other mid-European cities, as well as Calcutta and Australia. Her compositions were solicited for the Columbia World Exhibition of 1893, and one of them won first prize in an international cello competition.

Le Beau's wide-ranging career brought her into contact with many of the major musical figures of the late nineteenth century, including Johannes Brahms, Franz Liszt, Eduard Hanslick, and Hermann Levi. Early in her life she studied with Clara Schumann, Franz Lachner, and Josef Rheinberger; and Hans von Bülow showed a special interest in her, referring to her as "a laudable exception among women."[1] Le Beau's impact on the major music critics of her time, including Hanslick, August Bungert, Alfred Kalischer, and Wilhelm Tappert, was also impressive. Through Le Beau's example they saw for the first time that women were capable of the musical invention, conceptualization, and control of basic compositional techniques necessary to successfully write large vocal and instrumental works.

Le Beau's musical career and her associations with major German composers and critics are remarkably well documented through her autobiography,[2] two almost complete collections of her works,[3] and a collection of over three hundred reviews of her works.[4] Although she was active and recognized as a pianist and a critic,[5] Le Beau defined herself primarily as a composer. Her *Lebenserin-*

nerungen einer Komponistin, which is one of the few autobiographical documents of women composers active in the nineteenth century, covers a unique and broad geographical range.[6]

Various themes found throughout the autobiography include Le Beau's systematic development of her career, her parents' unusual contribution to it, and obstacles that made it necessary for Le Beau to reestablish her career many times in different cities in Germany. Also emphasized are the difficulties and roadblocks Le Beau encountered as a composer because of her gender. The major outlines of Le Beau's life and career as developed in her autobiography follow.

Luise Adolpha Le Beau was born 25 April 1850 in Rastatt in the Duchy of Baden. Her father, a general in the Baden army and an amateur singer and conductor, was transferred to nearby Karlsruhe shortly after her birth; it is there that Luise grew up. Her interest in music manifested itself at an early age. She reports that she could sing back a melody before she could speak, and she includes among her earliest memories her experiments at the piano. By the age of eight she had composed her first piece. Her parents responded to her interest by allowing her to study voice, piano, and composition with local musicians. At eighteen she made her debut with the Baden Court Orchestra playing Mendelssohn's Piano Concerto in G Minor. A tour of Basel, Heidelberg, and Augsburg followed, in which she played Mozart's Piano Concerto in D Major with cadenzas she composed herself.

Le Beau describes how the provincial musical society of Karlsruhe repeatedly expressed disapproval of her parents' allowing her to study music seriously.[7] In the early 1870s, in response to this disapproval, the family began to seek musical opportunities farther afield. In the summer of 1873, on the advice of Hermann Levi, the conductor of the Baden Court Orchestra, Le Beau went to study piano with Clara Schumann, who had settled in Baden-Baden. Hans von Bülow, who was also summering in Baden-Baden, was requested to evaluate the younger woman's skills in both piano and composition. Amazed by both, Bülow urged Le Beau to move to a larger city to study and provided her with letters of recommendation to Josef Rheinberger, who was well regarded as a composer and as a teacher of composition in Munich.

In 1874 Wilhelm Le Beau retired, and after Luise had made a concert tour of Holland, the entire family moved to Munich to facilitate her studies. On her arrival in Munich, Le Beau delivered her letter of recommendation to Rheinberger, who assigned her to one of his students to review her compositional studies. Shortly thereafter, on the strength of her Violin Sonata, opus 10, which he found "manly, and not sounding as if composed by a woman,"[8] Rheinberger made an exception to his rule of not teaching women and accepted Le Beau as a student of composition. Le Beau received private lessons, making her training much more intensive than it would have been at the Königliche Musikschule, where Rheinberger taught four students at a time (she was apparently not formally enrolled at the school), and she began to make great strides in her studies.

She also continued performing. On 30 December 1878 she played her first recital, consisting of lieder, a solo piano piece, and a piano trio, all of which she had composed, as well as a Rheinberger string quartet the composer had dedicated to her. Soon afterward, in response to suggestions that her skills in composition and piano merited a school of her own, Le Beau established a "Private Music Course in Piano and Theory for Daughters of Educated Station."[9] Her program was rigorous, and even the youngest of her students was required to practice at least two hours a day.

Le Beau's eleven years in Munich were probably her most rewarding as a composer. There she produced some of her best works, among them lieder, choral works, a viola suite, two cello works, a piano trio, a piano quartet, a piano fantasy with orchestra, and a cantata. Much of her published output appeared at this time. She played her Piano Fantasy, opus 25, with a number of orchestras, including the Münchener Orchesterverein and the Baden Court Orchestra in a concert for Kaiser Wilhelm I. Other musicians performed her works and sent her printed programs and reviews of their concerts. She played her own works on a number of tours throughout central Europe, often receiving rave notices from the critics.[10] Her cantata *Ruth*, opus 27, translated into English and Dutch, was performed in Holland, Switzerland, Austria, and many German cities.

In May 1882, her Four Pieces for Cello with Piano Accompaniment, opus 24, won first place in an international competition in Hamburg, at which Carl Reinecke served as one of the judges. Le Beau writes of the surprise the judges showed upon discovering that the prize work was written by a woman: "It appeared rather comical that 'Herr' had been printed everywhere on the enclosed certificates; it was now crossed out and replaced with 'Fräulein.' The judges themselves were certainly not a little amazed when the name of a lady appeared out of the sealed envelope!"[11]

On a tour to Vienna in 1884, Le Beau met Johannes Brahms and the music critic Eduard Hanslick. They both invited her to show

Plate 17
Luise Adolpha Le Beau, 1880

Source: Luise Adolpha Le Beau, *Lebenserinnerungen einer Komponistin*
(Baden-Baden: Emil Sommermayer, 1910), facing page 80
Reproduction from the collections of the Library of Congress

them her works and later congratulated her on them. Liszt, whom she met in Weimar in the fall of 1883, called her Piano Fantasy brilliant and idiomatic (*dankbar*).[12] In March 1884, she was named an honorary member of the Salzburg Mozarteum after performing two highly successful concerts there. Also in 1884, Le Beau's Piano Quartet, opus 28, was performed in the Leipzig Gewandhaus to overwhelming acclaim. Indeed, Julius Riedel, who was in charge of concerts there, told her he could not remember as great a success as hers in the Gewandhaus.

Le Beau's stay in Munich was not without problems, however. Although her first years of study with Rheinberger were positive, as she became more successful, she experienced conflict with him and his wife. Rheinberger nicknamed her "an emancipated lady"—for him a rather derogatory term. After a number of unpleasant incidents, Le Beau gradually withdrew from her association with the Rheinbergers, ending her period of formal compositional study.

Further, while the Munich musical society lionized its local composers, it regarded Le Beau as an outsider, and she experienced a lack of patronage as a result. She was also affected by the upheaval created by conflicts between advocates of "new music" who aligned themselves with Wagner, and the more conservative, established musicians. From the moment of his arrival in the Bavarian Court in Munich in 1864 at the summons of King Ludwig II, Wagner's influence had been felt throughout the entire musical establishment, including the Court Opera and the Königliche Musikschule. Rheinberger himself bore much of the criticism of the Wagnerites.

Le Beau's position in the controversy was ambiguous. She sturdily refused to take sides. While her refusal to criticize Wagner contributed to her problems with Rheinberger, she believed her association with him and the conservative compositional style in which she was schooled earned her the animosity of the Munich and Karlsruhe court orchestras. After a benefit concert she gave for the Mozart House in Salzburg, important musicians were discouraged from playing with Le Beau in her home as well as in public. Another benefit concert given by Le Beau received an extremely negative and cruel review from the *Süddeutsche Presse*, the main organ of the Wagner camp.[13] Although Le Beau continued to find support in such groups as the Oratorienverein, the family grew discouraged with the conflicts and resolved to leave Munich, preferably to return to Baden.

After first considering Baden-Baden for their new home, a course discouraged by the mayor of that town for fear of Le Beau's competition with local musicians, the family settled in Wiesbaden in October 1885. Le Beau's fame had preceded her and she found herself much in demand as a pianist and teacher. Her reputation also spread abroad, and her Piano Quartet was performed in Sydney, Australia, and *Ruth* in Constantinople. Her biography appeared in both the *Deutsche Frauenblätter* and the *Musikalische Tagesfragen*.[14]

Unfortunately, in 1886, the management of the local *Theaterkapelle* changed, and the new managers, whose posts gave them control over most concert activities in Wiesbaden, deprived Le Beau of most of her chances for performances in her own town. The Le Beaus reacted to this change of affairs as they had to their changing fortunes in Munich, only much more intensely. Seeing her loss of opportunities as the result of a sort of conspiracy against Luise, the family turned inward upon itself and decided again to move.[15]

Eva Weissweiler, in her *Komponistinnen aus 500 Jahren*, emphasizes the growing insularity of the Le Beau family, which from this point signaled an increasing bitterness and withdrawal from the musical community.[16] She cites these tendencies in particular regarding Le Beau's activity in Berlin, the family's next place of residence, for the years 1890–93. While Le Beau deplored her lack of performance opportunities, Weissweiler states, "The large concert agencies repeatedly offered her contracts for tours and the director of a conservatory wanted to engage her as a lecturer on harmony. Luise, however, always declined categorically."[17] Weissweiler also notes Le Beau's refusal to submit manuscripts when her works were requested for the Columbia World Exhibition in Chicago in 1893.

Even though Le Beau was not active on the musical scene, she retained a reputation as a distinguished musician. Her biography appeared in the *Neue Berliner Musikzeitung* and the Brockhaus *Konversations-Lexikon*, the major household encyclopedia of the time. The *Berliner Neueste Nachrichten* described her as "perhaps the most talented [woman composer] of today; in any case the first who was unconditionally accepted by her male colleagues."[18]

Le Beau occupied her time by attending concerts and studying scores of such composers as Bach, Palestrina, Orlando di Lasso, Mozart, Schubert, Méhul, Weber, and Cornelius at the Königliche Bibliothek. She also completed work on *Hadumoth*, opus 40, a *Märchenoper* she had begun to compose in the fall of 1888.[19] Knowing that no opera company would consider the work without orchestra and chorus parts, the Le Beaus rented a printing press and prepared the parts themselves. It took them an entire year. Even with the parts, however, Le Beau could not book a performance, though she applied to opera houses throughout Germany. The repeated refusals had as much to do with the large orchestral resources demanded by the work as with Le Beau's lack of an advocate in any of the opera house directorates to which she applied. Still, they contributed to her growing despair about her situation.

Further disillusionment was to follow. Le Beau's publisher, Paul Simon of the firm Kahnt Nachfolger, sponsored a review of the work by Alfred Kalischer, a well-known music critic at the *Neue Zeitschrift für Musik*.[20] The review interested Georg Vierling, composer, conductor, and professor at the Staatliche Hochschule für Musik. Vierling sent for Le Beau, to examine her compositions. He praised her invention and instrumentation, and told her, "No woman has yet produced such a work [as *Hadumoth*]." She records that:

The friendly old man who was, after all, a member of the Senate and was to decide along with the others about the conferring of the title "Professor" or "Königliche Musikdirektor" [Imperial Music Director] would have gladly used such a title for me. I could more than fulfill the stipulations regarding compositions to be submitted; they had not received such a work as *Hadumoth* in years! I could also submit lieder and the prize-winning cello pieces. The question was only whether this title could be conferred on a woman at all, and especially in Berlin, which was fifty years behind the times, it could not even be considered.[21]

This block to her reputation and recognition was a cruel blow to Le Beau. It meant she could not formally hold an academic position as a teacher or a composer within the Prussian school system, which included music conservatories. She knew men with such titles who were far inferior to her in musical ability.

Le Beau's comprehension of the full limitations of her position was now brought into focus. She explored blocks to women's career development in the arts in a circle of women performers and writers to whom she was introduced by a colleague at the *Neue Berliner Musikzeitung* (for which Le Beau wrote reviews). Berlin, as one of the most conservative cities in Germany, appears to have been one of the earliest to develop such women's groups. The circle included a Frau Schepeler-Lette, who was probably the daughter-in-law of W. A. Lette, founder of the major German women's professional federation, the Lette Society. Schepeler-Lette had spoken with the Prussian cultural minister about difficulties experienced by professional women in Germany and in Prussia, and had been rebuffed with the comment that women existed only to serve the state.[22] Le Beau's discussions with Frau Schepeler-Lette seem to have intensified her feelings of hopelessness.

On 30 September 1893 the Le Beau family moved to Baden-Baden. Here *Hadumoth* was at last performed using local resources and was favorably reviewed throughout western Germany. Le Beau became an active participant in chamber concerts and formed her own circle. *Ruth, Hadumoth,* and her symphonic tone poem *Hohenbaden,* opus 43, were performed again and again. But in 1896, when the death of both of her parents deprived her of the only people in her life who she felt had fully understood her emotionally and intellectually, she was devastated. She attempted to maintain herself emotionally with her composition, performance, and music criticism in the *Badener Badeblatt.* However, when her criticism of a locally popular singer aroused bad feeling, she decided to stop performing in the area and writing for the newspaper. A new Märchenoper, *Der verzauberte Kalif,* opus 55, was denied performance in Karlsruhe in spite of the efforts of the grand duchess of Baden, one of Le Beau's oldest supporters.

The conclusion to Le Beau's autobiography indicates the depth of resignation she was experiencing at the time she completed it in 1910:

It is difficult to come to terms with such circumstances, when one has dedicated her entire life to a profession; but one must be satisfied with the consciousness of having helped to build the temple of art according to one's best knowledge and with honest intentions. . . . I also feel satisfied that I—even with the disregard of all my musical interests—am completely free in thought and deed. I have attained this highest and most worthy goal of humankind; all of the successes of the world could not replace that for me.[23]

Le Beau subsequently declined to perform except in special cases. Still, many of her works continued to be performed locally and abroad, and she composed a few new choral and piano works. In 1925 Le Beau's friends in Baden-Baden sponsored a seventy-fifth birthday concert for her. In 1927 she died in her home, attended by friends.

What observations may be made, on the basis of Le Beau's life, about social preconceptions of the abilities of women and how society has treated women composers? Primarily we may note the tremendous skepticism Le Beau encountered in almost all of her professional contacts. For example, she reports of a visit Hermann Levi offered to pay the Le Beaus: "Naturally he was invited to come. I played the 'Variations' and it was amusing to see how he regarded me from all sides and openly stated his amazement."[24]

Critics were seldom shy about noting the doubt they brought to a review of Le Beau's work. August Bungert wrote in 1876: "Why shouldn't I state openly that I always feel mistrust when I pick up a work bearing the name of a woman?"[25] Otto Schamm began a review in 1883, "Certainly many a man, when he finds a feminine name listed on the program of the fourth chamber music concert, would cherish a slight misgiving concerning the worth and success of this composition, for, in general, one cannot trust all that much the productive capacity of women in the area of music."[26]

Occasionally when Le Beau presented her works to directorates for performance consideration or herself for special honors, she was dismissed out of hand, because such recognition of a woman was considered inappropriate. As noted above, Vierling felt that although she was competent, it would be futile to present her name for the title of Imperial Music Director because the qualifications of a woman for such a post would not even be considered. We do not know how often Le Beau's work was denied consideration on these grounds without its being explicitly stated.

In spite of the resistance of male musicians and critics to the idea that a woman could be a competent composer, there is also evidence of their willingness to take Le Beau's works in hand and give them a fair evaluation. This was a much more favorable situation than that which existed earlier in the century when a reviewer at the *Neue Zeitschrift für Musik* could state that a true critique of Clara Wieck's Piano Concerto in A Minor was out of the question, "since we are dealing here with the work of a woman."[27]

Le Beau's success in maintaining a role in German compositional life in comparison to other composing women of a few decades earlier may be related to the changing social situation in Germany in the 1870s and 1880s. She reached maturity in the wake of the Industrial Revolution, when the growing need of women to support themselves transformed the question of women's right to work and hold professional posts into an issue of great economic significance.[28] This question was brought before the public eye through the efforts of two major organizations, the Association for the Education of Women, founded in Leipzig in 1865, and the Society for Promoting the Employment of Women (later the Lette Society), founded in Berlin in 1866.[29] Separate educational systems for boys and girls were challenged, because under the prevailing system boys were given preprofessional training denied to girls. Women were prevented from taking qualifying examinations for the universities because they were inadequately prepared to take the tests by their limited prior training. The efforts of these organizations resulted in the admission of women to German universities in the first decade of the twentieth century[30] and, ultimately, to women's suffrage in 1918.

The new ideas introduced by these social changes may have predisposed musicians to give Le Beau's works a hearing. However, they also resulted in a strong reactionary swing. It was stated that such an opening up of educational doors to women would decrease the seriousness of professional study and lead to a "watering down" of the system. This was to happen as a result of the exposure of young men to a variety of potentially seductive feminine character flaws (such as moral and physical weakness and superficiality) and the flooding of the system with inferior (and, again, flawed) products of women's work.[31] One aspect of such thinking in musical circles appeared in an article, entitled "On the Reform of Our Music Schools," by Eugen Lüning. Lüning asserted that the admission of women as composition students to the conservatories would result in a feminization (*Verweiblichung*) of the art and its inevitable deterioration.[32]

Many musicians brought such fears to their evaluation of Le Beau. In some cases they were set aside. A number of Le Beau's critics asserted that the quality of her work raised her above their censure of "Blaustrumph-Arbeit" (the work of "bluestockings" or female literati), to them identifiable by low quality.[33] In Le Beau's study with Rheinberger, however, her teacher's antipathy toward "emancipated ladies" contributed to the schism between them.

Moreover, in the earliest stages of Le Beau's musical training in Karlsruhe, at the critical time when she was in the process of deciding her future, she encountered many expressions of social censure. A group of young boys would often stand outside her window when she was practicing her violin, imitating her movements with their arms.[34] The parents of her best friend told her they highly disapproved of her being allowed to study so seriously.[35]

In these early days and throughout her life, Le Beau's main support came from her parents. Le Beau notes in the introduction to her autobiography that she is writing it at the wish of her father, who wanted her to tell "of the many obstacles that confront a woman in the field of musical composition."[36] Her father's concern was borne out in action. Luise's parents fostered their daughter's interests and career to a degree that would be unusual in any century. Her father taught her subjects, such as geometry, not offered in girls' schools. The family willingly moved from city to city to try to improve the chances for performance of her works. She notes that her many disappointments hurt them more than they did her.

The support of her parents lent her an air of respectability in an age when many considered a single woman an embarrassment: her father made technical arrangements for her concerts; her mother often traveled with her on tour.[37] In addition, they supported her financially to a great extent throughout their lives, encouraging her to put away the money she earned from teaching, concerts, and music sales to live on after their deaths. This made it possible for her to refuse honoraria for concerts in cities in which she lived, perhaps improving her chances to obtain concert engagements. The emotional and monetary support they provided Le Beau also freed her from the necessity of a, perhaps, limiting marriage[38] or an exhausting teaching schedule. Her ineligibility—because of her sex—for a professional title[39] would undoubtedly have prevented her from earning high enough fees to give her much free time to compose.

The positive support the Le Beaus brought to their daughter's career stands in great contrast to the attitudes shown by the families or husbands of such compositionally talented women as Fanny Mendelssohn Hensel and Alma Mahler Werfel. The degree to which these women were required to sublimate their talents to the emotional support of others or to responsibility for their households is receiving more and more attention in recent studies of their lives.[40] Mendelssohn Hensel's father and brother repeatedly discouraged her from considering composition as a career or from publishing her works.[41] Gustav Mahler told his wife-to-be she must stop composing and attend to their home before he had even seen any of her pieces.[42]

Nevertheless, that a woman composer could be acknowledged and accepted by her contemporaries in late nineteenth-century Germany is demonstrated by the critical reception of Le Beau's works. The interest taken in her works by major critics, the sheer number of reviews of them, and the overwhelmingly positive tone of the reviews all indicate that Le Beau was granted a firm place on the German musical scene. Critics defined Le Beau as a successful composer by noting the degree to which they felt she excelled among women composers and qualified among men.[43] As one critic noted, "We believe we can give the works of Le Beau no more worthy honor than to say from the outset that everything we have heard from her deserves to be judged by the standards we are accustomed to using—not for her female colleagues—but for her contemporary male colleagues."[44]

What aspects of Le Beau's works and style were cited to draw this distinction? Eduard Hanslick's analysis of Le Beau's style at the time he saw her works during her Viennese tour in 1884 provides us with a starting point to answer this question:

What especially characterizes Frl. Le Beau is the solid musical training that enables her to put herself to the test in larger artistic forms which are otherwise only mastered by the strong sex. The good classical masters, through whom she trained herself under the eyes of Franz Lachner and Joseph [*sic*] Rheinberger, speak unmistakably from her Piano Quartet, Piano Trio, and Fantasy with Orchestra. [One finds] everywhere symmetrical relationships, sound harmony and modulation, and a correct and separately progressing bass one would hardly look for in [compositions by] a woman. One will scarcely encounter a bold turn or startling episode with this woman, and should she nevertheless once fall into a distant modulation, so, genuinely female, she ponders immediately how she can most quickly find her way home again. The larger chamber music forms that Fräulein Le Beau is the first of her sex to cultivate exhort from us our respect for the composer; [her use of these forms,] however, also justifies much apprehension, for they necessarily carry a not-rich inventiveness into danger [in attempting] to be broad and loquacious. Indeed, [Le Beau is] insatiable in repetition only to fill out the large formats. For these reasons I give preference to a small "Gavotte" for Piano, opus 32, among the compositions of Le Beau; it is a very characteristic, resolute piece in which even a slightly humorous touch in the sonorous middle section is noticeable. The Fantasy with Orchestra seems to suit the public taste the most; [it is] a short piano concerto, quite effectively set in three movements, in which fantasy, to be sure, plays the weakest role.[45]

Le Beau's compositions thus reveal a musical conceptualization expressed according to traditional structural and stylistic principles. In her large instrumental works, movements in sonata form predominate, and in those movements the themes exhibit affective characteristics typical of that form as, for example, in the bold opening of her Symphony in F Minor for Large Orchestra, opus 41 (figure 17). Le Beau's vocal and small instrumental pieces, likewise, follow established forms, for example, the early Piano Variations, opus 8, and the Gavotte for Piano, opus 32 (figure 18), cited above by Hanslick. Le Beau's lieder are typically strophic and often include short refrains at the end of verses, as in her popular *Kornblumen und Haidekraut*, opus 11, no. 1, and programmatic accompaniments reminiscent of Schubert, as in her *Spielmannslied*, opus 33, no. 2.

Critics based their approval of Le Beau and their recognition of her as different from other women composers to a large extent upon her mastery of traditional forms and her understanding of various standard compositional techniques, obviously developed through lengthy study. Review after review reiterated that Le Beau's willingness to attempt the composition of large forms (including those of chamber music) made her unique. According to some reviewers, Le Beau's compositions lacked the "mawkishness" and generally

Figure 17
Symphony in F Minor (composed 1894), opening of first movement

Source: Luise Adolpha Le Beau, Symphony in F Minor for Large Orchestra, Opus 41. A transcription according to the manuscript in the collections of the Deutsche Staatsbibliothek, Berlin, GDR

Figure 18
Gavotte (composed 1884), opening

Source: L. A. Le Beau, Gavotte, Opus 32 (Hamburg: Verlag von Aug. Cranz [1885]).
Print courtesy of Bayerische Staatsbibliothek, Munich

"pessimistic outlook" they usually associated with works by women.

Certain characteristics of Le Beau's style, especially her control of form and her power, energy, and spirit, were consistently referred to by critics and reviewers as *männlich* (manly). August Bungert, for example, wrote concerning her Piano Variations, opus 3: "[The final variation] subsequently plunges passionately and boldly on and becomes so violent, that one has quite forgotten by the end that the composer is a woman; indeed, one could think that one were dealing with a capable man, who can truly strike earnestly and hard as here."[46] Her most striking "masculine" characteristic was her capacity for musical conceptualization. As one critic put it, "Her abilities include solidity in development, taste, and a feeling for beauty and pleasing sound, as well as earnest, we should like to say, masculine ways of thinking, in relation to the comprehension of the independent tasks of the art."[47] For some reviewers the ultimate compliment they felt they could give to Le Beau was to divorce her from her own sex completely; this was to say, not that she composed well, but that she composed like a man. Wilhelm Tappert wrote concerning the *Nordmännerlied*, opus 19:

[Frl. Le Beau] shows here also that her knowledge and abilities extend far beyond the boundaries Mother Nature usually sets for her daughters who compose music. In most cases, it doesn't go beyond a certain point, as anyone who teaches young women will understand. Frl. Le Beau belongs to the exceptions who go farther; if many men did not write truly bad music, I would clothe my praise in the words: she composes like a man![48]

Such critiques illustrate the degree to which control of even the most basic skills of composition and affective musical language was considered masculine and beyond the capabilities of most women composers.

Le Beau herself explored the reasons why critics continued to perceive a low level of competence in women composers, and she told how she had been able to escape this syndrome in an article entitled "On the Musical Education of Young Women."[49] In the article she stated that the lack of musical understanding many women were said to exhibit was due, not to a genetic inability of the female sex, but rather to the "incomplete, often too late education of women." She criticized the double standard of encouraging a woman to earn her own living when she did not succeed in her "true profession" (nurturing the achievements of others) and calling her unfeminine when she strove for a thorough education for herself. She stated that, before the possibilities of women in music could be properly evaluated, young women must be allowed to dedicate themselves to music as if they were preparing for a profession.

Just do not limit, then, the training of girls. Rather, teach them the same things that are taught to boys. Grow accustomed to a system that has this same fundamental condition for every education, and then see what [girls] can do after acquiring technical skills and intellectual independence, rather than entrench yourselves against female capabilities by limiting the education of women![50]

Another way of assessing Le Beau's achievement as a composer, besides noting the recognition she received from her contemporaries, is to consider the degree to which she was able to realize her artistic potential. In her early years in Munich she demonstrated an unusual comprehension of compositional technique and openness to new compositional ideas. This is indicated by the special status she enjoyed for a time with Rheinberger. In addition, Weissweiler notes Le Beau's private study of Berlioz's *Treatise on Instrumentation and Orchestration* and her development of an unusual understanding of orchestral sound, especially that of stringed instruments.[51] She also attempted the composition of a piece according to a literary program (her String Quartet, opus 34), and she used leitmotivs to characterize contrasting emotions (in *Ruth*). The thematic originality of many works, such as the Three Pieces for Viola with Piano Accompaniment, opus 26, and the expressive melodic writing seen in an aria from *Ruth* (figure 19), showed the promise of a deep musical sensitivity and personal style.

Yet the promise of Le Beau's early talents was not fulfilled in her later works. Her style progressed little beyond the "classical" principles she learned from Rheinberger, and the works for which she was best known date, for the most part, from early in her career. Could it be that the social reaction to Le Beau explored early in this study was related to her failure to develop?

Throughout her autobiography, Le Beau attributes many of the difficulties she experienced to prejudice against women composers. She cites the misunderstanding of her talent as the primary reason for her increasing withdrawal from the musical community. This withdrawal was not only from active involvement in the musical life of the various cities in which she lived, but also from the stimulation of the works of her younger contemporaries—over the years she limited her personal study primarily to works of the accepted masters and her more conservative contemporaries. Thus Le Beau did not truly give herself the chance to fulfill her potential.

Figure 19
Ruth (composed 1882), scene 1, number 2

Source: Luise Adolpha Le Beau, *Ruth*, Opus 27, piano-vocal
reduction (Leipzig: C. F. Kahnt [1885]), pp. 13–15

We cannot know what Le Beau could have accomplished had she been spared the constant battle to prove herself occasioned by the special status to which she was relegated by her society. Perhaps she would have been able to realize her promise by studying at length with a major composer and by remaining in direct contact with, performing for, and exchanging ideas with the musical establishment. As it was, Le Beau's greatest achievement may have been that she was the first of her sex to be widely appreciated as a composer in the heavily male-dominated German musical tradition.

NOTES

Research for this study was undertaken with the support of a Deutscher Akademischer Austauschdienst fellowship for the year 1976–77.

1. Luise Adolpha Le Beau, *Lebenserinnerungen einer Komponistin* (Baden-Baden: Emil Sommermayer, 1910), p. 60. All translations in this study are mine.

2. Ibid.

3. Le Beau left copies of all her works either in published form or in manuscript to the Bayerische Staatsbibliothek in Munich and the Königliche Bibliothek in Berlin (now divided between the Staatliches Institut für Musikforschung [Stiftung Preussischer Kulturbesitz] in West Berlin and the Deutsche Staatsbibliothek in East Berlin). Other materials, primarily orchestral and vocal parts, were left to the Grossherzoglich Badische Hof- und Landesbibliothek in Karlsruhe, whose collection was destroyed by bombing in World War II. Some orchestral parts are in the Munich collection. A list of works appears in Le Beau, *Lebenserinnerungen*, pp. 280–82. Publishers of first printings are noted.

4. "Kritiken über Kompositionen von L. A. Le Beau, 1876–1925," 4 vols., Deutsche Staatsbibliothek, East Berlin, call no. 129 (available on microfilm) (hereafter referred to as "Kritiken"). The clippings, which were taken from major newspapers (many of them musical) published throughout central Europe and England, are pasted in scrapbooks whose compilers are not identified. The scrapbooks are numbered 1 to 4, with clippings numbered consecutively throughout each book.

5. Le Beau's piano repertory ranged from Scarlatti to Liszt and also included her own works. She was the Munich correspondent for the *Allgemeine Deutsche Musik-Zeitung* (Berlin) from 1878; and she later wrote for the *Neue Zeitschrift für Musik* (Leipzig), the *Neue Berliner Musikzeitung*, and the *Badener Badeblatt* (Baden-Baden).

6. Cf. Ethel Smyth, *Impressions That Remained*, 2 vols. (London: Longmans, Green & Co., 1919); and for a somewhat later composer, Alma Mahler Werfel, *Mein Leben* (Frankfurt am Main: S. Fischer, 1960). See also Johanna

Kinkel's autobiographical story, "Hausfrau und Künstlerin," *Frankfurter Zeitung* (30 November 1885); id., novella, "Musikalische Orthodoxie," in *Erzählungen von Gottfried und Johanna Kinkel* (Stuttgart, 1849); and id., *Hans Ibeles in London—ein Familienbild aus dem Flüchtlings-Leben*, 2 vols. (Stuttgart, 1860), cited in Eva Weissweiler, *Komponistinnen aus 500 Jahren* (Frankfurt am Main: Fischer Taschenbuch Verlag, 1981), p. 222ff. I am grateful to Renate Hüsken of Cologne, Germany, for suggesting or procuring for me books by Weissweiler and Eva Rieger (see n. 50) noted in this study.

7. See, e.g., p. 291.

8. Le Beau, *Lebenserinnerungen*, p. 60.

9. "Private-Musikkursus für Klavier und Theorie für Töchter gebildete Stände." See Le Beau, *Lebenserinnerungen*, pp. 66, 125–27.

10. See the reviews in "Kritiken."

11. Le Beau, *Lebenserinnerungen*, p. 74.

12. Ibid., p. 96.

13. Ibid., p. 76.

14. It had appeared earlier in music journals, such as *Die Tonkunst*, and in a calendar of composers produced by the music publisher Otto Brandstetter.

15. Le Beau, *Lebenserinnerungen*, pp. 160–61.

16. Weissweiler, *Komponistinnen*, p. 289ff.

17. Ibid., pp. 290–91.

18. *Berliner Neueste Nachrichten*, August 1890, quoted in Le Beau, *Lebenserinnerungen*, p. 171.

19. For excerpts from Le Beau, *Lebenserinnerungen*, covering the conception of *Hadumoth* to its eventual acceptance, see Judith E. Olson, trans., "Luise Adolpha Le Beau," in *Women in Music: An Anthology of Source Materials from the Middle Ages to the Present*, ed. Carol Neuls-Bates (New York: Harper & Row, 1982), pp. 167–74.

20. 28 September 1892, cited in Le Beau, *Lebenserinnerungen*, p. 189.

21. Le Beau, *Lebenserinnerungen*, p. 193.

22. Ibid., p. 182.

23. Ibid., p. 279.

24. Ibid., p. 60.

25. *Allgemeine Deutsche Musik-Zeitung* 3 (30 May 1876), "Kritiken," bk. 1, no. 3.

26. *Erste Beilage zum Leipziger Tageblatt und Anzeiger* 77 (3 December 1883), ibid., bk. 2, no. 27.

27. Cited in Weissweiler, *Komponistinnen*, p. 262.

28. Works on the status of women and the women's movement in Germany in the late nineteenth century include: Katherine Anthony, *Feminism in Germany and Scandinavia* (New York: Henry Holt & Co., 1915); Helena Lange, "Fünfzig Jahre deutscher Frauenbewegung," *Die Frau, Monatsschrift für das gesamte Frauenleben unserer Zeit* 23 (October 1915): 1–20; Helena Lange and Gertrud Bäumer, eds., *Handbuch der Frauenbewegung*, 5 vols. (Berlin: W. Moeser, 1901–6); Hugh Wiley Puckett, *Germany's Women Go*

Forward (New York: Columbia University Press, 1970); Werner Thönnessen, *Die Frauenemanzipation in Politik und Literatur der Deutschen Sozial-democratie, 1863–1933* (Frankfurt am Main: Bund Verlag, 1958), trans. Joris de Bres, under the title *The Emancipation of Women: The Rise and Decline of the Women's Movement in the German Social Democracy, 1863–1933* (London: Pluto Press, 1973); and Margrit Twellmann, *Die deutsche Frauenbewegung: Ihre Anfänge und erste Entwicklung: Quellen 1843–1899* (Meisenheim am Glan: Verlag Anton Hain, 1972). I am grateful to Professor Doris Starr Guilloton for calling my attention to several of the sources cited above.

29. The Frauenbildungsverein, later the Allgemeiner Deutscher Frauenverein (National Association of German Women), and the Verein zur Förderung der Erwerbstätigkeit des Weiblichen Geschlechts, later the Lette Verein.

30. For a general overview of women's entrance to German universities, see Puckett, *Germany's Women Go Forward*, pp. 187–88. For more detailed information, see Gertrud Bäumer, "Geschichte und Stand der Frauenbildung in Deutschland," in *Handbuch der Frauenbewegung*, ed. Lange and Bäumer, vol. 3: *Der Stand der Frauenbildung in den Kulturländern* (1902), pp. 1–128, tables 1–9; and ibid., vol. 5: *Die deutsche Frau in Beruf: Praktische Ratschläge zur Berufwahl*, ed. Josephine Levy-Rathenau and Lisbeth Wilbrandt (1906). In the latter volume, pages 224–62 treat factors affecting the study of specific professions at various universities by women, statistics concerning women students, and stipends available to women. Eva Rieger, *Frau, Musik, und Männerherrschaft* (Frankfurt am Main: Ullstein, 1981), includes a study of women in music pedagogy.

31. Numerous documents pertaining to such arguments may be found in Twellmann, *Die deutsche Frauenbewegung*.

32. Eugen Lüning, "Ueber die Reform unserer Musik-Schulen," *Allgemeine Deutsche Musik-Zeitung* 5 (11 and 18 October 1878): 341–43 and 349–51 respectively.

33. For example, a Dr. L. St. wrote in *Ueber Land und Meer*, no. 17, "Kritiken," bk. 1, no. 10, concerning Le Beau's Sonata for Piano, op. 8: "[This is] no *Blaustrumph-Arbeit*, on the contrary [it is] rather correct and stylistic." Otto Wangemann wrote in *Die Tonkunst* 8 (1 October 1882), ibid., bk. 2, no. 1, concerning *Ruth*, "[Le Beau's compositions] are not to be compared with the work of such *Blaustrümpfe*, who currently [are found] by the hundreds in our conservatories; rather, Frl. Le Beau is an artist in the most noble sense of the word."

34. Le Beau, *Lebenserinnerungen*, p. 17.

35. Ibid., pp. 20–21.

36. Ibid., p. 7.

37. The importance of this aspect of their support is substantiated by the difficulties Clara Wieck experienced in attempting to conduct performance tours on her own after her father refused to travel with her. See Rieger, *Frau, Musik, und Männerherrschaft*, pp. 179–82.

38. The legal rights and cultural standing of married and single women differed strikingly. Only with the German Civil Code of 1900 were even single women allowed equal footing with men in property ownership. Every aspect of the married woman's life continued to be liable to her husband's wishes. The statement in the code, "The husband has the right of decision in all matters affecting the common married life," was subject to a very broad interpretation.

39. Even in 1981 only one woman held a professorship in composition in a German country: Ruth Zechlin of the German Democratic Republic. See Rieger, *Frau, Musik, und Männerherrschaft*, p. 245.

40. See esp. ibid., pp. 170–209; Weissweiler, *Komponistinnen*, pp. 183–237, 255–95. Both authors make the same point concerning Clara Wieck Schumann.

41. Although Wilhelm Hensel encouraged his wife to publish her works, Rieger, in *Frau, Musik, und Männerherrschaft*, pp. 200–204, paints an extremely negative picture of Felix Mendelssohn's reaction to his sister's wish to publish and have her works known, and notes the effect of her limited public exposure on her productivity and feelings about herself. See also chap. 9 above.

42. Rieger, *Frau, Musik, und Männerherrschaft*, p. 204. See also Susan Filler, "A Composer's Wife as Composer: The Songs of Alma Mahler," *Journal of Musicological Research* 4 (1983): 427–41.

43. Throughout this discussion, note similarities in the sex-typing of compositional traits by German critics with the sexual aesthetics of American critics cited in chapter 13 below.

44. *Musikalisches Centralblatt* (Leipzig) 2 (7 December 1882), "Kritiken," bk. 2, no. 9.

45. *Concerte, Componisten, und Virtuosen der letzten fünfzehn Jahre: 1870–1885* (Berlin: Allgemeiner Verein für Deutsche Literatur, 1886), pp. 444–47.

46. *Allgemeine Deutsche Musik-Zeitung* 3 (30 May 1876), "Kritiken," bk. 1, no. 3.

47. *Die Tonkunst* 8 (15 January 1883), ibid., bk. 2, no. 14.

48. *Allgemeine Deutsche Musik-Zeitung* 7 (10 December 1880), ibid., bk. 1, no. 36.

49. L. B. [Le Beau], "Ueber die musikalische Erziehung der weiblichen Jugend," *Allgemeine Deutsche Musik-Zeitung* 5 (1 November 1878): 365–66. (The text is reprinted in its entirety in *Frau und Musik*, ed. Eva Rieger [Frankfurt am Main: Fischer Taschenbuch Verlag, 1980], pp. 56–59.) Le Beau prepared the article in response to the Lüning article cited in n. 32 above on the suggestion of the periodical's editors. Le Beau, *Lebenserinnerungen*, p. 128.

50. Le Beau, "Ueber die musikalische Erziehung der weiblichen Jugend," p. 366.

51. Weissweiler, *Komponistinnen*, pp. 278–81.

12

"Shout, Shout, Up with Your Song!" Dame Ethel Smyth and the Changing Role of the British Woman Composer

JANE A. BERNSTEIN

"When E. M. Smyth's heroically brassy overture to *Anthony and Cleopatra* was finished, and the composer called to the platform, it was observed with stupefaction that all that tremendous noise had been made by a lady."[1] Even in 1892, when George Bernard Shaw wrote this review, British society still maintained a double standard in its judgment of the artistic abilities of men and women. Since all women ought to be trained as ladies, how could a "lady composer" write music that was powerful, well-crafted, and complex? The achievements of nineteenth-century women composers, like those of their literary counterparts, could only be measured against feminine ideals of delicacy, grace, and refinement.[2] Although by the 1850s women writers such as Elizabeth Barrett Browning, the Brontës, and George Eliot confounded these stereotypes, it was not until the end of the century that a woman composer openly challenged the accepted double standard. That woman was Ethel Smyth (1858–1944).

One of the most gifted women of her day, Ethel Smyth attained international recognition as an opera composer. Besides her musical activities, she was an author of considerable distinction. As a feminist, she actively took part in the suffragist movement, and later she fought for the rights of women musicians. Her friendships with many notable people of her time and her candid and outspoken nature brought her further fame. In short, Smyth was one of the most colorful British women of the Victorian-Edwardian period.[3]

Although virtually unknown today, Smyth's music received much acclaim from her contemporaries. Critics, impressed with the strength and craftsmanship of her works, praised them in masculine terms as "virile, masterly in construction and workmanship," devoid "of the qualities that are usually associated with feminine productions."[4] They heralded Smyth as the first woman composer, "the most remarkable of her sex,"[5] the only woman to make "a name for herself in the field of opera."[6] Yet, recent research has shown that Ethel Smyth was neither "the only (so far) successful woman opera composer"[7] nor the first British woman to write music.[8] She was, in fact, preceded by a long line of hitherto unknown British women composers whose music has been left to languish in libraries.

England witnessed a tremendous increase in the number of women composers in the nineteenth century. While these women came from a variety of musical and socioeconomic backgrounds, by and large the majority were dilettantes from the middle and upper classes. Music became the highest of feminine accomplishments for the culturally acquisitive young lady. No etiquette book or domestic guide of the period fails to make the point that "An English lady without her piano, or her pencil, or her fancy work, or her favorite French authors and German poets, is an object of wonder, and perhaps of pity."[9]

The step from amateur pianist and singer to composer became an easy one for the talented dilettante. Encouraged by the demand for drawing-room ballads and easy dances for the piano, women such as Charlotte Alington Barnard [Claribel, pseud.] and Ellen Dickson [Dolores, pseud.] churned out hundreds of songs, some of which achieved extraordinary popularity. *In the Gloaming*, by Annie Fortescue Harrison [Lady Arthur Hill], for example, sold more than 140,000 copies between 1880 and 1889.[10]

The writers of fashionable parlor music, for whom composition seemed to be a genteel occupation, should be distinguished from the other more serious female composers to emerge in the nineteenth century—the performer-teachers. Many of these professional women were born into musical families and received their training from fathers and/or husbands. The most notable family of musicians in early nineteenth-century England was the Dusseks. The best known member of this family was Jan Ladislav, the brilliant pianist and composer. Among the women musicians in the Dussek clan were Ladislav's wife, Sophia Giustina Corri (1775–c.1830),[11] her daughter

Olivia Dussek (later Mrs. George Buckley) (1801–47),[12] and Veronica Rosalie Dussek (1779–1833), the sister of Ladislav and the wife of music publisher Francesco Cianchettini.[13]

By the middle decades of the nineteenth century, the main professional roles for British women musicians expanded to include pianist and church organist as well as singer and actress. Considering the long tradition of music for church and choral institutions in England, it is not surprising to find an emergence of female organists and church composers in the Victorian period. One of the first to claim recognition was Elizabeth Stirling (1819–95), who in 1837 performed the works of J. S. Bach at a public recital.[14] She composed organ music and part-songs for choir, and in 1856 became the first woman to pass the Oxford bachelor-of-music examination. She did not, however, receive an Oxford degree. The university did not confer music degrees on women until 1921.[15]

The most versatile organist-composer was Ann Sheppard Mounsey (Mrs. William Bartholomew) (1811–91).[16] Her works transcend those of the typical church composer. They consist of an oratorio, cantatas, German lieder, solo piano works, and part-songs, as well as the more typical hymns and organ pieces. At the age of nine, when she was a pupil of the musical pedagogue Logier, Mounsey attracted the interest of the German composer Louis Spohr, who published her harmonization of a melody in his *Autobiography*.[17] She later studied with Samuel Wesley and Thomas Attwood. Mounsey also became a good friend of Felix Mendelssohn; she premiered his famous anthem *Hear My Prayer*, which was written especially for her Crosby Hall Classical Concerts. Her oratorio *The Nativity* was first performed in 1855. Among her lieder, her setting of Goethe's *Erlkönig* can be favorably compared to those of her German contemporaries, such as Carl Loewe.

Female pianists abounded in the Victorian era. The piano, labeled along with the guitar and harp as an instrument most suitable for the Victorian lady to learn, became a fixture in every upper-middle-class parlor and a status symbol for the lower classes.[18] The need for teachers to instruct young ladies in the art of piano playing opened up a new field for British women musicians, and the best soon sought careers as pianists—concertizing, teaching, and composing on the side.

The most impressive of the pianist-composers was Caroline Orger (1818–92).[19] Her husband, organist and teacher Alexander Reinagle, was the third generation of a musical family. Orger, who was predominantly a piano teacher, composed many didactic pieces for the piano. Her other musical compositions, unlike those of her female contemporaries, did not emulate the brilliant style of Parisian salon music. Instead, they aspired to the more complex forms of the sonata, quartet, trio, and concerto. Her A Major Piano Sonata, opus 6, for example, demonstrates her skill in sudden modulations and handling of sonata form.[20]

Crucial to the emergence of the nineteenth-century woman composer in England was the establishment in 1822 of the first national school of music. By 1839 it received its charter as the Royal Academy of Music. From its inception, the academy was a coeducational institution, which accepted an equal number of male and female students. Although by the middle of the century the quality of instruction in comparison to continental equivalents was on the decline, the Royal Academy of Music became a haven for women musicians who, banned from taking music degrees at Oxford and Cambridge, found it difficult to study abroad. Among the women who acquired their musical training at the academy, Maude Valerie White (1855–1937), composer of songs, was the first woman to win the academy's Mendelssohn scholarship in composition.[21]

Thus, British women played an active role in the field of music during the nineteenth century, not just as parlor-music dilettantes, but also as professional performers and composers. Unfortunately these distinguished musicians were too few to change the general societal view of the woman as amateur. By the end of the nineteenth century, the British music establishment still insisted that women maintain subordinate positions as dilettantes and teachers.

Ethel Smyth, unlike her predecessors, fit neither the mold of performer-teacher nor that of parlor-music composer. Although she was a proficient pianist and a competent singer, she was by no means a performer. She did not even have the advantage of being born into a musical family. Her father was a major-general in the British Army, and her family, though not aristocratic, belonged to the prosperous middle class of Victorian society. If Ethel Smyth sought a musical career, her status as a woman dictated that it be as an amateur performer or composer of parlor music. Throughout her life Smyth struggled against this dictum, and it was this struggle that set her apart from the other women musicians of her day.

Ethel Mary Smyth was born on 23 April 1858, one of eight children. Her early education reflected the typical training of the Victorian young lady: after private tutoring at home, she was sent to boarding school at Putney, where she learned the usual curriculum of music, drawing, French, German, astronomy, chemistry, literature and "how to darn stockings."[22] Smyth's first book of memoirs, *Impressions That Remained*, tells very little about her musical training as a child. She mentions a governess who studied at the Leipzig Conservatory;[23] but only at the age of seventeen did she begin formal musical training, taking harmony lessons with Alexander Ewing (writer of the popular hymn *Jerusalem the Golden*). Besides studying harmony, she read through Wagner operas with Ewing and taught herself orchestration with a borrowed copy of Berlioz's *Treatise on Instrumentation*.

By 1876 the young woman firmly decided that she must go to Leipzig to study composition. The Leipzig Conservatory was considered the best European music school, and since musical studies on the Continent were believed to be essential for the education of the serious musician, Smyth never even considered the Royal Academy of Music. On 26 July 1877, at the age of nineteen, she set out for Leipzig with the begrudging consent of her family under the charge of her brother-in-law. She was by no means the first British woman to study on the Continent,[24] but it was still highly unusual during the Victorian period for a young lady to do so.

At the Leipzig Conservatory she studied composition with Carl Heinrich Reinecke, the conductor of the Gewandhaus Orchestra, counterpoint and harmony with Salomon Jadassohn, and piano with Joseph Maas. Of her teachers, she considered Reinecke and Jadassohn "rather a farce" and Maas "a conscientious but dull teacher." She was also surprised to find that many of the students came to the conservatory not for serious musical studies but to qualify for teachers' certificates.[25] After one year she quit the conservatory in disgust and took up private tuition with the Austrian composer Heinrich von Herzogenberg, who was the director of the Bach Verein in Leipzig. Both Herzogenberg and his talented and beautiful wife Elizabeth (Lisl) were close friends of Johannes Brahms, and through them Smyth gained entrance into the musical circle of Brahms and Clara Schumann.[26] During her stay in Leipzig, the young composer also made the acquaintance of Grieg, Dvorak, and Tschaikovsky, all of whom were students at the conservatory.

Smyth's apprentice works consist of small chamber pieces, which include her String Quartet, opus 1 (first performed in Leipzig in 1884), the Sonata for Violin and Piano, opus 7 (1887), and the Sonata for Cello and Piano, opus 5 (1887). Two sets of German lieder, opera 3 and 4 (c. 1886), also date from this period.[27] These chamber compositions, written in a Brahmsian vein, demonstrate the technical skill in counterpoint and harmony the young woman acquired from Herzogenberg, a skill that proved exceedingly valuable in her later years.

At the time of her apprenticeship in Leipzig, Ethel Smyth embarked upon her career as a professional composer when, in 1878, she took her German lieder to the famous music publishing house, Breitkopf and Härtel. Her interview with Dr. Hase, the "nephew who conducts the business," demonstrates the prejudice that existed at this time against professional women composers. Hase told Smyth that "no composeress had ever succeeded, barring Frau Schumann and Fräulein Mendelssohn, whose songs had been published together with those of their husband and brother respectively" and "that a certain Frau Lang had written some really very good songs but they had no sale." In her account of the interview, Smyth continues: "I played him [my songs] . . . and he expressed himself very willing to take the risk and print them. But . . . having listened to all he said about women composers, . . . I asked for no fee! Did you ever hear of such a donkey!"[28]

It did not take Smyth much time to realize that her Leipzig training excluded an essential aspect of musical composition. Taking the advice of Tschaikovsky, she continued to study orchestration on her own, and by the end of 1889 she had composed a four-movement *Serenade* and an overture for orchestra.[29] On 26 April 1890 Ethel Smyth made her orchestral debut in her native country with the *Serenade*, which was performed at the Crystal Palace in London under the baton of August Manns, who also premiered the overture to *Antony and Cleopatra* some six months later. Ethel Smyth had already reached her thirty-third year when she was heralded by some critics as a "promising young composer."

The success of her orchestral works inspired Smyth to compose the Mass in D, which she finished in the summer of 1891. The Royal Choral Society, under the direction of Sir Joseph Barnby, first performed this, her most important work of the decade, at the Royal Albert Hall. The Mass demonstrated Ethel Smyth's command of larger musical structures. Tovey thought so highly of the Mass that he included it in his *Essays in Musical Analysis*, among the choral works of Bach, Beethoven, and Brahms—not to mention such contemporaries as Joachim, Parry, and Bantock. Impressed with the vocal writing, Tovey felt that the score was a *locus classicus* in choral orchestration.[30]

There is a strong temptation to compare this strikingly powerful work, as Tovey does, to Beethoven's *Missa Solemnis*. Both are in the key of D, and both exude a grandiose yet personal musical style. Smyth was certainly well aware of the earlier work; for in her memoirs she speaks of a visit to Munich in 1892 when she played her Mass for the great German conductor, Hermann Levi, and "once more [had] the bliss of hearing him conduct *Tristan* and the *Missa Solemnis.*"[31] Indeed, the composer's use of rhythmic themes, intervals of fourths and fifths, and carefully worked-out developments of motives as seen in the passacaglia theme of the *Kyrie* and the rhythmic subject of *Et vitam venturi* from the *Credo* (figure 20), coupled with masterful orchestration, place her not with her English contemporaries, but in the German tradition that led from Beethoven to Brahms and Mahler. When Smyth showed Levi her Mass, he was so struck by her dramatic abilities that he said, "You must at once sit down and write an opera."[32] This was a turning point in the English composer's musical career, for from that time onward she devoted herself to the writing of musicodramatic works.

After her interview with Levi, Smyth spent the next eighteen months composing her first opera, *Fantasio.* She and her closest male friend, Henry Brewster, fashioned a libretto from Alfred de Musset's comedy;[33] and in 1898, at the age of forty, Smyth made her debut in Weimar as an opera composer. The Weimar premiere received a bad press, with critics praising only its rich orchestration. Three years later, however, the Wagnerian conductor Felix Mottl made amends with an excellent performance of *Fantasio* in Karlsruhe; but by this time the composer had given up on her first operatic attempt and was already hard at work finishing her second opera, *Der Wald.*

Much of the libretto for *Der Wald*, with its forest setting and theme of salvation through death, suggests Wagnerian influence. Yet, in contrast to Wagnerian drama, the main protagonist is not the hero but the chorus of forest spirits who introduce, conclude, and participate at the climax of the opera. These spirits evoke the tranquillity of the forest, as Henry Brewster, who again provided Smyth with the story and helped her with the libretto, explained: "I have tried . . . to frame the passionate human story, to 'set' it, in the impression of the forest, which must be the abiding impression. Its peace must close over the victims of the tragedy."[34] To some extent this idea pervades another early twentieth-century musical drama, Debussy's *Pelleas et Melisande.*

Der Wald was first performed in Berlin on 21 April 1902.[35] Smyth had her first opportunity to conduct an orchestra when Karl Muck, the conductor of the Berlin Opera, was indisposed and she was

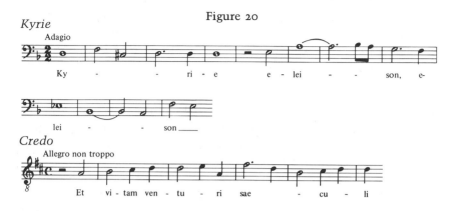

Source: Ethel Smyth, *Mass in D*, with a new introduction by
Jane A. Bernstein (New York: Da Capo Press, 1980)

compelled to direct the "cut rehearsal" after the premiere. Three
months later *Der Wald* was produced at Covent Garden.[36] The next
year, on 11 March,[37] it made history as the first opera by a woman to
be performed at the Metropolitan Opera House in New York. The
composer was present at the American premiere and "had an ovation
which some say lasted ten minutes."[38] A reviewer for the *New York
Times* wrote: "Miss Smyth is very serious, and the opera sounds the
note of sincerity and resolute endeavor. She uses the vocal and orchestral resources with masculine energy, and is not afraid of em-
ploying the most drastic means of modern expression."[39]

Both *Fantasio* and *Der Wald* were originally set to German
texts. It might seem strange that a British composer should write operas in German and go out of her way to have them produced on the
Continent rather than seek first performances in her own country. In
general, though, London musical life before the First World War, especially in the field of opera, was not propitious to native composers
of either sex. Martin Cooper notes that "opera [in England] at this
time was virtually confined to a summer season at Covent Garden
closely linked with the social life of London and provided almost entirely by foreign artists."[40] In her memoirs Smyth often laments the
stark contrast between English musical life and "the real thing" she
had known in Germany.[41]

If Smyth's first two operas reveal Germanic influence, her third
and best known opera, *The Wreckers*, hints at the composer's British
origins. A three-act drama in the grand opera style, *The Wreckers* (or

311

Les Naufrageurs, as it was originally entitled) has been considered by all (including the composer herself) to be her finest work. Sir Thomas Beecham, who conducted the first staged production in London, called it "one of the three or four English operas of real musical merit and vitality."[42]

The Wreckers concerns an eighteenth-century Cornish sea town that causes shipwrecks through the use of false lights. It is the story of "two lovers who, by kindling secret beacons, endeavored to counteract the savage policy of the community . . . how they were caught in the act by the Wrecker's committee—a sort of secret court which was the sole authority they recognized—and condemned to die in one of those sea-invaded caverns."[43] Smyth again collaborated with Henry Brewster on the libretto, which Brewster wished to write in French. Since rumor had it that André Messager of the Opéra comique would be the new artistic director of Covent Garden, they both felt that to compose the work in French "would be the best chance of a performance in England of an English opera!"[44] But ironically, *The Wreckers* was never presented in its original French version. Finished in 1904, it received its first two productions in Germany as *Strandrecht*.[45] Smyth then translated the opera into English, and on 28 May 1908 the London Symphony Orchestra under the direction of Artur Nikisch performed a concert version of the first two acts.[46] Beecham conducted the first English stage production on 22 June 1909 at His Majesty's Theatre; one year later, he included it in his debut season at Covent Garden.

Despite the protestations of the composer,[47] the music of *The Wreckers* contains many features of the Wagnerian style. The large and colorful orchestra, the use of leitmotifs, and the dense contrapuntal writing for the orchestra all harken back to Wagner. Smyth's use of ballad form for Mark's first aria and even the principal motive that pervades the storm scene and climactic love duet bear a close resemblance to Wagner's use of ballad form for Senta's aria and the main motive of *Der fliegende Holländer* (figure 21). German musical style aside, one can see many dramatic and musical features typical of an English opera. As a reviewer of the 1909 production astutely noted, "in *The Wreckers* the protagonist is the sea; and it is this that gives so much dramatic intensity to the situation."[48] Indeed, the evocation of the sea and characterization of an isolated sea town recalls to mind another English opera—Benjamin Britten's *Peter Grimes*.

Although Britten did not know Smyth's opera, his 1945 work bears some resemblance to it.[49] The main characters of *The Wreckers*, Mark and Thirza, are pitted against a savage community; the same

Figure 21

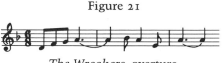

The Wreckers, overture
Ethel Smyth

Source: Ethel Smyth, *The Wreckers* (London: Forsyth Bros., 1916)

Der fliegender Holländer, overture
Richard Wagner

holds true for Peter Grimes, who as an outcast must face the wrath of his sea village. Other similarities between the two operas include the powerful use of chorus and the striking dramatic event of hymn singing offstage as an accompaniment to the soloists onstage. Most important, the portrayal of the sea in the orchestra interludes of both operas (*On the Cliffs of Cornwall*, prelude to act 2 of *The Wreckers*, and the *Four Sea Interludes* from *Peter Grimes*) demonstrates a common bond between these two operas.

By 1910 Ethel Smyth, at the age of fifty-two, had attained the musical recognition for which she had struggled. All of her operas had received stage productions, her Mass had been performed at the Royal Albert Hall, and in 1910 she was awarded an honorary Doctor of Music by the University of Durham.[50]

Yet amid this success, certain personal and political circumstances brought an end to this creative period in the composer's life. The death of her most intimate friend and collaborator, Henry Brewster, in 1908, had a profound effect upon Smyth. She writes, "I felt then like a rudderless ship aimlessly drifting hither and thither."[51] Meanwhile, the most important political issue of the day, the vote for women, attracted her attention. Lady Constance Lytton, one of the leaders of the suffrage movement, called upon the composer for her support; and Smyth, whose own life as an independent, professional woman naturally reflected the aims of the suffragists, decided to join the fight.

In 1903 the Women's Social and Political Union (W.S.P.U.), established by Emmeline Pankhurst and her daughters Christobel and Sylvia, embarked on a militant crusade to secure the vote for British women. By 1910 the struggle had reached a feverish pitch, with imprisonments, hunger strikes, and forcible feedings. During this year Ethel Smyth abandoned her musical activities and devoted two years to the suffragist cause. She soon became a close friend of Emmeline Pankhurst[52]—taking care of the charismatic leader during the final cat-and-mouse-act phase of the fight. In addition, Smyth played an active role in the movement itself, serving two months in Holloway Prison (1912) for smashing the window of a cabinet minister.[53] By far, Smyth's most important contribution to the movement was her *March of the Women*, which she composed for and dedicated to the W.S.P.U. membership. They sang it at meetings, at rallies, in the streets, and even in prison. The march, fitted with words by journalist Cicely Hamilton, had the passion and zeal of a national anthem (see figure 22). Smyth's biographer states, however, that the tune was not entirely devised by the composer but was adapted from an Italian song she had heard some years before in the Abruzzi.[54]

When her two years' service with the suffragists came to an end, Smyth set off in 1913 for Egypt, where she composed her fourth and most popular opera, *The Boatswain's Mate*. With this two-act comedy, the British composer ended her operatic exile, for not only was *The Boatswain's Mate* originally composed to an English text, but the first act was written in the traditional English ballad opera style with spoken dialogue and folk-song quotations.

The composer based the libretto on a short story by W. W. Jacobs, a choice that consciously reflects her identification with feminism. The plot concerns an exboatswain, Harry Benn, who vainly wooes Mrs. Waters, a widowed innkeeper. With the aid of his mate, Nick Travers, the boatswain stages a false burglary, hoping to rescue the widow and win her favor. Unfortunately, Mrs. Waters proves very capable in dealing with the supposed burglar and turns the joke on the boatswain.

For the overture of the opera, Smyth decided to rescue from the

Figure 22
March of the Women

Shout, shout, up with your song! Cry with the wind, for the dawn is break-ing!

Source: Ethel Smyth, *Songs of Sunrise* (London: n.p., 1911)

Plate 18
Ethel Smyth, 1916

Source: Ethel Smyth, *Impressions That Remained*, 2d ed.
(London: Longmans, Green & Co., 1919)
Photograph by Olive Edis

streets both the *March of the Women* and another suffragist choral work appropriately entitled *1910*.[55] Although Smyth states in a letter to Emmeline Pankhurst, "I simply stuck in the March because I like the tune!"[56] it was a fortuitous choice for this comedy, since the *March of the Women* and *1910*, like the earlier eighteenth-century ballad opera prototype, commented on the main political issue of the day.

Many critics of *The Boatswain's Mate* point to the inconsistent treatment of ballad opera techniques for the first act and a through-composed style for the second. Beecham, for example, states that "the first act with its mixture of lyrical numbers and dialogue is perfect in style and structure. But in the second this happy scheme is thrown overboard for an uninterrupted stream of music."[57] The change from spoken to sung dialogue, however, makes both musical and dramatic sense, since most of the action of this comedy occurs in the second act, while the first act merely serves to introduce the characters and the story.

What is most successful about *The Boatswain's Mate* is the composer's skill in setting its English text and her ability in portraying its characters. The self-assured ballad of the boatswain's mate in 5/4 time, *A Friend and I*, offers a fine example of text setting. Demonstrating Smyth's predilection for irregular rhythmic groupings, this strophic song actually takes the form of a passacaglia with the voice repeating the theme as the orchestral accompaniment performs a set of variations underneath (see figure 23).

In 1913 Ethel Smyth began to hear ringing in her ears, and by the end of World War I she realized that she was gradually going deaf. Despite this hardship, Smyth composed two more operas, the "dance-dream" *Fête Galante* (1922) and the comedy *Entente Cordiale* (1925). She also completed a Concerto for Violin, Horn, and Orchestra (1927) and a symphonic work for voices and orchestra entitled *The Prison* (1930).

Fête Galante is based on a short story by another friend, Maurice Baring. Set in a restrained, diatonic idiom, the music reflects the highly polished, rarefied atmosphere of Baring's tale of a king and queen and their commedia dell'arte players. Many of the opera's musical features, such as the use of baroque dances and an a cappella madrigal set to a poem by John Donne, capture the new musical idiom of neoclassicism that her more famous contemporary, Igor Stravinsky, had adopted just five years earlier. What became an important style for Stravinsky was evidently an isolated experiment for Smyth, since she never used it again in her later works.

Figure 23
A Friend and I

A friend and I were on the pier list'- ning to the band O, when

two young la - dies smart as paint came strol-ling down the strand O!

Source: Ethel Smyth, *The Boatswain's Mate* (London: Forsyth Bros., 1915)

In comparison to the fantasy world of *Fête Galante*, Smyth's other postwar opera, *Entente Cordiale*, deals with British soldiers and their language difficulties in a northern French town. Her last work, *The Prison*, is based upon a philosophical work by Henry Brewster. This was Smyth's memorial to the writer.

Ethel Smyth always considered herself first and foremost a composer; but when World War I put an end to performances of her music on the Continent, this remarkable woman decided to embark upon a second career—as a writer. She wrote ten books in all.[58] Although they remain an invaluable source of information on the composer's life, her books are perhaps more interesting for their brilliant portrayals of many notable people of her day, from Johannes Brahms, Queen Victoria, and Sir Thomas Beecham to Emmeline Pankhurst, Vernon Lee, and Maurice Baring. Written in a chatty, colloquial idiom, Smyth's books quickly became instant successes. Although one may agree with Virginia Woolf's severe criticism of Smyth's writing style,[59] one cannot help but be impressed with the composer's wit and candor. Woolf does admit, however, in a letter to Lytton Strachey, that Smyth's memoirs, *Impressions That Remained*, represented "the soul of the nineties."[60]

For their time Smyth's books were extraordinary in their unusual frankness about herself and her personal relationships. She had only one passionate affair with a man—Henry Brewster. For the most part, the other close attachments she formed were with other women. Smyth wrote:

Let me say here, that all my life, even when after years had brought me the seemingly unattainable, I have found in women's affection a peculiar understanding, mothering quality that is a thing apart. Perhaps too I had a foreknowledge of the difficulties that in a world arranged by man for man's convenience beset the woman who leaves the traditional path to compete for bread and butter, honours and emoluments. . . . The people who have helped me most at difficult moments of my musical career . . . have been members of my own sex.[61]

Smyth counted among her friends the writers Vernon Lee [Violet Paget], Edith Somerville, and Vita Sackville-West. Women also offered the composer financial support. The exiled Empress Eugénie of France helped out with the first performance of her Mass. Smyth's sister, Mrs. Mary Hunter, often stepped in during the production of the early operas, and American millionaire Mary Dodge financed the first British stage production of *The Wreckers*.

Of considerably greater interest was Smyth's last important friendship, with Virginia Woolf, to whom she dedicated her seventh book, *As Time Went On*. The two women met in 1930 when Smyth, near extreme deafness, was composing *The Prison* and Woolf was writing her most difficult book, *The Waves*. Smyth literally overwhelmed Woolf with her energy, barraging her in letters and meetings with questions and demanding much of the writer in their relationship. The often quoted passage from a letter that Woolf wrote to her nephew, Quentin Bell, betrays the writer's apprehension with the newly formed friendship: "An old woman of seventy-one has fallen in love with me. . . . It is at once hideous and horrid and melancholy-sad. It is like being caught by a giant crab."[62]

Yet, as their correspondence shows, Ethel Smyth was to Woolf, not just a nuisance, but an important confidante during a difficult period in her life:

What you give me is protection, so far as I am capable of it. I look at you and . . . think if Ethel can be so downright and plainspoken and on the spot, I need not fear instant dismemberment by wild horses. Its the child crying for the nurses [sic] hand in the dark. You do it by being so uninhibited: so magnificently unself-conscious.[63]

From time to time in her books, Smyth offered her opinions of other composers. Though sometimes wide of the mark, they are fascinating to read. Of Wagner she wrote: "Of all his works the only one I really love, and that only with ruthless cuts, is *Tristan*."[64] Smyth had great respect for Brahms, the composer, but this did not inhibit her from writing about her disdain for Brahms, the misogynist.[65] The British composer considered Gustav Mahler "the finest conductor [she] ever knew," but she was too young when she met him "to appreciate this grim personality."[66] In general Smyth's musical opinions tended toward the conservative side. Among her contemporaries she disliked Elgar, and she called Schönberg and his pupils "this school of impotent wrigglers."[67] She was deeply impressed with Holst's *Planets*,[68] and she felt that Hindemith's music was "exquisite in sound."[69]

Besides airing her views of other composers, Ethel Smyth also wrote many essays championing equal rights for women musicians.[70] In *Streaks of Life* she declaimed: "The whole English attitude towards women in fields of art is ludicrous and uncivilised. There is no sex in art. How you play the violin, paint, or compose is what matters."[71] Smyth's firm belief in the creativity of women led her to campaign in both newspaper articles and books to secure places for women in orchestras. Her friend Sir Henry Wood was the first conductor to start "mixed bathing in the sea of music and so successful was the innovation that many other orchestras followed suit."[72]

In general, Ethel Smyth stands out as one of the most original figures of British music history. Armed with a solid background in counterpoint, harmony, and orchestration, she forged ahead into the musical world, where she ranked with such contemporaries as Parry, Stanford, Sullivan, and even Elgar. A courageous, passionate woman, Smyth did not quietly plead for her right to be a composer; she defiantly demanded it. She proved, in the age of the amateur lady musician, that a woman could attain the status of a professional opera composer. In this sense Ethel Smyth stands alone as an important pioneer whose fight for recognition and efforts as a composer, writer, and feminist paved the way toward a new age in music.

NOTES

1. George Bernard Shaw, *Music in London, 1890–94*, 3 vols. (London: Constable, 1932), 2:37.

2. For information on the double standard in Victorian literature, see Elaine Showalter's excellent article, "Women Writers and the Double Standard," in *Woman in Sexist Society: Studies in Power and Powerlessness*, ed. Vivian Gornick and Barbara K. Moran (New York: New American Library, 1971), pp. 452–79.

3. The best source on the composer's life is Christopher [Marie] St. John, *Ethel Smyth: A Biography* (London: Longmans, Green & Co., 1959).

4. J. A. Fuller-Maitland, in *Grove's Dictionary of Music and Musicians*, 2d ed. (London: Macmillan, 1910), s.v. "Ethel Smyth," 4:490. This edition is hereafter referred to as *Grove's Dictionary*.

5. Sir Thomas Beecham, *A Mingled Chime: An Autobiography* (New York: G. P. Putnam's Sons, 1943), p. 137.

6. Eric W. White, *The Rise of English Opera* (London: John Lehmann, 1951), p. 129.

7. Donald J. Grout, *A Short History of Opera*, 2d ed. (New York: Columbia Univ. Press, 1965), p. 530, makes this claim. There were, of course, many women who wrote operas before Ethel Smyth. The early seventeenth-century Italian, Francesca Caccini, was not only a successful composer, but is also considered to be the first woman to have composed musicodramatic works. See Caroline Raney, "Francesca Caccini's *Primo Libro*," *Music and Letters* 48 (1967): 350–57; for biographical information, see also *Dizionario biografico degli italiani* (Rome: Istituto della Enciclopedia italiana, 1973), s.v. "Francesca Caccini," 16:19–23, and chap. 6 above.

8. Very little has been written on pre-twentieth-century British women composers. Jessica M. Kerr, "Mary Harvey—The Lady Dering," *Music and Letters* 25 (1944): 33, does mention a few eighteenth- and nineteenth-century composers, such as Mrs. Chazel (née Elisabetta de Gambarini), Maria Parke, and Mary Linwood, in her study of the seventeenth-century amateur composer, Lady Dering.

9. [Mrs. Jane Aster, pseud.,] *The Habits of Good Society: A Handbook for Ladies and Gentlemen . . . from the Last London Edition* (New York, 1868), p. 259. For discussion of accomplishments, see among other places Barbara Corrado Pope, "Angels in the Devil's Workshop: Leisured and Charitable Women in Nineteenth-Century England and France," in *Becoming Visible: Women in European History*, ed. Renate Bridenthal and Claudia Koonz (Boston: Houghton Mifflin, 1977), pp. 296–324; Arthur Loesser, *Men, Women, and Pianos* (New York: Simon & Schuster, 1954), pp. 267–79.

10. Ronald Pearsall, *Victorian Popular Music* (London: David & Charles Ltd., 1973), p. 91.

11. The best biographical information on Sophia Dussek appears in Philip H. Highfill, Jr., Kalman A. Burnim, and Edward A. Langhan, *A Biographical Dictionary of Actors, Actresses, Musicians, Dancers, Managers, and Other Stage Personnel in London 1660–1800*, 8 vols. to date (Carbondale: Southern Illinois University Press, 1973–), 4:527–28; see also *The New Grove Dictionary of Music and Musicians* (London: Macmillan, 1980), 5:758. This edition is hereafter cited as *New Grove Dictionary*.

12. Olivia Dussek Buckley, who became a well-known organist, was not actually the daughter of Jan Ladislav Dussek, since she was born of Sophia Dussek over a year after her father departed from London; see Highfill, Burnim, and Langhan, *Biographical Dictionary*, 4:527. The best information on her life appears in the *New Grove Dictionary*, 5:758; and in James Brown and Stephen Stratton, *British Musical Biography* (London: Wm. Reeves, 1897), pp. 67–68.

13. For more information on Veronica Dussek, see the *New Grove Dictionary*, 5:758; and Brown and Stratton, *British Musical Biography*, pp. 88–89.

14. Percy Scholes, *The Mirror of Music 1844–1944*, 2 vols. (London:

Novello and Oxford University Press, 1947), 2:729; see also Brown and Stratton, *British Musical Biography*, p. 396.

15. The first two women to receive Oxford degrees in 1921 were Evelyn Alice Sharp and Emily Rosa Daymond. Cambridge in 1927 awarded the B.Mus. degree to Elsie Baron Briggs, who had qualified for it in 1915; see Scholes, *Mirror of Music*, 2:680–82. For an overview of women and higher education in nineteenth-century England, see Rita McWilliams-Tullberg, "Women and Degrees at Cambridge University, 1862–1897," in *A Widening Sphere: Changing Roles of Victorian Women*, ed. Martha Vicinus (Bloomington: Indiana University Press, 1977), pp. 117–45.

16. For Mounsey's biography, see the *New Grove Dictionary*, 12:653; and Brown and Stratton, *British Musical Biography*, p. 33. A portrait of the composer appears as a frontispiece to a collection of her published works now housed in the British Library (shelfmark H 1587 b).

17. Louis Spohr, *Autobiography*, trans. from German, 2 vols. in 1 (London: Longmans, Green & Co., 1865), 2:99–100.

18. Patricia Branca, "Image and Reality: The Myth of the Idle Victorian Woman," in *Clio's Consciousness Raised: New Perspectives on the History of Women*, ed. Mary S. Hartman and Lois Banner (New York: Harper & Row, 1974), p. 188, believes that most middle-class families could not afford to own a piano.

19. *Grove's Dictionary*, 4:57; Brown and Stratton, *British Musical Biography*, p. 304.

20. Caroline Reinagle, *Sonata for the Pianoforte, Opus 6* (London: Cramer, Beale & Co., 1850?), British Library, shelfmark H 1485 z (38).

21. Maude White provides a fascinating account of the Mendelssohn competition she won in 1879 in her book, *Friends and Memories* (London: Edward Arnold, 1914). Her winning compositions were the songs *Espoir en Dieu, Chantez, chantez, jeune inspirée!* and *My ain kind dearie O!* and an *Agnus Dei* scored for solo voices, chorus, and orchestra. All three songs appear in a collection of her songs in the New York Public Library.

22. Ethel Smyth, *Impressions That Remained*, 2 vols. (London: Longmans, Green & Co., 1919), 1:95.

23. Ibid., 1:85.

24. In a letter dated Passion Week 1878, Smyth relates to her mother a meeting with a composer named Kirchner who "spoke much of the industry of the English in the (Leipzig) Conservatorium—how nearly all the ladies composed!" Ibid., 1:238. Among the other British women who studied music in Germany toward the end of the nineteenth century were Mary Wurm, Dora Schirmacher, Amina Goodwin, and Florence May. May is best known for her biography of Brahms.

25. Ibid., 1:165.

26. The Herzogenberg-Brahms correspondence often made reference to Ethel Smyth, who was nicknamed "our little English friend." Max Kalbeck, ed., *Johannes Brahms im Briefwechsel mit Heinrich und Elisabeth von*

Herzogenberg (Berlin: Deutsche Brahms-Gesellschaft, 1907). In a letter to Brahms, Clara Schumann mentioned Smyth, who was visiting the famous pianist. She stated, "I am surprised at the progress she has made and even if she has no originality as a composer, I cannot help feeling respect for such ability in a girl." Berthold Litzmann, ed., *The Letters of Clara Schumann and Johannes Brahms 1853–1896*, trans. A. M. Ludovici, 2 vols. (London: E. Arnold, 1927), 2:86. Although Brahms was not really interested in Smyth's compositions, he on occasion was shown a fugue by the English composer, and he praised a two-part invention in the style of Bach that she wrote as an exercise for Herzogenberg. Smyth, *Impressions That Remained*, 1:268.

27. For more information on Smyth's compositions from the Leipzig years, see Kathleen Dale, "Ethel Smyth's Prentice Work," *Music and Letters* 30 (1949): 329–36. A list of Ethel Smyth's works assembled by Kathleen Dale appears in St. John, *Ethel Smyth*, app. C, pp. 305–8.

28. Ethel Smyth to her mother, April 1878, in Smyth, *Impressions That Remained*, 2:236–37. Dr. Hase was referring to six songs by Fanny Mendelssohn that appeared under her brother Felix's name in two sets of his songs, opera 8 and 9; see Jack Werner, "Felix and Fanny Mendelssohn," *Music and Letters* 28 (1947): 303–36; and Rudolf Elvers, *Fanny Hensel, geb. Mendelssohn Bartholdy: Dokumente ihres Lebens, Ausstellung zum 125. Todestag im Mendelssohn-Archiv der Staatsbibliothek Preussischer Kulturbesitz* (Berlin, 1972). Three songs of Clara Schumann were published in 1841 by Breitkopf and Härtel in Robert Schumann's Opus 37; see Pamela Susskind, "Clara Wieck Schumann as Pianist and Composer: A Study of Her Life and Works," (Ph.D. diss., University of California–Berkeley, 1977). "A certain Frau Lang" is Josephine Lang (1815–80), a composer of songs and friend to the Mendelssohns and Clara Schumann. Her published works consist of forty-six opus numbers.

29. Smyth relates a conversation with the Russian composer: "he earnestly begged me to turn my attention at once to the orchestra and not be prudish about using the medium for all it is worth. 'What happens,' he asked, 'in ordinary conversation? If you have to do with really alive people, listen to the inflections in the voices . . . there's instrumentation for you!'" Smyth, *Impressions That Remained*, 2:168.

30. Donald F. Tovey, *Essays in Musical Analysis*, 6 vols. (London: Oxford University Press, 1937), 5:236.

31. Ethel Smyth, *As Time Went On* (London: Longmans, Green & Co., 1936), p. 46.

32. Ibid., p. 47.

33. In 1872 Offenbach also composed an opera on this comedy. See Alfred Loewenberg, *Annals of Opera 1597–1940*, 2d ed. (Geneva: Societas Bibliographica [1955]), p. 1020.

34. Henry Brewster to Ethel Smyth, 1896, in St. John, *Ethel Smyth*, p. 98.

35. See Ethel Smyth, "A Winter of Storm," in *Streaks of Life* (London:

Longmans, Green & Co., 1921), pp. 139–205, for an account of the Berlin production of *Der Wald*.

36. Ethel Smyth, *What Happened Next* (London: Longmans & Co., 1940), p. 205, gives the incorrect date of 14 July 1902 as the Covent Garden premiere. The first performance actually took place on 18 July; see, among other places, Loewenberg, *Annals of Opera*, p. 1240.

37. Not 14 March 1903 as stated by St. John, *Ethel Smyth*, p. 104; for correct date, see, among other places, Richard Aldrich, "Operatic Novelty at the Season's End," *New York Times*, 15 March 1903, p. 25, cols. 4–5.

38. Quoted in St. John, *Ethel Smyth*, p. 104.

39. Aldrich, "Operatic Novelties," p. 25, cols. 4–5.

40. Martin Cooper, "Stage Works: 1890–1918," in *New Oxford History of Music*, vol. 10, *The Modern Age, 1890–1960*, ed. Martin Cooper (London: Oxford University Press, 1974), p. 187.

41. Smyth, *As Time Went On*, p. 22. Smyth was not the only British composer to seek opera productions in Germany. Charles Villiers Stanford's first two operas, *Der Verschleierte Profet* (*The Veiled Prophet of Korassan*) and *Savanarola*, premiered in Hanover in 1881 and 1884 respectively. *Romeo und Julia auf dem Dorfe* (*A Village Romeo and Juliet*) by the expatriate Frederick Delius received its first production in Berlin in 1907.

42. Beecham, *A Mingled Chime*, p. 139.

43. Smyth, *What Happened Next*, p. 234.

44. Ibid.

45. The German translation was by Decker and Bernhoff; see White, *Rise of English Opera*, p. 263.

46. Earlier that month Nikisch conducted *On the Cliffs of Cornwall*, the prelude to act 2 of *The Wreckers*, at a London Symphony concert.

47. "I never was, nor am I now, a Wagnerite in the extreme sense of the word." Smyth, *As Time Went On*, p. 62.

48. Anonymous review in *London Times*, 23 June 1909, p. 10.

49. According to Sir Peter Pears and the archivist at the Britten-Pears Library in Aldeburgh, Britten did not know Smyth's opera, and the copy of *The Wreckers* in the Britten-Pears Library is a recent acquisition by Sir Peter Pears. I am grateful to Dr. Donald Mitchell for this information.

50. In 1922 Ethel Smyth was created Dame Commander of the Order of the British Empire. Four years later, Oxford conferred an honorary Doctorate of Music upon the composer.

51. Quoted in St. John, *Ethel Smyth*, p. 131.

52. Smyth included a brilliant study of Pankhurst and the composer's years with the suffragists in her book, *Female Pipings in Eden* (London: Peter Davies, 1933), pp. 185–290.

53. For an amusing account of Beecham's visit to Smyth in Holloway Prison, see Beecham, *A Mingled Chime*, pp. 138 ff.

54. St. John, *Ethel Smyth*, p. 151.

55. *1910*, for mixed chorus with (or without) band, like *March of the*

Women, was meant to inspire the suffragists to action. Although the lyrics of *1910* are trite ("Sounds of the battle raging around us, / Up and defy them, laugh in their faces!"), the music is more complicated both in harmony and part-writing than is that of *March of the Women*. These two choruses, along with *Laggard Dawn* for female chorus unaccompanied, were published by the composer in 1911.

56. Mentioned by Kathleen Dale, "Ethel Smyth's Music: A Critical Study," in St. John, *Ethel Smyth*, p. 301.

57. Beecham, *A Mingled Chime*, p. 139.

58. Not nine as stated and listed in *New Grove Dictionary*, 17:426. The complete list includes: *Impressions That Remained*, 2 vols. (London: Longmans, Green & Co., 1918); *Streaks of Life* (London: Longmans, Green & Co., 1921); *A Three-Legged Tour in Greece* (London: Wm. Heinemann, 1927); *A Final Burning of Boats* (London: Longmans, Green & Co., 1928); *Female Pipings in Eden* (London: Peter Davies, 1933); *Beecham and Pharoah* (London: Chapman & Hall, 1935); *As Time Went On* (London: Longmans, Green & Co., 1936); *Inordinate (?) Affection* (London: Cresset, 1936); *Maurice Baring* (London: Wm. Heinemann, 1938); and *What Happened Next* (London: Longmans, Green & Co., 1940).

59. In a letter to Smyth dated 6 June 1933 Woolf wrote: "I hate any writer to talk about himself; anonymity I adore. And this may be an obsession. I blush, I fidget, I turn hot and cold. I want to pull the curtain over this indecency." Quoted in St. John, *Ethel Smyth*, pp. 227–28.

60. Virginia Woolf to Lytton Strachey, 30 November 1919, in Virginia Woolf, *The Letters of Virginia Woolf*, 6 vols., ed. Nigel Nicolson and Joanne Trautman (London: Hogarth, 1975–80), vol. 2, *1912–1922* (1976), p. 405.

61. Smyth, *Impressions That Remained*, 2:6.

62. Quoted in Quentin Bell, *Virginia Woolf: A Biography*, 2 vols. in 1 (New York: Harcourt Brace Jovanovich, 1972), 2:151. See also Woolf, *Letters*, vol. 4, *1929–1931* (1978), p. 171.

63. Woolf, *Letters*, 4:302, gives the reader an excellent view of the Smyth-Woolf friendship, since Ethel Smyth played a dominant role in the writer's life during these three years. The main source for the Woolf-Smyth letters is the Henry W. and Albert A. Berg Collection of English and American Literature in the New York Public Library.

64. Smyth, *A Final Burning of Boats*, p. 115.

65. Smyth, *Impressions That Remained*, 1:261–70; see also "Recollections of Brahms," in id., *Female Pipings in Eden*, pp. 57–70.

66. Smyth, *Impressions That Remained*, 2:166.

67. Smyth, *A Final Burning of Boats*, p. 119.

68. St. John, *Ethel Smyth*, p. 176.

69. Smyth, *A Final Burning of Boats*, p. 120.

70. Her major feminist writings are *Female Pipings in Eden*, *A Final Burning of Boats*, and "An Open Secret," in *Streaks of Life*, pp. 231–46.

71. Smyth, *Streaks of Life*, p. 242.

72. Ibid., p. 239.

13

Passed Away Is the Piano Girl: Changes in American Musical Life, 1870–1900

JUDITH TICK

In 1904 James Huneker, noted critic and music journalist, sounded the death of a nineteenth-century stereotype, whom he called the "piano girl":

Passed away is the girl who played the piano in the stiff Victorian drawing rooms of our mothers. It has always seemed to me that slippery hair-cloth sofas and the "Battle of Prague" dwelt in mutual harmony. And now at the beginning of the century the girls who devote time to the keyboard merely for the purpose of social display are almost as rare as the lavender water ladies of morbid sensibilities in the Richardson and Fielding novels. . . . I wonder if the musical girl of the old sort may not also set down for study—the study we accord to rare and disappearing types. Yet never has America been so musical. . . . Here is a pretty paradox: the piano is passing and with it the piano girl—there really was a piano girl—and more music was never made before in the land![1]

However lovingly she had been portrayed in genre paintings or popular illustrations of the early nineteenth-century artists, in the literary world of music criticism and in the polemical world of cultural feminism she was the archsymbol of the dilettante. According to Huneker, she had been replaced by the "new girl":

The piano girl was forced to practice at the keyboard, even if without talent. Every girl played the piano, not to play was a stigma of poverty. The new girl is too busy to play the piano unless she has the gift; then she plays with consuming earnestness. We listen to her, for we know that this is an age of specialization, an age when woman is coming into her own, be it nursing, electoral suffrage, or the writing of plays; so our poets no longer make sonnets to our Ladies of Ivories, nor are budding girls chained to the keyboard.[2]

There is an earnestness that marks all self-conscious periods of change. Because we know that many people continue to practice without talent and that, even yet, girls are more likely to take piano lessons than are boys, it is difficult to believe in the demise of the piano girl entirely. But that level of human truth need not obscure the real issue of social and economic change. For women musicians, the late nineteenth century, particularly the 1890s, was one such period.

Whereas in 1870 women played the piano, harp, or guitar for the most part, by 1900 there were professional violinists and professional all-women orchestras. In 1870 women composers wrote parlor songs; even fewer wrote parlor piano music. By 1900 there had been premieres of concertos and a symphony by American women.

The change involved more than numbers. From a sociological viewpoint, instrumental performance and composition can be seen as occupations whose sexual definitions were in transition as well: they were no longer exclusively sex-typed as male.[3] The concept of occupational sex-typing, therefore, includes cultural values and beliefs that justify sexual distribution on normative grounds. Thus rationalizations of the division of labor within music that had previously excluded women from professional musicianship were also affected by changes in the definition of women's work.

Census data between 1870 and 1900 document this trend. As table 4 indicates, the percentage of women employed in music between those years rose dramatically from 36 percent to 56.4 percent. Music was, according to the 1900 census, one of the professions whose sex distribution altered most between 1880 and 1900.

Because the census after 1870 does not distinguish between musician and music teacher, we can only infer the distribution of employment increase from other kinds of evidence. It seems likely, however, that women were heavily represented within music teaching. In 1870, for example, women constituted only 2 percent of the professional musicians but 60 percent of the teachers. In 1897 the president of the Music Teachers National Association estimated that half the membership was female.[4] Many music teachers outside of the big cities did not belong to the association but were tallied in the census data. They were invariably women.

As teaching became increasingly competitive, the shortage of work also stimulated women into expanding their occupational ambitions within music. Caroline Nichols, the conductor of a celebrated female orchestra in the 1890s, cited unemployment and the

Table 4
Women in Music and Music Teaching, 1870–1910
Percent Female

	1870	1880	1890	1900	1910
Musicians	2 (6,519)**	*	*	*	*
Music teachers	60 (9,491)**	*	*	*	*
Total	36	43	55	56.4	66
Total employed in profession	(16,010)**	(30,477)	(62,155)	(92,174)	(139,310)

*Not available. After 1870 the census does not distinguish between music and music teaching.

**Numbers in parentheses indicate total number of males and females in the occupation.

SOURCE: U.S. Census Reports, 1870–1910.

oversupply of teachers as the major motivation behind her work.[5] Similarly, Camilla Urso, the famous violinist, demanded that women be admitted to theater orchestras for reasons of livelihood. In a paper delivered before the Women's Musical Congress at the 1893 Chicago World's Fair, Urso cited the "many hundred good female violinists who are now without work." Five years later, in a letter to the *Musical Courier*, Urso reiterated her position that women should be admitted to orchestras on an equal footing with men: "Let my sisters agitate this question and assert their rights. It will in time benefit women with scanty means who have spent their time and money, when now men alone profit."[6]

The mere existence of large numbers of professional female violinists, in or out of work, marked a significant change from the past. Tradition decreed that the piano, harp, and guitar were the appropriate feminine instruments.[7] They were instruments for domestic entertainment and required no facial exertions or body movements that interfered with the portrait of grace the lady musician was to emanate. Scanty evidence reassures us that such strictures were not regarded as natural laws. We know of a female seminary (or girls' school) in Madison, Georgia, that dared to teach its young pupils string instruments in the 1850s.[8] The activities of all-women brass bands were reported in local newspapers; and a female cornet player became famous in the 1870s, as also did a female saxophonist in the 1890s.[9] But, by and large, women did not learn orchestral instruments to any significant degree until the 1870s, and here change was focused on string instruments rather than on winds or brass.

By 1900 the violin had become an accepted instrument for women. In an article on "Woman as a Violinist" (March 1882), the editor of the *Musical World* commented on the changing attitudes. As a vernacular instrument, the "fiddle" was "accused of evil influences"; as a cultivated instrument, it lost its lower-class connotations and was respectable enough for women to play. The climate of opinion changed for a number of reasons. For one thing, two women became famous concert violinists during the 1870s and 1880s. Both Maud Powell and Camilla Urso established precedents for other women and advocated equal opportunities for women instrumentalists.[10]

Another factor was the influence of Julius Eichberg, the founder of the Boston Conservatory of Music. Eichberg, who taught both male and female pupils to play the violin, received considerable publicity from recitals at which his female pupils performed.[11] In an article on "Lady Violinists" for *Town and Country* (April 1879), Eichberg wrote, "We gladly espouse the cause of women's right to play upon all the instruments of the orchestra." By the 1880s Eichberg's female pupils had formed the Eichberg Ladies String Quartette and the Eichberg String Orchestra, giving concerts in New York as well as Boston.

The friendly press Eichberg received reflected civic pride in the establishment of musical groups that enhanced Boston's leadership in the cultivated tradition, as well as the relative ease with which prejudice against women playing string instruments was altered. For example, on 20 January 1888, the *Boston Herald* published an article on "Girl Violinists: An Innovation That Has Been Followed by Good Results," which included the following:

At the present time nothing is more common than to see upon the streets of our towns and cities, and especially in Boston, girls carrying jauntily a violin case. . . .

Twenty-five years ago, a girl appearing upon frequented streets with such a burden would have been subjected to much staring and muttered comment . . . if not downright persecution. But a good many things may happen within 25 years, and under the modern view of things girls may aspire to almost any attainment of which humanity is capable. The girl of today will astonish no one, even if she carries about the cornet or trombone, as well as the violin. . . .

The change in situation is due to Julius Eichberg. . . . He declares that girls are in every respect the equal of boys. And thus it happened that in his department of musical teaching and performance, as in so many others, Boston long since took the lead, and today representatives of her violinists of the "softer sex" astonish audiences.

At a concert given in New York by the Eichberg Ladies String Quartette the critic for the *Musical Review* (1 January 1880) acknowledged that a "regular string quartette of ladies is an unusual phenomenon: Boston really has something we can not match."

But female musicians in New York were turning their marginal status in the musical world to advantage by organizing "lady orchestras." While Eichberg was teaching young Bostonian ladies, New Yorkers were patronizing female musicians in the theatres and music halls. Lady orchestras became popular attractions in New York during the 1870s. Their model was probably the Vienna Damen Orchestra, led by Josephine Weinlich, which performed in the United States in 1871.[12] They originated as a feature of German-American life in the city, most of them playing the German music halls in lower Manhattan, such as the Volksgarten and the Atlantic Garten. The musicians in the 1870s were typically German, and the earliest such groups are listed by Odell, in his *Chronicles of the New York Stage*, as "Damen Orchesters."

Lady orchestras were a standard feature of New York entertainment for the rest of the century (see table 5). Like the female minstrel troupes, they exploited the prejudice that made them oddities, since the curiosity value of women playing cornets or double basses could attract audiences on that basis alone. Indeed, so important were their reputations as all-female troupes that if a musician were needed and a woman could not be found, then a man would dress as a woman in order to substitute.[13]

The most famous local lady orchestra in New York was the Ladies' Elite at the Atlantic Garden, a feature there for over thirty-five years.[14] In the 1880s the troupe was managed by Charles Eschert, xylophonist and general musician about town. As a manager of a musical bureau, Eschert capitalized on the popularity of the group by advertising "lady orchestras" as his specialty, available for "concerts, private entertainments, dinners, and parties."[15] The size and repertory of the Ladies' Elite varied over the years. The songwriter Ed Marks recalled in his memoirs a cornetist, bass player, and drum-

Table 5
Lady Orchestras in New York and Boston

1871	Vienna Damen Orchester
1873	Damen-Orchester (Bowery Garden)
1879	Berlin Lady Orchestra (Tivoli Garden)
1880–81	Marie Roller's "Elite Kapelle" (Atlantic Garden)
	Carl Eschert's Ladies' Elite (Atlantic Garden)
1882	The Ladies' Philharmony (Koster and Bial's Concert Hall)
	Marie Roller's Damen Orchester
	California Damen Orchester (Volksgarten)
1888	Ladies' Amateur Orchestra (Lyceum Theater)
	Boston Fadette Lady Orchestra
1891	Ladies Schubert Quartette
1891–92	Blanche Walters's Damen-Orchester (Volksgarten)
1891	Marion Osgood's Ladies Orchestra of Boston (YMCA Hall, Brooklyn)
1892	Eschert's Ladies Elite (Atlantic Garden)
1894	New York Ladies Orchestra
1896	Women's String Orchestra of New York
1898	Women's String Quartette of New York

SOURCE: Mainly George Odell, *Annals of the New York Stage*, 10 vols. (New York: Columbia University Press, 1927–31).

mer playing *Daisy, Daisy* in the 1890s.[16] But the orchestra numbers interspersed between the vaudeville acts could also include Johann Strauss and Meyerbeer.[17]

Only in this special capacity were female instrumentalists tolerated by the more conservative elements of the musical establishment. In 1895 the *Musical Courier* noted that "with a *light repertoire*, no traveling to do and no arduous rehearsals, they [all-women orchestras] might make a success as a unique feature in social engagements."[18] The idea that women ought to play only the light repertoire was simply a further elaboration of prejudice. Consequently, any occasion that demonstrated woman's ability to play the best of the cultivated tradition was celebrated as proof of her musical equality. One such concert was held in conjunction with the Columbian Exposition. A publication of the suffrage movement reported it with great pleasure:

Women as players and composers are coming into prominence in musical festivals and on great public occasions. A grand orchestra of 65 women players is to take part in the concerts of the Columbian festival to be given in

Boston on May 4, 5, 6, & 7. . . . So far as is known, this will be the first festival event of such magnitude in which women players have been given such prominence. The orchestra is to perform in conjunction with a great Sousa band the same compositions played by the N.Y. Symphony Orchestra and the Sousa band at the Carnegie Music Hall, April 16, i.e., Meyerbeer's Torchlight Dance and . . . the "Battle Hymn" from Wagner's "Rienzi," and the "Gathering of the Armies" from "Lohengrin". . . . The thanks of all women are due to Manager D. Blakely for this recognition of women as orchestral players in the higher class of compositions.[19]

By 1900 a number of reputable female orchestras and string quartets were playing the "higher class of compositions," among them the New York Women's String Orchestra and the Schubert Quartette of Boston. The most famous women's group, the Boston Fadette Orchestra, was organized in 1888. Unlike the Ladies' Elite, the Fadettes were not attached to a local theatre but became a major entertainment attraction with a national reputation. The Fadettes were organized by a pioneer woman conductor, Caroline Nichols. The original group of six expanded to twenty by 1898, when the vaudeville manager B. F. Keith booked them into his theatres all over the United States. Between 1890 and 1920 Nichols claimed that the Fadettes gave over 6,000 concerts, half of them as headliners in first-class vaudeville theatres.[20]

In some ways the Fadettes were a hybrid form of entertainment. As a vaudeville act they had comic routines, such as that described by the vaudeville performer Joe Laurie: "They had a bit where the all-girl group got mad and walked out and Caroline replaced them, playing ten different instruments."[21] The Fadettes naturally traveled in more polite society in Boston, where they were patronized by prominent people in the musical world, such as B. F. Lang and George Chickering. Their repertory showed equal diversity. Nichols describes it as "classical, standard, and popular." It included "many symphonies, all the classic overtures of 75 grand operas and numberless salon pieces of popular appeal as well as a complete collection of dramatic descriptive numbers which were used in the early silent moving pictures at Roxy's Theatre."[22] The mixture of vaudeville routines with symphonies reflects the peculiar position of the female instrumentalist in an orchestral world defined as masculine. Since women were excluded from permanent city or theatre orchestras, the best option was the free-lance performing organization that required a flexible repertory for survival.

The entrance of women into the orchestral world thus reflects the ways in which occupational sex-typing used prejudice to support

331

economic discrimination. The prejudice against women instrumentalists and the expansion of their musical opportunities to include
all instruments of the orchestra produced relatively little friction in
the musical world until it was accompanied by the threat of economic
competition. This threat was then met through the elaboration of
social segregation.[23] The institution of lady orchestras simultaneously removed women from the open job market while it exploited
their difference from the majority group. Just as black performers entered the entertainment world through genres that exploited racial
stereotypes, women formed their own separate orchestras. They too
got their start within vernacular rather than cultivated institutions.
Therefore by 1900 orchestral performance modified its sex-typed
connotations as a masculine field just enough to allow women room
on the periphery.

What most female players wanted, however, was just what union
discrimination denied them: the "strain of competition with men."[24]
As one member of the Ladies' Elite Orchestra said:

If I had the chance to substitute for a man I should do so in a minute and
should look for more and better opportunities to follow. By accepting them
we women gain a foothold in the orchestra world, and that is what we are all
ambitious for. Now we are limited to concert work or to musical organizations composed entirely of women. I am sure a great many of us could hold
our own with the majority of men. . . .[25]

Until 1904 the Musicians Union legally excluded women from
playing in union controlled public orchestras. However, when the
union became affiliated with the American Federation of Labor, it
could no longer legally deny women membership. At that point, the
union enrolled 4,500 members in New York City, thirty-one of them
women. Ten of those women were members of the still surviving
Ladies' Elite Orchestra at Atlantic Garden.

The change of policy was, of course, an inadvertent by-product of
the new labor affiliation. It caught New York conductors by surprise
and they reacted accordingly. The *Musical Standard* collected their
reactions in an article entitled "Opinions of Some New York Leaders
on Women as Orchestral Players." The consensus of opinion was
negative, as most of those interviewed resurrected the nineteenth-
century stereotype about feminine frailty—that women lacked the
strength to play wind or brass instruments:

Women harpists are most desirable in an orchestra but as cornetists, clarinet-
ists, flutists and the like, they are quite impossible, except in concert work.

Women cannot possibly play brass instruments and look pretty, and why should they spoil their looks? [26]

Women would derive only one real benefit from the new rules; they would now receive equal pay for equal work, whereas before "they had to take what was offered."

Lest any woman take offense at this low opinion of female musicians, one conductor of a theatre orchestra concluded his diatribe with gallantry: "Woman, lovely woman, is always to be admired, except when she is playing in an orchestra." Therefore, prejudice was simply the patina of belief glossing over the real fear of job competition. As the conductor of the Metropolitan Orchestra commented: "In a little while men will wake up to find that they are closely and successfully being pushed in one more sphere by the fair sex . . . fewer and fewer positions [will be] ready and waiting for them." [27]

The patterns described in the development of lady orchestras and instrumental training for women follow the sociological model of occupational change in which there is a correlation between social opinion and job opportunity. Prejudices against women players were rationalizations designed to protect the limited job market against competition. With respect to composition, however, the historical flow of opinion and the need for such prejudice is less obvious. There is no job market for composers equivalent to that for performers. Furthermore, the issues involved in the debate about women composers were weighty intellectual concepts about creativity and biological determinism rather than social propriety and money. The debate was all the more fierce for its abstractions.

The debate over women as composers began in the 1880s with the publication of George Upton's book *Woman in Music*. The opinions of Upton, who was a prominent critic for the *Chicago Tribune*, carried a great deal of weight. His work went through two editions by 1899 and was consistently referred to in articles of the period and of the 1900s.

Essentially, Upton's main concern was to resolve a central paradox in nineteenth-century beliefs. If music was the art of emotions, it logically followed that women, who were believed to be more emotional than men, should excel in its creation. According to Upton, however, woman failed because she could not objectify emotion by translating it into any other medium. She could experience and re-create, that is, execute; but she could not create. Furthermore, music was not *all* feeling. It also depended upon the ability to think logically and to abstract, both exclusively male powers:

Every technical detail of music is characterized by science in its most rigid forms. In this direction woman, except in rare instances, has never achieved great results. It does not seem that women will ever originate music in its fullest and grandest harmonic forms. She will always be the recipient and interpreter but there is little hope that she will be the creator.[28]

Musical creativity was, therefore, masculine by definition because it relied on male intellectual and psychological resources. Music was, as a writer in the *Atlantic Monthly* termed it, a "masculine idea." There neither had ever been nor ever could be a great female composer. Women did not have recourse to greater emotional resources, because men were actually more "emotional" than women: "Woman as the lesser man is comparatively deficient in active emotional force. . . . Much of what passes in women for true emotion is mere nervous excitability." Wagner's operas and Beethoven's symphonies are good examples of the kind of music women can't write because of their lack of emotional power.[29]

These arguments were countered by veterans of the women's rights movements and their sympathizers. Alice Stone Blackwell, a leading feminist and editor of the *Women's Journal*, wrote:

It is probably true that more women than men have received musical instruction of a sort, but not of the sort which qualifies anyone to become a composer. Girls are as a rule taught music superficially, simply as an accomplishment. To enable them to play and sing agreeably is the whole object of their music lessons. It is exceedingly rare that a girl's father cares to have her taught the underlying laws of harmony or the principles of musical composition.

In Germany and Italy, the countries where the greatest musical composers have originated, the standard of women's education is especially low and the idea of woman's sphere particularly restricted. The German or Italian girl who should confess an ambition to become a composer would be regarded by her friends as out her sphere, if not out of her mind.

When women have had for several centuries the same advantages of liberty, education, and social encouragement in the use of their brains that men have, it will be right to argue their mental inferiority if they have not produced their fair share of geniuses. But it is hardly reasonable to expect women during a few years of half liberty and half education to produce at once specimens of genius equal to the choicest men of all the ages.[30]

The role of patron was also attacked. The image of woman as muse, so precious to writers like Ruskin or George Upton, who filled his book on women in music with vignettes about composers' wives, was rejected with the kind of arguments Amy Fay, renowned pianist and teacher, used in 1900 to explain the lack of a great female composer:

Women have been too much taken with helping and encouraging men to place a proper value on their own talent, which they are prone to underestimate and to think not worth making the most of. Their whole training from time immemorial has tended to make them take an intense interest in the work of men and to stimulate them to their best efforts. Ruskin was quite right when he so patronizingly said that "Woman's chief function is praise." She has praised and praised and kept herself in abeyance.[31]

In the lead article for the *Etude* special issue, *Women in Music* (September 1901), Fanny Morris Smith specifically rebutted Upton's ideas, disparaging the looseness of most discussions of the "woman question." The contributions of women in the past were greater than Upton allowed, she argued, while their opportunities in the present were far less. The two major reasons why women as a class had not composed in the nineteenth century were thus stated:

The noble masculine spirit who cheered and upheld the fainting hopes of the feminine musical genius has yet to make his appearance in history. . . . The other great reason why women did not compose much before the last part of the nineteenth century is because they had, as a class, *no money*. They did not support themselves, as a rule, and had no control of the funds necessary for a composer's education or for publication.

The significance of feminist arguments is the mode in which they rebutted nineteenth-century attitudes toward women. In effect, they used arguments about socialization and environment to counter psychological and biological determinism. In so doing, they indirectly focused on the sociological aspects of musical creativity. In opposition to the romantic notions of the creative artist in artistic isolation and the romantic belief in the "rational male" as opposed to the "intuitive female," feminist musicians argued about the effect of class and status on creativity. Society could not determine which individual would be gifted with genius, but it could determine which groups had access to the institutions that support art. No one could become a musician in an Emily Dickinson attic. Society could also shape the expectations about the potentialities of groups that acted as self-fulfilling prophecies.

The "emancipated woman," of which the new female composer was one representative, knew better. She no longer believed that musical creativity was masculine. As Florence Sutro wrote in 1893:

Great intellectual effort and strong reasoning [are not] . . . the proprietary right of men. Fortunately my sex has already sufficiently advanced in its revolutionary progress through mental emancipation that it no longer accepts such doctrines as those as law.

We have begun to think for ourselves. And as we think for ourselves, we shall begin to compose.[32]

The politically charged cultural climate produced countless other articles repeating the charges of discrimination or claims of mental emancipation.[33] Certainly, the handbooks and dictionaries tended to inflate contributions of women composers, past and present. But they were provoked or countered by equally biased attacks on the music of women composers or on the women's movement in general. The reviewer of Otto Ebel's *Women Composers* wrote in 1903:

Some men and a few women, disposed to be just, have not hesitated to declare that until a woman produces a masterpiece the fair sex cannot hope to take high rank as composers. The strongminded sisterhood, on the other hand, looking as usual through lurid glasses, claim that there are some great women composers, and the reason there are not more is wholly the fault of man's selfishness and tyranny. Education and independence were denied to women for centuries after these blessed privileges were vouchsafed to men; hence why expect women to be the equal of men in all things? No one expects it, dear sisters.[34]

The polemics surrounding the female composer inevitably affected the kind of music she wrote and the ways in which it was received. The conflict between her role as a woman and her role as a composer was resolved through the development of sexual aesthetics, which analyzed music as a combination of masculine and feminine traits; therefore, music written by women should and did express "femininity." As descriptive metaphors, the terms *masculine* and *feminine* were hardly alien to nineteenth-century music criticism. Schumann, for example, described a pair of Schubert trios in just such terms: Opus 99 was "more passive, lyric and feminine," while Opus 100 was "active, masculine and dramatic."[35] Furthermore, as metaphors used to describe the expressive range of music, such language did not *logically* need to confine the woman composer. She, like Schubert, could write either masculine or feminine music. However, the language of Romantic music criticism degenerated into the language of sexual aesthetics, in which the potentialities of the individual female composer were defined through the application of sexual stereotypes.

Femininity in music was alleged to be delicate, graceful, refined,

Table 6
"Femininity" and "Masculinity" in Music c. 1900

	Eternal Feminine (ewige weibliche)	*Man-tone*[36] *(virile)*
1. Emotive content	delicate, sensitive, graceful, refined, spontaneous	powerful, broad, noble
2. Musical qualities	lyrical, melodious	intellectual, theoretical (e.g., use of harmony or counterpoint)
3. Genres	songs, piano pieces (the "smaller forms")	symphonies, opera, chamber music (the "higher class" of compositions)
4. Model composers	Chopin, Mendelssohn	Beethoven, Wagner

and sensitive. It was defined as the *eternal feminine* (sometimes by the German phrase *ewige weibliche*), which was drawn from Goethe's concept of womanhood. (Because of the great vogue of German music, especially Wagnerian opera, in the late nineteenth century, the German term was frequently used by American critics.) Through 1900 the aesthetics of the eternal feminine in music included both form and style, as well as emotive content (see table 6 for a summary comparison). Vocal music was the essence of ewige weibliche because it "appeals more directly to the heart."[37] Since harmony and counterpoint were "logical," they were alien to femininity. Instead of musical intellect, women were supposed to rely on their imaginations, from which "beautiful melodies could flow." The concert pianist Fanny Bloomfield-Zeisler believed in this allegedly inherent sex difference. She wrote:

I am no "woman's emancipator." There are many fields of intellectual activity which women never do or can trespass without sacrificing their more delicate or sensitive nature, the *ewige weibliche* (ever womanly). . . . What we need now is not to imitate man and try to become great in a field in which he has achieved success, but to develop those qualities which specifically belong to woman . . . that is, beautiful melodies.[38]

Romantic ideology traditionally defined women as emotional and passive and men as objective and active. Probably the hardening of the polarities in music criticism was no different from that taking place in other intellectual spheres.[39] Theories of evolution had raised the issue of biological determinism; and creativity, like power, was seen as fixed by genetic heritage. For women composers, the belief in sex-determined achievement reinforced centuries of traditional discrimination.

The eternal-feminine aesthetic, therefore, provided a referential vocabulary in which the music of composers could be judged by a double standard that placed them in a double bind. If, on the one hand, they composed in the smaller "feminine" forms, such as songs and piano pieces, they were thereby demonstrating their sexually derived inadequacies to think in the larger abstract forms. If, on the other hand, they attempted the larger forms, they were betraying their sexual identities by writing "man-tone" music. Sexual aesthetics therefore functioned as a way of keeping female composers on the traditional periphery of composition.

Even Rupert Hughes, a critic sympathetic to women composers, distinguished between the eternal feminine and the man-tone music of symphonies and operas. He charitably allowed that "art knows no sex"; nonetheless, women writing in "man-tone" were "seeking after virility."[40] Hughes cited the songs of Margaret Lang as examples of the "supremely womanly" in art:

Some of Miss Lang's frailer songs show the qualities many people expect in womanliness more than the works of any of these other writers. . . . The "Spinning Song" is inexpressibly sad, and such music as women best understand, and therefore ought to make best. But womanliness equally marks "The Grief of Love" . . . marks the bitterness of "Oh, What Comes over the Sea." Her "Lament" I consider one of the greatest of songs, and proof positive of woman's high capabilities for composition.

Hughes judged Lang's work by the degree to which the emotive content of her work corresponded to his ideas about womanliness: "Personally, I see in Miss Lang's composition such a depth of psychology that I place the general quality of her work above that of any other composer. It is devoid of meretriciousness and of any suspicion of seeking after virility."

Despite all of this, the late nineteenth century witnessed two constructive changes for women composers. One, a correlate of the debate over the woman question, was an enormous increase in women composers' visibility, that is to say, public acknowledgment that they existed. Even though numbers of women had published sheet music before 1870, they had never achieved public status comparable to that of their contemporaries in literature. By the 1890s this was changing. In an article for *Century Magazine*, critic Rupert Hughes wrote: "Only yesterday it was being said how strange it was that women could not write music. Today their compositions make up a surprisingly large portion of the total publication. . . . Now the manuscripts submitted by women outnumber those of the men two to one."[41] Those who in the past had denied female creativity would no doubt change their views if they could but hear the music of American women. For it was "the very dawn of what . . . is to be a great epoch of composition by women." Otto Ebel echoed these sentiments a few years later:

Scarcely 50 years ago the subjects of harmony and counterpoint had been considered outside the province of women's education, and the acquirement of such knowledge, other than as a pastime, would have been regarded as a mental aberration. . . . It therefore must be considered a great point gained that it is no longer looked upon as an eccentricity for women to compose.[42]

Music journals, concert societies, and professional organizations acknowledged women composers in a variety of ways quite similar to those in the 1970s. Both the *Etude*[43] and the *Musician* instituted feature columns on women's work in music, the latter designed to celebrate "the increasing activity of women in all phases of musical life, her aggressive and authoritative entrance in spheres heretofore monopolized by men."[44] The percentage of women in the New York Manuscript Society, a professional composers' organization, doubled between 1892 and 1898. In 1895 and 1900 the society gave concerts devoted entirely to women composers.[45] (See plate 19.) At the annual meetings of the Music Teachers National Association in 1897, a "woman's department" was headed by Florence Sutro; it included lectures on women's history, an exhibition, and concerts.[46] Sutro was also the first president of the National Federation of Music Clubs, which was founded in 1898. From its inception, the federation provided an arena for the promotion and performance of music by women.[47]

All this is not to suggest that there were no women composers in the United States before the Civil War. By the 1870s women had indeed been accepted as composers within the proscribed sphere of parlor music, which in fact was the dominating musical culture of prewar American urban life.[48] English composers, such as Virginia

Plate 19
Program of an early concert of music by women composers

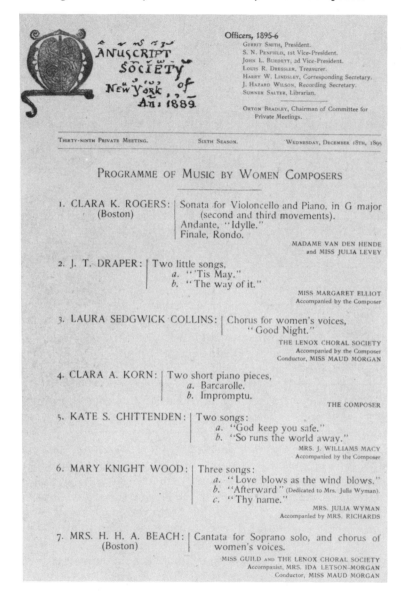

Officers, 1895-6
GERRIT SMITH, President.
S. N. PENFIELD, 1st Vice-President.
JOHN L. BURDETT, 2d Vice-President.
LOUIS R. DRESSLER, Treasurer.
HARRY W. LINDSLEY, Corresponding Secretary.
J. HAZARD WILSON, Recording Secretary.
SUMNER SALTER, Librarian.

ORTON BRADLEY, Chairman of Committee for
Private Meetings.

THIRTY-NINTH PRIVATE MEETING.   SIXTH SEASON.   WEDNESDAY, DECEMBER 18TH, 1895

PROGRAMME OF MUSIC BY WOMEN COMPOSERS

1. CLARA K. ROGERS: | Sonata for Violoncello and Piano, in G major
   (Boston) | (second and third movements).
                      | Andante, "Idylle."
                      | Finale, Rondo.
                                MADAME VAN DEN HENDE
                                and MISS JULIA LEVEY

2. J. T. DRAPER: | Two little songs,
                 | a. "'Tis May."
                 | b. "The way of it."
                                MISS MARGARET ELLIOT
                                Accompanied by the Composer

3. LAURA SEDGWICK COLLINS: | Chorus for women's voices,
                           | "Good Night."
                                THE LENOX CHORAL SOCIETY
                                Accompanied by the Composer
                                Conductor, MISS MAUD MORGAN

4. CLARA A. KORN: | Two short piano pieces,
                  | a. Barcarolle.
                  | b. Impromptu.
                                THE COMPOSER

5. KATE S. CHITTENDEN: | Two songs:
                       | a. "God keep you safe."
                       | b. "So runs the world away."
                                MRS. J. WILLIAMS MACY
                                Accompanied by the Composer

6. MARY KNIGHT WOOD: | Three songs:
                     | a. "Love blows as the wind blows."
                     | b. "Afterward" (Dedicated to Mrs. Julia Wyman).
                     | c. "Thy name."
                                MRS. JULIA WYMAN
                                Accompanied by MRS. RICHARDS

7. MRS. H. H. A. BEACH: | Cantata for Soprano solo, and chorus of
   (Boston) | women's voices.
                                MISS GUILD AND THE LENOX CHORAL SOCIETY
                                Accompanist, MRS. IDA LETSON-MORGAN
                                Conductor, MISS MAUD MORGAN

Source: Music Division, New York Public Library at Lincoln Center,
Astor, Lenox, and Tilden Foundations

Gabriel and Charlotte Allington Barnard,[49] and their far fewer American counterparts, such as Faustina Hodges (1822–95) and Mrs. E. A. (Susan) Parkhurst (1836–1918), both wrote parlor songs that musicalized upper-middle-class notions of a woman's "sphere." It is telling that Hodges's famous song, *The Rose Bush* (1859), was described by a critic as "an epitome of woman's life."[50]

Between 1870 and 1900 parlor music lost its dominating hold on taste, partly because musical forms at opposite ends of the spectrum developed larger audiences, economic foundations, and greater commercial potential. For women these created new options to a certain extent, and most of these options came within the world of classical rather than popular music. With respect to composition, only a very few women seem to have benefited from the enormous growth of the popular-song industry in the 1890s. To be sure, there were more women performers within minstrel shows and early vaudeville. After 1870 the barrier against the appearance of women on the stage as actress-singers in minstrel shows was broken, with the rise of burlesque and the eclectic postwar minstrel troupes that included blacks as well as women.[51] But apart from an occasional singer-turned-songwriter, such as Maud Nugent, and a few ragtime composers, Tin Pan Alley was not the milieu to which women songwriters gravitated.[52]

Despite the large number of women writing songs, the whole tradition of music as an "accomplishment" predisposed them toward what is still regarded as the margins of popular song—the semi-classical genres—rather than the urban ethnic song that fed Tin Pan Alley. It is significant that the most successful female song composer of this period—Carrie Jacobs-Bond—had to start her own music publishing company to print the songs that were rejected by Tin Pan Alley publishers for being too "classical."[53] Bond and other composers like Mary Turner Salter and Mary Knight Wood continued to write Victorian parlor songs through the turn of the century. Such songs as Salter's *The Cry of Rachel* (1905) and Wood's *Ashes of Roses* (1892) are descendants of Hodges's *The Rose Bush*.

In contrast, women made more striking progress as classical composers. The 1890s witnessed a number of historic firsts in the composition and performance of their works in the "higher forms" of orchestral and choral music: among them the first orchestral composition by a woman to be performed by a major American symphony orchestra; the first symphony, the first concerto, and the first large-scale choral composition. It is beyond the scope of this study to examine the lives and works of individual composers in detail, but the major achievements of the period are worth noting.[54]

The outstanding figures in the 1890s were Margaret Ruthven Lang (1867–1972), Helen Hopekirk (1856–1945), and Amy Cheney Beach (1867–1943). To Lang goes the honor of having the first performance of an orchestral work. Her *Dramatic Overture* was played by the Boston Symphony in 1893. Between 1893 and 1896 she also wrote two other orchestral overtures, *Totila* and *Wichitis*, and three arias for solo voice and orchestra, all of which received performances. Helen Hopekirk was a Scottish concert pianist who emigrated to Boston in 1897. Her American premiere tour included a performance with the Boston Symphony Orchestra in 1883, and she performed her Piano Concerto in D Major with that orchestra in 1900. The concerto was her second work for piano and orchestra; an early *Concertstück*, written in Europe, had been played in 1894.

The most famous and by far the most important of the turn-of-the-century women composers was Amy Cheney Beach, known throughout her long career as Mrs. H. H. A. Beach. Beach was the first American woman to achieve an international reputation as a composer of orchestral and chamber music, in addition to many compositions for piano and voice.[55] Her Mass in E-flat was performed by the Boston Handel and Haydn Society in 1892; her Gaelic Symphony in E Minor (1896) was a landmark work. It was followed in 1899 by a Piano Concerto in C-sharp Minor, which Beach performed with the Boston Symphony Orchestra.

How is the intense activity of this particular decade to be explained? Without doubt some of the factors that led to the growth of lady orchestras contributed here as well. More women were entering the labor force. A sense prevailed that the "superfluous women"— who might never marry—had to take work seriously, and more women were attending the newly founded conservatories. There was also an ideology of cultural feminism, at least for the upper-middle classes, and we have already mentioned the activities of the National Federation of Music Clubs in promoting works by women composers. Further evidence of political mobilization can be seen in the founding of the Women's Philharmonic Society in New York in 1899 by Amy Fay, the pianist, and her sister, Melusina Fay Pierce. The society was deliberately intended to "promote effort and achievement— in the performance, composition, theory, and history of music."[56]

More particularly there was a factor of place. Just as the court of Ferrara had served to nurture the talents of women singers in late sixteenth-century Italy, the city of Boston served as a similar hub in the 1890s. It took its role as cultural center seriously, and the education of women and their role in the community were matters of civic consciousness. Not for nothing did Henry James place his novel about feminism in that city.[57] Boston had a tradition of supporting American composers; it also had a publishing house—that of Arthur P. Schmidt—which printed contemporary music. More to the point, we have already mentioned the influence of Julius Eichberg in training female instrumentalists. Boston was also the home of a group of composers sufficiently focused there to become known as the "Boston group": George Chadwick, who taught Margaret Lang and Helen Hood; Arthur Foote; and John Knowles Paine.

The women active in composition also had strong ties to the cultural institutions of the city, such as the Boston Symphony Orchestra, the Handel and Haydn Society, and the Caecilia Club. Amy Beach and Helen Hopekirk were performers and soloists with the orchestra. Margaret Lang was the daughter of a prominent local musician. Her "easy and casual access to the Symphony," to quote music-historian Laurine Elkins-Marlow, was remarkable. Lang recalled in an interview late in her life: "They told me to take some Grieg to the orchestra and hear how it sounded so I could learn about orchestration. So I went to one of Nikisch's rehearsals and they played it for me. Things were so easy in those days."[58]

The significance of the achievements of this generation of women composers can be gauged by the number of years that passed before their work was matched. Beach's Symphony in E Minor (1896) retained its singularity until 1932. Her concerto (1899) and that of Hopekirk (1900) were followed by one in 1908, the work of another Boston composer, Mabel Daniels, and then by no other until 1925.[59] In addition, the 1890s—their fledgling years as composers—were obviously special, since what followed tended to be smaller works: in some cases pieces for women's chorus, in others chamber music and solo piano compositions.[60]

Obviously the process by which women composers came of age was begun but not completed in the 1890s. Their compositions were not, surprisingly, treated without a certain amount of ambivalence, given their exceptional status and the critical climate of which we have already spoken. The social grammar of sexual judgment was there to be used. To take one example, both virility and femininity were ascribed to Beach's symphony. Its premiere on 30 October 1896 was a controversial event. Both its virtues and its faults were alleged illustrations of the "eternal feminine." The *Women's Journal* chronicled the event on 6 November as one that gave them "no slight satisfaction and pride."

The Boston critic Philip Hale was equally impressed: "It is fortunately not necessary to say of the *Gaelic Symphony* 'this is a creditable work for woman.' Such patronage is uncalled for, and it would be offensive. . . . This symphony is the fullest exhibition of Mrs. Beach's indisputable talent." Nevertheless, despite Hale's praise for the "elemental swing, force and grandeur of the finale," he still related the defects of the orchestration to Beach's sex: "Occasionally she is noisy rather than sonorous. Here she is eminently feminine. A woman who writes for orchestra thinks 'I must be virile at any cost. . . .' The only trace of woman I find in this symphony is this boisterousness."[61] What Hale meant by virility was excessively heavy orchestration. The implication is that, because of prejudice against women composers, Beach overcompensated by overwriting.

Then, too, women who sought after "virility" by writing in the higher forms defeated themselves. A critic for the *Musical Courier* wrote in a review of a performance of Beach's symphony:

The symphony of Mrs. Beach is too long, too strenuously worked over and attempts too much. . . . Almost every modern composer has left a trace in her score, which in its efforts to be Gaelic and masculine ends in being monotonous and spasmodic. . . . There is no gainsaying her industry, her gift for melody . . . and her lack of logic. Contrapuntally she is not strong. Of grace and delicacy there are evidences in the Sicilana [sic], and there she is at her best, "but yet a woman."[62]

But, ironically, the composer George Chadwick, who was a personal friend of Beach, allegedly had the opposite reaction. According to a story in the *Etude*, "When George Wakefield Chadwick first heard Mrs. Beach's symphony, 'Gaelic,' he is said to have exclaimed: 'Why was not I born a woman?' It was the delicacy of thought and finish in her musical expression that had struck him, an expression of true womanliness, absolute in its sincerity."[63]

The critical reception of Beach's symphony symbolizes the ambiguities and tensions that accompanied the emergence of the woman composer from the parlor into the professional world of music as art. Women composers had to combat the stereotypes of dilettante and "piano girl" that were the legacy of the tradition of musical "accomplishment" for women. Still, the piano girl slowly gave way to, or at least found a strong competitor in, the "new woman." The tradition declined under social and economic pressures and a healthier, freer climate for creative American women. No doubt one could trace its vestiges today, and certainly its influence was not limited to women but affected men as well, in ways that have yet to be explored.

Beach's music stands on its own artistic merits. But her achievements and those of her generation shine even brighter in historical context, for they created options for other women who had remained within the traditional world of parlor music. By the turn of the century, women shared a vision of a future in which economic and social self-determination would have deep artistic parallels. Fanny Morris Smith proudly summed up the change in 1901:

The first practical entrance of women into music as composers has been within the last twenty-five years. . . . Within this time women have been pressed into self-support; colleges have been established; women have competed for and obtained university degrees; women dentists, lawyers, clergy, physicians, scientists, painters, architects, farmers, inventors, and merchants have all made their advent. Side by side with them has arrived the woman composer. She has come to stay.[64]

NOTES

Portions of this essay have appeared in Judith Tick, "Women as Professional Musicians in the United States, 1870–1900," *Yearbook for Inter-American Research* 9 (1973): 95–133, and appear here with permission. Portions have also appeared in id., *American Women Composers before 1870* (Ann Arbor, ©1983), and are reprinted here courtesy of UMI Research Press.

1. James Huneker, *Overtones* (New York, 1904), p. 286.

2. Ibid.

3. Sex-typed occupations are defined by sociologist Robert Merton as those "in which a very large majority of those in them are of one sex and when there is an associated normative expectation that this is as it should be." See Cynthia Epstein, *Woman's Place* (Berkeley: University of California Press, 1971), p. 154.

4. *Proceedings of the Nineteenth Annual Meeting of the Music Teachers National Association*, 24–28 June 1897, p. 172.

5. Blanche Naylor, *The Anthology of the Fadettes* (Boston, 1937), p. 8.

6. Camilla Urso, "Woman Violinists as Performers in the Orchestras," quoted in *Freund's Weekly*, 16 July 1893, p. 5. For the letter, see *Musical Courier*, 9 March 1898.

7. See Judith Tick, *American Women Composers before 1870* (Ann Arbor: UMI Research Press, 1983), for a discussion of music as a feminine accomplishment.

8. Ibid., p. 45.

9. Christine Ammer, *Unsung* (Westport, Conn.: Greenwood Press, 1980), pp. 100–101.

10. See Camilla Urso, "On Maud Powell," in *My Adventures in the Golden Age of Music*, by Henry T. Finck (New York: Funk & Wagnalls, 1926), p. 311. "Maud Powell, one of the pioneers of women musicians in America. When she was a girl there was still a strong prejudice against women in instrumental music. Pianists of the fair sex were beginning to be tolerated, but the violin—surely the line must be drawn there!" When Huneker accused Maud Powell of not sufficiently emphasizing the feminine traits of music, she explained that she did this purposely because of the existing prejudice against women violinists.

11. Julius Eichberg, Scrapbooks, Music Research Division, Boston Public Library.

12. For a reprint of the review from the *New York Times*, 13 September 1871, see Carol Neuls-Bates, *Women in Music: An Anthology of Source Readings from the Middle Ages to the Present* (New York: Harper & Row, 1982), p. 192ff.

13. According to the *American Art Journal*, 6 September 1884, the vaudeville theater manager John Braham "dressed up a young man as a woman to play the double bass to keep up the reputation of the group as a lady orchestra."

14. Atlantic Garden clippings, Theater Collection, New York Public Library, *New York Telegraph*, 23 March 1916: "The Atlantic Garden had the first woman's orchestra ever used in America, and the playing of its members was cause of argument, many holding, while others disagreed, that they did not perform as well as men."

15. *Atlantic Garden Programme*, 28 September 1896, advertisement. The cover of the program shows a female performer in a white dress, the trademark of the Ladies' Elite.

16. Edward Marks, *They All Sang* (New York: Viking Press, 1935), p. 6. Marks claims the tunes were arranged to suit the women: "Four-bar schmalz I used to call him [the arranger for the orchestra], because he would fix every tune so that there would be four bars of melody and then four of rest, or harmonic accompaniment, to give the ladies a chance to catch their wind."

17. The program for 28 September 1896 included *March, the Niagara*, N. D. Mann; selection from *Robert Le Diable*, Meyerbeer; *Galop*, Strauss; medley of songs of the day; *Waltz*, Vollstedt; *Overture*, Suppe.

18. Quoted in John Mueller, *The American Symphony Orchestra* (Bloomington: Indiana University Press, 1951), p. 309. Emphasis added.

19. "Women Musicians in Festival Works," *Woman's Journal*, 29 April 1893.

20. Naylor, *The Fadettes*, p. 13. The instruments included were four first violins, two second violins, one viola, one cello, two basses, one flute, one clarinet, two cornets, two horns, one trombone, tympani, snare drum, bass drum, traps, and harp.

21. Joe Laurie, Jr., *Vaudeville: From the Honky-Tonks to the Palace* (New York: Henry Holt, 1953), p. 67.

22. Naylor, *The Fadettes*, p. 8.

346

23. E. C. Hughes, "Dilemmas and Contradictions of Status," in *The Sociological Eye* (New York: Aldine-Atherton Press, 1971), p. 149, develops this concept as one that reconciles status conflicts, e.g., women doctors serve in those branches of medicine that are compatible with stereotypes about women, such as pediatrics.

24. Mueller, *American Symphony Orchestra*, p. 309. This is the reason the *Musical Courier* was against integrated orchestras—women allegedly "could not endure" such competition.

25. "Opinions of New York Leaders on Women as Orchestral Players," *Musical Standard*, 2 April 1904.

26. Ibid.

27. Ibid. Whether or not there is still de facto segregation is open to question. Mueller says it was "a matter of public comment" when Cleveland included four women in 1923.

28. George Upton, *Woman in Music* (Chicago, 1880), p. 23.

29. Edith Brower, "Is the Musical Idea Masculine?" *Atlantic Monthly*, March 1894, pp. 332–39.

30. *Woman's Journal*, 29 August 1891.

31. Amy Fay, "Women and Music," *Music* 18 (October 1900): 505–7.

32. Florence Sutro, *Women in Music and Law* (New York, 1895), p. 10, a paper read for the Clef Club in 1893.

33. For example, John Towers, *Women in Music* (Winchester, Va., 1897); Adolph Willhartitz, *Some Facts about Women in Music* (Los Angeles, 1902).

34. "Women Composers of All Lands," a review of *Women Composers*, by Otto Ebel, *Musical Courier* (January 1903): 19.

35. R. Schumann, *On Music and Musicians*, trans. P. Rosenfeld (New York: McGraw-Hill, 1964), p. 121.

36. The phrase *man-tone* comes from Rupert Hughes, *Contemporary American Composers* (New York, 1900), p. 434.

37. T. L. Krebs, "Women as Musicians," *Sewanee Review* 2 (1893): 77.

38. Fanny Bloomfield-Zeisler, "Women in Music," *American Art Journal* (17 October 1891).

39. See Jill Conway, "Stereotypes of Femininity in a Theory of Sexual Evolution," *Victorian Studies* 14 (September 1970): 47–61.

40. Hughes, *Contemporary American Composers*, p. 434.

41. Rupert Hughes, "Women Composers," *Century Magazine* (March 1898): 768–79. This estimate was from an unnamed "prominent publisher."

42. Otto Ebel, *Women Composers* (Brooklyn: F. H. Chandler, 1902), preface.

43. *Etude* began its series in 1901.

44. *Musician* 5 (6 March 1900).

45. The percentage of women's membership increased from 6 percent (5 out of 82) in 1892 to 14.5 percent (19 out of 130) in 1898. This statistic was computed from membership lists in the scrapbook on the Manuscript Society in the New York Public Library. The program on 18 December 1895 was entirely by "the women composers who were members of the society

and it was interpreted by women." Sumner Salter, "Early Encouragements to American Composers," *Musical Quarterly* 18 (January 1932): 76–105.

46. *Proceedings of . . . Annual Meeting of the Music Teachers National Association,* 1897, pp. 171–72.

47. *Musical Age* 21 (17 March 1898): 6.

48. Tick, *American Women Composers,* p. 73.

49. Charles Hamm, *Yesterdays* (New York: W. W. Norton, 1979), p. 185. Hamm calls Barnard, known as Claribel, "one of the most skilled and sensitive writers of the entire nineteenth century in Great Britain."

50. Tick, *American Women Composers,* p. 171.

51. Robert Toll, *Blacking Up: The Minstrel Show in Nineteenth-Century America* (New York: Oxford University Press, 1974), p. 149.

52. Nugent wrote *Sweet Rosie O'Grady* in 1896.

53. Hamm, *Yesterdays,* p. 323.

54. For more details, see Ammer, *Unsung,* chap. 4.

55. For information, see Burnet Tuthill, "Mrs. H. H. A. Beach," *Musical Quarterly* 26 (1940): 297–310; E. Lindsay Merrill, "Mrs. H. H. A. Beach: Her Life and Work" (Ph.D. diss., University of Rochester, 1963). A new study of Beach would be welcome. In the last few years a number of recordings of her work have been issued, among them the Piano Quintet in F-sharp Minor (op. 67), the Trio in A Minor for Violin, Cello, and Piano (op. 150), the Piano Concerto in C-sharp Minor (op. 45), and the Sonata in A Minor for Violin and Piano (op. 34).

56. Margaret W. McCarthy, "A Critical Study of the Career of Amy Fay in America," a paper delivered at the national convention of the College Music Society, fall 1978, p. 7.

57. Henry James, *The Bostonians.*

58. Laurine Elkins-Marlow, "American Women as Orchestral Composers, 1890–1960: An Unfamiliar Heritage," author's papers; Margo Miller, "Oldest BSO Subscriber Recalls Gentle World of the Past," *Boston Globe,* February 1967, Margaret Ruthven Lang Collection, Boston Public Library.

59. Laurine Elkins-Marlow, "What Have Women in This Country Written for Full Orchestra?" *Symphony News* 27 (April 1976): 15–19.

60. Ammer, *Unsung,* chap. 4 passim.

61. Philip Hale, *Musical and Drama Criticism 1892–1900,* microfilm, New York Public Library, p. 317. Also "Beach's Gaelic Symphony," *Boston Tribune,* 1 November 1896; "Women as Symphony Makers," ibid., 4 November 1896.

62. *Musical Courier* (23 February 1898), pp. 29–30.

63. *Etude* (February 1904).

64. Fanny Morris Smith, "The Record of Woman in Music," ibid. (September 1901), p. 317.

14

Women's Orchestras in the United States, 1925–45

CAROL NEULS-BATES

During the 1920s American musical life underwent great expansion in keeping with the economic boom experienced by the country as a whole. More concert halls were constructed, the concert season was considerably lengthened, and symphony orchestras—the hallmark of cultural respectability in the United States—increased dramatically in number. The new symphony orchestras included a number composed of women. These were founded as alternative institutions, because the standard orchestras typically excluded women. The establishment of women's symphony orchestras around 1925 sparked a period of increased activity that continued through the 1930s, as American women moved ahead boldly to seek recognition as orchestral musicians and to create the so-called "mixed" orchestra made up of both men and women chosen on the basis of ability.

There is a strange irony in the history of women's participation in art music, especially in the symphony orchestra, in the United States in 1925. While the editors of *Musical America* noted in October 1925 that women constituted the major share of the nation's music students,[1] with the exception of operatic, choral, and solo concert work, women were barred from the professional mainstream. Moreover, the activity of women as patrons had long been vital to the dissemination of music throughout the country. For symphony orchestras in particular, women's committees provided the chief source of fund raising. But these same symphony orchestras—as well as opera and theater orchestras, most orchestras in movie theaters and at radio stations, and chamber ensembles—did not accept women players in their ranks.

In fact, the discrimination against women instrumentalists that

Tick describes for the period 1870 through 1900 remained constant through the years of World War I. Although increasing numbers of women took up an ever-widening variety of instruments, only harpists were to find acceptance in standard all-male orchestras.[2] Otherwise women were confined to all-female groups, playing a mixture of popular, light classical, and classical music, often in hotel and restaurant settings.[3] The sole alternative income for these musicians lay in teaching.[4]

A new phase in the history of women as orchestral musicians opened in the 1920s. In the prosperous aftermath of World War I, the number of graduates from the nation's conservatories and college departments of music grew rapidly.[5] Also, three leading conservatories were founded in the early 1920s—the Eastman School (1921), the Curtis Institute (1924), and the Juilliard School (1924)—and soon their highly qualified graduates entered the labor market. As a result of these developments, a pool accumulated of especially well-trained female instrumentalists who were intent on leaving behind hotel and restaurant work in favor of the symphonic concert hall. Since the all-male symphony orchestras continued to exclude them, women sought employment and professional experience by establishing their own orchestras, with full complements of eighty or more players, which specialized in the performance of strictly symphonic repertory.

It must be remembered that in the 1920s standard symphonic organizations were made up mainly of European-born men and that, when new members were needed, conductors as a rule looked to Europe. Consequently, men born and trained in America faced some of the same problems in finding work as did American women. To deal with this restrictive situation and ultimately to open the major symphonies to more and more Americans, two graduate-level training orchestras were established in 1920: the American Orchestral Society in New York and the Civic Orchestra in Chicago. Women made their way into both orchestras—chiefly as violinists and harpists—and, while their presence increased during the decade, the overall percentage of women was small.[6] More important to the progress of women as orchestral musicians were the women's symphony orchestras.

Close to thirty women's symphonies flourished from coast to coast from the 1920s through the 1940s and in some cases even later. Table 7 lists them in the chronological order of their establishment, together with information about the dates of their disbanding (or the latest date of traceable activity) and their conductors. The data was

Table 7
Women's Orchestras * in the U.S., c. 1925–45

	Founded	Dis-banded	Last Traceable	Conductors

Los Angeles Woman's Orchestra
  Los Angeles Woman's Symphony Orchestra 1920s–50s
  California Women's Symphony Orchestra 1950s–1961
	1893	—	1961	Henry Hamilton, 1893–c.1913
				Henry Schoenefeld, c.1913–?
				C. D. Gianfoni, 1930s
				William Ulrich, 1937–39
				Ruth Haroldson, 1939–61

Philadelphia Women's Symphony Orchestra	1921	—	1952	J. W. F. Lehman
Chicago Woman's Symphony Orchestra	1924	—	1928	Elena Moneak
Woman's Symphony Orchestra of Chicago	1924	After WWII	—	Richard Czerwonky, 1924–27 Ethel Leginska, 1927–29 Ebba Sundstrom, 1929–38 Gladys Welge, 1938–? Izler Solomon, 1940–44 Jerry Bojanowski, 1944–45
[New York] American Women's Symphony Orchestra	1924	1925	—	Elizabeth Kuyper
Long Beach [California] Woman's Symphony Orchestra	1925	1948	—	Eva Anderson
Boston Woman's Symphony Orchestra	1926	1930	—	Ethel Leginska
[New York] National Women's Symphony Orchestra	1932	—	1932	Ethel Leginska
[New York] Orchestrette Classique Orchestrette of New York 1941–43	1932	1943	—	Frederique Petrides

Table 7 (continued)

	Founded	Dis-banded	Last Traceable	Conductors
Portland [Oregon] Women's Symphony Orchestra	1934	c.1955	—	D'Zama Murielle
New York Women's Symphony Orchestra	1934	1938	—	Antonia Brico
Cleveland Women's Symphony Orchestra	1935	—	Still active in 1985	Hyman Schandler
Cleveland Women's Little Symphony Orchestra	1935	1936	—	Ruth Sandra Rothstein
Pittsburgh Women's Symphony Orchestra	1935	—	1938	Carl Simonis
Stockton [California] Women's Sinfonetta	1936	1938	—	Virginia L. Short
Baltimore Women's String Orchestra	1936	c.1942	—	Stephen Deak, 1936–? Wolfgang Martin ?
Women's Concert Ensemble of Chicago	1936	—	1938	Fanny Arnsten-Hassler
St. Louis Women's Symphony Orchestra	1937	1941	—	Edith Gordon
Women's Chamber Orchestra of New York	1937	1941	—	Jeannette Scheerer
Women's Symphony of Mason City [Iowa]	1937	1945	—	Marjorie B. Smith
[Boston] Commonwealth Women's Symphony Orchestra (WPA)	1937	—	1943	Solomon Branslavsky Ruth Kemper
Women's Symphony Orchestra of Minneapolis	1938	—	1938	Harry Anderson
Boston Women's Symphony Orchestra	1938	—	1942	Stanley Hassel Alexander Thiede

Table 7 (continued)

	Founded	Dis-banded	Last Traceable	Conductors
Pittsburgh Women's String Sinfonetta	1938	—	1938	Gwen Treasure
All-Feminine Ensemble of Pittsburgh's Tuesday Musical Clubs	1938	—	1939	Margaret Horne
Montreal [Canada] Women's Symphony Orchestra	1940	1965	—	Ethel Stark
New York Woman's Symphony Orchestra	1941	—	1941	Maxim Walde
Detroit Women's Symphony Orchestra	1947	—	1971	Victor Kolar, 1947–57

*In the 1920s and earlier the term *Woman's Orchestra* was preferred; in the 1930s *Women's Orchestra* became common.

culled from a wide variety of sources, among them music magazines such as *Musical Courier, Musical America,* and *Etude,* correspondence with historical societies and public libraries in cities where women's orchestras were known to have existed, and interviews with female players and conductors who were active in the 1920s to 1940s. As the table indicates, the first group of women's symphonies— founded around 1925, with one earlier exception—was quite expectedly located in the largest and, in most instances, oldest cities, e.g., Philadelphia, Chicago, New York, Los Angeles and adjacent Long Beach, and finally Boston. The Woman's Orchestra of Los Angeles, established in 1893, was expanded by the 1920s into the Los Angeles Woman's Symphony Orchestra.

The backgrounds of the pioneer organizers of the women's symphonies are notable. Mabel Swint Ewer, who founded the Philadelphia Women's Symphony Orchestra in 1921, was a trumpet player and the mother of eight children. A graduate of the New England Conservatory, she played in the orchestra there under the direction of George W. Chadwick. She also played in brass ensembles in her native New England and Philadelphia.[7] Elizabeth Kuyper, a composer and conductor from Europe, accomplished the preliminary organization of the American Women's Symphony Orchestra in New York in 1924, surely somewhat as a vehicle for her own conducting interests. Kuyper had earlier attempted to establish women's symphonies in Berlin in 1910 and in The Hague and London in 1922, only to be forced to withdraw because of inadequate finances.[8] Her experience with the American Women's Symphony Orchestra in New York unfortunately had a similar end.

The organizers of the Woman's Symphony Orchestra of Chicago included two recent graduates from the local Bush Conservatory: Lillian Poenisch, a clarinetist, and Adeline Schmidt, a flutist.[9] The early history of the Woman's Symphony is typical of the new all-female organizations. The founders began with the modest plan of bringing together professionals in the Chicago area to read through repertory. As conductor they enlisted Richard Czerwonky, under whom Poenisch and Schmidt had played at Bush. Within a year the incentive of public performance was deemed necessary, and the orchestra made its debut in May 1925 with forty-five members, including a few amateurs. Later, in the 1930s, the orchestra grew to a fuller complement of ninety professional players.[10] From its beginnings the Woman's Symphony was seen as having a definite niche in the city's burgeoning musical life, and local critics reviewed its concerts encouragingly. As with most of the women's symphonies, finances were a problem; and while the founders were able to secure some financial backing, a lower than normal pay scale had to be devised with the consent of the union. Furthermore, in its early years the orchestra gave only six major concerts—hardly a very full season.

The Chicago women had a strong commitment to both their orchestra and to improving the status of women as orchestral musicians. Aside from the issues of fuller employment and better pay, they wanted to eliminate the initial assistance of a few male players of oboe, French horn, and trombone. Their solution was to award scholarships to women pianists and violinists for the purpose of retraining them on these instruments, which at the time were still considered unusual for women, as well as to high-school students who were studying winds and brass. The result was that male assistance was totally eliminated within five years of the orchestra's founding.

Another notable and forward-looking aspect of the orchestra's activity was its interest—shared by several of the women's symphonies—in performing works of American composers, specifically works by American women.[11] Gena Branscombe's music was featured on a program with the composer conducting in February 1930.[12]

354

Other programs in the late 1920s and 1930s included Amy Marcy Beach's Piano Concerto in C-sharp Minor, opus 45, Eleanor Everest Freer's Four Modern Dances, Florence Price's piano concerto (performed by the pianist-composer Margaret Bonds), Hazel Feldman's *Good Morning, America,* and Radie Briton's Symphonic Intermezzo.

After the first two seasons, the Women's Symphony Orchestra of Chicago hired a woman conductor. She was Ethel Leginska (plate 20), the leading pianist from England, who in the early 1920s decided to pursue orchestral conducting even though it was an occupation traditionally considered to be a male prerogative. A woman of feminist leanings, Leginska began, between 1915 and 1920, to speak out in the press about the handicaps facing professional women, such as the problems inherent in combining childrearing with a career and, also, about the need for sensible concert dress for women musicians. For herself she decided, in 1915, upon an outfit that remained standard throughout her career: a black velvet jacket, a trim skirt, and a white shirt. She commented that the attire was "always the same and always comfortable, so that I can forget my appearance and concentrate upon my art."[13] In a 1917 interview, Leginska urged women to strike out in new directions, and she also forecast her own bold move into conducting:

> [Just] because women haven't done anything in the past is supposed to be reason enough why they shouldn't do it in the future. We are always hearing about the "traditional woman." Why not for a change about the "traditional man?" Why are we always being generalized about? And why, why are we so docile and obedient in abiding by our traditions? If only we women would sometimes rebel, . . . break loose from traditions and go our own way! . . . We will never be original, do great work, until we get some courage and daring and trust our own way instead of the eternal beaten paths on which we are always asked to poke along.[14]

In establishing herself as a conductor, Leginska planned carefully. During 1923 she studied with Eugene Goossens in London and Robert Hager in Munich. Subsequently, in 1924, she appeared as guest conductor with both men's orchestras and also with major orchestras in Paris and Berlin. To be sure, Leginska had these contacts from her years as a pianist; she likewise seems to have capitalized on her fine reputation as a pianist in securing most of the conducting engagements she did in both Europe and the United States by agreeing to play a concerto on the program.

Leginska was not the first woman to achieve prominence as an orchestral conductor in the United States. Rather, Caroline B.

Plate 20
Ethel Leginska, 1928

Source: Music Division, New York Public Library at Lincoln Center,
Astor, Lenox, and Tilden Foundations
Photograph by Elzin

Nichols, the conductor of the Boston Fadette Lady Orchestra from 1888 to 1920, and Emma Roberto Steiner, who conducted light opera companies on tour in the same period, share that distinction. Nonetheless, in 1925 Ethel Leginska became the first woman to put herself forward as a conductor of leading American symphony orchestras. She made her United States debut with the New York Symphony Orchestra on 9 January 1925 and followed it by appearances with the Boston People's Orchestra in the spring and fall and by a triumphant performance at the Hollywood Bowl in the summer. Clearly she was a novelty and, as the reviews indicate, skepticism abounded. The legitimacy of Leginska's conducting, however, won over the majority of her critics, who in turn announced that a new field had been opened to women. A review of a Boston concert illustrates the climate in which Leginska had to work:

> She has made strides as a conductor, and although we are handicapped by an unexplainable distaste for women as orchestral leaders, it is only fair to report that she sensed and projected the grave beauty of the Brahms Symphony [no. 1 in C Minor, opus 68] and that the Prelude to Wagner's masterpiece [*Die Meistersinger*] was performed in a way that revealed its essential spirit.[15]

While in 1926 and afterwards Leginska secured isolated guest appearances with the New York Philharmonic, the St. Louis Symphony Orchestra, and directed the Boston Philharmonic, which she founded in 1926, her work as a conductor became confined mainly to women's orchestras; the likelihood that her contemporaries thought this was her appropriate sphere of activity is strong. And although she clearly sought conducting engagements with all-male orchestras, Leginska was nevertheless a strong advocate of the advancement of women as orchestral musicians. In fact, she held a highly successful tenure with the Woman's Symphony Orchestra of Chicago from 1927 to 1929, at the time she directed the Boston Woman's Symphony Orchestra from 1926 to 1930.

The Boston Woman's Symphony Orchestra was in existence for just four seasons; yet it occupies an important place in the history of women as orchestral musicians because of the visibility it gave to women players through two extensive tours throughout the eastern half of the United States in 1928 and 1929. The tours also provided encouragement to countless women to take up orchestral instruments. The 1928 tour consisted of fifty-five concerts in forty-three days, "a task that would make the managements of the largest symphony orchestras gasp," the *Musical Courier* reported.[16] The repertory included Beethoven's Symphony no. 5 in C Minor, opus 67, the Mendelssohn Piano Concerto no. 1 in G Minor, opus 25, the overture to *Rienzi*, and Liszt's Hungarian Fantasia. A second tour covered seventy-five cities with performances of Schubert's Symphony no. 8 in B Minor (the *Unfinished*), the overture to *Die Meistersinger*, and Liszt's Les Préludes and Hungarian Fantasia. Reviews indicate that in numerous locales Leginska and her band were initially greeted with derision, but that many audience members came away from performances convinced that women players and a woman conductor were equal to the task of symphonic repertory. For instance, the critic of the *Roanoke* [Virginia] *Times* wrote on 19 October 1929: "Roanoke music lovers gathered to hear a symphony orchestra of women led by a woman. They stayed to hear a symphony orchestra played by a great conductor."[17]

Meanwhile, during the 1920s, women orchestral musicians were also making progress outside the confines of the all-female orchestra, chiefly in the growing numbers of secondary-level orchestras. Between 1920 and 1930, fifty-five orchestras—almost all on the secondary level—were newly established in the United States; and small numbers of women found positions in locales from Springfield, Illinois, to Portland, Maine, for the most part in string sections.[18] The thirteen major orchestras, however, continued to exclude women other than harpists, with the noteworthy exception of the San Francisco Symphony Orchestra, which hired four female string players at the mid-decade point: Modesta Mortonsen, Mary Passmore, Frances Simonsen, violinists; Dorothy Passmore, cellist.[19] This early acceptance of women was no doubt due to the western locale of the host city, where musicians were not as numerous as in the East, and also to the orchestra's lesser rank in prestige among the major symphonies.

The Depression of the 1930s hit orchestral musicians especially hard. Bad economic times forced hotels, restaurants, and resorts to dispense with orchestras, and musical theater to retrench both on Broadway and on tour. Another special employment problem was caused by the advent of the talking movie picture, which was first introduced in 1928. Within a few years' time the movie-theater orchestra became obsolete, and thousands of musicians lost employment. Somewhat paradoxically, the demise of jobs in the hotel, movie, and musical-theater areas fostered the establishment of new symphony orchestras. Displaced musicians were eager to retain their professional skills; they tended to do so by forming new symphonic groups, which in time came to enjoy community interest and financial support. As a result, more than 120 new symphonic organizations were founded in the 1930s, practically all on the secondary level.[20]

Some women, of course, secured positions in the new organizations—especially in the thirty-six federally funded orchestras sponsored by the Works Progress Administration (WPA)[21]—and women in the 1930s were able to gain entrance to secondary orchestras that previously had been all-male strongholds, such as the Seattle Symphony Orchestra.[22] Nonetheless, there clearly were more trained women looking for opportunities than the standard institutions permitted, because during the 1930s there were enough women active to staff nearly twenty new all-female orchestras.

It is significant that the majority of the new women's groups were organized in cities that earlier had not had a women's orchestra in their midst, e.g., Cleveland, St. Louis, Portland (Oregon), and Stockton (California): the concept of woman as symphonic musician was spreading throughout the country. Meanwhile, the older women's orchestras in Philadelphia, Chicago, Long Beach, and Los Angeles endured. The Chicago orchestra was certainly the best known nationally of this group; it even grew in stature to the point of being featured in a nationwide radio series during the 1940–41 season.

The one orchestra that came to rival the Woman's Symphony Orchestra of Chicago was the New York Women's Symphony Orchestra, which was organized and conducted by Antonia Brico (plate 21). Although Ethel Leginska's stock as a conductor fell in the 1930s (or perhaps it should be said her novelty wore off), the path she charted was followed by a number of women in the 1930s, among them Ebba Sundstrom and Gladys Welge—who conducted the Chicago women's orchestra—and Antonia Brico. Brico, like Leginska, strove to work with standard orchestras besides being identified with all-female groups.

After graduation from the University of California at Berkeley in 1923, Antonia Brico worked in radio in the San Francisco area, studied piano with Sigismund Stojowski in New York from 1925 to 1927, and then received a fellowship that enabled her to realize her youthful ambitions in Berlin.[23] She described her quest as follows:

"People try to come up with such complicated reasons for what I thought or did, but it is really all so simple! From the earliest time I can remember I wanted to conduct, and Germany became my goal when I was

Plate 21
Antonia Brico and the Women's Symphony Orchestra of New York

Source: Music Division, New York Public Library at Lincoln Center,
Astor, Lenox, and Tilden Foundations

about ten years of age and reading stories about the beautiful Bavarian countryside. Around age eleven I fell in love with Beethoven. I played the *Moonlight* Sonata [no. 14, in C-sharp Minor (opus 27, no. 2)], and not very well, I might add. So after that I wanted to go to the country of Beethoven.

"In all, I spent six years in Germany—from 1927 to 1932—although I came back to the States in 1930 to make my American debut at the Hollywood Bowl. Yes, I was the first American to graduate from the [Staatliche] Hochschule für Musik in Berlin. As I recall twenty people applied to the Hochschule in conducting when I did, and two of us were accepted—a young man and myself. . . .

"The whole German conducting field was based on the premise that once you completed your training you would embark on the 'route' through the different opera houses, and this route called for you to play at rehearsals at the piano and to coach the singers. A conductor would progress, say, from being the third conductor in a small house to the second conductor in a larger house, and then perhaps back to the small house as first conductor, and so forth up the ladder. I am quite sure I could have followed that route [upon completion of the conducting course at the Hochschule] if World War II had not intervened.

"I returned to the United States in September 1932 for the simple reason that all foreigners were booted out of Germany by the Hitler business, which was getting very serious. . . . And so I arrived in New York at the height of the Depression with thousands of musicians out of work! I had spent years and years training: I had conducted in Berlin, Hamburg, the Hollywood Bowl, San Francisco, Warsaw, Lodz, Posnan, and Riga, and yet I had no opportunities forthcoming to me at that time. I even owed money for the trip back!"[24]

After raising $1,000 Brico was able to secure two conducting engagements at the Metropolitan Opera House with the Musicians Symphony Orchestra—a group that had been brought together by the exigencies of the Depression—and she received excellent reviews from Olin Downes in the *New York Times*,[25] among others. Subsequently she was hired to conduct the Civic Symphony Orchestra, one of the two WPA orchestras in New York in the mid-1930s.

Brico's plans for the New York Women's Symphony Orchestra developed in 1934. She recruited several wealthy women as financial backers, and her sponsors also came to include Bruno Walter, Harold Bauer, Sigismund Stojowski, Eleanor Roosevelt, and Mayor and Mrs. Fiorello La Guardia. It was not difficult to staff the orchestra of approximately eighty players, Brico recalled: there were "stacks" of women available for work, even though they had to rehearse for the first three months without remuneration.

"Yes, the women who made up the orchestra were well-trained. Some were young; and some had played a lot, like Betty Barry (first trombone) and Muriel Watson (tympani), both of whom had done a considerable amount of work in Boston. Lois Wann (first oboe) was a phenomenal player, who has since taught just about everywhere; and my concertmistress, Elfrieda Bos Mesteschkin, was an excellent violinist. So many women in the orchestra were very fine players, but they had limited opportunities for good engagements."[26]

Typically the New York Women's Symphony Orchestra gave four major concerts a season in Carnegie Hall, and reviews of the performances in the *New York Times* trace its evolution from a "good start" in 1935—with wind and brass choirs that definitely needed improvement—to a polished orchestra in 1937 that enabled Brico "to do justice to herself."[27] Brico was ambitious for the orchestra in planning programs, which reflect the then current vogue for late nineteenth-century Russian repertory and also an interest in furthering compositions by Americans. Among the American works was Elinor Remick Warren's *The Harpweaver*, which was given its premiere by the orchestra during the 1935–36 season. Brico liked to devote the final concert of a season to an especially large-scale work—e.g., Horatio Parker's *Hora Novissima* in 1937 and the Verdi Requiem in 1938. The choruses for these occasions were made up of several groups Brico conducted in the metropolitan area. Both performances received highly enthusiastic reviews from the *Times* and other New York newspapers.[28]

For the 1938–39 season Brico announced that, having accomplished the first stage of her campaign by proving women were indeed competent orchestral musicians, she would reorganize the New York Women's Symphony Orchestra as a mixed group, to demonstrate further the cooperation of both sexes in an orchestra—cooperation she had already known through her WPA experience. Unfortunately her board of directors felt, to quote Brico, "the female aspect of the orchestra was its interesting feature, and since the orchestra had no capital, that was that."[29] After three concerts in the winter and spring of 1939 the new orchestra disbanded.

Brico's belief in the validity of the mixed orchestra came to be shared by many women in the field in the late 1930s, as they began to develop a new consciousness about their professional goals. Not only had the pool of qualified women players grown substantially, but women felt they had proven themselves through their work in all-female orchestras, the secondary orchestras—in which they secured a place—and also in free-lance groups that were on the rise in major centers. Accordingly, women went on record demanding that all orchestras—but most especially the major symphonies—be mixed institutions made up of men and women chosen on the basis of ability. During the 1930s American men had at last become well entrenched in the major orchestras, whereas women were still barely visible there. Only a handful of women over the ten-year period 1930–40 had joined the ranks of the major institutions. Elsa Hilger began playing in the last row of the cello section of the Philadelphia Orchestra in 1935 amid much comment in the contemporary press. Lois Putlitz, violinist, was hired by the Philadelphia Orchestra the following season. Ellen Stone, French horn player, joined the Pittsburgh Symphony Orchestra in 1937. And two string players—Nina Wolfe, violinist, and Elizabeth Greenschpoon, cellist—became members of the Los Angeles Philharmonic with the 1937–38 season.[30]

Why shouldn't more qualified women be employed across the board? This was the premise of Frederique Petrides's newsletter *Women in Music*, which—despite its broad title—was devoted exclusively to women as orchestral players and conductors.[31] Petrides, who was also the conductor of the all-female Orchestrette Classique in New York in 1932–43, published the newsletter from 1935 until

1940, when she ran out of funds. In capsule form, this publication traces the activities of Petrides's own and other women's orchestras across the country, together with women's rising demands for mixed groups. Petrides's aim was to be supportive of women in the field:

"I began the newsletter *Women in Music* because I wanted to show that women in previous times had been orchestral musicians and that their activity in the 1930s—if indeed more extensive—was just another phase in the history. Therefore I placed, for example, an item about the female orchestras in orphanages in eighteenth-century Venice alongside of a report on the current work of the Portland Women's Symphony Orchestra [founded in 1934]. By reporting on their nationwide activity as orchestral musicians [in the 1930s] I wanted to encourage women to keep on working and to tell them that they would move ahead."[32]

The year 1938 was a high point in the movement for orchestral activity by women. The subject of women players in orchestras received more journalistic coverage than ever before, while the National Federation of Music Clubs in New York endorsed the principle of the mixed ensemble. At least sixteen women's orchestras, involving nine hundred players, were active. And in Chicago and New York women formed committees for the recognition of women as musicians to publicize the need for better professional opportunities in all areas of orchestral work. Dedicated to "combat an unjust discrimination for which there is absolutely no reason except habit," the New York committee asked that women be granted auditions for all jobs and further proposed auditions behind screens—an idea that was accepted only with the 1960s.[33] The New York organization also contemplated a boycott of products advertised by radio stations that did not hire women musicians.

One can only speculate about the outcome of this heightened militancy, for the war effort of the 1940s drastically altered the employment pattern. It depleted the ranks of men and thereby made possible the entrance of female players of all instruments into the major symphony orchestras, as well as the orchestras in opera, radio, and the movie and recording industries, from which they had formerly been excluded. The impact of the draft first became apparent with the 1942–43 season; then all but three of the nation's leading nineteen symphony orchestras included women.[34] True, the number of women employed by major orchestras was small—140 in 1943, 150 in 1947—and has remained so until recent years.[35] Nevertheless, during World War II women achieved general recognition as orchestral musicians and made the mixed orchestra a reality. Furthermore, in contrast to postwar employment patterns in other fields, women orchestral players for the most part held their own after the return of the veterans. That this was possible was surely due in part to Hans Kindler, conductor of the National Symphony Orchestra, who was singularly outspoken in support of women musicians for their contributions in wartime. For instance, in 1946 in response to a statement by the English conductor Thomas Beecham that "women in symphony orchestras constitute a disturbing element," Kindler wrote a letter to the *New York Times* in which he argued:

The women in the orchestras I have had the pleasure of conducting, not only in my own National Symphony Orchestra, but recently in Mexico City, Guatemala, Panama, Chile, Peru, and Canada as well, all proved themselves to be not only fully equal to the men, but to be sometimes more imaginative and always especially cooperative.

Hence I think Sir Thomas's jibe "if the ladies are ill-favored the men do not want to play next to them, and if they are well-favored they [the men] can't," though funny is also slightly unfair, and, as far as American orchestras are concerned, quite untrue. If anything their ability and enthusiasm constitute an added stimulant for the male performer to do as well. And as they were a veritable godsend to most conductors during the war years, and I think to Sir Thomas as well, it doesn't seem quite "cricket" (to use his vernacular) to drop them now.[36]

Once the mixed orchestra became the rule, there was less need for the all-female group, and most women's symphonies did not survive the war years. Frederique Petrides recalled the demise of the Orchestrette Classique in 1943 after ten seasons of successful activity:

"It was not financial considerations [although finances had been problematical] that led to the disbanding of the orchestra in 1943. Rather the first desk players all found positions with major orchestras, replacing men who had left because of the war. I didn't want to stand in the way of their advancement, and it would have been difficult to replace them right away. Besides, at that time the idea of preserving an orchestra seemed insignificant in the face of a world war."[37]

Other women's symphony orchestras did persevere, and they continued to fill a need in their communities. The Philadelphia and Los Angeles orchestras endured until the 1950s and 1960s respectively. The Detroit Women's Symphony Orchestra, which, indeed, was founded after the war, remained active until 1971. The women's symphony in Cleveland was still active as of 1985.

What about the woman conductor, though, who had figured significantly in the late 1920s and 1930s as head of the women's symphonies and elsewhere? During the 1940s men born and trained in America began assuming the directorships of many secondary-level orchestras. In 1943 Alfred Wallenstein became the first American to head a major orchestra—the Los Angeles Philharmonic.[38] American women, however, did not enjoy a similar career path; and given the loss in popularity of the women's symphony orchestras after the war, opportunities for women conductors diminished until recent years, when the new wave of the women's movement once again focused attention on women as conductors.

Feminist historians, who are in the process of investigating the decline of the women's movement after suffrage was won in 1920, have isolated several areas of strong activity that indicate the decade of the 1920s was not a period of total decline in professional and social commitment for all women.[39] The work of women as orchestral musicians is another such "pocket" of activity, beginning around 1925, when significant numbers of women put themselves forward as players and conductors, establishing their own institutions when necessary to secure experience and gainful employment. While the events of World War II finally opened better opportunities to women players, the visibility and experience women collectively gained during the 1920s and 1930s made them poised to move as they did.

NOTES

1. *Musical America* 42 (24 October 1925): 86.

2. See ch. 13 above. The supply of qualified male harpists was never adequate to fill more than the most prestigious posts.

3. *Musical Courier*, 1900–1919 passim. Groups formed after 1900 that were devoted chiefly to classical music included the orchestra of the Women's Philharmonic Society of New York (c. 1900–1920), the Cremona Ladies' Orchestra of New York (1906–7), the Pittsburgh Ladies' Orchestra (1911–13), and the Salt Lake Women's Orchestra (1915). See also Edith Lynwood Wynn, "How the War Helped Women Orchestral and Hotel Musicians," *Musical Observer* 18 (October 1919): 47. Due to the shortage of male players during World War I, women were able to find employment in some hotel and restaurant orchestras. They generally received equal pay with men, but in some instances they were not permitted to play for dancing during late hours.

4. Frederique Petrides to Carol Neuls-Bates, interview, 2 September 1981: "Teaching at that time [i.e., the 1920s and 1930s] was the major means of livelihood for women instrumentalists [other than solo work], and if you didn't like teaching, well, that was just too bad!" For the complete interview, see Carol Neuls-Bates, ed., *Women in Music: An Anthology of Source Read-*

ings from the Middle Ages to the Present (New York: Harper & Row, 1982), pp. 259–64. Richard Hageman, in "Shall the Young Woman Choose Music as a Profession?" *Musician* 30 (March 1925): 9–10, discusses teaching as the major option for female musicians, although he also mentions employment for women as choir singers and organists in small towns.

5. At the New England Conservatory, for instance, graduating classes grew from 78 students in 1919 to 118 in 1926. See *New England Conservatory of Music Bulletin* 1 (July 1919): 5–6; 7 (July 1926): 5–7.

6. Programs for concerts of the American Orchestral Society indicate that in April 1923 women constituted 11 percent of the student members of the orchestra and that in April 1927 they constituted 17 percent. Women were not included among the faculty players in the orchestra, who presumably occupied the first stands in sections. Figures for the Chicago Civic Orchestra were unavailable. Jeannette Scheerer, a clarinetist who played with that orchestra from 1920 to 1924, reported that "there were seven of us in the beginning, I think; and in my fourth year the concertmaster was a concertmistress, Mildred Brown." Jeannette Scheerer to Carol Neuls-Bates, interview, 9–10 July 1978. For the complete interview, see Neuls–Bates, *Women in Music*, pp. 265–72.

7. "Philadelphia Women's Orchestra," *Musical Courier* 76 (17 May 1923): 12.

8. Betsy Ross, "The American Women's Symphony Orchestra," ibid. 79 (2 October 1924): 17, 52.

9. "Bush Conservatory Orchestra," ibid. 77 (13 December 1923): 29.

10. Ibid., 1926–49 passim; Dorothea Kahn, "Women Build a Symphony Orchestra," *Christian Science Monitor*, 4 January 1941, pp. 5, 13.

11. For orchestral works by American women composers, consult Adrienne Fried Block and Carol Neuls-Bates, eds., *Women in American Music: A Bibliography of Music and Literature* (Westport, Conn.: Greenwood Press, 1979); Laurine Elkins-Marlow, "What Have Women in This Country Written for Full Orchestra?" *Symphony News* 27 (April 1976): 15–19.

12. Gena Branscombe recalled about this concert (to Carol Neuls-Bates, interview, 29 April 1976), "I thought it was a good orchestra with a lovely spirit."

13. New York Public Library, Music Division, clipping files, *Minneapolis Journal*, 11 October 1915. These files and the *Musical Courier*, 1913–42 passim, aided in the reconstruction of Leginska's career. See this author's article on Leginska in *Notable American Women: The Modern Period*, ed. Barbara Sicherman and Carol Hurd Green (Cambridge, Mass.: Belknap Press, 1980), pp. 415–17.

14. *Duluth Herald*, 17 February 1917.

15. "Leginska Conducts Last of Three Concerts for People's Symphony," *Musical Courier* 91 (26 November 1925): 24.

16. "Ethel Leginska to Return," ibid. 97 (13 December 1928): 24.

17. Quoted from an ad for Leginska in ibid. 99 (16 November 1929): 19.

18. Margaret Grant and Herman S. Hettinger, *America's Symphony*

Orchestras and How They Are Supported (New York: W. W. Norton, 1940), p. 23. Secondary-level symphony orchestras, in contrast with the major orchestras, were less prestigious and had smaller budgets and shorter seasons. The secondary category embraced a wide variety of orchestras ranging from all-professional to mixed groups of professionals and amateurs. Programs for the Springfield, Illinois, and Portland, Maine, orchestras—among many others—were consulted.

19. The thirteen major orchestras in the 1920s were the following: New York Philharmonic, New York Symphony Orchestra (merged with the Philharmonic in 1928), St. Louis Symphony Orchestra, Boston Symphony Orchestra, Chicago Symphony Orchestra, Cincinnati Symphony Orchestra, Philadelphia Orchestra, Minneapolis Symphony Orchestra, San Francisco Symphony Orchestra, Cleveland Orchestra, Detroit Symphony Orchestra, Los Angeles Philharmonic, and Pittsburgh Symphony Orchestra. Programs for the San Francisco Symphony Orchestra, 1925–26, list the designated women.

20. Grant and Hettinger, *America's Symphony Orchestras*, pp. 23–24, 60.

21. National Archives, Washington, D.C., miscellaneous programs of WPA-sponsored orchestras.

22. Programs indicate that several women played in the Seattle Symphony Orchestra by the 1934–35 season.

23. Clippings at the Music Division of the New York Public Library aided the reconstruction of Brico's career. See the author's article on Brico in the *New Grove Dictionary of Music in the United States* (forthcoming).

24. Antonia Brico to Carol Neuls-Bates, interview, 15 May 1976. Other parts of the interview are published in Neuls-Bates, *Women in Music*, pp. 254–59.

25. Olin Downes, "Successful Debut by Antonia Brico," *New York Times*, 11 January 1933, p. 19; id., "Brico and Musicians Symphony," ibid., 8 February 1933, p. 17.

26. Brico to Neuls-Bates, interview, 15 May 1976.

27. Howard Taubman, "Miss Brico Leads Women Musicians," *New York Times*, 19 February 1935, p. 27; Olin Downes, "Women's Ensemble in Varied Program," ibid., 24 February 1937, p. 18.

28. Olin Downes, "250 in Chorus Sing *Hora Novissima*," ibid., 31 March 1937, p. 28; id., "Verdi's Requiem Heard in Concert," ibid., 27 April 1938, p. 19.

29. Brico to Neuls-Bates, interview, 15 May 1976.

30. Programs: Philadelphia Orchestra, 1935–37; Pittsburgh Symphony Orchestra, 1937. For the Los Angeles musicians, see "Three Young, Native American Girls in Orchestra Personnel," *Philharmonic Orchestra of Los Angeles: Symphony Magazine 1937–38* (11–12 November), p. 15. The third young woman in the Los Angeles Philharmonic was harpist Ann Mason, who joined for the 1936–37 season.

31. *Women in Music* 1–4 (1935–40), newsletter of the Orchestrette

Classique, ed. Frederique Petrides; selections are reprinted in Neuls-Bates, *Women in Music*, pp. 247–50.

32. Frederique Petrides to Carol Neuls-Bates, interview, 4 October 1975. Petrides refers here to *Women in Music* 1 (September 1935).

33. "Women Musicians Urge Equal Rights," *New York Times*, 19 May 1938, p. 24, reprinted in Neuls-Bates, *Women in Music*, pp. 251–52; Elizabeth La Hines, "Orchestral Posts Urged for Women," *New York Times*, 2 October 1938, sec. 2, p. 5. Following its bold start with meetings in May and October 1938, the activities of the New York Committee for the Recognition of Women in the Musical Profession proved untraceable. Joyce Barthelson, an officer of the committee, noted her feeling that the committee was not especially influential. She recalled a meeting of committee members at which Abram Chasins, pianist-composer and radio commentator, advised that the women would best make progress by going home and practicing their instruments. Joyce Barthelson to Carol Neuls-Bates, interview, 1 April 1976. The Organized Women Musicians of Chicago was formed in 1938 by Lillian Poenisch, who, as noted above, was a founder of and clarinetist with the Woman's Symphony Orchestra of Chicago. The organization was not able to accomplish very much in the face of the Depression, but it brought together women musicians from a variety of pursuits: "The symphony girls were more militant and better educated, and therefore were more active in the movement." Norma Zuzanek to Carol Neuls-Bates, letter, 2 July 1976. Also, for the Chicago committee, see "Organized Women Musicians," *Musical Leader* 70 (26 March 1938): 16.

34. "The Symphony Goes Co-ed," *Newsweek*, 6 December 1943, pp. 86–87. For wartime shifts in women's employment and women in the 1940s in general, see Susan M. Hartmann, *The Home Front and Beyond: American Women in the 1940s* (Boston: Twayne Publishers, 1982).

35. See "Symphony Goes Co-ed," pp. 86–87, for the 1943 figures. See Hope Stoddard, "Women's Activities in the Field of Music," *International Musician* 47 (June 1948): 24–25, for the 1947 figures. The total number of women in eighteen of the same nineteen orchestras (San Francisco was surely omitted as an oversight) for the 1953–54 season was 199. Frances Q. Eaton, "Women Come into Their Own in Our Orchestras," *Musical America* 75 (February 1955): 30. A recent report states that while in 1964–65 the average number of women in major orchestras was 18.3%, the average rose to 21.8% in 1974–75 and further to 24.9% in 1975. The number of women players in secondary-level orchestras in the period 1964–74 rose from 36.5% to 39.7%. In 1975 women constituted 40.6% of the ranks of secondary orchestras. American Symphony Orchestra League, "Women in American Symphony Orchestras," *Symphony News* 27 (April 1976): 13–14.

36. Hans Kindler, "Support for Women Players," *New York Times*, 20 October 1946, sec. 2, p. 7.

37. Petrides to Neuls-Bates, interview, 4 October 1975. Petrides chose to state this information in a slightly different manner for the 2 September 1981 interview incorporated in Neuls-Bates, *Women in Music*, p. 263.

38. Hope Stoddard, *Symphony Conductors of the U.S.A.* (New York: Thomas V. Crowell, 1957), pp. 274–79 and passim.

39. Estelle B. Freedman, "The New Woman: Changing Views of Women in the 1920s," *Journal of American History* 61 (September 1974): 372–93. These areas include the work of women within the Women's Joint Congressional Committee for state legislation for child welfare, women's legal rights, social hygiene, and education, as well as the efforts of southern women for social and political reform in the 1920s.

15

Ruth Crawford Seeger

MATILDA GAUME

Ruth Crawford Seeger was a composer of uncommon creative gifts, whose place in American music has been increasingly acknowledged in recent years. As a member of the avant garde in the 1920s, she was an innovative—indeed, prophetic—composer who was dedicated to the cause of modern music. In the 1930s and 1940s she helped preserve and disseminate American folk song through her transcriptions and arrangements. She was a woman of integrity, resoluteness, and idealism, qualities that are found in both her life and her music.

Ruth Crawford was born on 3 July 1901, the daughter of a Methodist minister who held a pastorate in East Liverpool, Ohio. The family moved to several other midwestern towns before settling in Jacksonville, Florida. Ruth's father suffered ill health for several years and then died when she was thirteen years old. After his death, her mother kept a rooming house to help support Ruth and her brother Carl.[1]

In her youth Ruth Crawford manifested rich intellectual and philosophical curiosity as well as musicality. She began piano lessons when she was six years old.[2] Various diaries, poems, and stories have been preserved from at least her twelfth year. Much of her correspondence and several diaries from later years also survive. More than once during her youth she voiced the ambition to become a writer, and the perceptiveness and vivid imagery in her journals reveal her literary gifts.

Her high-school diary entries (1915–18) often reveal her remarkable aptitude for self-assessment, as she constantly strove to improve herself according to her own rather strict standards. She exhorted herself to practice self-discipline and reproached herself for procrastination:

> And listen to me, Ruth. You will never make a success of yourself in this world, unless you learn to exercise your will power, and to *tackle* tasks

which are to be done, not put them off. Suppose you are writing a book, and get a wee bit tired of it—for authorship is not all pleasure. How will you ever finish it if you have not trained your will power? Buckle to![3]

Although her father died when Ruth was young, his puritanical attitudes made a strong impression on her, as did his humaneness and altruism. Her mother was also influenced by her husband's moralizing, but she also had tolerance for the unknown or unfamiliar and a strong trust in people. Both her father and her mother had low-keyed personalities, with no hint of the extrovert in either of them. At an early age Ruth Crawford showed both her father's idealism and concern for people and her mother's trust in them. She was open and curious, despite her socially conservative upbringing.

After high school, Crawford was asked to teach piano at the School of Musical Art in Jacksonville; she also continued her own piano study, took a few lessons in harmony, and wrote a few compositions on her own. In the fall of 1920, when a small amount of money was made available to her (apparently through some relative), she chose to enter the American Conservatory of Music in Chicago.[4] This was an important step. Her years there changed her from a fledgling pianist and incipient composer into a woman whose intellectual and musical attainments were commensurate with her talents. Crawford soon earned the respect and love of her teachers as her talents blossomed under the guidance of such mentors as Heniot Levy, Louise Robyn, Adolf Weidig, and John Palmer.

During her first two years at the conservatory, Crawford suffered serious discomfort in her arms from muscular tension, and since her original concern was to develop her skills as a pianist, her redirection as a composer was perhaps as much a matter of fate as it was an act of will. This handicap was so debilitating that she began to question her previous goals. As justification for continuing her education as a musician, Crawford turned to her theoretical studies:

What am I gaining that is worth it all? . . . Again and again the debate has raged, and always peace and contentment come in the answer: my theoretical work. Yes, it alone is worth my being here. I feel myself broadening; my ear—the inner ear, whose good judgment and training is of infinite value to composers—is hearing better than it did last year. Tho we have not begun composition yet, I am working on little ideas that come to me.[5]

After receiving her graduate diploma in 1923 and her bachelor's degree in 1924, Crawford continued to study composition with Weidig, completing her master's degree in 1927. She also taught piano at the American Conservatory from 1924 to 1929 and at the Elmhurst College of Music from 1926 to 1929.

In 1924 Crawford started private piano study with Mme Djane Lavoie-Herz, an independent teacher. Mme Herz and her husband Siegfried had previously lived in Toronto and New York, where they were both active in musical circles. Mme Herz, a strong protagonist of modern music in Chicago, was a dynamic, self-assured woman who cannot have failed to impress Crawford with her leading position in the kind of musical milieu she aspired to enter. Herz was able to introduce Crawford to important avant-garde figures, such as Henry Cowell, who took an active interest in her compositional activities, and Dane Rudhyar, whose devotion to theosophy and the music of Scriabin were to influence her both intellectually and musically.[6] Mme Herz soon became more than a piano teacher to Crawford, and their friendship brought her into contact with a much more sophisticated way of life, socially and musically, than she had previously known.

Crawford also developed a close friendship with Alfred Frankenstein, who took her to Mme Herz's musical soirees, where young composers could play their own music. Frankenstein, who was then a clarinetist with the Civic Orchestra of Chicago, later became well known as a music and art critic for the *San Francisco Chronicle* and program annotator for the San Francisco Symphony Orchestra. Crawford lived close to the Frankensteins and often visited in their home, where Frankenstein played for her recordings of contemporary music that he had brought back from a recent visit to Europe. Frankenstein also introduced Crawford to Carl Sandburg and to the world of folk music. Later, when Sandburg's publishers decided to add accompaniments to the words and tunes in the *American Songbag*, Crawford shared in their preparation.[7]

Crawford's friendship with Carl Sandburg and his family accounts for the spark that ignited her lifelong interest in folk song. It also explains her use of his poetry for the texts of her solo vocal music. Strongly attracted to the man and his philosophy of life, she relied on his poems almost exclusively as texts for her songs. Sandburg had manifested socialist sympathies through his work for the Social Democratic party in Wisconsin and as secretary to the first socialist mayor of Milwaukee, and it is safe to assume that Crawford became acquainted with socialist ideas at this time. Sandburg probably influenced Crawford in still another way, in that both he and she became successful authors of children's books.

It is not known how many works Crawford composed during her

Plate 22
Carl Bohnen, *Ruth Crawford*, portrait from life

Source: Courtesy of the estate of Carl Crawford, deceased

years in Chicago. The Five Preludes for Piano (1924–25) are the earliest works she felt were worth public acknowledgment. Her piece *The Adventures of Tom Thumb*, for piano and narrator, designed to appeal to children, won first prize in the Sigma Alpha Iota national composition contest in 1927. A Suite for Small Orchestra (1926), though still unpublished, was nevertheless recently recorded (see appendix 2). A newly discovered Sonata for Violin and Piano (1926) was played in New York in 1927 and in Chicago in 1928.[8] In a review of the Chicago performance, which was without doubt intended to be flattering—although the term *virile* could be considered condescending—the *Musical Courier* reported: "The most ambitious work on the program, Miss Crawford's Sonata for Violin and Piano, is boldly energetic and virile, with a bittersweet harmonic flavor. The composer writes with palpable sincerity and poetic intent."[9]

The second set of piano preludes, Four Preludes for Piano (1927–28), was printed by Henry Cowell in his *New Music Quarterly* (October 1927). The Suite for Five Wind Instruments and Piano (1927) was revised by Crawford in 1929, after she went to New York. The Suite no. 2 for Piano and Strings, which probably originated in Chicago, was also composed in 1929. Both suites remain in manuscript.

The piano preludes and the instrumental suites share certain stylistic traits that characterize the music from Crawford's years in Chicago. The harmonic vocabulary in particular is reminiscent of both Debussy and Scriabin. These works reflect Crawford's concept of melody as nonlyric, her use of cell-like formations and octave displacements, her avoidance of scalar and triadic patterns, and her preference for dissonant intervals or nondirectional harmonies.

In the summer of 1929 Crawford was in residence at the MacDowell Colony in Peterboro, New Hampshire. There she met many important writers and musicians—among them the composer Marion Bauer, a well-known writer and teacher, who also enjoyed a reputation as a somewhat conservative composer. Bauer took an interest in Crawford, recognized her unusual talents, and encouraged her to continue composing.

Only three works, songs with texts by Sandburg, appear to have been composed during this summer: *Joy*, *Sunsets*, and *Loam*. Two other songs, *Home Thoughts* and *White Moon*, both also with Sandburg texts, were apparently written later that year. All five songs appear as a set in a manuscript dated 1929. These songs are all related texturally, rhythmically, and formally. The three-part structure of each is defined largely through the alternation of declamatory and lyrical vocal lines in a chordal, tonally unstable fabric with much use of tone clusters. Traces of impressionism appear in the rhythm and in floating chords often present in the accompaniment. The pan-chromatic harmony of the tone clusters is often varied through use of both diatonic and whole-tone scale patterns.

Crawford's decision to leave Chicago in 1929 for New York was a turning point in her career. Henry Cowell is generally credited with playing a vital role in this move, since he arranged for her to spend the winter of 1929–30 in the New York home of Blanche Walton, a wealthy widow who was a patron and friend of several American avant-garde composers and musicians, including Cowell, Dane Rudhyar, Richard Buhlig (a concert pianist), Carl Ruggles, and Charles Seeger.[10] One of Cowell's intentions in helping Crawford to make the New York move was to interest his friend and former teacher, Charles Seeger, in her music so that Seeger would accept her as his student in composition.[11] This was accomplished, but not until Cowell had convinced Seeger that Crawford had sufficient talent to warrant his acceptance of her as a pupil. The skeptical Seeger admittedly questioned the role of women in the field of musical composition.

"My opinions of women composers were quite often expressed and not very high, based mostly on the absence of mention of them in the histories of music; but, of course, there were some early women composers who were quite famous. So that when I was approached by Henry Cowell with the idea of teaching Ruth, I was a little bit skeptical of the value of the undertaking."[12]

During Seeger's tenure as professor of music at the University of California at Berkeley (1912–18), he had become one of Cowell's first music teachers. Later, in New York, they both continued their interest in avant-garde composing techniques, although by the time Seeger left California his interest in the sociological aspects of music had already superseded his compositional activities.[13]

In the course of Crawford's first winter in New York, she not only revised the Suite for Five Wind Instruments and Piano, but she also wrote four Diaphonic suites as assignments for Seeger. These suites utilize Seeger's ideas of dissonant rhythm and dissonant counterpoint and the dissonating of a single melody as long as possible.[14] (A melodic line is "dissonated" by the avoidance of triadic implications on successive notes of the melody.) Three of the four suites are for two instruments. The first suite, for flute or oboe—the only one for solo performance—is perhaps the most interesting of the set. Its third movement uses a seven-note pitch set in ⅞ meter and features an ostinato rhythm organized in eight-measure phrases.

Other works from this period show a similar concern for ordering different parameters of music in a methodical formal design. Crawford's last work for piano, Piano Study in Mixed Accents (1930), is built completely around the idea of a dissonated melodic line, constantly rising and falling, played by both hands an octave apart. Retrograde motion, introduced at midpoint in the study, is also worked out through a sophisticated and unconventional rhythmic design. The work also orders dynamics in an innovative manner, by using three optional dynamic patterns, each of which is likewise reversed at midpoint.

Crawford also wrote one song, *Rat Riddles*, based on a poem by Sandburg, during her first winter in New York. A powerful and imaginative work, it later became part of the set called Three Songs for Contralto, Oboe, Piano, and Percussion.

In 1930, when Crawford was awarded a Guggenheim Foundation fellowship for European study in composition, she was the first woman to be so honored. Before she left for Europe, however, another important event occurred that was to change her life. Her student-teacher relationship with Charles Seeger had gradually changed to a warm friendship and finally, not long before time to sail, to love. When Seeger put Crawford on the boat in Quebec, each had mixed feelings—anticipation of a year's valuable musical experience and distress at the thought of being apart for so long.[15]

Crawford's year in Europe was devoted to composing, attending concerts, interviewing publishers, and meeting leading European composers and theorists, to whom she showed her compositions when the occasion presented itself. She did not study composition with anyone because of a combination of circumstances. She had studied composition since 1922 and Charles Seeger felt she was already a mature composer. In addition, Crawford undoubtedly felt challenged to prove she could do independent work successfully.

Through letters of introduction from the Guggenheim Foundation she was able to arrange valuable visits with people like Alban Berg, Béla Bartók, Josef Rufer, and Maurice Ravel. They received her kindly and in no way rebuffed her because she was a woman. Her single unpleasant encounter occurred during a visit with the director of Universal Editions in Vienna, who remarked that it would be especially difficult for a woman to get anything published (presumably a general policy statement).[16]

Crawford also began to realize the importance of having studied with a well known composer-teacher, of knowing the right people, and of making important connections. However, all these concepts were distasteful to her and she avoided them as much as possible. She wrote, "If in several ways I had concentrated on 'pull' this year, it would have been a different story. . . . But I'm fighting against this pull idea, and annoyed that just because you studied with [   ] you get your music published."[17]

During this year abroad Crawford produced her most important compositions. The Three Chants for Women's Chorus were completed in Berlin; all three use meaningless phonemes for texts. *Chant, 1930,* for four-part mixed a cappella chorus with soprano solo, published in 1971, is a slightly revised version of one of these chants. The scores of the other two chants, long thought to be lost, were located by Charles Seeger a few years before his death. All three chants are studies in dissonant counterpoint and in shifting masses of sound. The third chant is the most complex of the group both texturally and rhythmically; it has twelve vocal parts and uses complicated polyrhythms.

The most famous and distinguished of Crawford's works is her String Quartet (1931), which was written partly in Berlin and partly in Paris. From its first performance in 1933 to the present, this work has constantly gained recognition, as an increasing number of performances, both live and on record, allow its unique qualities to become more widely known. The two most progressive movements are the third and fourth. In the third movement all instruments play legatissimo, and each of the four parts has its own elaborate ever-changing dynamic pattern. Charles Seeger called this movement a study in "dynamic counterpoint."[18] The last movement is an example of total organization of pitch, rests, rhythm, dynamics, tempo, instrumentation, and form. All of these elements are worked out in a prescribed pattern, and as in some of Crawford's earlier works, the second half of the movement is a retrograde of the first. The string quartet deserves its position as one of the most important in contemporary literature, not only for its use of techniques unusual at the time of its composition, but also for its artistic unfolding of musical ideas.[19]

While in Berlin, Crawford also wrote *In Tall Grass,* one of the set of Three Songs. Another of the set, *Prayers of Steel,* was written later in New York; and the third, *Rat Riddles,* had been written in New York the previous winter. The Three Songs, all settings of Sandburg poems, employ experimental techniques, such as serialization of several parameters of music and retrograde motion. The instrumental parts are highly organized, whereas the vocal lines are free and declamatory.

Crawford expressed the opinion that the works she composed in Europe were her best to that time: "I am sure that the work I did during this time was by far the best I had done—a fact which I attribute not so much to Europe itself (though the experience abroad was invaluable to me in a general sort of way) as to the financial freedom to work, and to the natural course of my growth."[20]

She wrote Charles Seeger from Berlin about the desirability of renewing her fellowship for a second year. She wanted the time to compose, but she did not want to spend another year apart. Since one of the men she knew had been permitted, as a Guggenheim fellow, to spend part of the year in New York and part in Europe, why couldn't she ask for the same privilege? Although she apparently sent in her application for a second year, the fellowship was not renewed.

After her return to New York in November 1931, Crawford wrote *Prayers of Steel*; she also added optional orchestral "ostinati" to the Three Songs and readied various manuscripts for photoduplication.[21] Her subsequent marriage to Charles Seeger in 1932 brought about a major change in her life; she now anticipated fulfilling a long held hope of raising a family.[22] The Seegers' only son, Michael, was born in 1933; their first daughter, Peggy, in 1935. From that time on, much of Ruth Crawford Seeger's energy and interest was centered on her children, although her ideals and ambitions in composing remained the same.

Several events of the 1930s were to change her commitment about the kind of music she wanted to write and were soon to trigger her abandonment of avant-garde dissonant music for the next several years. The Great Depression affected the Seegers economically, as it reduced Charles's source of income from teaching. Equally important, it sparked further his long-standing interest in music's relevance to social and political issues. The Seegers began to consider seriously the obligations composers had to serve a broadly based audience rather than an artistic elite. Such questions were extremely important to them and were, in fact, to alter dramatically the course of Crawford Seeger's career as a musician. It should be pointed out that the Seegers were not alone in their decision to pursue political and economic aims through music. Many other composers and artists were affected by the times. Eric Salzman aptly described the general situation when he stated that during the 1930s "under the influence of populist ideologies, avant garde ideas and forms were set aside."[23]

In 1932 Henry Cowell introduced the Seegers to a group of musicians in New York known as the Composers Collective. The goal of the group, as Charles Seeger recalls, was "to connect music somehow or other with the economic situation."[24] During this same year Crawford Seeger composed two songs that were inspired by the ideals of the Composers Collective. These songs, *Sacco, Vanzetti*, and *Chinaman, Laundryman*, along with the previously mentioned *Prayers of Steel*, are the only original compositions written by Crawford Seeger in New York after her return from Europe. The two songs, in their exploitation of structural devices, represent her most sophisticated works. They are not, however, as successful artistically as the earlier Three Songs, perhaps because of a certain self-conscious quality that pervades them in the wake of their social message.

The Seegers soon began to realize that their kind of music making for the Composers Collective, no matter how well intentioned, was not filling the needs of the people for whom it was intended, namely, those caught up in the political and economic maelstrom of the time. The "people" responded more readily to familiar tunes, such as folk songs, as well as to lyrics that reflected their daily interests.

So they decided to set aside their composition in dissonant counterpoint temporarily to study folk music, which they now regarded as the true "music of the people." As they began intensive research on Anglo-American folk music, they quickly perceived the discrepancies between the published versions of the music and the recorded performances made in the field. Crawford Seeger, who had already been introduced to folk music through her association with Carl Sandburg in Chicago in the twenties, resumed and intensified her activities in the transcription and arrangement of folk songs.

The Seegers' involvement in folk music was shared by a number of musicians living in New York in the early 1930s. Two who greatly influenced the course of Crawford Seeger's career were John and Alan Lomax, with whom both the Seegers formed lasting and fruitful friendships. When the Lomaxes asked Crawford Seeger to take the responsibility of making musical transcriptions for *Our Singing Country*,[25] she accepted. She then studied the scholarly aspects of transcription to notate as closely as possible the style of the music she heard in the field recordings. Her introductory remarks to *Our Singing Country* contain much valuable information for the performer of folk music.

In 1935 the Seegers moved to Washington, D.C., where they

found further support for their interest in folk music. While Charles Seeger worked there with the Resettlement Administration and later also worked on the Federal Music Project, a whole new world was opening to the Seegers through the Archives of American Folk Song in the Library of Congress. While Crawford Seeger was transcribing and arranging folk music for the Lomax book, Seeger was also working intensively with folk materials. Crawford Seeger accompanied her husband on some of the field trips he made as part of his job responsibilities.[26]

In the Capitol their family continued to expand: Barbara was born in 1937, Penelope in 1943. With no outside help and young children to raise, Crawford Seeger scarcely had time to even think about original composition. Work on the Lomax book took practically all the spare time she had, and it is not surprising that she wrote only one composition during this period. In 1939 she composed *Rissolty, Rossolty,* her second and final essay for orchestra, on commission for CBS, which presented it on a program entitled "School of the Air." She based it on three folk tunes that were transcribed from recordings in the Library of Congress. Had she lived longer, she probably would have written other original compositions using folk materials.[27]

During the 1940s, while Charles Seeger worked at the Pan American Union, Ruth Crawford Seeger helped support the family through a variety of musical activities. She gave private piano lessons at home and also taught music in several cooperative nursery schools. These schools were projects organized by groups of women who were interested in this kind of education for their children. A gifted teacher, Crawford Seeger was patient, resourceful, and especially empathetic with young children. She had an almost uncanny ability to hold their attention. Almost in spite of herself, she became one of the leaders of the group of women who organized the cooperative Silver Spring (Maryland) Nursery School, the Washington, D.C., suburb where the Seegers were living.[28]

As an outgrowth of her work with the children in the nursery schools, Crawford Seeger also compiled books of folk songs, which she arranged for voice and piano: *American Folk Songs for Children* (1948), *Animal Folk Songs for Children* (1950), and *Christmas Folk Songs for Children* (1953). Her pioneering in this field received critical acclaim and recognition from music educators.[29]

Despite all of these interests, which took time and energy from composition, Crawford Seeger did not abandon her ambitions as a composer. She made more than one reference to her hope of returning to her own composition. One of her diaries recounts such thoughts along with others concerning the feasibility of joining with a group of neighborhood women to organize a cooperative nursery school. The extant entries date from 18 August to 29 August, presumably from the year 1941. The 20 August entry reads in part:

Mrs. Williams asked me last spring if I would be interested. And I answered, frank enough, that I would—if other people organized it! I'm no good at organizing. Besides, cooperation might mean some work for me, and I'm too busy as it is. How can anyone with three children and no maid, and a few ideas for books and compositions on the side, expect to cooperate with anything except her own inter-tangled can-do's and can-not-do's? On the other hand, it would help both Barbara and me (and I might be able to get back to my own music every morning at least) if Barbara could be in school.

In the 25 August entry she recorded a similar hope: "Maybe I can resume my 'career' when Michael can learn to type my letters for me."

Yet, after writing these diary excerpts, the only work she completed was the Suite for Wind Quintet (1952). Unlike *Rissolty, Rossolty*, which drew on folk materials, it returned to the more abstract contrapuntal style of her earlier works. It won the first-place award in a competition for woodwind quintets sponsored by the District of Columbia chapter of the National Association of American Composers and Conductors.

At the time of Crawford Seeger's death in 1953, many of the projects she had planned—among them additional collections of folk songs and compositions—were unfinished. During her last years she drove herself relentlessly, "as though she was almost conscious that she was going to die early and wanted to get it all in before she went."[30] At what point she first realized she was seriously ill is not ascertainable; however, she suffered through three or four months of severe illness prior to her death from cancer.

Many tributes were paid to Crawford Seeger's memory after her death on 18 November 1953. One of the finest was written by her friend and co-worker, Sidney Robertson Cowell, who knew her through their work in folk music at the Library of Congress: "For all her great creative gifts and wide musical knowledge, Mrs. Seeger was a sturdy personality of the utmost simplicity and naturalness. She had the widest possible sympathies, the quickest loyalty and kindness—a memorably rich and generous human being who was a most rewarding friend."[31]

Ruth Crawford Seeger was a multifaceted, reflective individual, who from her youth continually worked to understand herself. She obviously accepted her roles as a woman as they were defined during her lifetime, for she did not, at least overtly, question her place in a male-dominated society. She also seems, however, to have assumed equality with the men she met professionally. As a woman musician she encountered a minimum of discrimination. No question was ever raised regarding the propriety of her study of composition at the American Conservatory. Likewise, the men she met through Henry Cowell and Charles Seeger were most generous in their support of her talents. Her recognition by the Guggenheim Foundation has already been mentioned.

Why did Crawford Seeger give up composing for so many years? Her daughter Peggy, in discussing her mother's career as a composer, cited the many family responsibilities that claimed her time and attention. She described the problems of a "woman composer" in familiar terms:

"I don't think you have so many problems unless you have an overweening husband who won't let you go out or won't let you do anything for yourself, but my father was never like that. He absolutely gloried in my mother's independence, and it was such a good relationship that you had the feeling that anything she wanted to do would meet with his approval. But the problems of a woman composer—I can really understand now what her problems were, because I've got three children. Time just doesn't exist for doing things of your own."[32]

Even before Crawford Seeger married, she saw her choices in rather conventional terms. Her husband, while reminiscing about his visit with her in Paris during the summer of 1931, recalled one of the letters in which she wrote of the obstacles marriage might pose to her composing life. Unfortunately no further information about her thoughts on this provocative subject is available.[33]

There is a consensus among her children that Crawford Seeger felt a real conflict between her composing and her family. Peggy recalls that her mother wanted freedom to compose; but she also wanted her children, took tremendous pleasure in them, and always had time for them. Peggy theorized:

"I think a lot of women who have a motherhood period have to exorcise it and I think this is why she started taking up her composing later on in life, as she felt that her period of motherhood had been exorcised. . . . She was really, I would say, sunk in her family life up until about the time I was thirteen or fourteen."

When her Suite for Wind Quintet won a prize in 1953, she was "so pleased as to be almost frightened by the fact that something she had done had been recognized by someone else."[34]

Other reasons also account for the long compositional hiatus. Economic necessity was the most obvious, especially during the Depression years when she (and many other composers) had to turn to other activities to help make a living. Other less obvious but still important factors must also be mentioned: her disillusionment with the commercial aspects of composing, her broadened concept of music that valued folk music as a legitimate concern of the professional musician, and her belief that music exists within a large social framework. Charles Seeger explained that, although she knew her compositions were good,

"she was willing to give it up because of the idea that that kind of music was just the frosting on the musical life of a country. She wanted to get down to the real thing and the real thing for her and me at that time was contained in the records in the Library of Congress and what we were making ourselves. It wasn't anything like a descent from the heights to the depths; it was simply going up to a higher level of understanding of the whole Western culture, American version."[35]

The Seegers' concern for folk music and music of the people was shared, in the thirties and forties, by many intellectuals who became interested in them from a radical leftist political viewpoint. For the Seegers, however, the larger view of music they both came to espouse, which we call ethnomusicology, cannot be confined within the tenets of a particular ideology. Folk-song scholarship became for them a matter worthy of their best intellectual and musical efforts.

In spite of the small amount of music Crawford Seeger composed, she is considered one of the important American modernists, and her name belongs to the generation of American composers who formed the avant garde of the 1920s, including Cowell, Varèse, Riegger, and Ruggles. Her reputation as a composer is based on a small number of works: the String Quartet, the songs *Sacco, Vanzetti* and *Chinaman, Laundryman*, the Three Songs, the piano preludes, the Piano Study in Mixed Accents, the four Diaphonic suites, and the Suite for Wind Quintet.[36] (For a complete list of her works, see appendix 1.) These works are in small forms and are for small performing groups. Crawford Seeger had no ambition to write the definitive American symphony; neither was she interested in large dramatic forms such as opera. The composition of a large work for orchestra mentioned in her application for the Guggenheim Foundation fellowship was apparently not even begun. She seriously considered this project but was never able to convince herself of its rightness for her.

Although stylistic analysis is beyond the scope and purpose of this essay, a few of the techniques that characterize the inquiring spirit of her compositions merit acknowledgment, however brief. Many of her compositions foreshadowed techniques that were to be exploited a generation later. Although common now, they were rarely encountered when she first employed them.[37] Among these techniques is the use of total serial control, already discussed in connection with the last movement of the String Quartet. Others include extensive use of a dissonated melodic line (third movement of Diaphonic Suite no. 1); chords that, if reduced to their closest position, produce a cluster of tones (Piano Prelude no. 4); three- and four-note cells that are often permuted (Diaphonic Suite no. 3 contains forty such three-note patterns); and octave displacements used in many different kinds of note groupings, probably for their dissonance value (Diaphonic Suite no. 1). Characteristic also are the use of a sound mass per se (String Quartet, third movement), dynamic counterpoint (String Quartet, third movement), juxtaposed layers of sound (*Rat Riddles*), patterned vibrato (*In Tall Grass*), the serialization of pitch and rests (*Prayers of Steel*), the use of unordered as well as ordered sets of twelve pitches (*Prayers of Steel*), and glissandi in the strings marked *alto possibile* (*In Tall Grass*).

In a musical society dominated by men, Ruth Crawford Seeger was encouraged by them to enter the competition, which she did successfully. By and large, Crawford Seeger was free to make the major decisions that determined her life patterns, although she sensed the hazards of these choices. She wanted to go to Chicago, to New York, to Europe, to marry, to raise a family, and to compose; she enjoyed her teaching and her folk-song activities. She also longed for more time to devote to composition. Charles Seeger once described her in the following words: "Ruth had a marvelous serenity and sense of humor. She was very much a woman, not an imitation man, yet as you know, an ardent feminist."[38] Her rich and rewarding life left an indelible stamp on the musical heritage of her country and fulfilled her own personal creed: "We should not seek to become greater than others, but to discover the greatness in ourselves."[39]

NOTES

1. The biographical information in this essay is based largely upon Matilda Gaume, *Ruth Crawford Seeger: Her Life and Works* (Ann Arbor: University Microfilms, 1973). This was derived from Ruth Crawford Seeger's letters, diaries, and other writings, which were made available through the kindness of her husband, Charles Seeger; her children, Michael, Peggy, Barbara, and Penelope; and her brother, Carl Crawford.

2. Ruth Crawford, autobiographical data, n.d.

3. Ruth Crawford, diary, 14 January 1915.

4. Ruth Crawford to Nicolas Slonimsky, 29 January 1933.

5. Ruth Crawford to her mother, Chicago, 18 November 1922.

6. Crawford to Slonimsky.

7. Alfred Frankenstein, interview with author, San Francisco, March 1968.

8. The score to the Sonata for Violin and Piano was only recently recovered. A performance at the Library of Congress on 12 November 1982, with Vivian Fine at the piano and Ida Kavafian on the violin, brought a glowing review in the *Washington Post*. All manuscripts discussed in this essay are located in the Library of Congress, Washington, D.C.

9. *Musical Courier*, 13 February 1927.

10. Charles Seeger, interview with author, Santa Monica, Calif., March 1968.

11. Charles Seeger, recollections taped for author, London, July 1967.

12. Ibid. (It can only be inferred that Cowell convinced Seeger of Ruth Crawford's talent by showing him the piano preludes and other selected compositions from her Chicago days.)

13. Ibid.

14. See Charles Seeger, "On Dissonant Counterpoint," *Modern Music* 7 (June-July 1930): 25–31.

15. C. Seeger, recollections.

16. Ruth Crawford to Charles Seeger, Vienna, 6 May 1931.

17. Ibid.

18. Charles Seeger, "Ruth Crawford," in *American Composers on American Music*, 2d ed., ed. Henry Cowell (New York: Frederick Ungar, 1962), p. 115.

19. The String Quartet has been recorded more than any other work by Crawford Seeger; see app. 2. The third movement has been reprinted in the *Norton Scores: An Anthology for Listening*, 3d ed. (New York: W. W. Norton & Co., 1977), 2:747–50.

20. Crawford to Slonimsky.

21. Charles Seeger, interview with author, Bridgewater, Conn., 8 October 1974.

22. Ruth Crawford to her mother, Chicago, 20 November 1921.

23. Eric Salzman, *Twentieth-Century Music: An Introduction*, 2d ed.

(Englewood Cliffs, N.J.: Prentice-Hall, 1974), p. 135.

24. C. Seeger, recollections.

25. John A. Lomax, Alan Lomax, and Ruth Crawford Seeger, *Our Singing Country* (New York: Macmillan, 1941).

26. Michael Seeger, interview with author, Globe, Ariz., 7 November 1977.

27. C. Seeger, interview, March 1968.

28. Peggy Seeger, recollections taped for author, Kent, England, April 1976.

29. For reviews, see *New York Herald-Tribune*, 31 December 1950; *Music Library Association Notes* 8 (1951): 388–89.

30. Peggy Seeger, recollections taped for author, Kent, England, 22 July 1977.

31. Sidney Robertson Cowell, "Ruth Crawford Seeger," *International Folk Music Journal* 7 (1955): 55–56.

32. P. Seeger, recollections, April 1976.

33. Charles Seeger, interview with author, Bridgewater, Conn., 7 October 1974.

34. P. Seeger, recollections, April 1976.

35. C. Seeger, interview, 8 October 1974.

36. For a list of Crawford Seeger's recorded works, see app. 2.

37. For a discussion of Crawford Seeger's innovative style, see George Perle, "Atonality and the Twelve-Tone System in the United States," *Score* 27 (July 1960): 51–66.

38. Charles Seeger to author, 18 August 1973.

39. Crawford, diary, 8 November 1928.

APPENDIX I

Oeuvre of Ruth Crawford Seeger

Published Works:

Chant, 1930, for SATB chorus and soprano solo a cappella (1930) (New York: Continuo Music Press, 1971), 5 pp.

Chinaman, Laundryman, for voice and piano (1932) (Bryn Mawr, Pa.: Merion Music, 1976), 12 pp.

Diaphonic Suite no. 1, for solo flute or oboe (1930) (New York: New Music Edition, 1933; New York: Continuo Music Press, 1972), 6 pp.

Diaphonic Suite no. 2, for bassoon and cello or two celli (1930) (New York: Continuo Music Press, 1972), 8 pp.

Diaphonic Suite no. 3, for two B-flat clarinets (1930) (New York: Continuo Music Press, 1972), 8 pp.

Diaphonic Suite no. 4, for oboe and cello (1930) (New York: Continuo Music Press, 1972), 12 pp.

Four Preludes for Piano (1927–28) (San Francisco: New Music Edition, 1930), 14 pp.; (reprint, Bryn Mawr, Pa.: Theodore Presser, 1983).

Piano Study in Mixed Accents (1930) (San Francisco: New Music Edition, 1932), 4 pp.; (reprint, Bryn Mawr, Pa.: Theodore Presser, 1983).

Sacco, Vanzetti, for voice and piano (1932) (Bryn Mawr, Pa.: Merion Music, 1976), 12 pp.

String Quartet (1931) (New York: New Music Edition, 1941), 21 pp.; (Bryn Mawr, Pa.: Merion Music, 1941), 21 pp.

Suite for Wind Quintet (1952) (New York: Continuo Music Press, 1969), 26 pp.

Three Songs for Contralto, Oboe, Piano, and Percussion (1930–32) (San Francisco: New Music Edition, 1933), 58 pp.

Unpublished Works:

The Adventures of Tom Thumb, for piano and narrator (1925)

Five Preludes for Piano (1924–25)

Five Songs (1929)

Rissolty, Rossolty (1939)

Sonata for Violin and Piano (1925–26)

Suite for Five Wind Instruments and Piano (1927; rev. 1929)

Suite for Small Orchestra (1926)

Suite no. 2 for Four Strings and Piano (1929)

Two Chants for Women's Chorus (1930)

APPENDIX 2

Discography of Works by Ruth Crawford Seeger

Chant, 1930, Gregg Smith Singers (New York: Vox, 1979), SVBX-5353

Diaphonic Suite no. 1, with oboe solo (New York: CRI, 1980), S-423

Diaphonic Suite no. 2, with bassoon and cello (Nashville: Gasparo, 1981), GS-108CX

Nine Preludes for Piano (1924–28) (New York: CRI, 1968), S-247; (Columbus, Ohio: Coronet Records, 1983), 3121

Piano Study in Mixed Accents (New York: CRI, 1968), S-247; (Boston: Northeastern Records, 1981), NR 204; (Columbus, Ohio: Coronet Records, 1983), 3121

Preludes for Piano, nos. 6–9 (1927–28) (Boston: Northeastern Records, 1981), NR 204

Sonata for Violin and Piano (New York: CRI, 1985), SD-508

String Quartet, andante only (New York: New Music Quarterly Records, 1934)

String Quartet (New York: Columbia, 1960), ML 5477; (New York: Nonesuch, 1973), 71280; (Nashville: Gasparo, n.d.), 205

Suite for Wind Quintet (New York: CRI, 1970), SD-249

Suite no. 2 for Four Strings and Piano (New York: New World Records, 1984), NW 319.

Three Songs, for Contralto, Oboe, Piano, and Percussion (New York: New World Records, 1978), NW 285

Two Movements for Chamber Orchestra (Suite for Small Orchestra) (Pacific Palisades, Calif.: Delos, 1975), 25405

The Contributors

JANE A. BERNSTEIN has published widely in the fields of Renaissance and nineteenth-century music. Her work in women's studies includes the introduction to a recent edition of Ethel Smyth's *Mass in D* (Da Capo Press, 1980). She is associate professor of music at Tufts University.

JANE BOWERS has published articles on French flute music and on the history of the flute as well as an edition of Michel de La Barre's *Pièces pour la flûte traversière* (Heugel, 1978). She is currently working on a cross-cultural study of women musicians and on a study of the blues singer Mama Yancey. She has taught flute, music history, and women's studies at various universities and is now associate professor of music history at the University of Wisconsin–Milwaukee. She also performs on the Baroque flute.

HOWARD MAYER BROWN'S extensive writings on Renaissance music include *Music in the Renaissance* (Prentice-Hall, 1976), *Embellishing Sixteenth-Century Music* (Oxford University Press, 1976), and, most recently, *A Florentine Chansonnier from the Time of Lorenzo the Magnificent*, 2 vols. (University of Chicago Press, 1983). Brown is a past president of the American Musicological Society and the current vice-president of the International Musicological Society. He is the Ferdinand Schevill Distinguished Service Professor of Music at the University of Chicago.

MARCIA J. CITRON is the author of *Letters of Fanny Hensel to Felix Mendelssohn* (Pendragon Press, forthcoming) and of several articles on Fanny Mendelssohn Hensel and women lied composers in scholarly music journals. She is associate professor of music at the Shepherd School of Music of Rice University.

MARIA V. COLDWELL is the author of "*Guillaume de Dole* and Medieval Romances with Musical Interpolations," in *Musica Disciplina*

35 (1981). She is now completing a catalog of the Herbert and Ruth Steinkraus Cohen Collection of Keyboard and Chamber Music that will be published by Yale University Press. She has taught at the University of Chicago and is currently teaching at Yale University.

MATILDA GAUME, like Ruth Crawford Seeger, was born in the Midwest, experienced the Terrible Twenties, the Great Depression, and the Roosevelt New Deal. After the completion of her doctoral dissertation on the life and works of Crawford Seeger, her older contemporary, she continued her research on this outstanding American woman, and her articles appear in standard reference works. She is professor emerita of West Texas State University and has been a visiting professor of music at Tunghai University in Taiwan.

CAROL NEULS-BATES is the author, with Adrienne Fried Block, of *Women in American Music: A Bibliography of Music and Literature* (Greenwood Press, 1979), and editor of *Women in Music: An Anthology of Source Readings from the Middle Ages to the Present* (Harper & Row, 1982). She has taught on the faculties of the University of Connecticut, Yale, and Hunter and Brooklyn colleges of the City University of New York.

ANTHONY NEWCOMB's wide-ranging and numerous publications include *The Madrigal at Ferrara: 1579–1597* (Princeton University Press, 1979). He is professor of music history at the University of California at Berkeley.

JUDITH E. OLSON has done extensive research in nineteenth-century music criticism, particularly on Heinrich Porges and other writers in the Bayreuth Circle. She has been a translator and music archivist and has worked in the arts and business administration. She is a member of the editorial board and the foreign reports editor for *Current Musicology*.

NANCY B. REICH is the author of *Clara Schumann: The Artist and the Woman* (Cornell University Press, 1985). A musicologist with a special interest in the nineteenth century, she has written about Felix Mendelssohn, Franz Liszt, Johann Friedrich Reichardt, and Louise Reichardt. She has taught at New York University, Lehman College, and Manhattanville College, and has been a visiting scholar at the Stanford University Center for Research on Women.

ELLEN ROSAND has written on various topics in Venetian music and has edited a volume of cantatas by Barbara Strozzi to be published by Garland Press in a forthcoming series on the Italian Cantata in the

Seventeenth Century. She is now working on a book-length manuscript entitled "Opera in Seicento Venice: The Creation of a Genre." A former editor of the *Journal of the American Musicological Society*, she is currently professor of music history at Rutgers University.

JULIE ANNE SADIE is the author of *The Bass Viol in French Baroque Chamber Music* (UMI Research Press, 1980). She is currently compiling a companion to Baroque music. Sadie has taught in this country at the Eastman School of Music and has lectured in England at King's College. She now lives in London, where she has played the viol and Baroque cello with such groups as the English Bach Festival Orchestra and the Academy of Ancient Music.

JUDITH TICK is the author of *American Women Composers before 1870* (UMI Research Press, 1983) and the editor of *Selected Songs of Josephine Lang* (Da Capo Press, 1982). She is currently preparing an edition of Ruth Crawford Seeger's *Five Songs on Poems by Carl Sandburg* for Continuo Press. She has also contributed the article "Women and Music" to the *New Grove Dictionary of Music in the United States*. Tick is associate professor of music at Brooklyn College.

ANN BAGNALL YARDLEY is a performer with and musicologist for the Early Music Players of (Morristown,) New Jersey. She has taught music history at the University of Illinois and Drew University.

Index

Index

Index

Index

Index

379, 380; songs, 379, 383; *Rissolty, Rossolty*, 380, 381; Suite for Wind Quintet, 381, 383
Sessa, Claudia, 132, 143, 155n75; composer, 118, 126–27; published works, 163
Sforza, Alessandro, 100
Sforza, Bianca Maria, 68
Sforza, Caterina, 62
Sforza, Galeazzo Maria, 67, 68, 84n32
Shaw, George Bernard, 304
shawm, 44
singers, 5, 6, 7, 8, 15, 43–44, 46–47, 58n23, 58–59n27, 66, 99, 191; professional, 11, 67–70, 87n48, 99, 122; in convents, 17, 20, 25, 30, 81–82n13, 125–28; in medieval Europe, 41–44, 46; of the abbaids, 59n30; at Renaissance courts, 67–70, 73, 78–79, 92–94, 109; of woman's songs, 78–79; courtesans as, 84n33; as ladies-in-waiting, 93–96, 122; education of court, 94, 98, 99–100; engagements under ancien régime, 192, 200–203; salaries, 201, 202. *See also* opera singers, minstrels, troubadour, trouvère
Sirmen, Maddalena Laura Lombardini: violinist, 158–59n92, 207
Sixtus V, 135
Smyth, Ethel, 7, 8, 10, 12, 304–24; 323n50; feminism of, 304, 313–14, 316, 319, 323–24n55; writings, 304; on famous contemporaries, 317–19; compositional style, 305, 311; education, 307–9; and Tschaikovsky, 308, 309, 322n29; study with Herzogenberg, 308–9, 321n26; collaboration with Brewster, 310, 312, 313, 317; portrait, 315; deafness, 316, 318; and Virginia Woolf, 317, 318, 324n63; female supporters of, 317–18; acquaintance with Brahms and Clara Schumann, 321n26
—, works: criticism of, by Shaw, 304; orchestral, 304, 309; instrumental, 308; Mass in D, 309–10, 313; *Fantasio*, 310, 311; *Der Wald*, 310–11; *The Wreckers*, 311–13; criticism of, by Beecham, 312, 316; *The Boatswain's*

Mate, 314, 316; *Fête Galante* and *Entente Cordiale*, 316–17. *See also* Tovey, Donald F.
Somenza, Corona, 125, 152n52
songs, 12, 19; woman's, 47–55; in the Italian Renaissance, 74–78; with a woman's point of view, 75–79, 88–89n56. *See also* bergerette, chanson, lieder, madrigal, poetry, rondeau
Spaccini, Giovanni Battista, 120, 132
Spain, 17, 26, 39, 43, 44. *See also* Las Huelgas de Burgos
Spohr, Louis, 306
Stampa, Gaspara, 64, 133; poet, 106
Stein, Andreas, 252
Steiner, Emma Roberto: conductor, 357
Stirling, Elizabeth: organist, 306
Stockhausen, Julius. *See* Schumann, Clara Wieck
Striggio, Alessandro, 108–9
Strinasacchi, Regina: violinist, 256
Stravinsky, Igor, 316
strings, 358
Strozzi, Barbara, 5, 10, 12, 108, 118, 131, 132, 133, 140, 146, 168–89, 190n23, 224; "adoption" of, 169; published works, 165, 166, 173–78 passim, 187–88n1; Accademia degli Unisoni, 131, 169–70, 172, 183, 184; audience of, 169–70, 183, 184; courtesan, 172, 184–85; singer, 172–73, 183, 185; composer, 173, 175–76; income, 174–75; cantatas, 175–78; madrigals, 176; texts set, 176, 183–84; compositional techniques, 176–81; musical training, 178–79; portrait, 184–85, 186; sacred motet, 187–88n1. *See also* Loredano, Giovanni Francesco; Sagredo, Nicolò
Strozzi, Bernardo, 184–86, 190n23
Strozzi, Giulio, 118, 131, 168–70, 174–75, 190n23; feminism of, 175, 190n18
Strozzi, Ruperto, 105
Sutro, Florence, 335–36, 339
Switzerland, 26, 27
"Symphonia harmoniae caelestium revelationum." *See* Hildegard of Bingen
Syon Abbey, 22